RESEARCH IN EDUCATION

RESEARCH IN EDUCATION

Third edition

John W. Best

PRENTICE-HALL, INC., Englewood Cliffs, New Jersey 07632

Library of Congress Cataloging in Publication Data

BEST, JOHN W. (DATE)
   Research in education.

   Includes bibliographies and index.
   1. Educational research. I. Title.
LB1028.B4 1977   370′.78   76–44388
ISBN 0-13-774018-2

© 1977, 1970, 1959 by Prentice-Hall, Inc.,
Englewood Cliffs, New Jersey 07632

Printed in the United State of America

10 9 8 7 6 5 4 3 2 1

PRENTICE-HALL INTERNATIONAL, London
PRENTICE-HALL OF AUSTRALIA PTY. LIMITED, Sydney
PRENTICE-HALL OF CANADA, LTD., Toronto
PRENTICE-HALL OF INDIA PRIVATE LIMITED, New Delhi
PRENTICE-HALL OF JAPAN, INC., Tokyo
PRENTICE-HALL OF SOUTHEAST ASIA PTE. LTD., Singapore
WHITEHALL BOOKS LIMITED, Wellington, New Zealand

CONTENTS

CHAPTER 4

Experimental research   90

CHAPTER 5

Descriptive studies:
assessment, evaluation, and research   116

CHAPTER 6

The tools of research   156

CHAPTER 7
Descriptive data analysis   211

CHAPTER 8
Inferential data analysis   267

CHAPTER 9

The research report   309

CHAPTER 10

Historical research   340

PREFACE

This book has been written for use as a basic textbook in an introductory course in educational research, or as a reference for those interested in research, either as part of a graduate course, a thesis requirement, or as a professional activity.

All professional workers should be familiar with the methods of research in their fields and, if only as consumers, should understand some of the techniques of problem identification, hypothesis formulation, the design and use of data-gathering instruments and data analysis, and be able to interpret research reports that appear in professional publications.

An introductory course cannot be expected to confer research competence, nor can an introductory textbook present all of the relevant information. These skills and understandings cannot be achieved without the necessary intellectual qualities and the extensive training and experience that research demands. Graduate students may find it profitable to carry on a modest study as a way of learning about research through actual participation in the process.

This third edition of *Research in Education* has attempted to expand and clarify a number of ideas presented in previous editions. Additional concepts, examples, exercises and problems have been added. The similarities and distinctions between assessment, evaluation, and research have been emphasized. The statistical analysis of data has been reorganized and clarified and additional tests of significance have been included and illustrated.

The author is indebted to many students and colleagues, more than can be acknowledged by name. He is indebted to Dr. Gene V. Glass for his many helpful suggestions. To his wife, Solveig Ager Best, he is grateful for her constant encouragement.

John W. Best

THE MEANING OF RESEARCH

Chapter 1

Man is the unique product of his creation and evolution. In contrast to other forms of animal life, his more highly developed nervous system has enabled him to develop sounds and symbols (letters and numbers) that make possible the communication and recording of his questions, observations, experiences, and ideas.

It is understandable that his greater curiosity, implemented by his control of symbols, would lead him to speculate about the operation of the universe, the great forces beyond his own control. Over many centuries man began to develop what seemed to be plausible explanations. Attributing the forces of nature to the working of supernatural powers, he believed that the gods, at their whims, manipulated the sun, the stars, the wind, the rain, and the lightning.

The appearance of the medicine man or the priest, who claimed special channels of communication with the gods, led to the establishment of a system of religious authority passed on from one generation to another. A rigid tradition developed and a dogma of Nature's processes, explained in terms of mysticism and the authority of the priesthood, became firmly rooted, retarding for centuries further search for truth.

But gradually man began to see that the operations of the forces of

Nature were not as capricious as he had been led to believe. He began to observe an orderliness in the universe, certain cause-effect relationships, and discovered that, under certain conditions, events could be predicted with reasonable accuracy. However, these explanations were often rejected if they seemed to conflict with the dogma of religious authority. Curious men who raised questions were often punished and even put to death when they persisted in expressing doubts suggested by such unorthodox explanations of natural phenomena.

This reliance on empirical evidence or personal experience challenged the sanction of vested authority and represented an important step in the direction of scientific inquiry. Such pragmatic observation, however, was largely unsystematic and further limited by the lack of an objective method. The observer was likely to overgeneralize on the basis of incomplete experience or evidence, to ignore complex factors operating simultaneously, or to let his feelings and prejudices influence both his observations and his conclusions.

It was only when man began to think systematically about thinking itself that the era of logic began. The first systematic approach to reasoning, attributed to Aristotle and the Greeks, was the deductive method. The categorical syllogism was one model of thinking that prevailed among early philosophers. Syllogistic reasoning established a logical relationship between a *major premise*, a *minor premise*, and a *conclusion*. A major premise is a self-evident assumption, previously established by metaphysical truth or dogma, concerning a relationship; a minor premise is a particular case related to the major premise. Given the logical relationship of these premises, it leads to an inescapable conclusion.

A typical Aristotelian categorical syllogism follows:

Major premise .... All men are mortal.
Minor premise .... Socrates is a man.
   Conclusion .... Socrates is mortal.

This deductive method, moving from the general assumption to the specific application, made an important contribution to the development of modern problem solving. But it was not fruitful in arriving at new truths. The acceptance of incomplete or false major premises based on old dogmas or unreliable authority could only lead to error. Semantic difficulties often resulted from shifting definitions of the terms involved.

Centuries later, Francis Bacon advocated the application of direct observation of phenomena, arriving at conclusions or generalizations through the evidence of many individual observations. This inductive process of moving from specific observations to the generalization freed logic from some of the hazards and limitations of deductive thinking.

Bacon recognized the obstacle that the deductive process placed in the way of discovering new truths: It started with old dogmas that religious or intellectual authorities had already accepted and could be expected to arrive at few new truths. These impediments to the discovery of truth, which he termed "idols," were exposed in his *Novum Organum*, written in 1620.

The following story, attributed to Bacon, expresses his revolt against the authority of the written word, an authority that dominated the search for truth during the Middle Ages:

> In the year of our Lord, 1432, there arose a grievous quarrel among the brethren over the number of teeth in the mouth of a horse. For thirteen days the disputation raged without ceasing. All the ancient books and chronicles were fetched out, and wonderful and ponderous erudition was made manifest. At the beginning of the fourteenth day a youthful friar of goodly bearing asked his learned superiors for permission to add a word, and straightway, to the wonder of the disputants, whose deep wisdom he sorely vexed, he beseeched them in a manner coarse and unheard of, to look in the mouth of a horse and find answers to their questionings. At this, their dignity being grievously hurt, they waxed exceedingly wroth; and joining in a mighty uproar they flew upon him and smote him hip and thigh and cast him out forthwith. For, said they, "Surely Satan hath tempted this bold neophyte to declare unholy and unheard-of ways of finding truth, contrary to all the teachings of the fathers." After many days of grievous strife the dove of peace sat on the assembly, and they, as one man, declaring the problem to be an everlasting mystery because of a dearth of historical and theological evidence thereof, so ordered the same writ down.[1]

The method of inductive reasoning proposed by Bacon, a method new to the field of logic, but widely used by the scientists of his time, was not hampered by false premises, by the inadequacies and ambiguities of verbal symbolism, or by the absence of supporting evidence.

But the inductive method alone did not provide a completely satisfactory system for the solution of problems. Random collection of individual observations without a unifying concept or focus often obscured investigations, and therefore rarely led to a generalization or theory.

The deductive method of Aristotle and the inductive method of Bacon were fully integrated in the work of Charles Darwin in the nineteenth century. During his early career his observations of animal life failed to lead to a satisfactory theory of man's development. The concept of the struggle for existence in Thomas Malthus' *Essay on Population* intrigued Darwin and suggested the assumption that natural selection explains the origin of different species of animals. This hypothesis provided a needed

---

[1]Francis Bacon as cited by C. E. K. Mees, "Scientific Thought and Social Reconstruction," *American Scientist* 22 (1934): 13–24.

focus for his investigations. He proceeded to deduce specific consequences suggested by the hypothesis. The evidence gathered confirmed the hypothesis that biological change in the process of natural selection, in which favorable variations were preserved and unfavorable variations destroyed, resulted in the formation of new species.

The major premise of the older deductive method was gradually replaced by an assumption or hypothesis which was subsequently tested by the collection and logical analysis of data. This deductive-inductive method is now recognized as an example of a scientific approach.

John Dewey suggested a pattern that is helpful in identifying the elements of a deductive-inductive process:

A METHOD OF SCIENCE

1. Identification and definition of the problem
2. Formulation of a hypothesis—a hunch, an assumption, or an intelligent guess
3. Collection, organization, and analysis of data
4. Formulation of conclusions
5. Verification, rejection, or modification of the hypothesis by the test of its consequences in a specific situation

While this pattern is a useful reconstruction of some methods of scientific inquiry, it is not to be considered the *only* scientific method. There are many ways of applying logic and observation to problem solving. An overly rigid definition of the research process would omit many ways in which researchers go about their tasks. The planning of a study may include a great deal of exploratory activity, which is frequently intuitive or speculative and, at times, a bit disorderly. Although the researcher must eventually identify a precise and significant problem, his object may initially be vague and poorly defined. He may observe situations that seem to suggest certain possible cause-effect relationships and even gather some preliminary data to examine for possible relevancy to his vaguely conceived problem. At this stage imagination and much speculation are essential to the formulation of a clearly defined problem that is susceptible to the research process. Many students of research rightly feel that problem identification is one of the most difficult and most crucial steps of the research process.

A clearly defined problem may suggest one or several hypotheses. The hypothesis, which may be a hunch, an educated guess, or a speculation, must be expressed in operational terms and must lend itself to testing in a manner precise enough to determine whether or not it is probably true. The hypothesis, which gives focus to the data-gathering process and the confirming activity that follows, should be based upon a sound theory rather than upon wild speculation.

Hypothesis testing

Certain types of hypotheses may be tested directly. For example, if a lamp failed to light when the switch was turned on, several hypotheses could be stated:

1. There has been a power interruption.
2. The extension cord was not properly connected to the wall outlet.
3. The bulb was defective or burned out.
4. The fuse was burned out.

Each of these hypotheses could be tested directly, by noting whether or not other lights would go on, by checking the wall plug or the fuse, and by substituting a bulb known to be in working condition.

In behavioral research many hypotheses cannot be tested directly. Since they may deal with abstractions they must be tested indirectly. The researcher must set up some type of incident or sample of behavior that is concrete enough to observe directly. These observable incidents may then be judged to be consistent or inconsistent with the hypothesis, and the researcher may deduce the logical consequences of the hypothesis. If true, he would expect to observe a consistent occurrence of certain behavior; if not true, an inconsistent occurrence.

For example, one might propose the hypothesis that orphaned children receive greater intellectual stimulation if placed in carefully selected foster homes than if placed under institutional care. Separating pairs of orphaned identical twins, placing one of each pair in a foster home and the other in an institution, might provide evidence. After a period of several years a test of intellectual status might provide an indirect test of the hypothesis. If the hypothesis were true, the logical consequences would produce observations of significantly higher psychological test scores for those subjects placed in foster homes. Thus, we deduce the consequences of the hypothesis.

The role of theory

At this stage in the discussion, a statement about theory would be appropriate. To many people the term *theory* suggests an ivory tower, something unreal, something of little practical value. To the contrary, a theory establishes a cause-effect relationship between variables with the purpose of explaining and predicting phenomena. Those who engage in pure research devote their energies to the formulation of theories and may not be concerned with their practical application. When a theory has been established it may suggest many applications of practical value. John Dewey once said that there was nothing more practical than a good theory.

Theories about the relationship between the position of the earth and other moving celestial bodies were essential to the successful launching and return of manned space vehicles. Theories of the behavior of gases were essential to the development of refrigeration and air-conditioning. Controlled atomic energy could not have been achieved without the establishment of theories about the nature of mass and energy and the structure of the atom. The real purpose of scientific method is prediction, the discovery of certain theories or generalizations that anticipate future occurrences with maximum probability.

The social sciences

The term *science* may be thought of as an approach or attitude rather than a field of subject matter. By attempting to apply the rigorous controls of systematic observation and analysis used in the physical and biological sciences to areas of social behavior, the social sciences have grown and have advanced man's knowledge of himself. The fields of anthropology, economics, education, political science, psychology, and social psychology have become recognized as sciences by many authorities. To the extent that these studies are founded on scientific methodology, they are sciences. There are some who reject this concept, still defining science in terms of areas of subject matter rather than as methodology. Historically their position can be readily explained. Since scientific methods were first used in the investigation of physical phenomena, tradition has identified science with the physical world. Only within the last century has the methodology of science been applied to the study of various areas of human behavior. Since these are newer areas of investigation their results have not achieved the acceptance and status that come with the greater maturity and longer tradition of the physical sciences. There exist today bodies of opinion in politics, religion, and some academic disciplines that man is not the proper study of mankind.

Because human behavior is so complex, it is much more difficult to develop sound theories of human behavior than it is to develop theories that predict occurrences in the purely physical world.

1. No two persons are alike in feelings, drives, or emotions. What may be a reasonable prediction for one may be useless for another.
2. No one person is completely consistent from one moment to another. Human behavior is influenced by the interaction of the individual with every changing element in his environment, often in a way that is difficult to predict.

3. Human beings are influenced by the research process itself. They are influenced by the attention that is focused on them when under investigation and influenced by the knowledge that their own behavior is being observed.
4. The behavioral sciences have been limited by a lack of adequate definitions. Accurate operational definitions are essential to the development of a sophisticated science. Such traits as intelligence, learning, hostility, anxiety, or motivation are not directly observable. As constructs they can only be postulated, and since they cannot be seen, heard or felt, they can only be inferred by test scores, or by observed hostile or aggressive acts, skin responses, pulse rates, or persistence at a task.

Because satisfactory descriptive instruments or measuring devices have not yet been devised to precisely describe many of these constructs, research in the behavioral sciences has lagged behind research in the physical sciences.

But even constructs for which useful descriptive instruments *are* available account for only limited sources of variation; they yield only partial definitions. For example, intelligence, as defined operationally by a score on an intelligence test, is not a satisfactory measure of the type of intelligence that individuals are called upon to demonstrate in a variety of situations outside a formal academic environment.

In the physical sciences, complex constructs have been more effectively defined in operational terms. Time is one such construct; time is a function of the motion of the earth in relation to the sun, measured by the rotation of a hand on the face of a circular scale in precise units. Weight is a construct involving the laws of gravitation, measured by springs, torsion devices, levers, or electronic adaptations of these instruments.

The instruments which measure such constructs are devised so that they are consistent, to a maximum degree, with known physical laws and forces, and yield valid descriptions in a variety of situations. An international bureau prescribes standards for these devices so that they may provide precise operational definitions of the constructs.

Although the problems of discovering theories of human behavior are difficult, they may not be insoluble. Behavioral scientists will need to carry on their investigations as carefully and rigorously as have physical scientists. Subjective, qualitative judgments must be supplemented by more exact quantitative measurements, and variables must be more carefully controlled.

Progress is being made and there is a possibility that in time behavioral scientists will be able to develop more precise theories and definitions and better measuring instruments, seeking the exactness, consistency, and completeness that characterize investigation in the physical sciences.

Today we live in a world that attests to the miracles of physical science. Many diseases have been conquered. The Salk and Sabin vaccines promise to rid the world of poliomyelitis. Man's life span has been increased markedly in some countries, actually by almost two-thirds in the past century. Man has traveled at several times the speed of sound; he enjoys a more adequate diet, performs less physical labor, and suffers less from the discomforts of excessive heat and cold. He has entertainment available, at home or in his car, at the turn of a switch, and enjoys more leisure than he could have dreamed of a century ago. The splitting of the atom, space travel, and developments in the field of electronics such as the laser promise improvements and adventures that are beyond the scope of human imagination. All these improvements have resulted from the investigation of physical science.

However, there is less confidence about the improvement of the non-physical aspects of our culture. Despite all his marvelous gadgets there is some question about whether man is happier or more satisfied, or whether his basic needs are being fulfilled more effectively today than they were a century ago. The consequences of hot and cold wars and intergroup tensions and conflicts have become more frightening with the development of more sophisticated means of destruction.

Scientific methods must be employed with greater vigor and imagination to the behavioral aspects of our culture. The development of the behavioral sciences and their application to education and other human affairs presents one of the greatest challenges to twentieth-century man.

What is research?

How is research related to scientific method? The terms *research* and *scientific method* are sometimes used synonymously in educational discussions. Although it is true that the terms have some common elements of meaning, a distinction would be helpful.

For the purposes of this discussion, *research* is considered to be the more formal, systematic, and intensive process of carrying on a scientific method of analysis. Scientific method in problem solving may be an informal application of problem identification, hypothesis formulation, observation, analysis, and conclusion. One could reach a conclusion about the reason his car wouldn't start or why a fire occurred in an unoccupied house by employing a scientific method, but the processes involved would not likely be as structured as those of research. Research is a more systematic activity directed toward discovery and the development of an organized body of knowledge. Research may be defined as the systematic and objective analysis and recording of controlled observations that may lead to the development of generalizations, principles, or theories, resulting in prediction and ultimate control of many events that may be consequences or causes of specific activities.

Since definitions of this type are rather abstract, a summary of some of the characteristics of research may clarify its methodology:

1. Research is directed toward the solution of a problem. It may attempt to answer a question or to determine the relation between two or more variables.
2. Research emphasizes the development of generalizations, principles, or theories that will be helpful in predicting future occurrences. Research usually goes beyond the specific objects, groups, or situations investigated and infers characteristics of a target population from the sample observed. Research is more than information retrieval, the simple gathering of information. Although many school research departments gather and tabulate statistical information that may be useful in decision making, these activities are not properly termed research.
3. Research is based upon observable experience or empirical evidence. Certain interesting questions do not lend themselves to research procedures because they cannot be observed. Research rejects revelation and dogma as methods of establishing knowledge and accepts only what can be verified by observation.
4. Research demands accurate observation and description. The researcher uses quantitative, numerical measuring devices, the most precise means of description. The researcher selects or devises valid data-gathering instruments or procedures and employs appropriate mechanical, electronic, or psychometric devices to refine human observation, recording, computation, and analysis of data.
5. Research involves gathering new data from primary or first-hand sources or using existing data for a new purpose. Teachers frequently assign a so-called research project that involves writing a paper dealing with the life of a prominent person. The students are expected to read a number of encyclopedias, books, or periodical references, and synthesize the information in a written report. This is not research, for the data are not new. Merely reorganizing or restating what is already known and has already been written, valuable as it may be as a learning experience, is not research. It adds nothing to what is known.
6. Although research activity may at times be somewhat random and unsystematic, it is more often characterized by carefully designed procedures, always applying rigorous analysis. Although trial and error are often involved, research is rarely blind, shotgun investigation—trying something to see what happens.
7. Research requires expertise. The researcher knows what is already known about the problem and how others have investigated it. He has searched the related literature carefully. He is also thoroughly grounded in the terminology, the concepts, and the technical skill necessary to understand and analyze the data that he gathers.
8. Research strives to be objective and logical, applying every possible test to validate the procedures employed, the data collected, and the conclusions reached. The researcher attempts to eliminate personal bias. There is no attempt to persuade or to prove an emotionally held conviction. The emphasis is on testing rather than on proving the hypothesis. Although absolute

objectivity is as elusive as pure righteousness, the researcher tries to suppress bias and emotion in his analysis.

9. Research is characterized by patient and unhurried activity. It is rarely spectacular and the researcher must expect disappointment and discouragement as he pursues the answers to difficult questions.

10. Research is carefully recorded and reported. Each important term is defined, limiting factors are recognized, procedures are described in detail, references are carefully documented, results are objectively recorded, and conclusions are presented with scholarly caution and restraint. The written report and accompanying data are made available to the scrutiny of associates or other scholars. Any competent scholar will have the information necessary to analyze, evaluate, and even replicate the study.

11. Research sometimes requires courage. The history of science reveals that many important discoveries were made in spite of the opposition of political and religious authorities. The Polish scientist Copernicus (1473–1543) was condemned by church authorities when he announced his conclusion concerning the nature of the solar system. His theory that the sun, not the earth, was the center of the solar system, in direct conflict with the older Ptolemaic theory, angered supporters of prevailing religious dogma, who viewed his theory as a denial of the story of creation as described in the book of Genesis. Modern researchers in such fields as genetics, sexual behavior, and even business practices have aroused violent criticism from those whose personal convictions, experiences, or observations were in conflict with some of the research conclusions.

The rigorous standards of scientific research are apparent from an examination of these characteristics. The research worker should be a scholarly, imaginative person of the highest integrity, willing to spend long hours painstakingly seeking truth. However, it must be recognized that researchers are human beings. The ideals that have been listed are probably never completely realized. Like righteousness, they serve as goals to strive for, and are not all achieved by every researcher.

Many people have a superficial concept of research, picturing the research worker as a strange introverted individual who, shunning the company of his fellows, finds refuge in his laboratory. There, surrounded by test tubes, retorts, beakers, and other gadgets he carries on his mysterious activities. In reality the picture is quite different. Research is not at all mysterious, and is carried on by thousands of quite normal individuals, more often in teams than alone, very often in the factory, the school, or the community, as well as in the laboratory. Its importance is attested to by the tremendous amounts of time, manpower, and money spent on research by industry, universities, government agencies, and the professions. The key to the cultural development of the Western world has been research, reducing man's areas of ignorance by discovering new truths, which in turn lead to better predictions, better ways of doing things, and new and better products. We recognize the fruits of research: better consumer products, better ways of preventing and treating diseases, better ways of understanding the behavior of individuals and groups, and a better understanding of the world in which we live. In the field of education, we identify research with a better understanding of the individual, and a better understanding of the teaching-learning process and the conditions under which it is most successfully carried on.

Fundamental or pure research

The discussion to this point has described research in its more formal aspects. Research has drawn its pattern and spirit from the physical sciences and has represented a rigorous, structured type of analysis. The purpose of research has been seen as the development of theories by discovering broad generalizations or principles. It has employed careful sampling procedures in order to extend the findings beyond the group or situation studied. It has had little concern for the application of the findings to actual problems in areas considered to be the concern of people other than the investigator. This methodology is the approach of pure or fundamental research.

Fundamental research is usually carried on in a laboratory situation, often with animals as subjects. This type of research has been primarily the activity of psychologists rather than educators.

Applied research

Applied research has most of the characteristics of fundamental research, including the use of sampling techniques and the subsequent inferences about the target population. However, its purpose is improving a product or a proces—testing theoretical concepts in actual problem situations. Most educational research is applied research, for it attempts to develop generalizations about teaching-learning processes and instructional materials.

Fundamental research in the behavioral sciences may be concerned with the development and testing of theories of behavior. Educational research is concerned with the development and testing of theories of how students behave in an educational setting.

Action research

Since the late 1930s there has been great interest in social psychology and education in what has been called *action research*. In eduction this movement has had as its goal the involvement of both research specialist and classroom teacher in the study and application of research to educational problems in a particular classroom setting.

Action-research is focused on the immediate application, not on the development of theory, nor upon general application. It has placed its emphasis on a problem, here and now, in a local setting. Its findings are to be evaluated in terms of local applicability, not in terms of universal validity. Its purpose is to improve school practices and, at the same time, to improve those who try to improve the practices. The purpose of action research is to combine the research function with teacher growth in such qualities as objectivity, skill in research processes, habits of thinking, ability to work harmoniously with others, and professional spirit.

If most classroom teachers are to be involved in research activity it will probably be in the area of action-research. Modest studies may be made for the purpose of trying to improve local classroom practices. It is not likely that many teachers will have the time, resources, or technical background to engage in the more formal aspects of research activity. Fundamental research must continue to make its essential contribution to behavioral theory and applied research to the improvement of educational practices. These activities, however, will be primarily the function of research specialists, many of them subsidized by universities, private and government agencies, professional associations, and philanthropic foundations.

Stephen M. Corey, a leader in the field of action research, stated the case in this way:

> ... I have lost much of the faith I once had in the consequences of asking only the professional educational investigator to study the schools and to recommend what they should do. Incorporating these recommendations into the behavior pattern of practitioners involves some problems that so far have been insoluble. ... Most of the study of what should go and what should be added must be done in thousands of classrooms and American communities. These studies must be undertaken by those who may have to change the way they do things as a result of the studies. Our schools cannot keep up with the life they are supposed to sustain and improve unless teachers, pupils, supervisors, administrators, and school patrons continuously examine what they are doing. Singly and in groups, they must use their imaginations creatively and constructively to identify the practices that must be changed to meet the needs and demands of modern life, courageously try out those practices that give better promise, and methodically and systematically gather evidence to test their worth.
>
> This is the process I call action research. I hold no special brief for the name, but it has some currency and is sufficiently descriptive. What I will talk about is research that is undertaken by educational practitioners because they believe that by so doing they can make better decisions and engage in better actions.[2]

[2]Stephen M. Corey, *Action Research to Improve School Practices* (New York: Bureau of Publications, Teacher's College, Columbia University, 1953), p. vii. Used with permission of the publisher.

Many observers have deprecated action research as nothing more than the application of common sense or good management. All too frequently the action aspect has overshadowed the research element. To the extent that action is emphasized at the expense of research this type of activity fails to qualify as genuine research.

But whether or not it is worthy of the term *research* it does apply scientific thinking and methods to real-life problems and represents a great improvement over teachers' subjective judgments and decisions based upon folklore and their limited personal experiences.

In concluding this discussion it is important to realize that research may be carried on at various levels of complexity. Respectable research studies may be of the simple descriptive fact-finding variety that lead to useful generalizations. Actually many of the early studies in the behavioral sciences were useful in providing needed generalizations about the behavior or characteristics of individuals and of groups. Subsequent experimental studies of a more complex nature needed this groundwork information to suggest hypotheses for more precise analysis. The descriptive studies of the intellectually gifted, carried on since the early 1920s by the late Lewis M. Terman and his associates, have provided useful generalizations about the characteristics of this segment of the school population. Although these studies did not explain the factors underlying giftedness they did provide many hypotheses to be investigated by more sophisticated experimental methods.

Curriculum evaluation and research

The terms *curriculum evaluation* and *research* are sometimes used to describe the same type of activity, and perhaps the many similarities between them have tended to obscure their differences. Both evaluation and research employ the process of disciplined inquiry through the examination and logical analysis of empirical evidence. Both attempt to develop new knowledge and, to be done competently, require the expertise of the scientific investigator.

There are important differences. Research seeks to develop principles and generalizations by analyzing the relationships between variables. This body of knowledge attempts to provide a basis for prediction, extending its generalizations to other individuals, times, and settings.

Evaluation is concerned with a more immediate application, seeking to determine the merits of a particular educational product, process, or program in terms of carefully defined and agreed-upon objectives or values. Evaluation implies some judgment of the effectiveness, social utility, or desirability of the product, process, or program and is not concerned with generalizations that may be extended to other settings.

It answers such questions as: Which textbook should be adopted? Should a middle school program be instituted? Should an initial teaching alphabet program be introduced? Should the program in agriculture education be retained? Is the science curriculum developing the competencies that have been agreed upon by the faculty curriculum committee?

In summary, research seeks conclusions leading to new truths; evaluation seeks conclusions leading to recommendations and decisions.

ASSESSMENT

Assessment is concerned with the determination of progress that students have made toward educational goals at a particular time. The data are generated by a sampling process in such a way that no individual is tested over the whole test battery. It differs from evaluation in a significant way: It is not designed to evaluate the effectiveness of a particular process or program, but merely to estimate the achievement of large groups of individuals who have been exposed to many different educational and environmental influences.

Assessment also differs from research, for it does not seek to develop generalizations by analyzing the relationship between variables. It proposes no hypotheses and only attempts to reach broad generalizations without analysis of the variables involved.

The National Assessment of Educational Progress (NAEP), originally known as the Committee on Assessment of the Progress of Education, is now financed by the National Center for Educational Statistics, a division of the Department of Health, Education and Welfare. Since 1969, a nationwide testing program has been conducted in such fields as science, mathematics, literature, reading, and social studies, in four age groupings, in various geographical areas of the country, in communities of various sizes and in particular states, and has reported interesting, and sometimes alarming, evidence of the degree to which learning goals have or have not been realized.

Types of educational research

Any attempt to classify types of educational research poses a difficult problem. The fact that practically every textbook suggests a different system of classification provides convincing evidence that there is no generally accepted scheme.

To systematize a method of presentation, however, some pattern is desirable. At the risk of seeming arbitrary, and with a recognition of the danger of oversimplification, a framework is suggested that might clarify understanding of basic principles of research methodology. It should be noted that the system of classification is not important in itself, but only has value in making the analysis of research processes more comprehensible.

Actually, *all* research involves the elements of observation, description, and the analysis of what happens under certain circumstances. A rather simple three-point analysis may be used to classify educational research. Practically all studies fall under one, or a combination, of these types.

1. *Historical research* describes *what was.* The process involves investigating, recording, analyzing, and interpreting the events of the past for the purpose of discovering generalizations that are helpful in understanding the past, understanding the present, and to a limited extent, in anticipating the future.
2. *Descriptive research* describes *what is.* It involves the description, recording, analysis, and interpretation of conditions that now exist. It involves some type of comparison or contrast and may attempt to discover relationships that exist between existing nonmanipulated variables.
3. *Experimental research* describes *what will be* when certain variables are carefully controlled or manipulated. The focus is on variable relationships. As defined here, deliberate manipulation is always a part of the experimental method.

A complete chapter is devoted to each of these three types of research; to techniques of data-gathering, to areas of application, and to methods of analysis.

Summary

Man's desire to know about his world has led him from primitive superstition to modern scientific knowledge. From mysticism, dogma, and the limitations of unsystematic observation based upon personal experience, he has examined the process of thinking itself to develop the method of deductive-inductive thinking which has become the foundation of scientific method. Although first applied as a method of the physical sciences, the process of scientific inquiry has also become the prevailing method of the behavioral sciences.

Fundamental, or *pure*, research is the formal and systematic process of deductive-inductive analysis, leading to the development of theories. *Applied* research adapts the theories, developed through fundamental research, to the solution of problems. *Action* research, which may fail to attain the rigorous qualities of fundamental and applied research, attempts to apply the spirit of scientific method to the solution of problems in a particular setting, without any assumptions about the general application of findings beyond the situation studied.

Readers are reminded that research is essentially an intellectual and creative activity. The mastery of techniques and processes does not guarantee research competence, though these skills may help the creative problem-solver to reach his objectives more efficiently.

Suggested activities

1. Construct two syllogisms
   a. one that is logically sound
   b. one that is faulty; indicate the nature of the fallacy
2. Give two examples of inductive reasoning
   a. one that is sound
   b. one that is faulty; indicate the nature of the fallacy
3. Illustrate the application of Dewey's steps in problem solving. Choose one of the problems listed, or one of your own:
   a. brown patches on your lawn
   b. vandalism that you discover when you enter your classroom in the morning
   c. your car won't start when you leave for home
   d. getting an economical buy on canned peaches
   e. most of the members of your class failed an examination
4. Give an example of:
   a. a fundamental research problem
   b. an applied research problem
   c. an action research problem
5. To what extent have religious institutions resisted the claims of science?
6. Give an example of, and explain, a research study that could be profitably replicated.
7. Is there necessarily a conflict between the disciplines of the sciences and the humanities?
8. Explain why you agree or disagree with the following statements:
   a. excessive effort is spent on the development of theories because they don't usually work in real situations.
   b. science is more properly thought of as a method of problem solving, rather than as a field of knowledge.
   c. applied research is more important than basic research in contributing to man's welfare.

Bibliography

CONANT, JAMES B. *Science and Common Sense.* New Haven: Yale University Press, 1951.

CONANT, JAMES B. *Two Modes of Thought*. New York: Simon & Schuster, 1964.

DEWEY, JOHN. *How We Think*. Boston: Raytheon Education Co., 1933.

DEWEY, JOHN. *Logic: The Theory of Inquiry*. New York: Holt, Rinehart & Winston, 1938.

EBEL, ROBERT L. "Some Limitations of Basic Research in Education." *Phi Delta Kappan* 49 (Oct. 1967): 81–84.

FEIGL, HERBERT and MAY BROADBECK. *Readings in the Philosophy of Science*. New York: Appleton-Century-Crofts, 1953.

FRANK, PHILLIP G. *The Validation of Scientific Theories*. New York: Collier Books, 1961.

HAYS, W. L. *Quantification in Psychology*. Monterey, Calif.,: Brooks/Cole Publishing Co., 1967.

HELMSTADTER, GERALD C. *Research Concepts in Human Behavior*. New York: Appleton-Century-Crofts, 1970.

JONES, W. T. *The Sciences and the Humanities: Conflict and Reconciliation*. Berkeley: University of California Press, 1965.

KAPLAN, ABRAHAM. *The Conduct of Inquiry*. San Francisco: Chandler Publishing Co., 1964.

REAGAN, MICHAEL D. "Basic and Applied Research: A Meaningful Distinction?" *Science* 155 (Jan. 6, 1967): 1383–1386.

SKINNER, B. F. *Walden Two*. New York: Macmillan Co., 1948.

SNOW, C. P. *Two Cultures and the Scientific Revolution*. New York: Cambridge University Press, 1959.

SELECTING A PROBLEM
AND PREPARING
A RESEARCH PROPOSAL

Chapter 2

One of the most difficult phases of the graduate research project is the choice of a suitable problem. The beginner is likely to select a problem that is much too broad in scope. This may be due to his lack of understanding of the nature of research and systematic problem-solving activity. It may also be due to his enthusiastic, but naïve, desire to solve an important problem quickly and immediately.

Those who are more experienced know that research is often tedious, painfully slow, and rarely spectacular. They realize that the search for truth and the solution of important problems take a great deal of time and energy and the intensive application of logical thinking. Research makes its contribution to human welfare by countless small additions to knowledge. The researcher has some of the characteristics of the ant, who brings his single grain of sand to the anthill.

Before considering the ways in which problems may be identified, a discussion of a few of the characteristics of research and the activities of the researcher would seem appropriate. Research is more often a team endeavor than an individual activity. Researchers working in groups attack problems in different ways, pooling their knowledge and ideas and sharing the results of their efforts. Highly publicized discoveries usually result from the cumulative efforts of many, working as teams over long periods of time. They are rarely the product of a single individual working in isolation.

Great discoveries rarely happen by accident. When they do, the researcher is usually well-grounded and possesses the skill, known as serendipity, to recognize the significance of these fortunate occurrences. He is imaginative enough to seize the opportunity presented and to carry it through to a fruitful conclusion. Pasteur has observed that chance favors the prepared mind.

The researcher is a specialist, rather than a generalist. He employs the principle of the rifle rather than the shotgun, analyzing limited aspects of broad problems. Critics have complained that much social research consists of learning more and more about less and less until the researcher knows everything about nothing. This is a clever statement, but an exaggeration. The opposite statement, equally clever and exaggerated, characterizes much ineffective problem solving: learning less and less about more and more until one knows nothing about everything.

There is a danger, however, that research activity may focus upon such fragmentary aspects of a problem that it has little relevance to the formulation of a general theory. An analysis of the relationship between a few isolated factors in a complex situation may seem attractive as a research project, but it will make little or no contribution to a body of knowledge. Research is more than compiling, counting, and tabulating data. It involves deducing the consequences of hypotheses through careful observation and the application of rigorous logic.

It is sometimes important to discover that a generalization is probably *not* true. Beginning researchers frequently associate this type of conclusion with a sense of personal failure, for they become emotionally committed to their hypotheses. Research, however, is a process of *testing*, rather than *proving*, and implies an objectivity that lets the data lead where they will.

The academic research problem

Academic research projects have been subjected to much criticism, both by the academic community and by the general public. The academic research project is usually a requirement in partial fulfillment of the requirements of a graduate course or for an advanced degree. The initial motivation may not be the desire to engage in research, but the practical need of meeting a requirement. Unfortunately, few such studies make a significant contribution to the development or refinement of knowledge or to the improvement of practice. The lack of time, financial resources, experience, and expertise of the researcher, and the academic hazard of departing from a relatively safe, short-range project are, understandably, hindrances to significant contributions. But these projects are often justified on the grounds that, once the student develops some research competency, he will use his "know-how" to seek solutions to basic problems and will make a contribution to the body of knowledge upon which sound practices are based. Too often this expectation is not realized, for relatively few students, particularly in education, carry on further studies. This lack of a strong research tradition in education is regrettable, though it may be partially explained.

Few graduate students in education are full-time students, consequently they are often victims of the competing demands of teaching, supervising student activities, attending conferences and workshops, or participating in administrative activity. Many of them are not on campus while they are writing the thesis or dissertation, and they miss the continuing intellectual stimulation of the university faculty, discussions with fellow graduate students, the readily available resources of the library, and the opportunity of the full-time student to absorb the scholarly atmosphere of the university community.

These students tend to select narrow, practical problems that are closely related to their school experience. These problems are frequently low-level investigations, with little relevance to theory.

Perhaps more significant master's-degree or doctoral studies could be carried on under the direction of an advisor or major professor who is devoting his own energies to research on a significant problem. The efforts of degree candidates thus could be directed toward certain restricted phases of the major problem, making possible long-term longitudinal studies. Such studies as those by the late Lewis M. Terman at Stanford University of gifted children, followed over 40 years, represent the cumulative attack that is likely to yield more significant results than the uncoordinated investigations of candidates whose efforts lack this unifying direction and continuity.

It has also been noted that faculty members in schools of education have not been as productive in research as their colleagues in other parts of the university. Schools of education have placed great emphasis on teaching, coordinating conferences, conducting school surveys, and providing consulting services to schools and communities. Perhaps these activities have been emphasized at the expense of research.

Since the early 1960s, the massive participation of the federal government in the support of educational research has had great impact on schools of education. Funds have been made available for significant long-range studies, conducted by individuals and by teams of faculty researchers, and have provided financial support and valuable apprenticeship opportunity for graduate students.

LEVELS OF RESEARCH PROJECTS

In the light of the varied types and purposes of students' projects, the choice of a problem will depend upon the level at which the research is done. A problem appropriate for a beginner in a first course in research would be different from that selected for the more rigorous requirements of the master's thesis or the doctoral dissertation. The first topic will necessarily be a modest one which can be carried on by an inexperienced researcher in a limited period of time. The emphasis will be placed upon the learning process of the beginning researcher, rather than on his actual contribution to education. This statement does not imply that the product is necessarily unimportant. It merely recognizes that the limitations of the first research project place the emphasis on learning how, with the hope that subsequent investigations will progressively yield more significant contributions to the advancement of knowledge.

Some students choose a first problem that can be expanded later into a more comprehensive treatment at the level of the master's thesis or the doctoral dissertation. The first study thus serves as an exploratory process.

SOURCES OF PROBLEMS

The choice of a suitable problem is always difficult. Few beginners possess real problem awareness, and even the more experienced researcher hesitates at this step. It is a serious responsibility to commit oneself to a problem that will inevitably require much time and energy and which is so academically significant.

What are the most likely sources to which one may go for a suitable research problem, or from which one may develop a sense of problem awareness?

1. Many of the problems confronted in the classroom, the school, or the community lend themselves to investigation, and they are perhaps more appropriate for the beginning researcher than are problems more remote from his own teaching experience. What organizational or management procedures are employed? How is learning material presented? To what extent does one method yield more effective results than another? How do teachers feel about these procedures? How do pupils and parents feel about them? What out-of-school activities and influences seem to affect students and the teaching-learning process?

Teachers will discover "acres of diamonds" in their own back yards, and an inquisitive and imaginative mind may discover in one of these problem areas an interesting and worthwhile research project.

2. Technological changes and curricular developments are constantly bringing forth new problems and new opportunities for research. Perhaps more than ever before, educational innovations are being advocated in classroom organization, in teaching materials and procedures, and in

the application of technical devices and equipment. Such innovations as teaching by television, programmed instruction, modified alphabets, new subject matter concepts and approaches, flexible scheduling, and team teaching need to be carefully evaluated through the research process.

3. The graduate academic experience should stimulate the questioning attitude toward prevailing practices and effectively promote problem awareness. Classroom lectures, class discussions, seminar reports, and out-of-class exchanges of ideas with fellow students and professors will suggest many stimulating problems to be solved. Students who are fortunate enough to have graduate assistantships have an especially advantageous opportunity to profit from the stimulation of close professional relationships with faculty members and fellow assistants.

Reading assignments in textbooks, special assignments, research reports, and term papers will suggest additional areas of needed research. Research articles often suggest techniques and procedures for the attack on other problems. A critical evaluation may reveal faults or defects that made published findings inconclusive or misleading. Many research articles suggest problems for further investigation that may prove fruitful.

Such specialized sources as the *Encyclopedia of Educational Research, Dissertation Abstracts International, the Handbook of Research on Teaching*, and similar publications are rich sources for problem seekers.

4. Consultation with the course instructor, advisor, or major professor is helpful. Although the student should not expect research problems to be assigned, consultation with the more experienced faculty member is a desirable practice. Most students feel insecure as they approach the choice of a research problem. They wonder if the problem they may have in mind is significant enough, feasible, and reasonably free of unknown hazards. To expect the beginner to arrive at the advisor's office with a completely acceptable problem is quite unrealistic. One of the most important functions of the research advisor is to help the student clarify his thinking, achieve a sense of focus, and develop a manageable problem from one that may be vague and too complex.

The following list may suggest some problem areas from which research problems may be defined.

1. Programmed instruction—scrambled texts—teaching machines—computer-assisted instruction
2. Television instruction—closed circuit
3. Modified alphabets—Unifon—Initial Teaching Alphabet
4. Flexible scheduling
5. Team teaching
6. Evaluation of learning—reporting to parents
7. Student regulation/control
8. Evaluation of learning—practices—philosophies

9. Homework policies and practices
10. Field trips
11. School buildings and facilities—lighting—space—safety
12. Extracurricular programs
13. Student out-of-school activities—employment—recreation—cultural activity —reading—television viewing
14. Teacher out-of-school activities—employment—political activity—recreation
15. The open classroom
16. Linguistics
17. New approaches to biology/chemistry/physics
18. Language laboratries—foreign languages—reading
19. Multiple textbooks
20. Independent study programs
21. Advanced placement program
22. Audiovisual programs
23. Sociometry
24. Health services
25. Guidance-counseling programs
26. Teacher morale—annoyances and satisfactions
27. Teacher welfare—salaries—merit rating—retirement—tenure
28. Educational organizations—local, state, and national—NEA—AFT
29. Inner-city schools—the culturally deprived—Head Start—Upward Bound— tutoring
30. Preservice education of teachers—student teaching
31. In-service programs
32. Racial integration—student—teacher
33. Parochial/private school problems
34. Follow-up of graduates—early school leavers
35. Religion and education—released time programs—dismissed time—shared time
36. Non-school sponsored social organizations or clubs
37. School district reorganization
38. Community pressures on the school—academic freedom—controversial issues
39. Legal liability of teachers
40. Cadet teaching—teacher recruitment
41. Teaching internship
42. Sex education
43. Ability grouping—acceleration—retardation/promotion
44. Special education—speech therapy—clinical services—social services
45. Problems in higher education—selection—prediction of success—graduate programs
46. Work-study programs
47. Comparison of the effectiveness of two teaching methods/procedures
48. Self-image analysis
49. Vocational objectives of students
50. History of an institution, program, or organization
51. Factors associated with the selection of teaching/nursing/social work as a career
52. Case studies

For those members of the class who are not teachers, some of the problem areas listed may be appropriate in social agency, hospital, or industrial situations.

EVALUATING THE PROBLEM

Before the proposed research problem can be considered appropriate, several searching questions should be raised. Only when those questions are answered in the affirmative can the problem be considered a good one.

1. Is this the type of problem that can be effectively solved through the process of research? Can relevant data be gathered to test the theory or find the answer to the problem under consideration?
2. Is the problem significant? Is an important principle involved? Would the solution make any difference as far as educational theory or practice is concerned? If not, there are undoubtedly more significant problems waiting to be investigated.
3. Is the problem a new one? Is the answer already available? Ignorance of prior studies may lead a student to spend time needlessly on a problem already investigated by some other worker.

   Although novelty or originality is an important consideration, the fact that a problem has been investigated in the past does not mean that it is no longer worthy of study. There are times when it is appropriate to replicate (repeat) a study to verify its conclusions or to extend the validity of its findings to a different situation.
4. Is research on the problem feasible? After a research probject has been evaluated, there remains the problem of suitability for a particular researcher. Although the problem may be a good one, is it a good problem for me? Will I be able to carry it through to a successful conclusion? Some of the questions that should be raised are the following:
   a. Am I competent to plan and carry out a study of this type? Do I know enough about this field to understand its significant aspects and to interpret my findings? Am I skillful enough to develop, administer, and interpret the necessary data-gathering devices and procedures? Am I well grounded in the necessary knowledge of research design and statistical procedures?
   b. Are pertinent data accessible? Are valid and reliable data-gathering devices and procedures available? Will school authorities permit me to contact the students, conduct necessary experiments or administer necessary tests, interview teachers, or have access to important cumulative records? Will I be able to get the sponsorship necessary to open doors that otherwise would be closed to me?
   c. Will I have the necessary financial resources to carry on this study? What will be the expense involved in data-gathering equipment, printing, test materials, travel, and clerical help? If the project is an expensive one, what is the possibility of getting a grant from a philanthropic foundation or from the U. S. Office of Education?
   d. Will I have enough time to complete the project? Will there be time to devise the procedures, select the data-gathering devices, gather and analyze the data, and complete the research report? Since most academic programs impose time limitations, certain worthwhile projects of a longitudinal type are precluded.

e. Will I have the courage and determination to pursue the study in spite of the difficulties and social hazards that may be involved? Will I be willing to work aggressively when data are difficult to gather and when others are reluctant to cooperate? Sex education, racial integration, teaching about communism, and other controversial problem areas, however, may not be appropriate for a beginning research project.

The research proposal[1]

The preparation of a research proposal is an important step in the research process. Many institutions require that a proposal be submitted before any project is approved. This provides a basis for the evaluation of the project and gives the advisor a basis for assisting during the period of his direction. It also provides a systematic plan of procedure for the researcher to follow.

The proposal is comparable to the blueprint which the architect prepares before the bids are let and building commences. The initial draft proposal is subject to modification in the light of the analysis by the student and his project advisor. Since good research must be carefully planned and systematically carried out, procedures that are improvised from step to step will not suffice. A worthwhile research project is likely to result only from a well-designed proposal.

The outline which follows presents the essential parts of a research proposal, with a brief explanation of each step.

The statement of the problem, either in question form or as a declarative statement. This attempt to focus on a stated goal gives direction to the research process. It must be limited enough in scope to make a definite conclusion possible. The major statement or question may be followed by minor statements or questions. The problem areas that previously have been listed in this chapter are not statements of problems. They are merely broad areas of concern from which problems may be selected.

A problem suggests a specific answer or conclusion. Usually a controversy or a difference of opinion exists. A cause-effect relationship may be suggested upon the basis of personal observation and experience. Do children who have had kindergarten experience demonstrate greater academic achievement in the first grade than those who have not had this experience? Is participation in high school competitive athletics detrimental to academic achievement? Does racial segregation have a damaging effect upon the self-image of minority group children? Does knowledge of participation in an experiment have a stimulating effect upon

[1]Compare the research proposal described here with the format or outline of a research report described in Chapter 9.

the reading achievement of participants? These four questions are problem statements. They involve more than information gathering. They suggest answers or conclusions and provide a focus for research activity.

The hypothesis. It may be appropriate here to formulate a major hypothesis and several minor hypotheses. This approach clearly establishes the nature of the problem and the logic underlying the investigation, and gives direction to the data-gathering process. A good hypothesis has several basic characteristics:

a. It should be reasonable.
b. It should be consistent with known facts or theories.
c. It should be stated in such a way that it can be tested and found to be probably true or probably false.
d. It should be stated in the simplest possible terms.

The hypothesis is a tentative answer to a question. It is a hunch, or an educated guess, to be subjected to the process of verification or disconfirmation. The gathering of data and the logical analysis of data relationships provide a method of confirming or disconfirming the hypothesis by deducing its consequences.

The hypothesis should first be stated in positive or substantive form. "The academic achievement of high school athletes is significantly higher than the achievement of nonathletes." In the section on research procedures and in the section that presents the findings and conclusions, the statistical hypothesis should be stated in negative or null form. "There is no significant difference between the academic achievement of high school athletes and that of nonathletes." The null form may seem strange and unnecessarily obscure to the beginner in research. However, because of the logic of statistical analysis the null form is preferable. The understanding of the advantage of the null hypothesis necessitates an understanding of sampling error, a concept that is explained in the chapters on the experimental method and the inferential statistical interpretation of data (Chapters 4 and 8).

It is important that the hypothesis be formulated before data are gathered. Suppose that the researcher gathers some data and, on the basis of these, notes something that looks like the basis for an alternative hypothesis. Since any particular set of observations may display an extreme distribution, using it to test the hypothesis would possibly lead to an unwarranted conclusion.

The formulation of the hypothesis in advance of the data-gathering process is necessary for an unbiased investigation. It is not inappropriate to formulate additional hypotheses after data are collected, but they should be tested on the basis of new data, not on the old data that suggested them.

The significance of the problem.   It is important that the researcher point out how the answer to the question or the solution to the problem can influence educational theory or practice. Careful formulation and presentation of the implications or possible applications of knowledge helps to give the project an urgency, justifying its worth.

Failure to include this step in the proposal may well leave the researcher with a problem without significance—a search for data of little ultimate value. Many of the tabulating or "social bookkeeping" research problems should be abandoned if they do not pass the critical test of significance. Perhaps university library shelves would not groan with the weight of so many unread and forgotten dissertations if this criterion of significance had been rigorously applied. With so many gaps in educational theory, and so many areas of educational practice in need of analysis, there is little justification for the expenditure of research effort on trivial or superficial investigations.

Definitions, assumptions, and limitations.   It is important to define all unusual terms that could be misinterpreted. This definition helps to establish the frame of reference with which the researcher approaches the problem. The assumptions that the researcher makes, and the restrictions and limitations that he recognizes, must be frankly stated. This recognition helps to focus attention on valid objectives, and helps to minimize the dangers of overgeneralization.

The variables to be considered should be defined clearly and unambiguously in operational terms. Such terms as *academic achievement* and *intelligence* are useful concepts, but they cannot be used as criteria unless they are defined as observable samples of behavior. Academic grades assigned by teachers or scores on standardized achievement tests are operational definitions of *achievement*. A score on a standardized intelligence test is an operational definition of *intelligence*. These measures yield tangible numerical values that make statistical inferences possible.

A résumé of related literature.   A brief summary of previous research and the writings of recognized experts provides evidence that the researcher is familiar with what is already known, and with what is still unknown and untested. Since effective research must be based upon past knowledge, this step helps to eliminate the duplication of what has been done, and provides useful hypotheses and helpful suggestions for significant investigation.

In searching related literature the researcher should note certain important elements:

a. Reported problems or closely related problems that have been investigated
b. Design of the study, including procedures employed and data-gathering instruments used

c. Populations that were studied
d. Variables that could have affected the findings
e. Pitfalls or faults that were apparent
f. Recommendations for further research

The review of related literature should conclude with a summary of areas of agreement and disagreement in findings. Review articles, those that summarize related studies, are often useful in saving time and effort. Capitalizing on the review of expert researchers can be fruitful, for such reviews as those included in the *Review of Educational Research* are usually critical and provide helpful ideas and suggestions.

A careful and detailed analysis of proposed research procedures. This part of the proposal outlines the entire research plan. It describes just what must be done, how it will be done, what data will be needed, what data-gathering devices will be employed (with an evaluation of their validity and reliability), how sources of data will be selected, and how the data will be analyzed and conclusions reached.

A time schedule. A schedule should be prepared so that the researcher may budget his time and energy effectively. Dividing the project into parts and assigning dates for the completion of each part help to systematize the project and minimize the natural tendency to procrastinate.

Some phases of the problem cannot be started until other phases have been completed. Some parts of the final research report, such as the review of related literature, can be completed and typed while waiting for the data to be gathered. Since academic research projects usually involve rather critical time limitations and definite deadlines for filing the completed report, this preplanning of procedures with definite date goals is most important.

From time to time the major professor or advisor may request a progress report indicating how well the project is progressing. This device also serves as a stimulus, helping the researcher to move systematically toward the goal of completing the project.

The first research project

Experience has indicated that one way to understand the methodology and processes of research is actually to engage in research. Such a project may be very modest in nature and necessarily limited by time, the experience of the student, and many other factors associated with the graduate student's home and teaching obligations. However, the methodology may be learned by this doing and thinking under the careful supervision of the instructor of the beginning course in research. Respectable research projects have been undertaken and reported on within a semester's time, even within an eight-week summer session. Although most of these studies have been of the descriptive-survey type, some simple historical and experimental studies have also been completed. The emphasis must necessarily be placed on the process rather than on the product or its contribution to the improvement of educational practice. A study chosen for this first project, however, may not be of great enough significance to serve as an appropriate thesis problem.

The full-scale project may be either an individual or a group enterprise. Groups of three to five graduate students can profitably work together on the planning of the study. Data-gathering devices may be chosen or constructed through joint enterprise. Data may be gathered within the university graduate class, or in the classrooms, schools, or communities in which the group's members teach. However, it is recommended that the next steps—organization and analysis of data and the writing of the final report—be an individual project. There is always the danger in a group project of "letting George do it," and incidentally letting George get all of the values of the experience.

This recommended combination of group effort in the initial stages and individual effort in the later stages represents a compromise that seems effective and enables students to carry through a study in a limited amount of time with reasonable opportunity for personal growth. For some of those who plan to write a thesis in partial fulfillment of degree requirements, this first project may serve as preparation. For others, it may initiate a study capable of subsequent expansion into a thesis or dissertation.

Many research course instructors believe that a more practicable requirement would be the preparation of a carefully designed research proposal, rather than a limited-scope study. There is much to be said for this point of view, for the beginning research student is inexperienced, the time is short, and there is a real danger of conveying a superficial concept of sound research. The author has assigned the study as part of the course requirement, but other instructors may find the research proposal a more effective exercise.

Topics used by students in a beginning graduate course in educational research

1. An Analysis of Master's-Degree-in-Education Programs at a Group of Midwest Universities
2. The Status of Latin in Indiana High Schools
3. A Comparative Study of the Self-Concept of Two Groups of Negro Youth Attending a Segregated and an Integrated High School

4. Attitudes of a Group of High School Seniors toward Selective Military Service
5. Discipline Problems at Washington High School As Viewed by the Teachers
6. Discipline Problems at Washington High School As Viewed by Senior Students
7. A Comparison between Two Methods of Teaching Typing
8. The Treatment of Educational Topics in the Indianapolis *Star*
9. Truancy in Marion County High Schools
10. Class Size in Wayne Township Elementary Schools
11. The Summer Employment of Arlington High School Juniors
12. Attitudes of a Group of Students toward Substitute Teachers
13. Absenteeism among Freshmen at Southport High School
14. A Follow-up Study of the 1963 Graduates of Grace Lutheran School
15. A History of the Indiana Boy's School, Plainfield, Indiana
16. The Self-Concept of a Group of Gifted and Retarded Children
17. The Relationship between Automobile Ownership and Academic Achievement at Lincoln High School
18. An Analysis of the Reading Content of the Shortridge *Daily Echo*
19. The Influence of Entering Age upon Subsequent Achievement at First, Second, and Third Grade Levels in Washington Township
20. The Attitudes of a Group of Fifth Grade Teachers toward the Weekday Religious Education Program
21. A Survey of Organizational Structures and Resources of Curriculum Laboratories in Colleges of Teacher Education in a Three-State Area
22. Problems of a Selected Group of High School Freshmen As Indicated by the SRA Youth Inventory
23. A Survey of Library Facilities in Warren Township Elementary Schools
24. A Comparison of the Academic Achievement of Athletes and Nonathletes at Kokomo High School
25. A Follow-up Study of Nonpromoted Students at School #86
26. The Reading Habits of a Selected Group of Teachers
27. The Attitudes of a Group of Teachers toward Professional Organizations
28. Why a Group of Freshmen Chose Butler University
29. The Attitudes of a Group of High School Seniors toward Academic Dishonesty
30. The Instrumental Music Budgets of a Group of Central Illinois High Schools
31. Attitudes of a Group of High School Students toward Secret Societies
32. The Predictive Value of Entrance Examinations at the Methodist Hospital School of Nursing
33. An Analysis of the Effect of Trial Promotion on the Achievement of a Group of Underachievers
34. The Influence of Color Combinations in the Teaching of Spelling
35. Attitudes of a Group of Parents toward Homework Assignments
36. A History of Shortridge High School
37. A Comparison of Vocabulary Levels in Three Textbook Series in Reading
38. A Survey of the Buying Practices of a Group of Teenagers
39. An Analysis of Selected Factors Associated with Dropouts at Arlington High School
40. Why a Group of Teachers Left Teaching
41. Allowances and Earnings of Pike Township High School Seniors
42. Attitudes of a Group of College Seniors toward Social Protest Movements
43. The Political Activities of a Group of High School Teachers

44. A Comparison of the Television Viewing Habits of a Group of Gifted and Slow-Learning Pupils
45. The Views of Selected Baptist Laymen, Ministers, and National Church Leaders Concerning Issues Related to the Tradition of Separation of Church and State
46. A Study of the Religious Orthodoxy of Five Hundred Elementary and Secondary School Teachers
47. Authority Images of a Selected Group of Inner-City Children
48. A Study of Socioeconomic Status in the Butler-Tarkington Area, a Racially Integrated Community
49. Pupil and Teacher Reactions toward a Midwest Airborn Television Instruction Program
50. A Comparative Analysis of Programmed Instruction and Traditional Classroom Instruction As Measured by the Algebra Achievement Test
51. Student Participation in the Activity Program at Lawrence Central High School
52. The Status of Music in the Western Yearly Meeting of the Society of Friends
53. Two Methods of Teaching Algebra, Modern and Traditional
54. Civic and Community Activities of the Professional Staff of the Indianapolis Public Schools
55. The Leisure Activities of Gifted and Nongifted Students at School #86
56. The Influence of Hearing and Visual Acuity on the Reading Ability of a Selected Group of Second Grade Pupils
57. The Attitudes and Behavior of Freshmen and Seniors Regarding Classroom Dishonesty at Sheridan High School
58. The Influence of Kindergarten Experience on the Subsequent Reading Achievement of a Group of First Grade Pupils
59. The Achievement of Twins, Both Identical and Fraternal, in the Lebanon, Indiana, Metropolitan School District
60. Apathy Regarding Poliomyelitis Vaccination of a Selected Group of Graduate Students
61. Factors Associated with Withdrawal from a Diploma School of Nursing
62. An Analysis of Emergency Admissions at St. Vincent's Hospital
63. The Attitudes of a Group of Parents toward the Cooperative Nursery Program
64. The Interests of a Three-Year-Old Boy
65. The Influence of Selected Experiences upon a Group of Culturally Deprived Children
66. The Attitudes of a Group of Parents toward Busing to Achieve Racial Integration

The topics listed above were selected by inexperienced student researchers who were carrying on a project in partial fulfillment of the requirements of a beginning course in educational research. Most of the topics were short, action-type descriptive studies, not based upon random selection and random assignment of subjects or observations. Notice that the wording of the titles did not imply generalization of the conclusions to a wider population. The primary purpose was a learning exercise, not a contribution to a field of knowledge.

For experienced researchers projects would necessarily be more theory-oriented with conclusions generalized beyond the specific group observed. At this more advanced level a careful process of randomization would be desirable, if not necessary, and the research design would be much more rigorous. The details of some of the more sophisticated procedures are partially explained in subsequent chapters of this text and in other relevant sources, particularly discussion of experimental and descriptive research processes, the selection or construction of data-gathering devices, and the statistical analysis of data.

Seasoned researchers may plan to submit research proposals to foundations or government agencies for financial support. The beginning researcher may not feel the need for suggestions, but it may be helpful to understand the detailed type of information that a foundation or agency would expect to receive before committing support funds.

The following is a list of suggestions for those who seek financial support:

1. Write the proposal very carefully. A carelessly written proposal suggests to the evaluators that the research project would be carelessly done.
2. State your problem in such a way that the proposal evaluators, who are capable and experienced in judging research proposals, but know nothing about your project, will be able to judge its worth and the likelihood of its contributing to a significant area of knowledge.
3. Indicate how your study will add to or refine present knowledge.
4. State your hypothesis or hypotheses in both conceptual and operational terms and in both substantive and null form.
5. Indicate that you are completely familiar with the field of investigation and are aware of all recent studies in the problem area.
6. Indicate how you propose to test your hypotheses, describing your research design, and the data-gathering instruments or procedures that you will use, indicating their known validity and reliability.
7. Describe your sampling procedures, indicating how you will randomly select and randomly assign your subjects or observations.
8. Indicate the extraneous variables that must be recognized and explain how you propose to minimize their influence.
9. Explain the statistical procedures that you will employ, indicating any computer application that you will use.
10. Prepare a budget proposal estimating the funds required for:
    a. wages, including any fringe benefits
    b. purchase or rental of special equipment or supplies
    c. travel expense
    d. clerical expense
    e. additional overhead expense that may be involved
    f. publication costs
11. Provide some tangible evidence of your competence by listing:
    a. research projects that you have carried on or actively participated in
    b. a list of your scholarly journal articles, including abstracts of your studies
    c. personal letters of recommendation from researchers who are recognized authorities in your area of investigation

Summary

Academic research projects are usually required in partial fulfillment of the requirements of a course or a degree program. The motivation is not always a genuine desire to engage in research, and in addition, limitations of time, money, and experience usually preclude the consideration of problems that could make significant contributions to educational theory and practice.

The choice of a suitable problem is one of the most difficult tasks facing the beginning researcher. Students tend to define problems that are too broad in scope or that deal with too fragmentary aspects of the problem. Consultation with the course instructor or advisor is particularly helpful in identifying a problem that is manageable and significant enough to justify the time and effort that will be required.

Problems are found in the teachers' daily classroom, school, and community experiences. Technological and social changes call for research evidence to chart new courses in educational practice. Graduate academic experience helps to promote problem awareness through classroom activities, the reading of research studies, and interaction with instructors, advisors, and fellow students.

A good research problem has the qualities of significance, originality, and feasibility. The researcher should evaluate a proposed problem in the light of his competence, the availability of data, the financial demands of the project, the limitations of time, and the possible difficulties and social hazards involved.

A research proposal is required by many institutions, and serves as a useful basis for the evaluation of a project as well as a guide for the researcher. The agendum contains a clear and concise statement of the problem, the hypothesis or hypotheses involved, a recognition of the significance of the problem, definitions of important terms, assumptions and limitations, a résumé of related literature, an analysis of proposed research procedures, and a time schedule. Some advisors request a progress report from time to time in order to evaluate the progress of the investigation.

One effective way to learn about research is to conduct a study in connection with the beginning research course. Another way is to write a research proposal which may involve all of the steps in the research process except the gathering and analysis of data and the formulation of conclusions. Either of these exercises gives a focus to the discusssions about research and may help in developing some competence and the research point of view. It may even encourage some teachers to conduct modest studies in their own schools during or after the completion of their graduate programs.

Exercises

1. The following research topics are faulty or are completely inappropriate. Revise each one, if possible, so that it describes a feasible project or proposal for this course.
   a. The Attitudes of Teachers toward Merit Rating
   b. How to Teach Poetry Most Effectively
   c. The Best Way to Teach Spelling
   d. The Evils of Alcohol
   e. Does Ability Grouping Meet the Needs of Students?
   f. The Adequacy of Law Enforcement
   g. The Hazards of Smoking
   h. Why the Discussion Method Is Better Than the Lecture Method
   i. The Fallacy of Evolution
2. State a hypothesis, first in positive or substantive form and then in null or statistical form.
3. Define the following terms in operational form:
   a. intelligence
   b. creativity
   c. coordination
   d. authoritarian
   e. memory
4. In a research study is a hypothesis to be tested always preferable to a question to be answered? Why or why not?
5. What are some of the more effective ways to find a suitable research problem?

Bibliography

AGIN, AVIS P. "Overview of Recent Research in Reading." *Elementary English* 52 (March 1975): 370-375.

ANDERSON, RICHARD C. ET AL., eds. *Current Research on Instruction.* Englewood Cliffs, N.J.: Prentice-Hall, 1969.

EARLY, MARGARET. "Important Research on Reading and Writing." *Phi Delta Kappan* 57 (Jan. 1976): 298-301.

ENNIS, ROBERT H. "Operational Definitions." *American Educational Research Journal* 1 (May 1964): 183-201.

GAGE, N. L. *Handbook of Research on Teaching.* Chicago: Rand McNally & Co., 1963.

HEARN, D. D., JOEL BURDIN, and LILLIAN KATZ, eds. *Current Research and Perspectives in Open Education.* Washington, D.C.: American Association of Elementary-Kindergarten-Nursery School Education, 1973.

KERLINGER, FRED N. ET AL., eds. *Review of Research in Education*. Itasca, Ill.: F. E. Peacock, Publishers, 1973–date.

LEHMANN, IRVIN J. and WILLIAM A. MEHERENS, eds. *Educational Research: Readings in Focus*. New York: Holt, Rinehart & Winston, 1971.

MARTIN, LYN S. and BARBARA N. PAVAN. "Current Research on Open Space, Non-Grading, Vertical Grouping, and Team Teaching." *Phi Delta Kappan* 57 (January 1976): 310–315.

ROSENAU, M. J. "Serendipity." *Journal of Bacteriology* 29 (February 1935): 91–98.

TRAVERS, R. M. W., ed. *Handbook of Research on Teaching*. 2d ed. Chicago: Rand McNally & Co., 1973.

WARD, A. W. ET AL., "Evaluation of Published Research in Education." *American Educational Research Journal* 12 (Spring 1975): 109–128.

WESTBURY, IAN and ARNOLD A. BELLACK, eds. *Research into Classroom Procedures*. New York: Teachers College Press, 1971.

THE USE OF REFERENCE MATERIALS

Chapter 3

Practically all human knowledge can be found in books and libraries. Unlike other animals that must start anew with each generation, man builds upon the accumulated and recorded knowledge of the past. His constant adding to the vast store of knowledge makes possible progress in all areas of human endeavor.

Undergraduate students sometimes receive special instruction in the use of the library and its facilities, but too often their library activites are confined to assigned and suggested readings. Graduate students must find their own references. Few graduate students, however, and not all faculty members, have adequate knowledge of the library and its many resources for the effective search for specialized knowledge.

Extensive use of the library and thorough investigation of related literature are essential in preparing graduate term papers, seminar reports, and in planning and carrying out the kind of searching involved in special field problems, theses, and dissertations.

The search for reference material is a time-consuming but fruitful phase of the graduate program. A familiarity with the literature in any problem area helps the student to discover what is already known, what others have attempted to find out, what methods of attack have been promising or disappointing, and what problems remain to be solved. Knowing how to use the library effectively should receive primary emphasis in the graduate program in education. To know what sources to use, what sources are available, and where and how to find them will save many hours of aimless activity.

Using the library

The graduate student should become thoroughly acquainted with the university library, the location of its varied facilities, and the regulations governing the use and circulation of materials. Many university libraries have a printed guide that contains helpful information. A diagram may indicate the location of the stacks, the periodicals room, the reference division, reading rooms, and special collections of books, microfilm or microcard equipment, clippings, manuscripts, or pamphlets. Another useful part of the guide may list the periodicals to which the library subscribes and the names of special indexes, abstracts, and other references available. A third section may deal with the regulations concerning the use of the stacks, the use of reserve books, and the procedures for securing materials held by the library or those that may be procured from another library.

It is well to use the skill and knowledge of librarians, who are anxious to help the student find reference materials. The graduate student should not depend too much on the librarian, however, but should learn to find his own references.

Ordinarily, undergraduates fill out call slips for presentation at the circulation desk when they wish to use a book. Faculty members and graduate students are usually issued a card giving them access to the stacks, and thus may carry on the independent searching and browsing not possible when each book must be requested by name.

Most libraries prefer that students not replace books on the shelves after they have been used, for a misplaced book creates confusion both for librarians and for other students seeking it. If students leave the books with which they are finished on the tables, the librarians will return them to their proper position on the shelves.

Sometimes a student learns of a reference that is not available in the local library. Many libraries subscribe to a "union" catalog, which lists references found in other libraries. Most libraries have a union list of serials to indicate the libraries where particular serial publications may be obtained. There are a number of ways in which these materials may be obtained by a library.

1. *By interlibrary loan.* The library may request that the work be sent and then checked out to the user. Note that the library must request this material. It is never sent directly to the user.
2. *By requesting a photostatic copy* of a page or of a number of pages of a desired reference.
3. *By requesting a microfilm or microfiche.* For an established fee a microfilm may be purchased. This may be projected on library microfilm equipment.
4. *By an abstracting or translating service.* Some large libraries provide copied or translated portions of needed materials at an established fee.

In connection with any of the above services, the user is expected to bear the costs involved in reproducing, handling, and shipping the materials.

MICROFICHE

The development of the microfiche has been one of the most significant contributions to library services by providing economy and convenience of storing and distribution of scholarly materials.

A microfiche is a sheet of film that contains micro-images of printed materials. Filmed at a reduction of 1 to 24 or higher, it is possible to reproduce nearly one hundred $8\frac{1}{2}'' \times 11''$ pages of copy on one $4'' \times 6''$ film card. Microfiche readers that magnify the micro-images to original or larger copy size are available at libraries that subscribe to microfiche services. Some microfiche readers provide up to $40\times$ magnification on screens as large as $15'' \times 21''$.

There are many document reproduction services that supply microfiche to libraries upon subscription or upon special order.

The Educational Resources Information Center (ERIC) has prepared for the National Institute of Education a directory of nearly 600 libraries that possess extensive collections or receive regular periodic shipments of ERIC microfiche collections. These libraries receive approximately 17,000 microfiche per year. Other document reproduction sources that provide microfiche to libraries or individuals are described later in this chapter.

SUPER- AND ULTRA-MICROFICHE

Recent developments in the field of micro-printing will transform the process of storage, retrieval, and distribution of published materials in libraries of the future. A super-microfiche has been developed that contains up to 1000 pages of printed material on a single $4'' \times 6''$ transparent card, the equivalent of two or more books. An even more spectacular development is the ultra-microfiche that contains up to 3200 micro-dots on a single card. When projected each dot contains the equivalent of several pages. Thus, seven to ten volumes could be contained on a single $4'' \times 6''$ transparent card. Reader printers make hard copy printouts (full-page reproductions) of any page in a few seconds.

The card catalog

The card catalog, an alphabetical listing, may be compared to the index of a book. It is the index to the entire library, listing the contents of all publications found in the library, with the exception of serially published periodicals. These compact 3″ × 5″ card forms provide a quick and convenient way to find all of the books, monographs, or pamphlets found on the library shelves.

The cabinet drawers of the card catalog are alphabetically labeled, and also numbered sequentially, to facilitate replacing them in the proper place when they have been removed. Printed cards are prepared by the H. W. Wilson Company or by the Library of Congress. College and university libraries usually use these prepared cards. Smaller libraries often prepare their own.

When printed cards are used, they contain a great deal of useful information. The card illustrated in Figure 3–1 is a typical Library of Congress card. The "call number" in the upper left corner is written in by the librarian. For the sake of convenience in finding books, the card catalog has two and often three listings for each book. A few libraries have a fourth card for some books.

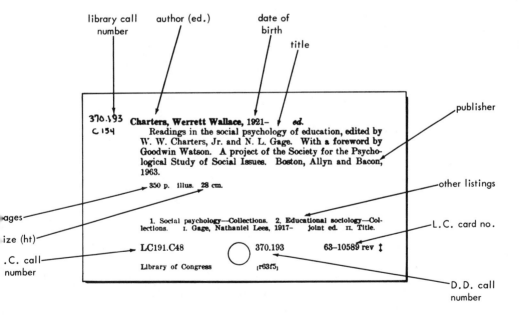

FIGURE 3–1   Library of Congress Author Card

1. author card
2. subject card
3. title card
4. analytical card

The author card is filed, last name first (Conant, James B.). One can find any or all publications credited to the author. In the case of joint authorship a card is filed separately for each author. Societies, associations, editors of yearbooks, committees, a government departments are listed as authors when no author is credited with the publication.

The subject card is filed under the appropriate heading. Since headings run from general to specific, *counseling*, a subtopic, would follow *guidance*. When a book is about an author, his name is considered a subject. Books about John Dewey are listed under the subject, *Dewey, John*.

The title card is filed under the actual name of the book. Initial articles, *a*, *an*, or *the* are disregarded. Thus, *The Elements of Research* is field under *Elements of Research*.

The analytical card, used by some large libraries, provides a reference to important sections of a book that deal with an important subject or person. For example, De Kruif's *Microbe Hunters* has a section on Ehrlich which can be called to the attention of the reader by the special analytical card. This title, filed separately, indicates that the volume has a section on the person or topic cited.

Ordinarily, the card catalog covers only the books in that specific library. In very large university libraries there may be found the union catalog, which contains duplicates of the card catalog of the Library of Congress, or duplicates of cards found in other important libraries in the United States. Instead of a union catalog, some libraries have a photo-printed, bound-book copy of the Library of Congress catalog, eighteen cards to a page.

Library classification

Library systems of book classification are complex but ingenious ways of systematizing the placement and location of books. There is a tremendous amount of detail involved in these systems, but they have been devised in a logical and neat way. Library classification is a science based upon a methodology that is logical and orderly to the smallest detail. Although it is beyond the scope of this chapter to explain all of the details of book classification, a few principles and procedures are presented that should prove helpful to the library user.

000		General references, periodicals, cyclopedias, biography
100		Philosophy, psychology
200		Religion
300		Social Sciences
	310	Statistics
	320	Political Science
	330	Economics
	340	Law
	350	Administration
	360	Welfare Assns. and Institutions
	370	Education (General)
	370.1	Theory and Philosophy of Education
	370.9	History of Education
	371	Teachers—Methods
	372	Elementary Education
	373	Secondary Education
	374	Adult Education
	375	Curriculum
	376	Education of Women
	377	Religious, Ethical Education
	378	Higher Education
	379	Public Schools (Relation of State to Education)
	379.14	School Law
	379.15	Supervision and Control
	380	Commerce, Communications
	390	Customs
400		Linguistics
500		Pure Science
600		Applied Science
700		Arts and Recreation
800		Literature
900		History

THE CALL NUMBER

Most libraries use the Dewey Decimal system of classification, as published by Melvil Dewey (1851–1931) in 1876 and adopted by the Amherst College Library in 1873. The system, or some modification of it, is now used in 89 percent of the college and university libraries, 96 percent of public libraries, and in 64 percent of all special libraries in the United States. It is also widely used in libraries in England and in other parts of the world.

It will be noted that the Dewey Decimal system is, as its title indicates, a decimal plan, the numbers running from 001 to 999.99. Following is a typical breakdown:

001	−300
300	−370
370	−379
379.1	−379.9
379.91	−379.99

LIBRARY OF CONGRESS SYSTEM

Some of the more extensive libraries, particularly in large universities, use the Library of Congress system of book classification. This system, divised by Dr. Herbert Putnam and authorized by an act of Congress in 1880, is especially useful in large libraries consisting of individual collec-

A		General Works
B		Philosophy, Religion
C		History
D		World History
EF		American History
G		Geography, Anthropology
H		Social Sciences
I		vacant
J		Political Science
K		Law
L		Education
	LA	History of Education
	LB	Theory of Education
	LC	Special forms and applications
	LD	U. S. Schools
	LE	American Education (Outside U. S.)
	LF	European Education
	LG	Asia, Africa, Oceana
	LH	School Periodicals
	LI	vacant
	LJ	Fraternities, Societies
	LT	Textbooks
M		Music
N		Fine Arts
O		vacant
P		Language, Literature
Q		Science
R		Medicine
S		Agriculture
T		Technology
U		Military Science
V		Naval Science
W		vacant
X		vacant
Y		vacant
Z		Library Science—Bibliography

tions housed separately. It provides for twenty main classes instead of the ten of the Dewey Decimal system. Letters of the alphabet are used for the principal headings, but numerals are used for further subgrouping in a fashion somewhat similar to the Dewey Decimal system.

The tremendous size of the national Library of Congress at Washington is evidenced by its growth from two million volumes in 1899 to over 32 million volumes in 1960.

The main classifications in the Library of Congress system have been listed.

BOOK PLACEMENT

All books have a call number or letter that appears in the upper left-hand corner of the author, subject, or title card, and on the spine of the book itself. Books are placed on the library shelves serially by call numbers or letters. Within each classification the books are arranged alphabetically by author's last name. An exception to this rule is that biographies are placed under the subject, rather than the author, of the book.

Most libraries use an additional classification device known as the Cutter-Sanborn system. This system adds author numbers to the basic classification to represent the first letter of the author's name, and additional numbers to distinguish between authors whose names begin with the same initial.

Other systems such as the Bliss, Quinn Brown, Universal Decimal, and Colon systems are described in the specialized literature of book classification in library science.

Reference materials

There are hundreds of references that may be useful to the graduate student in education. A rather comprehensive list, with a brief description of each source, is presented. Those that are considered basic are marked with an asterisk (*); others may be of value when choosing a problem or when requiring information in a particular area.

Since the names given to many publications have little common meaning, it is difficult to classify them by title. The contents and information treatment have been used as a basis for classification. Since editorship changes frequently, some editor names have not been included.

REFERENCES ABOUT REFERENCES

There are a number of publications that identify specific references that cover particular areas of knowledge.

Constance M. Winchell, ed. *A Guide to Reference Books.* **8th ed.   Chicago: American Library Association, 1967.**

This comprehensive work lists, without evaluation, subject area, by type and by author or editor, the most important reference books printed in a number of languages. A section is devoted to education. Supplements appear every two or three years.

> Wynar, Christine L. *Guide to Reference Books for School Media Centers.* Littleton, Colo.: Libraries Unlimited, 1973. 475 pp.

This guide includes 2575 entries with evaluative comments on reference books and selection tools for use in elementary schools, junior and senior high schools, and community and junior colleges. It is indexed by author, subject, and title.

> *Cheney, Frances N. *Fundamental Reference Sources.* Chicago: American Library Association, 1971. 318 pp.

This work is a fairly comprehensive review of all types of references, with a description and evaluation of each source.

> *American Reference Books Annual.* Littleton, Colo.: Libraries Unlimited, 1970.

All reference books published or distributed in the United States are reviewed. The reviews, written by more than 200 library specialists, vary from 75 to 300 words, and are not cumulated from year to year.

> *Booklist.* Chicago: American Library Association, 1905–date.

Published biweekly and cumulated every two years, this reference presents an unbiased critical analysis by expert librarians of atlases, encyclopedias, biographical works, dictionaries, and other reference materials in terms of their usefulness and reliability for libraries or homes. Every two years some of the more important reviews are published in a separate publication titled,

> *Reference and Subscription Books Reviews.* Chicago: American Library Association, 1956–date.

> *Cumulative Book Index.* New York: H. W. Wilson Co., 1898–date.

This monthly publication, cumulated semiannually and in one- and two-year cumulations, indexes all books published in the English language by author, title, and subject. It is helpful in assuring the student that all pertinent books have been covered in his searches.

> *Books in Print.* New York: R. R. Bowker Co., 1948–date.

Vol. I Authors
Vol. II Titles and Publishers

This a two-volume comprehensive listing of in-print titles, lists names of publishers and other publication information.

*Union List of Serials in Libraries of the United States and Canada. **New York: H. W. Wilson Co., 1965. 5 vols.**

This listing of periodicals, foreign and domestic, held by more than 225 libraries does not include government periodicals and other highly specialized materials. *Union List of Serials* is kept up to date by:

New Serial Titles. **Washington, D.C.: Library of Congress, 1961–date.**

Issued monthly and indexed in the December issue, it lists periodicals, loose-leaf publications, government series, motion pictures, and filmstrips, both domestic and foreign. Also listed are holdings of the Library of Congress and hundreds of participating libraries.

*The Standard Periodicals Directory. **New York: Oxbridge Publishing Co., 1964–date.**

Published every other year, this directory of over 30,000 entries covers every type of periodical, with the exception of local newspapers. Periodicals are defined as publications appearing at least once every two years. Two hundred classifications are arranged by subject. An alphabetical index is provided.

Ulrich's International Periodicals Directory. **New York: R. R. Bowker Co., 1966–date, 2 vols.**

This classified list of more than 11,000 foreign and domestic periodicals is arranged by subject and title. Publication information is provided.

Irregular Serials and Annuals. An International Directory: Excepting Periodicals Issued More Frequently than Once a Year. **R. R. Bowker Co., 1972.**

Published irregularly, this directory includes more than 20,000 publications.

Sources of Information in the Social Sciences. **Chicago: American Library Association, 1973.**

Organized by subject area and indexed by author and title, this work contains a comprehensive listing and brief description of reference books, monographs, and scholarly journals.

Pohle, Linda A. *A Guide to Popular Government Publications for Libraries and Home Reference.* **Littleton, Colo.: Libraries Unlimited, 1972.**

Describing almost 1400 current free and inexpensive Government publications on a wide variety of topics, this volume updates Leidy's *Popular Guide to Government Publications*, published in 1968.

Schmeckebier, Laurence F. and Roy B. Eastin. *Government Publications and their Uses.* **Washington, D.C.: Brookings Institution, 1969.**

This work explains the uses and limitations of the basic guides to government publications and provides directions for obtaining them.

William L. Camp, Guide to Periodicals in Education. Metuchen, N.J.: Scarecrow Press, 1968. Indexes 449 periodicals.

L. Joseph Lins and Robert A. Rees, eds., Scholar's Guide to Journals of Education and Educational Psychology. Madison, Wis.: Dembar Press, 1965. Indexes 134 periodicals.

These two references are particularly helpful to those who are planning to submit manuscripts for publication. Information is provided about editorial policies, type of readers, and how to submit manuscripts.

Periodicals

Up-to-date treatment of educational problems, contemporary opinions, and the latest reviews and reports of educational research will be found in periodicals or serials. A periodical or serial is defined as a publication issued in successive parts, usually at regular intervals, and, as a rule, intended to be continued indefinitely. Included in this definition are almanacs, yearbooks, directories, handbooks, government documents, publications of societies and associations, newspapers, and magazines.

Periodicals change frequently. More than 80 percent published today did not exist before 1940. More than 60 percent of those now published are no longer published under their original name.

Without comprehensive guides the search of tens of thousands of periodicals would be a nearly impossible task. Fortunately, a number of indexes and abstracts are available to help scholars in their search for relevant information.

The index

A periodical index serves much the same purpose as the index of a book or the card file of a library. Usually listing articles alphabetically under subject, title, and author headings, the sources of periodical articles are indicated. Readers should read the directions for the use of an index before trying to locate references. Most indexes provide complete directions, as well as a list of the periodicals covered, the issue dates included, and a key to all abbreviations used.

*Education Index. New York: H. W. Wilson Co., 1929–date. Published monthly (September through June), and cumulated annually.

Since its first publication in 1929, the *Education Index* has served as a comprehensive index of practically all publications in the area of education; it indexes more than 250 educational periodicals, and many yearbooks, bulletins, and monographs published in the United States, Canada, and Great Britain. It includes materials on adult education, business education, curriculum and curriculum materials, educational administration, educational psychology, educational research, exceptional children, guidance, health and physical education, higher education, international education, religious education, secondary education, teacher education, and related subjects.

The cited references listed by subject and title appear in the paperbound monthly edition two or three months after the articles appear in the periodicals. College and university libraries and most public libraries subscribe to the *Index*. The cost of the service is determined by the number of listed periodicals to which the library subscribes, making it less expensive for smaller libraries that do not take as many periodicals.

In using the *Index*, it is often advisable to use past cumulative issues, for references are not carried from one year to the next. It is often helpful to know when a particular problem or topic was of current interest, for *Index* issues from that period will yield better references. For example, in 1968 the author found few citations of articles dealing with cheating or dishonesty in the classroom. However, many references were found in the 1952 and 1965 cumulative issues, for public interest and professional concern had been aroused by the exposures of academic dishonesty at the United States Military Academy and the Air Force Academy in those years.

Canadian Education Index. Ottawa, Ontario: Canadian Council for Educational Research, 1965–date.

Issued quarterly, this publication indexes periodicals, books, pamphlets, and reports published in Canada.

Current Contents: Education. Philadelphia: Institute for Scientific Information and Encyclopedia Britannica Educational Corporation, 1969–date.

PETERSON, John E.
Life education: a new concept in health education instruction. J Sch Health 45:542-4 N '75
PETERSON, Leo C. and Sawyer, R. C.
How to perpetuate our profession. pors Agric Educ 48:53 S '75
PETERSON, Sterling, and Buttschau, Ray
Innovations in purchasing industrial arts supplies. Ind Educ 64:34-6 D '75
PETROSKY, Anthony R. See Cooper, C. R. jt. auth.

PHARIS, William L.
Principalship; where are we? Natl El Prin 55:4-8 N '75

PHENOMENOLOGY
From phenomenology to subjective method. R. Poole. Univ Q 29:412-40 Aut '75

PHILADELPHIA

E. Washington Rhodes middle school
Philadelphia school study about attitude in inner city students. E. L. Stranix. bibl Education 96:95-100 Fall '75

Public schools
Schools do make a difference. A. A. Summers and B. L. Wolfe. il Todays Educ 64:24-7; Discussion. 27-31 N '75

PHILOSOPHY
See also
Dialectical materialism
Political philosophy
Subjectivity
Values (philosophy and logic)

PHONOLOGY
See also
Bengali language—Phonology

PHONORECORDS
Wider distribution of serious contemporary music. R. C. Sheldon. Intellect 104:149 N '75

PHOTOCHEMISTRY

Experiments
Preparation and photochemistry of stilbenes; a synthetic organic chemistry experiment. J. R. Davy and others. bibl il J Chem Educ 52:747-8 N '75

PHOTOGRAMS. See Shadowgrams

PHOTOGRAPHY
See also
Nature photography
Shadowgrams

Printing processes
Darkroom; cropping, burning-in and vignetting. R. W. Cooke. il Sch Arts 75:4-7 D '75

PHOTOGRAPHY, Aerial
Take to the air for a solidly unflighty view of your district; aerial photomaps. il Am Sch Bd J 162:44-5 N '75

PHOTOGRAPHY, Artistic
Photography: an isolated approach. B. R. Carmenati. il Sch Arts 75:12-13 D '75

PHOTOGRAPHY in education
Self-concept and the camera. D. C. Locke. Sch Counsel 23:139 N '75

PHYSICAL defects. See Deformities

PHYSICAL directors

Correspondence, reminiscences, etc.
Boy, a rope, and a truth. E. R. Hill. Todays Educ 64:108 N '75

Duties
Nobody looks at me. B. Bing. J Phys Educ & Rec 46:55-6 F '75

Rating
O.S.U. teacher behavior rating scale. D. Siedentop and C. Hughley. J Phys Educ & Rec 46:45 F '75

PHYSICAL education
See also
Physical education for girls and women

Activities
Ahoy. J. Kautz. J Phys Educ & Rec 46:89 F '75
How we teach it; ed. by M. Hannigan. See issues of Journal of physical education and recreation

Bibliography
Books. See issues of Journal of physical education and recreation

Correlation with other subjects
Interdisciplinary bike tour. il J Phys Educ & Rec 46:40-1 F '75

Curriculum
Education of the whole child: fact or fiction? P. Hunsicker and G. Reiff. NASSP Bull 59: 82-5 D '75
Fresh ideas for college physical education; symposium. il J Phys Educ & Rec 46:37-44 F '75

Research
Research; ed. by P. B. Johnson. See issues of Journal of physical education and recreation
Why research? T. P. Martin. J Phys Educ & Rec 46:56+ F '75

Teaching aids and devices
Audiovisual aids. See issues of Journal of physical education and recreation

Teaching methods
Play cards. S. Ravitz. J Phys Educ & Rec 46:30 F '75

Theories and principles
Elementary games and humanism. M. Riley. il J Phys Educ & Rec 46:46-9 F '75

Colleges and universities
Cheyney's phys ed goes co-ed. D. T. Wirth. J Phys Educ & Rec 46:29 Ja '75
Fresh ideas for college physical education; symposium. il J Phys Educ & Rec 46:37-44 F '75
HPER directory of professional preparation institutions. American alliance for health, physical education and recreation. JOHPER 45:37-48 S '74 (cont as) J Phys Educ & Rec 46:26 Ja; 14+ My '75

Elementary schools
Alphabet dance. G. Blanchard. J Phys Educ & Rec 46:65 F '75
Elementary games and humanism. M. Riley. il J Phys Educ & Rec 46:46-9 F '75
Play cards. S. Ravitz. J Phys Educ & Rec 46:30 F '75

High schools
Exercise physiology in secondary schools; a three dimensional approach. E. J. Meyers. J Phys Educ & Rec 46:30-1 Ja '75

PHYSICAL education associations
See also
International federation for university sport

PHYSICAL education departments. See Colleges and universities—Departments of physical education

PHYSICAL education facilities
New Texas-size facilities. A. E. Coleman. J Phys Educ & Rec 46:28 Ja '75
Phys ed facility invites participation; Robert Crown center. Hampshire college, Amherst, Mass. il Am Sch & Univ 48:39 D '75
See also
Playgrounds

PHYSICAL education for girls and women
Self-defense for women. il J Phys Educ & Rec 46:44 F '75
Third HISPA seminar; tr by M. Spiegel. J. P. Massicotte. J Phys Educ & Rec 46:61-2 F '75

PHYSICAL education for the handicapped
IRUC: what's going on? ed. by J. U. Stein. See issues of Journal of physical education and recreation
Project I CAN' individualized curriculum designed for mentally retarded children and youth. C. Knowles and others. Educ & Train Men Retard 10:155-60 O '75

PHYSICAL education students
Students; ed. by R. Ciszek. See issues of Journal of physical education and recreation

PHYSICAL examinations
See also
School children—Medical inspection

PHYSICAL therapy
Physical activity guidelines for children with developmental hip disorders. R. Adams and M. Puthoff. bibl il J Phys Educ & Rec 46: 69-70+ F '75

PHYSICIANS
New oath for physicians. il Intellect 104:147-8 N '75
See also
Pediatricians

PHYSICS

Graduate work
Observations on an obstacle course; U.S. graduate education for the deserving Asian physics student. F. E. Dart and others. Int Educ & Cul Exch 11:29-32 Fall '75

Laboratory work
Developing a laser holographic laboratory for use in secondary school science curriculum. D. J. Record. bibl il Sch Sci & Math 75: 691-704 D '75

Teaching
High schools
Developing a laser holographic laboratory for use in secondary school science curriculum. D. J. Record. bibl il Sch Sci & Math 75: 691-704 D '75

PHYSIOLOGY
See also
Flexibility (physiology)
Neurophysiology

FIGURE 3-2   Page from the Education Index. Used with permission of the H. W. Wilson Company, New York. Education Index copyright © 1976 by The H. W. Wilson Company.

Issued weekly, this publication reproduces the table of contents of more than 500 foreign and domestic educational periodicals. It contains an author index and address directory to facilitate writing for reprints of the articles and to identify the author's organization. Reprints are available directly from the Institute for Scientific Information.

Current Index to Journals in Education. New York: Macmillan Information, 1969–date.

This index is issued monthly and cumulated semiannually and annually, and indexes by subject and author approximately 20,000 articles each year from more than 700 education and education-related journals, a joint venture with the National Institute of Education.

ERIC Educational Documents Index. Washington, D.C.: National Institute of Education, Government Printing Office, 1966–date.

This index to all research documents in the Educational Resources Information Center collection is published annually.

State Educational Journal Index. Westminster, Colo.: State Educational Journal Index, 1964–date.

Issued twice each year, this publication indexes state educational journals, most of which are not indexed by *Education Index.*

Index of Doctoral Dissertations International. Ann Arbor, Mich.: Xerox University Microfilms, 1956–date.

Published as the issue 13 of *Dissertation Abstracts International* each year, this work consolidates into one list all dissertations accepted by American, Canadian, and some European universities during the academic year, as well as those available in microfilm. It indexes by author and key words selected from dissertation titles.

Comprehensive Dissertation Index (1861–1972). Ann Arbor, Mich.: Xerox University Microfilms, 1974.

This volume indexes by author name and key word 417,000 doctoral dissertations accepted at 362 accredited institutions from 1861–1972.

Master's Theses in Education. Cedar Falls, Iowa: Research Publications, 1952–date.

Issued annually, this publication lists most theses written in Canadian and American colleges and universities. Titles are listed by academic area, state, institution, and author.

Indignation, An Impetus for Change: Implications for the Professional Home Economist, *Illinois Teacher of Home Economics* v18 n1, pp10-13, Sep/Oct 74 EJ 105 412

The Disadvantages of a College Degree, *Liberal Education* v60 n3, pp304-307, Oct 74 EJ 106 116

What Are Law Related Studies?, *California Council for the Social Studies Review* v14 n1, pp4-6, F 74 EJ 106 516

Dissent and Disobedience: Teaching Political Science, *Teaching Political Science* v2 n1, pp95-99, Oct 74 EJ 106 564

Ethnic Education: Can It Be Relevant?, *Massachusetts Teacher* v53 n5, pp36-41, Feb 74 EJ 106 725

Religion

Self Reported Religious Concerns of University Underclassmen, *Adolescence* v9 n35, pp333-38, F 74 EJ 105 234

A Clash over 'Dirty Books' Is Dividing a School Board, Threatening a Superintendent, and Shattering a Community, *American School Board Journal* v161 n11, pp31-32,41-43, Nov 74 EJ 105 891

American Civil Religion and the Sunday School, *Notre Dame Journal of Education* v5 n3, pp206-210, F 74 EJ 106 548

Work, Play, and Worship: Toward a New Moral Economy, *Journal of Health, Physical Education, Recreation* v45 n9, pp38-40, Nov/Dec 74 EJ 106 688

Religious Cultural Groups

What Jewish Studies Can Do, *Commentary* v58 n4, pp71-77, Oct 74 EJ 106 736

Religious Education

Theory and Practice in Religious Education: The Discrepancy, *Notre Dame Journal of Education* v5 n3, pp197-205, F 74 EJ 106 547

American Civil Religion and the Sunday School, *Notre Dame Journal of Education* v5 n3, pp206-210, F 74 EJ 106 548

Thoroughly Christian and Truly a School: Developing a Christian Secondary School, *Notre Dame Journal of Education* v5 n3, pp211-215, F 74 EJ 106 549

Toward a New Approach in Morality, *Notre Dame Journal of Education* v5 n3, pp216-220, F 74 EJ 106 550

Teaching Religion to Minority Groups, *Notre Dame Journal of Education* v5 n3, pp232-236, F 74 EJ 106 551

Religious Education as Symbol-Making, *Notre Dame Journal of Education* v5 n3, pp237-244, F 74 EJ 106 552

Religious Instruction in the Context of Catholic Schooling, *Notre Dame Journal of Education* v5 n3, pp259-274, F 74 EJ 106 553

"That You Do Unto Me", *Notre Dame Journal of Education* v5 n3, pp275-280, F 74 EJ 106 554

Religious Factors

A Modern Indian Speaks: Under One Flag, *Weewish Tree* v3 n1, pp17-18, Sep 74 EJ 106 312

The Story of Corn, *Weewish Tree* v3 n1, pp21-2, Sep 74 EJ 106 314

Remedial Courses

Dialect Features in the Compositions of Black and White College Students; The Same or Different?, *College Composition and Communication* v25 n4, pp259-63, Oct 74 EJ 105 750

Remedial Programs

An Exhortation for Teachers of English in Open-Admissions Programs, *College Composition and Communication* v25 n4, pp292-7, Oct 74 EJ 105 756

Remedial Reading

Beyond Decoding: Systematic Schoolwide Tutoring in Reading, *Reading Teacher* v28 n2, pp157-60, Nov 74 EJ 105 631

A Good Teacher and an Eclectic Approach: The Hopeful Answer to Successful Reading Instruction, *Reading Horizons* v15 n1, pp7-11, F 74 EJ 105 683

Remedial Reading Programs

A Hand-up for Slow Readers, *Learning* v3 n3, pp86-7, Nov 74 EJ 106 581

Repeated Testing

Acquisition of College Course Material under Conditions of Repeated Testing, *Journal of Educational Psychology* v66 n3, pp367-72, Jun 74 EJ 106 712

Report Cards

Computers: Report Cards, Security, *Nation's Schools and Colleges* v1 n1, pp31-32, Sep 74 EJ 105 867

Reprography

A "Third Force" In Photocopying Dispute?, *Library Resources and Technical Services* v18 n4, pp341-2, F 74 EJ 106 219

Research

Slippery Boundaries of Lipid Research, *Vestes* v17 n2, pp188-192, Aug 74 EJ 106 144

Participant-Observation in Nutrition Education Program Development, *Journal of Nutrition Education* v6 n3, pp89-92, Jul-Sep 74 EJ 106 335

Children's Behavior Responses to TV Food Advertisements, *Journal of Nutrition Education* v6 n3, pp93-96, Jul-Sep 74 EJ 106 336

Energy for America's Third Century, *MOSAIC* v5 n2, pp2-36, 74 EJ 106 340

Bloodless and Breathless, *Science News* v106 n13, pp202-203, Sep 74 EJ 106 347

Sinister Psychology - Tests and Studies Indicate That Left-Handedness Need Not and Should Not Be Considered an Undesirable Trait, *Science News* v106 n14, pp220-222, Oct 74 EJ 106 348

Skylab Report: Man's Role in Space Research, *Science* v186 n4160, pp219-226, Oct 74 EJ 106 349

High-Pressure Ion Exchange Chromatography, *Science* v186 n4160, pp226-233, Oct 74 EJ 106 350

Injury Data Collection and Analysis - The NEISS Model, *Journal of Environmental Health* v37 n2, pp167-169, Sep/Oct 74 EJ 106 355

Linear Measurement in the Elementary School, *Arithmetic Teacher* v21 n6, pp520-525, Oct 74 EJ 106 368

Intellectual Development Beyond Elementary School IV: Ratio, The Influence of Cognitive Style, *School Science and Mathematics* v74 n6, pp476-482, Oct 74 EJ 106 393

Altering Teacher and Pupil Behavior with Mastery Teaching, *School Science and Mathematics* v74 n6, pp530-535, Oct 74 EJ 106 400

Structure of Wet Specimens in Electron Microscopy, *Science* v186 n4162, pp407-414, Nov 74 EJ 106 421

Laser Spectroscopy: A New High Resolution Technique, *Science* v186 n4162, pp428-430, Nov 74 EJ 106 423

Computer Simulations: Inelegant Mathematics and Worse Social Science?, *International Journal of Mathematical Education in Science and Technology* v5 n2, pp139-155, Apr-Jun 74 EJ 106 425

A Plan to Combine Individualized Instruction with the Lecture Method, *Mathematics Teacher* v67 n7, pp647-651, Nov 74 EJ 106 449

Modern Versus Traditional Mathematics, *Australian Mathematics Teacher* v30 n4, pp139-48, Aug 74 EJ 106 468

Negative Instances in Mathematical Concept Acquisition: Transfer Effects Between the Concepts of Commutativity and Associativity, *Journal for Research in Mathematics Education* v5 n4, pp197-212, Nov 74 EJ 106 493

Determining the Best Predictors of Success and of Time of Completion or Dropout in an Individualized Course in Arithmetic at a Community College, *Journal for Research in Mathematics Education* v5 n4, pp213-223, Nov 74 EJ 106 494

On Comparing Error Patterns and the Effect of Maturation in a Unit on Sentential Logic, *Journal for Research in Mathematics Education* v5 n4, pp225-237, Nov 74 EJ 106 495

H.S. 1 Studies: Research on the Credit System, *Orbit 24* v5 n4, pp16-7, Oct 74 EJ 106 616

Research Design

Status Values of Professions and Vocational Preferences: Studying Vocational Development among 11 Pupils in an Indian School, *Adolescence* v9 n35, pp443-59, F 74 EJ 105 240

A Survey of Evaluations Performed on Elementary School Innovations, *Illinois School Research* v11 n1, pp38-42, F 74 EJ 105 304

Discussion: Developmental Gains in Reasoning *American Journal of Mental Deficiency* v79 n2, pp127-31, Sep 74 EJ 105 92

Stephen's Reply to Hunt's Discussion, *American Journal of Mental Deficiency* v79 n2, pp131-3, Sep 74 EJ 105 92

Stephens' Reply to Kohlberg's Discussion, *American Journal of Mental Deficiency* v79 n2 pp145-6, Sep 74 EJ 105 93

Research Methodology

Effects of Stress on the Performance of Normally Anxious and High-Anxious Subjects unde Chance and SkillConditions, *Journal of Abnormal Psychology* v83 n5, pp466-72, Oct 74 EJ 105 15

The Role of Language, Manipulation and Demonstration in the Acquistion, Retention, and Transfer of Conservation, *Alberta Journal of Educational Research* v20 n3, pp217-25, Sep 74 EJ 105 17

Teacher Quality Perceptions and Achievement in Rajasthan, *Alberta Journal of Educational Research* v20 n3, pp226-32, Sep 74 EJ 105 17

Cognitive Complexity as a Determinant of Information Processing, *Alberta Journal of Educational Research* v20 n3, pp233-43, Sep 74 EJ 105 17

Bilingual Education and Cognition, *Alberta Journal of Educational Research* v20 n3, pp259-69 Sep 74 EJ 105 18

Bicultural Excursion Programs: Their Effects on Students' Stereotypes, Attitudes and Motivation, *Alberta Journal of Educational Research* v20 n3, pp270-77, Sep 74 EJ 105 18

Relationship Between Children's Learning Disorders and Emotional Disorders at a Mental Health Clinic, *Journal of Clinical Psychology* v30 n4, pp450-58, Oct 74 EJ 105 18

Psychological Needs, Academic Achievement and Marijuana Consumption, *Journal of Clinical Psychology* v30 n4, pp496-98, Oct 74 EJ 105 18

The Relation Between the Altitude Quotient and Adjustment Potential, *Journal of Clinical Psychology* v30 n4, pp510-13, Oct 74 EJ 105 19

A Replacement for the Venerable Stanford Binet?, *Journal of Clinical Psychology* v30 n4 pp517-21, Oct 74 EJ 105 19

Personality Change in the Specially Admitted Disadvantaged Student After One Year in College, *Journal of Clinical Psychology* v30 n4 pp522-28, Oct 74 EJ 105 19

Sex Differences and Spatial Ability Factors in Witkin's "Differentiation" Construct, *Journal of Clinical Psychology* v30 n4, pp528-32, Oct 74 EJ 105 19

Sex Differences in the Endorsement of MMPI Critical Items, *Journal of Clinical Psychology* v30 n4, pp557-58, Oct 74 EJ 105 19

A Cross Validation of Seventeen Experimental MMPI Scales Related to Antisocial Behavior *Journal of Clinical Psychology* v30 n4, pp56-65, Oct 74 EJ 105 19

The Compatibility of Anxiety and Actualization *Journal of Clinical Psychology* v30 n4, pp56-68, Oct 74 EJ 105 19

An Examination of the Salience Hierarchy During Adolescence: The Influence of the Family, *Adolescence* v9 n35, pp317-32, F 74 EJ 105 23

Tobacco, Alcohol, Medicines and Illegal Drug Taking, *Adolescence* v9 n35, pp421-24, F 74 EJ 105 23

The Effects of Behavior Contracts and Behavior Proclamations on Social Conduct and Academic Achievement in a Ninth Grade English Class, *Adolescence* v9 n35, pp425-36, F 74 EJ 105 23

Choice and Source Attractiveness in Exposure to Discrepant Messages, *Journal of Experimental Social Psychology* v10 n6, pp516-27, Nov 74 EJ 105 26

Involvement and Response Language Effects in Attitude Scaling, *Journal of Experimental Social Psychology* v10 n6, pp572-84, Nov 74 EJ 105 26

Attitude Attribution When Behavior Is Constrained, *Journal of Experimental Social Psychology* v10 n6, pp585-600, Nov 74 EJ 105 26

The Increasing Emphasis of Quantitative Analysis and Computer Methods in Policy Oriented Educational Research, *UCLA Educator* v16 n pp10-3, Spr 74 EJ 105 2

FIGURE 3-3 Page from Current Index to Journals in Education.
Used with permission of Macmillan Publishing Co., Inc.

Research Studies in Education. Bloomington, Ind.: Phi Delta Kappa, 1953–date.

This annual publication includes doctoral dissertations in education, both completed and in progress, author and subject indexes, and a research methods bibliography.

Bibliographic Index. New York: H. W. Wilson Co., 1938–date.

Issued semiannually, this guide indexes by subject current bibliographies containing more than 40 citations, including those published in books, pamphlets and periodicals both in English and in foreign languages. More than 1500 periodicals are examined for bibliographic material.

*Readers' Guide to Periodic Literature. New York: H. W. Wilson Co., 1900–date.

Issued twice each month, *Readers' Guide* indexes by subject and author articles of a popular and general nature. Prior to 1929 *Readers' Guide* covered many of the educational periodicals. By 1929, the number of educational periodicals had become so great that the *Education Index* was established as a more specialized guide. *Readers' Guide* may be helpful to students in education for finding references to articles in areas outside the field of professional education.

Abridged Readers' Guide to Periodic Literature. New York: H. W. Wilson Co., 1935–date.

Forty-four selected periodicals most likely to be found in smaller libraries are indexed here.

*New York Times Index. New York, 1913–date.

This index is published biweekly with annual cumulation, and it classifies material in the *New York Times* alphabetically and chronologically under subject, title, person, and organization name. It is also useful in locating materials in other newspapers because it gives a clue to the date of events. Complete issues of the *New York Times* are available in microfilm form in many libraries.

Subject Index to the Christian Science Monitor. Boston: Christian Science Monitor, 1960–date.

This publication is issued monthly with annual cumulations.

*Social Sciences Index. New York: H. W. Wilson Co., 1974–date.

This guide indexes 263 periodicals.

Educational accountability
Accountability [symposium]. Nurs Outlook 23:496-516 Ag '75
Rating the teachers. M. Rodin. Center Mag 8:55-60 S '75
Educational anthropology
Ethnography and policymaking: the case of education [with discussion] F. Mulhauser. Hum Org 34:311-19 Fall '75
Positive stereotyping: the cultural relativist in the classroom. J. Kleinfeld. bibl Hum Org 34:269-74 Fall '75
Educational aspirations. See Student aspirations
Educational associations
Impact of voluntary association characteristics on selective attraction and socialization. M. Betz and B. Judkins. bibl Sociol Q 16:228-40 Spr '75
Educational attainment
City size and feelings of political competence. A. W. Finifter and P. R. Abramson. Pub Opinion Q 39:189-98 Summ '75
Cohort and sex changes in black educational achievement. O. L. Edwards. bibl Sociol & Soc Res 59:110-20 Ja '75
Does migration interfere with children's progress in school? L. H. Long. bibl Sociol Educ 48:369-81 Summ '75
Education, ethnic stereotypes, and question format. S. Hessel-bart. bibl Sociol & Soc Res 59:266-73 Ap '75
Educational level of the population of the USSR. G. Maksimov. Sov R 16:20-33 Spr '75
Extracurricular activities in the educational attainment process. L. B. Otto. bibl Rur Sociol 40:162-76 Summ '75
Occupational achievement process, 1940-1949: a cohort analysis. A. Lane. bibl Am Sociol R 40:472-82 Ag '75
Patterns of educational attainment in Great Britain. A. C. Kerckhoff. Am J Sociol 80:1428-37 My '75
Educational innovations
Innovation in governmental structures: Minnesota school district reorganization. J. L. Foster. bibl Am J Pol Sci 19:455-74 Ag '75
Educational progress. See School progress
Educational psychology
Education in psychological perspective. J. R. Kantor. Psychol Rec 25:315-23 Summ '75
Readability and human interest scores of thirty-six recently published introductory educational psychology texts. R. J. Hofmann and R. J. Vyhonsky. bibl Am Psychol 30:790-2 Jl '75
Educators
See also
Bissell, C. T.
Fine, B.
Wayland, F.
Edwards, Andrew W.
Toward a cohesive black community. Soc Casework 56:433-5 Jl '75
Edwards, John D.
Improving employment opportunities and the public image of social psychologists. Am Psychol 30:784-5 Jl '75
See McPeek, R. W. jt. auth.
Edwards, Ozzie L.
Cohort and sex changes in black educational achievement. bibl Sociol & Soc Res 59:110-20 Ja '75
Edwards, Richard C.
Social relations of production in the firm and labor market structure. bibl Pol & Soc 5 no 1:83-108 '75
Edwards personal preference schedule
Comparison of Edwards personal preference schedule norms with recent college samples. D. Murgatroyd and E. I. Gavurin. J Psychol 91:71-6 S '75
Efficiency, Industrial
Competition, information, redundancy: x-efficiency and the cybernetics of the firm. R. A. McCain. Kyklos 28 no2:286-308 '75
Productive efficiency in commercial banking. W. A. Longbrake and J. A. Haslem. J Money Cred Bank 7:317-30 Ag '75
Secretaries answer back. Economist 256:62 Ag 23 '75
See also
Time study
Efron, Vera
Vera Efron retiring. M. Keller. J Stud Alcohol 36:1000-1 Jl '75
Egeland, Byron
Effects of errorless training on teaching children to discriminate letters of the alphabet. J App Psychol 60:533-6 Ag '75
Ego (psychology)
Ego and the integration of violence in homicidal youth. C. H. King. bibl Am J Orthopsych 45:134-45 Ja '75
Ego strength and confidence thresholds in two methods of paired-associate learning. J. C. Duffy and N. J. Kanak. bibl Am J Psychol 88:245-52 Je '75
Egypt
See also
Cairo

Defenses
See also
Military assistance, Russian—Egypt

Foreign relations
Israel
Countdown to settlement. N. Shepherd. New Statesm 90:43-4 Jl 11 '75
Israel without a policy. N. Shepherd. New Statesm 89:795-6 Je 20 '75
One small step. Economist 256:12 Jl 12 '75
Package Rabin will say yes to. map Economist 256:39-40 Jl 12 '75
Wrong stick. Economist 256:37-8 Jl 19 '75
Libya
No entry. Economist 256:44 Ag 16 '75
Ehrenberg, Ronald G.
Heterogeneous labor, minimum hiring standards, and job vacancies in public employment. bibl J Pol Econ 81:1442-50 N '73
Ehrman, Myra L.
Sex education for the young. Nurs Outlook 23:583-5 S '75
Eisenbud, Jule
Case of Florence Marryat. bibl Am Soc Psychical Res J 69:-215-33 Jl '75
Eisenhower, Dwight David
General Patton: why they didn't let George do it [review article]. M. Evans. il Am Opinion 18:11-18+ S '75
Eitzen, D. Stanley
Athletics in the status system of male adolescents: a replication of Coleman's The adolescent society. Adolescence 10:-267-76 Summ '75
Elasticity (economics)
Central America: empirical evidence on the demand for money in the common market. J. M. Villasuso and W. T. Wilford. Soc & Econ Stud 24:209-20 Je '75
International comparisons of expenditure patterns. C. Lluch and A. Powell. bibl Eur Econ R 6:275-303 Jl '75
Measurement of income and price elasticities. A. S. Deaton. bibl Eur Econ R 6:261-73 Jl '75
El-Bushra, El-Sayed
Sudan's triple capital: morphology and functions. il maps Ekistics 39:246-50 Ap '75
Election forecasting
Accuracy of presidential-preference primary polls. M. Felson and S. Sudman. Pub Opinion Q 39:232-6 Summ '75
Simple and inexpensive election prediction: a practical alternative. W. R. Shaffer. W Pol Q 28:506-15 S '75
Election law
France
Distorted representation in France. B. Criddle. Parl Aff 28:-154-79 Spr '75
Great Britain
Electoral reform. map Economist 256:13+ Ag 2 '75
India
Final touches to Indira's make-up. L. Lifschultz. Far E Econ R 89:26-7 Ag 22 '75
Elections
See also
Nominations for office
Preferential ballot
Australia
Economy and polity in Australia: a quantification of commonsense. R. Douglas. Brit J Pol Sci 5:341-61 Jl '75
Tempting target for the opposition. K. Randall. Far E Econ R 89:23 Jl 11 '75
France
Developmental change and electoral cleavage in France: government and opposition in the Fifth republic. V. E. McHale and D. Paranzino. Can J Pol Sci 8:431-53 S '75
Distorted representation in France. B. Criddle. Parl Aff 28:-154-79 Spr '75
Great Britain
When rejects re-run: a study in independency. A. D. R. Dickson. Pol Q 46:271-9 Jl '75
Ireland
Used vote and electoral outcomes: the Irish general election of 1973. A. S. Cohan and others. Brit J Pol Sci 5:363-83 Jl '75
Malaysia
Election losers learn the hard way. K. Das. Far E Econ R 89:9-10 Jl 4 '75
New Zealand
Muldoon's confidence in election year. D. Wederell. Far E Econ R 89:18 Ag 8 '75
Sri Lanka
Hollow victory for Jayewardene. Far E Econ R 89:24 Ag 8 '75
United States
Belief systems: constraint, complexity, and the 1972 election. J. A. Stimson. bibl Am J Pol Sci 19:393-417 Ag '75
Impact of broadcast campaigning on electoral outcomes. G. C. Jacobson. J Pol 37:769-93 Ag '75
Participation in local policy making: the case of referenda. W. B. Shepard. Soc Sci Q 56:55-70 Je '75
Social-structural sources of cleavage on law and order policies. S. E. Bennett and A. J. Tuchfarber. bibl Am J Pol Sci 19:419-38 Ag '75

FIGURE 3-4   Page from Social Sciences Index. Used with permission of the H. W. Wilson Company, New York. Social Sciences Index copyright ©1975 by the H. W. Wilson Company.

Humanities Index. New York: H. W. Wilson Co., 1974–date.

Formerly published as *Social Sciences and Humanities Index* (1965–1973), the *Humanities Index* lists 260 periodicals. These two indexes, each issued quarterly and cumulated annually, index alphabetically by subject and title articles from more than 260 periodicals, including many published outside the United States.

New Studies: A Guide to Recent Publications in the Social and Behavioral Sciences. Beverly Hills, Calif.: Sage Publications, 1966–date.

New Studies indexes and annotates articles from over 400 journals, reviews, books, and pamphlets, both foreign and domestic. The annotations appear in the bimonthly journal, *American Behavioral Scientist*, and are bound each year into one volume.

Applied Science and Technology Index. New York: H. W. Wilson Co., 1958–date.

Formerly a part of the *Industrial Arts Index*, this subject index, issued monthly and cumulated annually, covers more than 225 periodicals in chemistry, physics, electricity, engineering, aerospace, metallurgy, machinery, and related subjects.

Business Periodicals Index. New York: H. W. Wilson Co., 1958–date.

Issued monthly and cumulated annually, this subject index covers more than 120 periodicals in the fields of business, accounting, labor and management, marketing, purchasing, office management, public administration, banking, finance, taxation, insurance, and related areas.

Air University Library Index. Maxwell Field, Ala.: Air University Library, United States Air Force, 1945–date.

This work indexes quarterly and cumulates every three years more than 76 military periodicals published in the English language.

Consumer Education Bibliography. New York: Office of Consumer Affairs, 1971.

This bibliography is a comprehensive listing of books, pamphlets, and audio-visual materials issued by public and private agencies concerned with consumer affairs.

Art Index. New York: H. W. Wilson Co., 1929–date.

Published quarterly with cumulation annually and every two years, this publication indexes by author and subject 110 periodicals and museum bulletins, both foreign and domestic. Subjects included are archaeology, architecture, art history, arts and crafts, fine arts, graphic arts, industrial design, interior decoration, photograph, planning, and landscape design.

Biological and Agricultural Index. New York: H. W. Wilson Co., 1916–date.

Formerly *Agricultural Index*, and issued monthly and cumulated annually, this work indexes by subject and title more than 190 periodicals in such fields of agriculture as chemicals, economics, engineering, animal husbandry, soil science, forestry, nutrition, biology, genetics, ecology, zoology, and veterinary medicine.

Occupational Index. New York: Occupational Index, 1936–date.

Issued quarterly, this work indexes more than 100 general and technical periodicals by subject, author, and title.

Cumulative Career Index. Moravia, N.Y.: Chronicle Guidance Publications, 1971–date.

This annual publication lists more than 1800 free and inexpensive materials on careers and work opportunities, listed by job titles.

Index to Legal Periodicals. New York: H. W. Wilson Co., 1908–date.

Issued monthly and cumulated annually, this index covers nearly 300 legal periodicals, indexed by subject with case notes.

State Law Index. Washington, D.C.: Library of Congress, 1929–date.

Index Medicus. Washington: National Library of Medicine, 1960.

Issued monthly, this index includes research reports from most medical journals, and is cumulated annually as:

Cumulated Index Medicus. Chicago: American Medical Association 1960–date.

Abridged Index Medicus. Washington: National Library of Medicine and the A.M.A., Superintendent of Documents, 1970–date.

Issued monthly, this work cross indexes articles from 100 English language medical journals by subject and author.

Hospital Literature Index. Chicago: American Hospital Association, 1945–date.

Issued quarterly with annual and five-year cumulations, this publication covers periodicals in the United States and the British Commonwealth dealing with public health, nursing, hospital administration, gerontology, and medicine.

Cumulative Index to Nursing Literature. Glendale, Calif.: Glendale Sanitorium and Hospital Public Service, 1961–date.

Issued quarterly with annual cumulation, this work indexes most nursing periodicals.

Rehabilitation Literature. Chicago: The National Society for Crippled Children and Adults, 1940–date.

Published monthly this index lists material on the physically handicapped.

Index to Religious Periodical Literature. Chicago: American Theological Library Association, McCormick Seminary, 1949–date.

This index to more than 100 religions periodicals is issued every two years.

Catholic Periodical Index. Haverford, Penn.: Catholic Library Association, 1930–date.

The quarterly publication indexes more than 60 Catholic periodicals, newspapers, and bulletins.

Index to Jewish Periodicals. Cleveland: Cleveland College of Jewish Studies, 1963–date.

This index is issued quarterly, and lists by subject and author articles from Jewish periodicals.

Index to Periodicals: Articles by and about Negroes. Boston: G. K. Hall and Co., 1961–date.

Issued annually, this work indexes about twenty black interest periodicals not indexed elsewhere.

Bibliographic Survey: The Negro in Print. Washington: Negro Bibliographic and Research Center, 1965–date.

Issued five times each year, the *Survey* indexes periodicals abstracts, bibliographies, and book reviews.

Public Affairs Information Service Bulletin. **New York: Public Affairs Information Service, 1915–date.**

Published weekly and cumulated quarterly and annually, this publication lists by subject articles in books, pamphlets, government publications, periodicals, and society publications dealing with social, political, and economic affairs throughout the world.

Book Review Index. **Detroit: Gale Research Co., 1965–date.**

This biweekly publication with quarterly cumulations lists book reviews by author name from more than 250 periodicals.

Mental Health Book Review Index. **New York: Research Center for Mental Health, 1956.**

Published annually and indexed by author, this work lists reviews from more than 200 English language journals.

Subject Guide to Microforms in Print. **Washington, D.C.: Microcard Editions Books, 1961–date.**

This annual cumulative guide to microfilms and microfiche does not include theses and dissertations.

Selected United States Government Publications. **Washington, D.C.: Superintendent of Documents, 1928–date.**

Issued biweekly, this small publication, available without cost, lists government books and pamphlets soon after publication.

Index to U.S. Government Periodicals. **Chicago: Infordot International, 1972–date.**

Issued quarterly and cumulated annually, this is a computer-generated guide to selective titles from over 100 major government periodicals.

International Guide to Educational Documentation. **Paris: UNESCO.**

Published every five years, this guide indexes annotated bibliographies covering major publications, bibliographies, and national directories, written in English, French, and Spanish.

United Nations Document Index. **New York: United Nations Library, 1950–date.**

All U.N. publications are listed by subject and issuing body in this monthly publication.

Abstracts

Another type of reference guide is the abstract, review, or digest. In addition to providing a systemized list of reference sources, it includes a summary of the contents. Usually the summaries are brief, but in some publications they are presented in greater detail.

> *Dissertation Abstracts International.* **Ann Arbor, Mich.: Xerox University Microfilms, 1955–date.**

Issued monthly and indexed annually, *Dissertation Abstracts* is divided into:

A. Humanities and Social Sciences
B. Sciences and Engineering

Dissertations accepted by all universities in the United States and Canada and some in foreign countries are indexed by author and key word. Libraries or individuals may purchase complete xerographic or microfiche copies of any dissertation.

> *Master's Abstracts.* **Ann Arbor, Mich.: Xerox University Microfilms, 1962– date.**

Issued quarterly, this guide abstracts those master's degree theses that are available on microfilm.

> *Resources in Education.* **Washington: Government Printing Office, 1966–date.**

This monthly abstract journal prepared by the National Educational Research Information Center reports new and completed research projects gathered by the 16 Educational Research Information Centers (ERIC).

> *ERIC Educational Documents Abstracts.* **Washington, D.C.: National Institute of Education, Government Printing Office, 1968–date.**

This annual publication includes abstracts of all reports which appeared in *Resources in Education* for the year. Author, source, publication date, and price of the original report are cited.

> *Complete Guide to ERIC Reports.* **Englewood Cliffs, N.J.: Prentice-Hall, 1970. 1388 pp.**

Résumés of the most significant research studies in education selected from the files of the *Educational Research Information Center* are alphabetically indexed by subject, author, clearinghouse, and numerical title.

Completed Research in Health, Physical Education and Recreation Including International Sources. Washington, D.C.: American Alliance for Health, Physical Education and Recreation, 1958–date.

Issued annually, this work indexes by subject and title abstracts of studies conducted throughout the world.

Child Development Abstracts and Bibliography. Chicago: University of Chicago Press, 1927–date.

Issued every four months and cumulated every three years, this publication abstracts more than 20 journals.

Review of Child Development Research. New York: Russell Sage Foundation, 1964–date.

Research Relating to Children. Washington, D.C.: Children's Bureau, Department of Health, Education and Welfare, 1948–date.

Published annually, these abstracts of studies related to the welfare of children are indexed by subject, author, and title.

Research Related to Emotionally Disturbed Children. Washington, D.C.: Dept. of Health, Education and Welfare, Children's Bureau, 1968.

These abstracts are issued irregularly.

How Effective Is Schooling? A Critical Review and Synthesis of Research Findings. Santa Monica, Calif.: RAND Corporation, 1971. 222 pp.

Mental Retardation Abstracts. Columbus, Ohio: American Association of Mental Deficiency, 1964–date.

Issued quarterly, this work abstracts more than 200 journals and books, both foreign and domestic.

Mental Health and Social Change. Rushville, Md.: National Institute of Mental Health, 1972.

These abstracts of research studies in scholarly journals, both foreign and domestic, are indexed by subject, title, and author.

Deafness, Speech and Hearing Abstracts. Washington, D.C.: Deafness, Speech and Hearing Publications, 1960–date.

This quarterly publication abstracts more than 1800 articles each year from over 250 domestic and foreign journals.

Selected RAND Abstracts. Santa Monica, Calif.: RAND Corporation, 1963–date.

Issued quarterly, these abstracts cover books and reports published by the corporation, many of which deal with education and other social sciences.

College Student Personnel Abstracts. Claremont, Calif.: College Student Personnel Institute, 1965–date.

Issued quarterly, the abstracts cover more than 275 periodicals. Summaries deal with research practices and developments relating to college students and student services.

*Psychological Abstracts. Washington, D.C.: American Psychological Association, 1927–date.

Issued bimonthly and indexed annually by subject and author, this publication has excellent signed summaries of psychological research reports. The December issue provides annual cumulative author and subject indexes. Beginning in 1963 each issue is also indexed by both subject and author. Libraries may also provide a cumulative subject index (1927–1960) and a cumulative author index (1927–1963).

*Annual Review of Psychology. Palo Alto, Calif.: Annual Reviews, 1950–date.

Each issue of this annual volume contains critical reviews of the literature in some 15 topical areas of contemporary psychology. Each review is written by a recognized authority on the topic. Although different authors writing in different years may vary considerably in their interpretation and handling of the same topic, all aim for comprehensive coverage of new developments.

*Psychological Bulletin. Washington, D.C.: American Psychological Association, 1904–date.

Issued bimonthly, the *Bulletin* evaluates reviews of research literature and methodology.

Sociological Abstracts. New York: Abstracts, 1952–date.

Issued five times a year, and cumulated annually, the *Abstracts* cover all areas of sociology including educational sociology. Abstracts articles and presents book reviews from several hundred periodicals, both domestic and foreign.

New Studies: A Guide to Recent Publications in the Social and Behavioral Sciences. **Beverly Hills, Calif.: Sage Publications, 1966–date.**

Published as part of the bimonthly journal, *American Behavioral Scientist*, this guide abstracts approximately 100 items in each issue from more than 400 journals, reviews, books, and pamphlets, both foreign and domestic.

Crime and Delinquency Abstracts. **Rockville, Md.: National Institute of Mental Health, 1966–1972.**

These abstracts cover published material on delinquency, crime, and penology.

Research Annual on Intergroup Relations. **New York: Anti-Defamation League of B'nai B'rith, 1965–date.**

This annual abstracts major studies in interracial and interfaith relations.

Religious and Theological Abstracts. **Youngstown, Ohio: Theological Abstracts, 1957–date.**

The quarterly publication abstracts articles on various phases of religion, including religious education.

Women Studies Abstracts. **Rush, N.Y.: Women Studies Abstracts, 1972–date.**

Issued quarterly, these abstracts cover articles and studies from many journals.

Education Abstracts. **Paris: UNESCO, 1949–1964.**

Issued monthly, this work covers fundamental education, listed by country and topic in English, French, and Spanish. Abstracts are indexed in each December issue.

National School Law Reporter. **New London, Conn.: Croft Educational Services, 1955–date.**

The biweekly publication abstracts court decisions on school law.

Book Review Digest. **New York: H. W. Wilson Co., 1905–date.**

Issued monthly and cumulated annually, this publication digests reviews of more than 6000 books each year taken from over 70 periodicals.

Braille Book Review. Washington, D.C.: American Foundation for the Blind and Physically Handicapped, Library of Congress, 1933–date.

This bimonthly abstracts articles about Braille materials and library services.

Specialized bibliographies

These specialized bibliographies present extensive lists of periodical articles, monographs, books, and reports.

*Department of Health, Education and Welfare.
Price List 31 Education
Price List 33a Occupations
Price List 71 Children
Washington, D.C.: Department of Health, Education and Welfare, Superintendent of Documents, Government Printing Office.

These annual publications list available government publications and are free upon request.

National Education Association Publications Catalogue. Washington, D.C.: National Education Association, 1930–date.

Published annually, the *Catalogue* lists all books, pamphlets, periodicals, audio-visual materials, research monographs, and procedings of the Association.

Current Documents in Higher Education: A Bibliography. Washington. American Association for Higher Education, 1969–date.

Occupational Literature. New York: H. W. Wilson Co., 1971.

This annotated bibliography of more than 7000 books, pamphlets, charts, and posters covers all phases of occupations.

Buros, Oscar K., ed. *Personality Tests and Reviews*. Highland Park, N.J.: Gryphon Press, 1972. 1679 pp.

This comprehensive bibliography on the literature of personality scales includes references on construction, use, and validation of specific tests.

Encyclopedias

Encyclopedias provide concise information on a number of subjects written by specialists. They provide a convenient source of information, and

often include illustrations and bibliographies. Only specialized encyclopedias dealing with restricted areas of knowledge are discussed in this
section.

*Encyclopedia of Educational Research. **New York: American Educational
Research Association, Macmillan Co.**

Published every ten years, this important reference work cites research
on educational problems. Each signed article is written by a specialist and
an excellent bibliography is included.

International Encyclopedia of the Social Sciences. **New York: Macmillan Co.,
1968. 17 vols.**

Prepared under the direction of ten learned societies, this reference
work treats topics in all of the social sciences.

Encyclopedia of Child Care and Guidance. **Garden City, N. Y.: Doubleday &
Co., 1968.**

A fairly comprehensive treatment of the nature of, and methods of
dealing with, problems of childhood.

Encyclopedia of Mental Health. **New York: Franklin Watts, 1970. 6 vols.**

An authoritative and comprehensive reference, this encyclopedia is
written by highly qualified contributors who are recognized authorities
in the field.

Encyclopedia of Social Work. **New York: National Association of Social
Workers, 1965–date. 2 vols.**

Published irregularly in intervals of several years, this work presents
extensive articles on all aspects of social work.

Facts on File. **New York: Facts on File, 1940–date.**

A weekly eight-page, current encyclopedia, *Facts on File* covers world
events indexed for quick fact finding, and is cumulated quarterly and
annually.

Encyclopedia of the Arts. **New York: Meredith Press, 1966.**

Articles deal with architecture, painting, theater, cinema, music, drama,
and ballet.

Larousse Encyclopedia of Music. New York: World, 1971. 576 pp.

An excellent reference work on all areas of music, it is well-written and comprehensive.

Grove's Dictionary of Music and Musicians. New York: St. Martin's Press, 1970.

This music encyclopedia includes signed contributions by more than 500 experts on music history, theory, composers, instruments, and artists.

Encyclopedia of Science and Technology. New York: McGraw-Hill Book Co., 1971. 15 vols.

More than 7000 articles written by more than 2000 contributors in all areas of science and engineering. Annual supplements are published.

Encyclopedia of Philosophy. New York: Macmillan–Free Press, 1967. 8 vols.

This outstanding authoritative encyclopedia covering both Western and Eastern thought, ancient, medieval, and modern is also available in a Four-volume edition.

Religions of the World from Primitive Belief to Modern Faiths. New York: Grosset & Dunlap, 1971.

This encyclopedic guide to the history and distinctive beliefs of all faiths includes facts and figures on membership and attendance, definitions of religious terms, and an extensive bibliography.

New Catholic Encyclopedia. New York: McGraw-Hill Book Co., 1967. 15 vols.

An international reference on the teachings, history, organization, and activities of the Roman Catholic Church, this work also covers all institutions, philosophies, and scientific and cultural movements affecting the church.

Encyclopedia Judaica. New York: Macmillan Co., 1972. 16 vols.

More than 25,000 entries, 11 million words, and 8000 illustrations present all phases of Jewish history and culture.

The Negro in America. Washington, D.C.: Howard University Press, 1970.

More than 6500 articles and studies about the Negro are provided, indexed by subject and title.

Corpus Juris Secundum. **Vols. 78 and 79. New York: American Law Book Co.**

This work has replaced the older volume, *Corpus Juris*, Vol. 56, long a standard encyclopedia of school law. Annual supplements are available.

American Jurisprudence. **Rochester, N. Y.: Lawyers Co-Operative Publishing Co.**

This series has replaced the older series, *Ruling Case Law.*

Yearbook of School Law. **Danville, Ill.: Interstate Printers and Publishers, 1950–date.**

This is a digest of federal, state, and appellate court decisions affecting schools.

Almanacs, handbooks, yearbooks, and guides

The name of a reference book does not always accurately describe its function, its frequency of publication, or the way in which the subject matter is organized. This general category of references includes those publications that present rather detailed, up-to-date information on a variety of subjects, organized around a given theme. They are the type of reference that one consults to find specific information, often of a statistical nature. Since they are ordinarily not comprehensive enough to be considered encyclopedic and the organization of topics is not alphabetical, they are classified together in this category. Generalized sources are listed first, followed by those with a more specialized emphasis.

World Almanac—Book of Facts. **New York: Newspaper Enterprise Association, 1868–date.**

Published annually, this inexpensive volume is the most comprehensive and most frequently consulted source of miscellaneous information. Statistical data in social, political, religious, geographic, commercial, sports, educational, and economic affairs are presented. One turns to this reference to find such information as the population of cities or countries, the state tax on gasoline in Wisconsin, the enrollment of Lawrence University, the date of the *Andrea Doria* disaster, or the world's record for the mile run. A chronology of important events of the previous year is included and all topics are indexed in detail. The following almanacs are similar to World Almanac:

Information Please Almanac. **New York: Simon & Schuster, 1947–date.**

Reader's Digest Almanac. Pleasantville, N.Y.: Reader's Digest Association, 1963–date.

The Official Associated Press Almanac. New York: Almanac Publishing Company, 1970–date.

Statistical Abstract of the United States. Washington, D.C.: Department of Commerce, Superintendent of Documents, Government Printing Office, 1879–date.

This important volume includes statistical data gathered by all agencies of the federal government, as well as by some private agencies. Of interest to students in education are the data on students, institutions, enrollment, salaries, expenditures, and literacy. All levels from preschool to higher education are covered.

The Fact Book: The American Almanac. New York: Grosset & Dunlap, 1964–date.

This is a privately printed, less expensive paperbound reprint of *Statistical Abstract of the United States.*

*Digest of Educational Statistics. Washington, D.C.: Department of Health, Education and Welfare, Government Printing Office, 1962–date.

Issued annually, this digest provides statistical information in the following volumes:

1. Elementary and secondary
2. Higher education
3. All levels of education
4. Federal programs of education
5. Miscellaneous

*Handbook of Research on Teaching. Chicago: Rand McNally & Co.
Vol. I 1963.
Vol. II 1973.

Comprehensive research on teaching is presented, with in-depth coverage of topics and extensive bibliographies.

Education Yearbook. New York: Macmillan Co., 1972–date.

This annual publication includes statistical data on major educational issues and movements with an extensive bibliography and reference guide.

Standard Education Almanac. Indianapolis, Ind.: Marquis Academic Media, 1968–date.

Published annually, this source of statistical information covers practically all aspects of education: elementary, secondary, higher, adult, and vocational; role of the federal government, legislation, finance, enrollments, construction of facilities, international education, and research.

Yearbook of Higher Education. **Indianapolis, Ind.: Marquis Academic Media, 1969–date.**

Up-to-date information on all aspects of higher education in the United States, Canada, and Mexico, for more than 3000 junior colleges, colleges, and universities.

The Annual Guide to Graduate Study. **Princeton, N.J.: Peterson's Guides, 1966–date.**

Extensive institutional information is published in eight separate books:

1. Graduate institutions
2. Undergraduate study
3. Biological and health sciences
4. Administrative, environment and social sciences
5. Arts, letters and communications
6. Education and nursing
7. Engineering and applied sciences
8. Physical sciences

A Guide to Graduate Study. **Washington, D.C.: American Council on Education, 1957–date.**

A useful reference to undergraduates planning graduate study, this book provides information for the selection of a graduate institution.

Requirements for Certification of Teachers, Counselors, Librarians and Administrators in Elementary and Secondary Schools and Junior Colleges. **Chicago: University of Chicago Press.**

Published annually, this guide presents information for the fifty states and territories of the United States.

Handbook of Adults Education in the United States. **Chicago: Adult Education Association of the United States, 1970–date.**

Signed articles deal with various aspects of adult education.

Handbook of Job Facts. **Chicago: Science Research Associates, 1972.**

This book of concise information about 300 occupational fields includes titles, nature of work, educational requirements, and income.

Occupational Outlook Handbook. Washington, D.C.: Bureau of Labor Statistics, Government Printing Office, 1949–date.

Published every two years, this volume describes job opportunities and requirements in the principal occupational categories. It is useful to guidance counselors, parents, and teachers.

*Mental Measurements Yearbook. Highland Park, N.J.: Gryphon Press, 1938–date.

This is the most comprehensive summary on psychological measurement and standardized tests and inventories. It contains reviews on all significant books on measurement and excerpts from book reviews appearing in professional journals. More than 800 standardized tests and inventories (achievement, aptitude, interest, and personality) are reviewed by one, two, or three reviewers. Published every four years, this work has been called the "bible of psychological testing." Readers are urged to refer to previous editions, for material is not duplicated from one edition to the next. The 1972 edition was the seventh.

*Tests in Print. Highland Park, N.J.: Gryphon Press, 1974.

This index to the contents of previous editions of the *Mental Measurements Yearbook* lists practically all standardized tests in print as well as those out of print.

The Student Psychologist's Handbook: A Guide to Sources. Cambridge, Mass.: Schenkman Publishing Co., 1969.

This handbook describes the major content areas of psychology, with sources of information, methods of data collection, and the use of reference materials.

Butler University Bulletin. Indianapolis, Ind.: Butler University, 1854–date.

A college or university bulletin or catalog yields a great deal of information about an institution, its history, course of study, admission requirements, degrees granted, campus building, tuition, fees, scholarships and grants, and faculty. This is often the best source of information about a particular school containing more detailed information than is found in any general source. Most institutions maintain a rather complete file of the catalog of other institutions, either in the library or in the registrar's office.

The College Blue Book. New York: C.C.M. Information Corporation, 1923–date. 4 vols.

Published every three years, the four volumes include nine books which are a most complete source of information on the characteristics of several thousand institutions.

Patterson's American Education. **Mt. Prospect, Ill.: Educational Directories, 1904–date.**

Published annually, this guide lists public and private schools, vocational and technical schools, colleges and universities by state and city with statistical data and names of administrative officials.

Handbook of Denominations in the United States. **Nashville: Abingdon Press.**

Detailed information is provided about the history and doctrine of more than 250 religious sects and denominations.

Catholic Dictionary. **New York: Macmillan Co.**

This reference work offers a concise treatment of topics related to Catholic history, philosophy, literature, and doctrine.

American Jewish Yearbook. **Philadelphia: American Jewish Committee, Jewish Publishing Society of America, 1899–date.**

This annual yearbook is a comprehensive statistical reference on all phases of Jewish life throughout the world.

Negro Almanac. **New York: Bellwether Publishing Co., 1971.**

A concise and comprehensive treatment of the Negro in American life, this volume includes biographical materials, and information on organizations, employment, business enterprise, the arts, sports, military life, and educational activities.

Data Processing Yearbook. **Detroit: Frank H. Gille, 1952–date.**

Published irregularly, this reference includes information on institutions offering data-processing and computer courses, and articles on equipment, techniques, and developments.

United Nations Statistical Yearbook. **New York: United Nations, 1949–date.**

This annual publication presents statistical data on population, trade, transportation, finance, health, and education.

References on international education

This section lists publications that deal with education outside the United States.

The World Yearbook of Education. **New York: Harcourt Brace Jovanovich, 1953–date.**

Issued annually, and prepared under the joint responsibility of the University of London Institute of Education and Teacher's College of Columbia University, each issue is devoted to some aspect of international education.

World Survey of Education. **New York: UNESCO Publications Center, 1959–date.**

Published irregularly, this reference includes statistical data on more than 90 countries.

International Yearbook of Education. **Geneva: International Bureau of Education, UNESCO, 1948–date.**

The *Yearbook* presents in English and French a review of educational developments for the previous year in the United States, Canada, and more than 40 foreign countries.

Education Abstracts. **Paris: UNESCO. New York: Columbia University Press, 1949–date.**

Issued ten times each year, this annotated guide deals with selected works from a number of international publications dealing with foreign education.

Paedagogica Europa: The European Yearbook of Education. **Amsterdam: Elsevier, 1965–date.**

An annual presentation of papers on educational research published in English, French, and German, the publication focuses on a single trend in contemporary educational research.

Educational Documentation and Information. **Geneva: International Bureau of Education, 1971–date.**

This quarterly provides short descriptive articles on national and international institutions, documentation, and research.

International Handbook of Universities. Paris: International Association of Universities, 1971. 1216 pp.

This book describes universities and other institutions of higher learning in more than 100 countries outside the United States and the British Commonwealth. It provides information about officials, facilities, history, structure, academic year, admission requirements, fees, scholarships, degree programs, libraries, publications, teaching staff, enrollment, and languages of instruction.

Commonwealth Universities Yearbook. Edinburgh: R. and R. Clark, 1964–date.

Issued annually, this volume gives detailed information on universities in the 23 Commonwealth countries.

World of Learning. London: Europa Publications, 1947–date.

Annual information is provided on universities, colleges, libraries, museums, art galleries, learned societies, and research institutions throughout the world.

Mathies, Lorraine and William G. Thomas. *Overseas Opportunities for American Educators and Students.* New York: Macmillan Co., 1973.

This is a useful guide for those who may be interested in teaching, studying, or conducting research outside continental United States.

Study Abroad, International Handbook. Paris: UNESCO, National Agency for International Publications, 1934–date.

Published every two years, this comprehensive guide to fellowships and awards for foreign study includes information on funds, foundations, activities, academic requirements, and teacher exchange.

Directory of Overseas Summer Jobs. Cincinnati: National Directory Service, 1972.

Designed primarily for young people, it describes summer employment opportunities with private employers as well as with various service organizations in Europe, North and South America, Africa, and Australia.

UNESCO Handbook of International Exchanges. Paris: UNESCO, 1965–date.

Information is provided on the purposes, programs, and activities of national and international organizations concerned with educational exchange programs.

Higher Education in Developing Countries. **Cambridge, Mass.: Harvard University Center for International Affairs, 1970.**

This is a selected bibliography on students, politics, and higher education.

Specialized dictionaries

*Dictionary of Education. **New York: McGraw-Hill Book Co., 1973.**

This educational dictionary covers 33,000 technical and professional terms. Foreign educational terms used in comparative education writings are included.

*Thesaurus of ERIC Descriptors. **Washington, D.C.: National Institute of Education, Superintendent of Documents.**

A definitive vocabulary of education, the *Thesaurus* is a major source of subject headings used for indexing and retrieval of documents and journals in the *Educational Resources Information Center* collection. It is a useful tool for students, teachers, and information specialists.

Comprehensive Dictionary of Psychological and Psychoanalytical Terms. **New York: David McKay Company.**

More than 13,000 terms are defined in nontechnical language.

Dictionary of Sociology. **Totowa, N.J.: Littlefield, Adams & Co.**

Most sociological terms are defined in nontechnical language.

Dictionary of Political Science. **Totowa, N.J.: Littlefield, Adams & Co.**

The McGraw-Hill Dictionary of Modern Economics. **New York: McGraw-Hill Book Co., 1973.**

Dictionary of the Social Sciences. **New York: Glencoe Press.**

This work defines approximately 2000 concepts used in the social sciences, and is compiled under the auspices of UNESCO.

Dictionary of Occupational Titles. **Washington, D.C.: Department of Labor, U.S. Government Printing Office.**

This lists of over 40,000 job titles and job descriptions is useful in the study of occupations and industrial processes, and in counseling.

Black's Law Dictionary. **St. Paul, Minn.: West Publishing Co.**

Black's contains definitions of the terms and phrases of American and English jurisprudence.

Ballentine's Law Dictionary with Pronunciations. **Rochester, N.Y.: Lawyers Cooperative Publishing Co., 1969. 1429 pp.**

This is a highly regarded law dictionary.

*Roget's International Thesaurus of Words and Phrases. **New York: Crowell, Collier and Macmillan.**

A thesaurus is the opposite of a dictionary. When you have an idea you look for the most appropriate word to convey it. Synonyms and antonyms are listed together. This reference should be used in conjunction with a good dictionary to insure precision of expression. Several inexpensive paper-bound editions are available.

Biographical references

Educational workers often need information about another educator or a prominent person outside the field of education. Some of these occasions relate to the conduct of educational research, while others concern professional contacts.

A partial list of situations in which biographical information would be helpful:

1. To help evaluate writings
2. To recommend a speaker for a professional meeting
3. To prepare a press release about a speaker
4. To introduce a speaker
5. To prepare for an important interview
6. To correspond with a person with greater understanding of his background
7. To choose an authority with whom to work professionally (This may involve the choice of a major professor or advisor for advanced study.)
8. To aid in recommending an individual for an honor, such as an award or an honorary degree

There are a number of sources of information about the famous and the not so famous. If a person is really outstanding, a general reference will supply the needed information, but if he is less prominent, a more specialized or limited source must be consulted.

Many of these references, particularly the autobiographical type, have been criticized as vanity publications, including in their listings persons of little distinction who are anxious to get their names listed. Hundreds of these autobiographical Who's Whos have been published, covering every city, state, section of the country, foreign country, vocation, profession, ethnic group, religious sect, or denomination. Another criticism concerns the possible lack of accuracy of the information, since persons listed usually send in their own data, which cannot be carefully checked. Another limitation is that important persons are not listed, for the listings are usually submitted as the results of a questionnaire, and some are not willing to respond.

Without questioning the motive of the publishers, who finance the publication largely by sales of the books to those listed, the reader is urged to evaluate the autobiographical data carefully. Many of these publications are found in libraries and can provide useful biographical data.

The brief sketches include information such as home address, business address, present position and title, former positions, date and place of birth, name of spouse, name of spouse's parents, names of children, schools attended, degrees, honorary positions, honors and awards, membership in professional and social organizations, books published, contributions to periodicals, military experience, travel, and hobbies.

Information about people is usually presented in one of three ways:

1. The Who's Who type. This information is compiled from responses to a questionnaire.
2. The biographical type. This information is taken from published sources which may range from feature articles to carefully documented investigations.
3. The dictionary type. This information usually consists of rather brief biographical data about a number of individuals, who have lived in the past, and were selected because of their historical importance.

AUTOBIOGRAPHICAL REFERENCES

*Who's Who in America. Chicago: Marquis Co., 1899–date.

Published every two years and listing more than 65,000 names, this general reference is considered one of the most reliable. This company also publishes Who's Who in the East, Who's Who in the Midwest, Who's Who in the West, Who's Who in the South and Southwest, Who's Who in the World, and Who's Who in Government. The information is autobiographical.

Who's Who of American Women. Chicago: Marquis Co., 1958–date.

This biennial reference is useful because few women have been listed in Who's Who in America.

Who Was Who in America. Chicago: Marquis Co., 1942–date.

Published approximately every ten years, this reference lists deceased persons who were prominent.

America's Men of Science. New York: R. R. Bowker Co., 1906–date.
Vol. I Physical Sciences
Vol. II Biological Sciences
Vol. III Behavioral Sciences

The information is autobiographical.

Contemporary Authors. Detroit: Gale Research Co., 1964–date.

Issued semiannually, this work lists autobiographical sketches of about 4000 authors each year.

Leaders in Education. New York: Bowker and Jacques Cattell Press, 1932–date.

This autobiographical publication lists some less-than-prominent as well as prominent educators.

Biographical references

*Current Biography. New York: H. W. Wilson Co., 1940–date.

Issued monthly and cumulated annually, this reference covers celebrities: kings, prime ministers, presidents, Nobel Prize winners, senators, cabinet members, congressmen, court justices; and sports, radio, film, television, and stage personalities. Biographies are abstracted from feature articles in hundreds of publications. The yearly cumulation is published as *Current Biography Yearbook*.

Directory of American Scholars. New York: R. R. Bowker Co., 1942–date.
Vol. I History
Vol. II English, Speech and Drama
Vol. III Foreign Languages
Vol. IV Philosophy, Religion and Law

This directory provides short biographical articles on leaders in various academic fields: teachers, authors, researchers, and administrators.

*Biography Index. New York: H. W. Wilson Co., 1946–date.

This quarterly index is cumulated annually of biographical material found in more than 2000 periodicals and in the various indexes of the H. W. Wilson Company. Biographies are indexed by name and profession or occupation.

Dictionary of American Biography. New York: Charles Scribner's Sons. 11 vols.

This reference, written by recognized authorities in their fields, contains information on more than 15,000 American men and women no longer living, and is prepared under the direction of the American Council of Learned Societies. A one-volume concise edition is available. This is an important source of information about individuals who had some influence upon history, but many of whom are not mentioned in history books.

Webster's Biographical Dictionary. **Springfield, Mass: G. & C. Merriam Company, 1969.**

This work contains more than 50,000 biographical sketches ranging from a few lines to more than a page in length. It is useful for finding information about persons of any nationality and from any period of history.

Directories

Directories provide information about the purposes and programs of institutions or agencies, and often include information about officers and staff.

Education Directory. **Washington, D.C.: U.S. Office of Education, Superintendent of Documents, 1912–date.**

This directory is issued annually in five parts dealing with names, educational agencies, officials, institutions, and other relevant data:

1. State Governments
2. Public School Systems
3. Higher Education
4. Educational Associations
5. Federal Government Agencies

NEA Handbook for Local, State, and National Associations. **Washington, D.C.: National Education Association, 1945–date.**

This annual publication contains listings and comprehensive reports of state and national officers of affiliated associations and departments. Information about purposes, membership, and publications is included.

Educator's World. **Englewood, Colo.: Fisher Publishing Co., 1972–date.**

This is an annual guide to more than 1600 education associations, publications, research centers, and foundations.

National Faculty Directory. **Detroit: Gale Research Co., 1964–date.**

Published annually, this work lists alphabetically the names and addresses of more than 300,000 full-time and part-time faculty members and administrative officials of junior colleges, colleges and universities in the United States.

American Education. **Mt. Prospect, Ill.: Educational Directories, 1904–date.**

School officials for practically all schools and school systems in the country, both private and public, are listed by state.

*Encyclopedia of Associations. **Detroit: Gale Research Co., 1964–date.**

This directory of more than 14,000 national associations includes business, scientific, educational, health, social welfare, and others of a more general nature. Listing is alphabetical and includes information on membership, address, name of executive secretary, and statement of purpose.

Foundations Directory. **New York: Russell Sage Foundation, 1964–date.**

Foundations are listed alphabetically by state, address, date of incorporation, donors, financial data, purposes, activities, and names of officers. A bimonthly publication, *Foundation News*, supplements the directory.

Directory for Exceptional Children. **Boston: Porter Sargent Publishing Co., 1962–date.**

This directory describes schools, camps, homes, clinics, hospitals, and services for the socially maladjusted, mentally retarded or physically handicapped. It is indexed by special need and by state location.

Mental Health Directory. **Washington, D.C.: National Institute of Mental Health, Government Printing Office, 1964–date.**

This annual publication lists national, state, and local mental health agencies, both public and private.

A National Catalogue of Financial Aids for Students Entering College. **Dubuque, Iowa: William C. Brown Co., 1966–date.**

More than 2000 institutional programs are described, with information on sponsors, eligibility, criteria, basis of awards, and application procedures.

Annual Register of Grant Support. **Indianapolis, Ind.: Academic Media, 1967–date.**

This list of more than 1000 sources of grants in all areas indicates available funds, purposes, and directions for applying.

American Library Directory. **New York: R. R. Bowker Co., 1923–date.**

This comprehensive biannual guide to private, state, municipal, institutional, and collegiate libraries in the United States and Canada includes information on special collections, number of holdings, staff salaries, budgets, and affiliations.

Instructional aids

The following publications list books, pamphlets, and audio-visual materials that are helpful to classroom teachers. Many are sent free on request; others may be obtained at a nominal cost.

New Educational Materials. **New York: Citation Press, Scholastic Magazines, 1967–date**

An annual reference and selection guide to recent educational materials this guide evaluates and reviews instructional aids, and books and articles of reference value, covering all levels, K–12.

Free and Inexpensive Learing Materials. **Nashville, Tenn.: Division of Surveys and Field Services, George Peabody College for Teachers, 1941–date.**

Published biennially, this list of more than 3000 items is indexed by curriculum-related categories.

Vertical File Index. **New York: H. W. Wilson Co., 1932–date.**

Issued monthly, the catalog indexes pamphlets and current free and inexpensive materials. Since these materials may soon be out of print, they should be ordered as soon as possible.

Programmed Instruction Guide. **Newburyport, Mass.: Entelek, 1967–date.**

This semiannual publication lists thousands of programmed instruction units available from more than 300 different sources.

Educators Guide to Free Curriculum Materials, **1944–date.**

Educators Guide to Free Guidance Materials, **1961–date.**

Educators Guide to Free Health, Physical Education and Recreation Materials, **1960–date.**

Educators Guide to Free Science Materials, **1959–date.**

Educators Guide to Free Social Studies Materials, **1960–date.**

Educators Guide to Free Films, **1941–date.**

Educators Guide to Free Filmstrips, **1949**–date.

Educators Guide to Free Tapes, Scripts and Transcriptions, **1955**–date.

Published annually at Randolph, Wisconsin, by Educators Progress Service, these eight references are indexed by subject and title, and include names and addresses of sources listed.

> *Index to 16 mm. Educational Films.* Los Angeles, Calif.: National Information Center for Education Media, 1973.
>
> *Index to 35 mm. Educational Films.* Los Angeles, Calif.: National Information Center for Education Media, 1973.

The two sources index more than 16,000 educational films by subject, title, length, color, description, producer, distributor, and year of release.

> *United States Government Films for Public Educational Use.* Washington, D.C.: Government Printing Office, 1964–date.

Films owned by government agencies and available for free use are listed.

> *National Center for Audio Tapes Catalogue.* Boulder, Colo.: National Center for Audio Tapes, 1965–date.

Hundreds of audio tapes are listed by subject and title. Duplicate tapes are furnished for a small recording fee.

Research-oriented periodicals

There are many publications in education and in closely-related areas that report research activity. Some of these publications are exclusively research-oriented. Others present both research reports and feature-type articles. It is possible that beginning researchers may not be familiar with many of the specialized publications that deal with a problem area selected. Browsing through these periodicals provides an effective introduction to the field. It is also possible that the student may find recent and current reports that have not yet appeared in the appropriate index.

The following list of periodicals may be helpful to those who are planning a research project. Since there is some overlapping between certain areas, appropriate periodicals may be located under several topic headings.

Administrator Quarterly

Adult Education

American Association of University Professors Bulletin

American Educational Research Journal

American Vocational Journal

Arbitration in the Schools

Arithmetic Teacher

Audio Visual Language Journal
Bulletin of the National Association of Secondary School Principals
Business Education Forum
California Journal of Educational Research
California Personnel and Guidance Association Journal
Canadian and International Education
Catholic Educational Review
Character Education Journal
Child Development
Childhood Education
Child Study Journal
Child Welfare
College Board Review
Community and Junior College Journal
Comparative Education
Comparative Education Review
Computer Education
Continuous Learning
Education and Urban Society
Educational Administration Quarterly
Educational Forum
Educational Leadership
Educational Researcher
Education Summary
Educational Technology
Education and Urban Society
Elementary School journal
Harvard Educational Review
High School Journal
History of Education Quarterly
Home Economics Research Journal
Independent School Bulletin
International Journal of Educational Science
International Review of Education
Jewish Education
Journal for the Scientific Study of Religion
Journal of Business Education
Journal of Communication
Journal of Creative Behavior
Journal of Educational Data Processing
Journal of Educational Measurement
Journal of Educational Research
Journal of Educational Statistics
Journal of Experimental Education
Journal of Higher Education
Journal of Home Economics
Journal of Industrial Teacher Education

Journal of Law and Education
Journal of Legal Education
Journal of Negro Education
Journal of Religion
Journal of Research and Development in Education
Journal of Research in Mathematics Education
Journal of Research in Music Education
Journal of Research in Science Teaching
Journal of Secondary Education
Journal of Teacher Education
Junior College Journal
Junior College Research Review
Kappa Delta Pi Record
Library Quarterly
Mathematics Teacher
Measurement in Education
Merrill Palmer Quarterly of Behavior and Development
Microfilm Review
Modern Language Journal
National Business Education Quarterly
National Catholic Educational Association Bulletin
National Education Association Research Bulletin
National Society for Programmed Instruction Journal
Negotiation Research Digest
Negro Educational Review
New England Association Review
North Central Association Quarterly
Peabody Journal of Education
Phi Delta Kappan
Pollution Abstracts
Programmed Instruction
Programmed Learning and Educational Technology
Public Opinion Quarterly
Religion Teachers Journal
Religious Education
Research in Higher Education
Review of Educational Research
Review of Religious Research
School and Society
School Law Journal
School Law Reporter
School Research Information Service Quarterly
School Review
School Science and Mathematics

Science Education
Science and Children
Social Education
Speech Monographs

Speech Teacher
Teachers College Record
Theory into Practice
Young Children

Sociology

American Anthropologist
American Behavioral Science
American Journal of Sociology
American Sociological Review
Ethnology
Federal Probation
Human Relations
Journal of American Indian Education
Journal of Applied Behavior Science
Journal of Correctional Education
Journal of Educational Sociology
Journal of Experimental Social Psychology
Journal of Marriage and the Family

Journal of Research in Crime and Delinquency
Rural Sociology
Social Case Work
Social Education
Social Forces
Social Problems
Sociological Methods and Research
Sociology of Education
Sociology and Social Research
Sociometry
Urban Education
Urban Review

Health and physical education

American Journal of Nursing
American Journal of Occupational Therapy
American Journal of Physical Medicine
American Journal of Public Health
Athletic Journal
Health and Education Journal
Health Education
Journal of the American Dietetic Association
Journal of the American Medical Association
Journal of the American Physical Therapy Association
Journal of Clinical Nutrition
Journal of Drug Education
Journal of Health and Social Behavior
Journal of Health, Physical Education and Recreation

Journal of Mental Health
Journal of Nursing Education
Journal of Nutrition
Journal of Psychedelic Drugs
Journal of Physical Education and Recreation
Journal of Rehabilitation
Journal of School Health
Nursing Mirror
Nursing Outlook
Nursing Research
Nursing Times
Quarterly Review of Pediatrics
Registered Nurse
Research Quarterly of the American Alliance for Health, Physical Education and Recreation

Psychology

American Journal of Orthopsychiatry
American Journal of Psychiatry
American Journal of Psychology
American Psychologist

British Journal of Educational Psychology
Catholic Psychological Record
Contemporary Psychology

Developmental Psychology
Educational And Psychological Measurement
Genetic Psychology Monographs
Journal of Abnormal Psychology
Journal of Applied Psychology
Journal of Child Psychology, Psychiatry, and Allied Disciplines
Journal of Clinical Psychology
Journal of Comparative and Physiological Psychology
Journal of Consulting and Clinical Psychology
Journal of Counseling Psychology
Journal of Creative Behavior
Journal of Educational Psychology
Journal of Experimental Child Psychology
Journal of General Psychology
Journal of Genetic Psychology
Journal of Nervous and Mental Disease
Journal of Personality
Journal of Personality and Social Psychology
Journal of Personal Assessment
Journal of Psychiatric Research
Journal of Psychology
Journal of Social Psychology
Journal of Verbal Learning and Verbal Behavior
Learning and Motivation
Mental Hygiene
Pastoral Psychology
Perceptual and Motor Skills
Personnel Psychology
Psychiatry
Psychoanalytic Quarterly
Psychological Abstracts
Psychological Bulletin
Psychological Monographs
Psychological Record
Psychological Reports
Psychological Review
Psychology in the Schools
Psychometrika
Small Group Behavior
Transactional Analysis Journal

Guidance and counseling

American Vocational Journal
Counselor Education and Supervision
Elementary School Counseling and Guidance
Focus on Guidance
Guidance Clinic
Measurement and Evaluation in Guidance
Personnel and Guidance Journal
School Counselor
Vocational Guidance Quarterly

Special education

Academic Therapy
American Annals of the Deaf
American Journal of Mental Deficiency
Braille Book Review
Digest of the Mentally Retarded
Education and Training of the Mentally Retarded
Exceptional Children
Exceptional Child Education Abstracts
Focus on Exceptional Children
Gifted Child Quarterly
Gifted Pupil
Hearing and Speech News
International Journal for the Education of the Blind
Journal of Learning Disabilities
Journal of Mental Deficiency Research
Journal of Special Education
Journal of Speech and Hearing Disorders
Journal of Speech and Hearing Research
Learning Disorders
Mental Retardation
Mental Retardation Abstracts
New Outlook for the Blind
Sight Saving Review
Special Education
Teacher of the Blind
Teaching Exceptional Children
Training School Bulletin
Volta Review

Reading

American Journal of Optometry	*Journal of Reading Behavior*
Elementary English	*Journalism Quarterly*
English Journal	*Reading Improvement*
Initial Teaching Alphabet Bulletin	*Reading Quarterly*
Journal of the Association for the	*Reading Research Quarterly*
Study of Perception	*Reading Teacher*
Journal of Reading	*Reading World*
Journal of Reading Specialists	

Computer-generated sources

There are a number of computer-generated reference sources that may save a great deal of time and effort and provide a more complete search of the literature.

School Research Information Service (SRIS)

This information retrieval service is operated by Phi Delta Kappa fraternity, Bloomington, Indiana. The Educational Resources Information Center, *Current Index to Journals in Education* and *Resources in Education* tapes serve as a base. A computer printout of abstracts will be furnished for a moderate fee.

Direct Access to Reference Information (DATRIX)

A development of the University Microfilms (Ann Arbor, Michigan), a division of the Xerox Corporation, this system provides computerized retrieval for *Dissertation Abstracts*, from 1928 to date. The researcher selects key words from a DATRIX Key Word List and dissertations will be cited by title, author, page and volume of *Dissertation Abstracts*, and name of university. Information on microfiche or Xerographic copy of the complete dissertation is provided and may be ordered from University Microfilms.

Psychological Abstracts Search and Retrieval Service (PASAR)

This search and retrieval service provides printouts of abstracts of psychological journal articles, monographs, reports, and parts of books. Each monthly issue of *Psychological Abstracts* provides a request form and search request guidelines. Consult the *Cumulative Subject Index to Psychological Abstracts* for appropriate key words or terms to use in making a request. A moderate fee is charged for the search.

Note taking

One of the most important research activities of the graduate student is note taking—putting materials in a form that can easily be recalled and used in the future. Notes will result from speeches and lectures, class discussions, conversation, from solitary meditation, and from reading reference materials. In preparing term papers and research reports the notes that result from reading will be most significant. Without a careful, systematic system of note taking, much of what is read is quickly forgotten.

Reading-reference notes have been classified under four principal categories:

1. *Quotation.* The exact words of an author are reproduced, enclosed in quotation marks. It is essential to copy each statement accurately, and to indicate the exact page reference so that the quotations may be properly footnoted in the written report.
2. *Paraphrase.* The reader restates the author's thoughts in his own words.
3. *Summary.* The reader states in condensed form the contents of the article.
4. *Evaluation.* The reader records his own reaction, indicating his agreement or disagreement, or interpreting the point of view of the writer.

A single note card may include several of these types when it seems appropriate.

A SUGGESTED METHOD FOR TAKING NOTES

1. Skim the reference source before copying any notes. A bird's-eye view is essential before one can decide what material to record and use. Selecting the most significant material is an art to be cultivated.
2. Use 4″ × 6″ index cards. They are easily sorted by subject headings, and are large enough to include a reasonable amount of material. Some students prefer 5″ × 8″ cards, which are less convenient to carry but provide more space for notes.
3. File each note card under a definite topic or heading. Place the subject heading at the top of the card for convenient filing. A complete bibliographic citation should be placed at the bottom of the note card. If a book has been used, the call number should be indicated to facilitate library location in the future.
4. Include only one topic on a card. This makes organization of notes flexible. If the notes are lengthy, use consecutively numbered cards, and slip a rubber band around them before filing.
5. Be sure that notes are complete and clearly understandable, for they are not likely to be used for some time after they have been copied.
6. Distinguish clearly between a summary, a direct quotation of the author, a reference to the author's source, and an evaluative statement.
7. Don't plan to recopy or type your notes. It wastes time and increases possibility of error and confusion. Copy your notes carefully the first time.
8. Keep a supply of note cards with you at all times, so that you can jot down ideas that come to you while waiting, riding the bus, or listening to a lecture or discussion.

Lateral dominance - reading achievement

Purpose: to study relationships between dominance and reading achievement specified by Dearborn (1931), Monroe (1932), + Harris (1957)

Hypothesis: there is no significant relationship between reading achievement and: 1. hand - eye dominance 2. strength or direction of hand dominance 3. strength or direction of eye dominance 4. early, late, or no establishment of consistent hand dominance

Sample: 250 second grade pupils in 13 randomly-selected classrooms in a middle-class St. Paul, Minnesota suburb

Tests: Lorge Thorndike Intelligence Test, Level I; Harris Test of Lateral Dominence; Gates Advanced Primary Reading Tests.

Analysis: Analysis of Covariance: IQ scores the covariate

Results: all three hypotheses confirmed; no significant differences at the .05 level. "Lateral dominance does not seem to be a fruitful area for seeking out determiners of individual differences in reading achievement." p.143.

Irving H. Balow and Bruce Balow, "Lateral Dominence and Reading Achievement in the Second Grade." American Educational Research Journal, 1: 139-43, May, 1964.

FIGURE 3-5   Note Card (4" × 6")

9. Be careful not to lose your notes. As soon as they are copied, file them in a card index box. If you must carry them with you, use the 4" × 6" or 5" × 8" accordion file folder, and be sure that your name and address is clearly printed on it.
10. Keep a permanent file of your notes. You may find the same notes useful in a number of courses or in writing a number of reports.

The bibliography

In preparing a formal report or paper, it is customary to include a bibliography, indicating the references that have been used in preparing the report. Writing a brief descriptive comment or annotation adds to the usefulness of the entries.

The most convenient way to assemble and organize the bibliography is by the use of 3" × 5" bibliography cards. The card includes the call number (if the reference is a book), the name of the author, the facts of

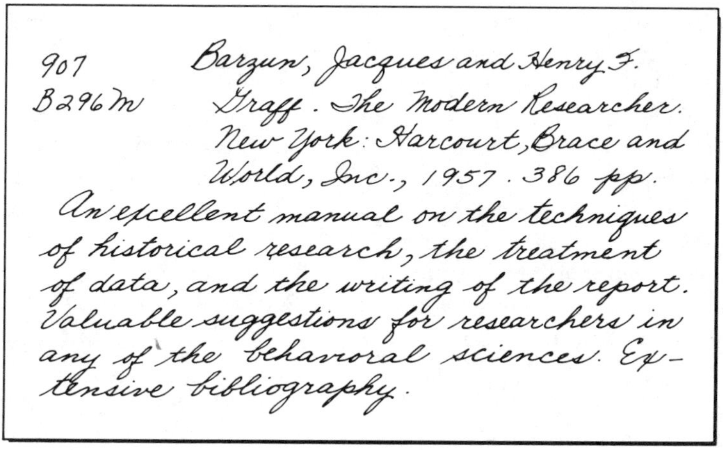

907
B296m   Barzun, Jacques and Henry F.
Graff. The Modern Researcher.
New York: Harcourt, Brace and
World, Inc., 1957. 386 pp.
An excellent manual on the techniques
of historical research, the treatment
of data, and the writing of the report.
Valuable suggestions for researchers in
any of the behavioral sciences. Ex-
tensive bibliography.

FIGURE 3–6   Bibliography Card (3″ × 5″)

publication, and the annotation. Placing the information on cards makes it easy to assemble the author's names in the alphabetical order in which they are listed in the bibliography of the report.

Finding related literature

Students often waste time searching for references in an unsystematic way. The search for references is an ever-expanding process, for each reference may lead to a new list of sources. Although the order suggested does not exhaust the process of compiling a bibliography, it does provide a systematic plan for getting underway.

Researchers may consider these sources as basic:

1. *The Education Index*
2. *Resources in Education*
3. *Current Index to Journals in Education*
4. *Index to Doctoral Dissertations* and *Dissertations Abstracts International*
5. *The Encyclopedia of Educational Research*
6. Other specialized indexes or abstracts indicated by the area of investigation

Summary

Practically all that man knows can be found in books and in libraries. Both the professional worker in education and the graduate student, as consumers if not producers of research, should be familiar with the library and its many facilities and services. They should know about the most important reference sources in education and its related fields.

An extensive list of references has been presented, including many more than a student should be expected to remember. Those considered basic have been designated by an asteriak (*). The course instructor may wish to indicate others. It is hoped that this chapter will serve as a useful ready reference when a particular need arises.

Skill in compiling a bibliography, and skill in taking, recording, and filing notes is essential for graduate students. The brief suggestions provided should be helpful to both students and professional workers in education.

Suggested Activities

REFERENCE EXERCISE
Choose the most likely source for the following information:

number

 1. A recently completed educational research project   ———
 2. List of encyclopedias published in several languages   ———
 3. All books on research in a particular library   ———
 4. Cost of school building construction in 1975   ———
 5. Book reviews on *Jaws*   ———
 6. Superintendent of schools at Davenport, Iowa   ———
 7. Summary of recent research on spelling   ———
 8. A more appropriate word than you have in mind   ———
 9. Birth date of the author of a particular book   ———
10. World record for the mile run   ———
11. Chemistry teaching requirements in Iowa   ———
12. Author, publisher, and price of a particular book   ———
13. Teacher liability for a playground accident   ———
14. President of the Illinois Educational Association   ———
15. Biographical sketch of Henry Kissinger   ———
16. Concise history and campus facilities of a college   ———
17. Divorce data for the United States in 1974   ———
18. Faculty rank of a faculty member at Duke University   ———
19. Information on the University of Copenhagen   ———

number

20. Articles on the Strategic Air Defense   _____
21. Autobiographical sketch of Senator Tower   _____
22. Quotations that deal with trees   _____
23. Computer printout of abstracts on ability grouping   _____
24. Listing of all books published in the English language   _____
25. Articles on homework in professional journals   _____
26. Summary of research on reading   _____
27. A Purdue master's thesis on administrator characteristics   _____
28. Information about a not-too-prominent educator   _____
29. Articles on computer-assisted instruction   _____
30. Definition of the term *core curriculum*   _____
31. Secretary of State under President Woodrow Wilson   _____
32. Up-to-date evaluation of *World Book Encyclopedia*   _____
33. Critical evaluation of the *Kuder Preference Record*   _____
34. A Syracuse University dissertation on merit rating   _____
35. Articles on academic dishonesty   _____
36. Concise information on Roman mythology   _____
37. Proper footnote form   _____
38. Date of the *Andrea Doria* disaster   _____
39. A chronology of events for 1975   _____
40. Enrollment of Temple University   _____
41. History of the word *sheriff*   _____
42. List of articles on co-insurance   _____
43. Honorary degrees held by Henry Kissinger   _____
44. Word opposite in meaning to *duplicity*   _____
45. List of articles on steel tempering   _____
46. Illinois tax on gasoline   _____
47. Expert evaluation of a recently published dictionary   _____
48. Information about Simon Vetch, revolutionary war personality   _____
49. Information about the Ford Foundation   _____
50. List of articles on Robert Frost   _____
51. Concise article on computers   _____
52. Article in a publication not available in a local library   _____

number

53. References on the middle school   _____
54. Price of a U.S. government pamphlet on classroom discipline   _____
55. Information about the Milwaukee city library   _____
56. University of Wisconsin dissertation on labor history   _____
57. Information about the author of a recently published book   _____
58. Articles on home nursing care   _____

LIST OF REFERENCES

1. Air University Library Index
2. Almanac: World/Information Please
3. American Library Directory
4. American Universities and Colleges
5. Applied Science and Technology Index
6. Bartlett's Familiar Quotations
7. Biography Index
8. Black's Law Dictionary
9. Books in Print
10. Book Review Digest
11. Book Review Index
12. Mental Measurements Yearbook
13. Business Periodicals Index
14. Card Catalogue/Index
15. College Blue Book
16. College/University Catalog/Bulletin
17. Contemporary Authors
18. Corpus Juris Secundum
19. Cumulative Book Index
20. Cumulated Index Medicus
21. Cumulative Index to Nursing Literature
22. Current Biography
23. Dictionary of American Biography
24. Dictionary of Education
25. Dictionary of Occupational Titles
26. Dictionary of Sociology
27. Digest of Educational Statistics
28. Dissertation Abstracts International
29. Documentation in Education
30. Education Index
31. Encyclopedia of Associations
32. Encyclopedia of Educational Research
33. Encyclopedia Americana/Britannica
34. Foundations Directory
35. Guide to Graduate Study
36. Handbook of Research on Teaching
37. Home Book of Quotations
38. Index to Legal Periodicals
39. International Handbook of Universities
40. Journal of Educational Research
41. Journal of Experimental Education
42. Master's Theses in Education
43. NEA Handbook of Local, State, and National Associations
44. National Tape Recording Catalogue
45. New Serial Titles
46. New York Times Index
47. Oxford English Dictionary
48. Patterson's American Education
49. Price List #31, USOE
50. Personality Tests and Reviews
51. Psychological Abstracts
52. Readers' Guide to Periodic Literature
53. Research Studies in Education
54. Resources in Education
55. Review of Educational Research
56. Roget's Thesaurus
57. School Research Information Service (SRIS)
58. Sociological Abstracts
59. Social Sciences Index

60. Statistical Abstract of the United States
61. Standard Periodicals Directory
62. Subject Guide to Books in Print
63. Twenty Thousand Words
64. Union List of Serials
65. USOE Directory
66. Vertical File Index
67. Webster's Biographical Dictionary
68. Who's Who in America
69. Who Was Who
70. Who's Who in American Education
71. Woelner and Wood: Requirements for Certification
72. World Yearbook of Education

EXPERIMENTAL
RESEARCH

Chapter 4

Experimental research provides a systematic and logical method for answering the question, "If this is done under carefully controlled conditions, what will happen?" The experimenter manipulates certain stimuli, treatments, or environmental conditions and observes how the condition or behavior of the subject is affected or changed. His manipulation is deliberate and systematic. He must be aware of other factors that could influence the outcome and remove or control them in such a way that he can establish a logical association between manipulated factors and observed effects.

Experimentation provides a method of hypothesis testing. After the experimenter defines a problem he proposes a tentative answer, or hypothesis. He tests the hypothesis and confirms or disconfirms it in the light of the controlled variable relationship that he has observed. It is important to note that the confirmations or rejection of the hypothesis is stated in terms of probability rather than certainty.

Experimentation is the classic method of the science laboratory, where elements manipulated and effects observed can be controlled. It is the most sophisticated, exacting, and powerful method for discovering and developing an organized body of knowledge.

Although the experimental method finds its greatest utility in the laboratory, it has been effectively applied within nonlaboratory settings such as the classroom, where significant factors or variables can be controlled to some degree. The immediate purpose of experimentation is to predict events in the experimental setting. The ultimate purpose is to generalize the variable relationships so that they may be applied outside the laboratory to a wider population of interest.

Early experimentation

The earliest assumptions of experimental research were based upon what was known as the *law of the single variable*. John Stuart Mill defined this principle in 1872 in his work "Methods of Experimental Inquiry." He stated five rules or canons that he believed would include all types of logical procedure required to establish order among controlled events.

One of his canons, known as the *method of difference*, states:

If an instance in which the phenomenon under investigation occurs, and an instance in which it does not occur have every circumstance in common save one, that one occurring only in the former, the circumstance in which alone the two instances differ is the effect, or the cause, or an indispensable part of the cause of the phenomenon.[1]

In simpler language, if two situations are alike in every respect and one element is added to one but not the other, any difference that develops is the effect of the added element; or, if two situations are alike in every respect and one element is removed from one, but not from the other, any difference that develops may be attributed to the subtracted element.

The law of the single variable provided the basis for much early laboratory experimentation. In 1662 Robert Boyle, an Irish physicist, used this method in arriving at a principle upon which he formulated his law of gases: When temperature is held constant the volume of an ideal gas is inversely proportional to the pressure exerted upon it. In other words, when pressure is raised, volume decreases; when pressure is lowered, volume increases.

$$\frac{V_1}{V_2} = \frac{P_2}{P_1} \quad \text{(In Boyle's Law, \textit{pressure} is the single variable.)}$$

A little more than a century later, Jacques A. C. Charles, a French physicist, discovered a companion principle, now known as Charles' Law.

[1]John Stuart Mill, *A System of Logic* (New York: Harper & Row, Publishers, 1873), p. 222.

He observed that when the pressure was held constant, the volume of an ideal gas was directly proportional to the temperature. When temperature is raised, volume increases; when temperature is lowered, volume decreases.

$$\frac{V_1}{V_2} = \frac{T_1}{T_2}$$ (In Charles' Law, *temperature* is the single variable.)

Factorial designs

Although the concept of the single variable proved useful in some areas of the physical sciences, it failed to provide a sound approach to experimentation in the behavioral sciences. Despite its appealing simplicity and apparent logic, it did not provide an adequate method for studying complex problems. It assumed a highly artificial and restricted relationship between single variables. Rarely, if ever, are human events the result of single causes. They are usually the result of the interaction of many variables, and an attempt to limit variables so that one can be isolated and observed proves impossible.

The contributions of R. A. Fisher, first applied in agricultural experimentation, have provided a much more effective way of conducting realistic experimentation in the behavioral sciences. His concept of achieving pre-experimental equation of conditions through random selection of subjects and random assignment of treatments, and his concepts of analysis of variance and analysis of covariance, made possible the study of complex interactions through factorial designs, in which the influence of more than one independent variable upon more than one dependent variable could be observed.

Experimental and control groups

An experiment involves the comparison of the effects of a particular treatment with that of a different treatment or of no treatment. In a simple conventional experiment reference is usually made to an *experimental group* and to a *control group*.

These groups are equated as nearly as possible. The experimental group is exposed to the influence of the factor under consideration; the control group is not. Observations are then made to determine what difference appears or what change or modification occurs in the experimental as contrasted with the control group.

However, experiments are not always characterized by a treatment-nontreatment comparison. Varying types, amounts, or degrees of the experimental factor may be applied to a number of groups. For example, an experiment to test the effectiveness of a particular medication in reducing body temperature might involve administering a massive dosage to one group, a normal dosage to a second, and a minimal dosage to a third. Since all the groups receive medication, there is no control group in the limited sense of the term, but control of the experimental factors and observation of their effects are essential elements.

Internal and external validity

The researcher has two major objectives:

1. He must attempt to determine whether the factors that have been modified actually have a systematic effect in the experimental setting and whether the observed occurrences were not influenced by extraneous or uncontrolled factors. The extent to which this goal is attained is a measure of the *internal validity* of the experiment. But the researcher would achieve little of practical value if these relationships were valid only in the contrived experimental situation and only for those individuals participating.

2. He must also determine whether the systematic relationships that have been identified, isolated, and measured can be generalized—used to predict relationships outside the experimental setting. The extent to which this goal is attained is a measure of the *external validity* of the experiment.

Independent and dependent variables

Variables are the conditions or characteristics that the experimenter manipulates, controls, or observes. The *independent* variables are the conditions or characteristics that the experimenter manipulates in his attempt to ascertain their relationship to observed phenomena. The *dependent* variables are the conditions or characteristics that appear, disappear, or change as the experimenter introduces, removes, or changes independent variables.

In educational research an independent variable may be a particular teaching method, a type of teaching material, a reward, or period of exposure to a particular condition. The dependent variable may be a test score, the number of errors, or measured speed in performing a task. Thus, the dependent variables are the measured changes in pupil performance attributable to the influence of the independent variables.

Operational definitions of experimental variables

Such variables as giftedness, academic achievement, and creativity are conceptual definitions that are defined as dictionary terms. But because they cannot be observed directly, they are vague and ambiguous and provide a poor basis for identifying variables. Much more precise and unambiguous definitions of variables would be stated in operational form, which stipulates the operation by which they could be observed and measured. Giftedness could be operationally defined as a score two or more standard deviations above the mean on the *Wechsler Adult Intelligence Scale*, academic achievement as a score on the 1973 edition of the *Stanford Achievement Test*, or creativity as a score on the *Torrance Tests of Creative Thinking*. When an operational definition is used there is no doubt about what the researcher means.

To be useful, however, operational definitions must be based upon a theory that is generally recognized as valid. Operational terms do not necessarily prove to be useful in describing variables, for they could conceivably be based upon irrelevant behavior. Defining degree of self-esteem in terms of the number of times an individual smiles per minute would not be a useful or realistic definition, even though such behavior could easily be observed and recorded.

Organismic or attribute variables

Organismic variables are those characteristics that cannot be altered by the experimenter. Such independent variables as age, sex, or race have already been determined, but they can be introduced or removed as variables. The question of whether eight-year-old girls show greater reading achievement than eight-year-old boys provides an example of sex as an organismic variable. The teaching procedure is the same for each group. Since sex is the variable it is not manipulated; it has already been determined.

Intervening variables

In many types of behavioral research the relationship between the independent and dependent variables is not a simple one of stimulus to response. Certain variables which cannot be controlled or measured directly may have an important effect upon the outcome. These modifying variables intervene between the cause and the effect.

In a language classroom experiment a researcher is interested in determining the effect of immediate reinforcement upon learning the parts of speech. He suspects that certain factors or variables may influence the relationship, even though they cannot be observed directly. Anxiety, fatigue, and motivation, for example, may be intervening variables and are difficult to define in operational terms. These intervening variables cannot be ignored, however, and must be accounted for.

Extraneous variables

Extraneous variables are those uncontrolled variables (i.e., variables not manipulated by the experimenter) that may have a significant influence upon the dependent variable. Many research conclusions are invalidated by the influence of these extraneous variables.

In a widely publicized study, the effectiveness of three methods of social studies teaching was compared. Intact classes were used and the researchers were unable to randomize or control such variables as teacher competence or enthusiasm, or the age, socioeconomic level, or academic ability of the student subjects. The criterion of effectiveness was achievement, measured by scores on standardized tests. It would seem clear that the many extraneous variables precluded valid conclusions about the relative effectiveness of the independent variables, which were teaching methods.

Although it is impossible to eliminate all extraneous variables, particularly in classroom research, sound experimental design enables the researcher to largely neutralize their influence.

Controlling extraneous variables

Variables that are not of direct interest to the researcher may be removed or their influence minimized by several methods:

Removing the variable. Variables may be controlled by eliminating them completely. Observer distraction may be removed by separating the observer from both experimental and control groups by a one-way-glass partition. Some variables between subjects may be eliminated by selecting cases with uniform characteristics. Using only female subjects removes sex as a variable. (Of course, it must be remembered that not all females have uniform physical or psychological characteristics.)

Matching cases. Selecting pairs or sets of individuals with identical or nearly identical characteristics and assigning one of them to the experimental group and the other to the control group provides another method of control. This method is limited by the difficulty of matching on more than one variable. It is also likely that some individuals will be excluded from the experiment if a matching subject is not available. Matching is not considered satisfactory unless the members of the pairs or sets are randomly assigned to the treatment groups, a method known as *blocking*.

Balancing cases. Balancing cases consists of assigning subjects to experimental and control groups in such a way that the means and the variances of the groups are as nearly equal as possible. Since identical balancing of groups is impossible, the researcher must decide how much departure from equality can be tolerated without loss of satisfactory control. This method also presents a similar difficulty noted in the matching method; namely, the difficulty of equating groups on the basis of more than one characteristic or variable.

Analysis of covariance. This method permits the experimenter to eliminate initial differences on several variables between the experimental and control groups by statistical methods. Using pretest mean scores as covariates, this method is considered preferable to the conventional matching of groups. Analysis of covariance is a rather complicated statistical procedure, beyond the scope of this elementary treatment. For a complete discussion readers may wish to consult the references by Edwards, Kerlinger, or Lindquist, listed in the chapter bibliography.

Randomization. Randomization involves pure chance selection and assignment of subjects to experimental and control groups from a limited supply of available subjects.

If two groups are involved, randomization could be achieved by tossing a coin, assigning a subject to one group if heads appeared, to the other if the toss were tails. When more than two groups are involved, dice or a table of random numbers could be used.

Randomization provides the most effective method of eliminating systematic bias and of minimizing the effect of extraneous variables. The principle is based upon the assumption that through random selection and assignment differences between groups result only from the operation of probability or chance. These differences are known as *sampling error* or *error variance*, and their magnitude can be estimated by the researcher.

In an experiment, differences in the dependent variables that may be attributed to the effect of the independent variables are known as *experimental variance*. The significance of an experiment may be tested by comparing experimental variance with error variance. If at the conclusion of the experiment the differences between experimental and control groups are too great to attribute to error variance it may be presumed that these differences are probably attributable to experimental variance.

Experimental validity

In order to make a significant contribution to the development of knowledge an experiment must have two types of validity, internal validity and external validity.

Internal validity.   An experiment has internal validity to the extent that the factors that have been manipulated (independent variables) actually have a genuine effect on the observed consequences (dependent variables) in the experimental setting.

External validity.   The researcher would achieve little of practical value if these observed variable relationships were valid only in the experimental setting and only for those participating. External validity is the extent to which the variable relationships can be generalized to nonexperimental situations—other settings, other treatment variables, other measurement variables, and other populations.

Experimental validity is an ideal to aspire to, for it is unlikely that it can ever be completely achieved. Internal validity is very difficult to achieve in the nonlaboratory setting of the behavioral experiment where there are so many extraneous variables to attempt to control. When experimental controls are tightened to achieve internal validity, the more artificial, less realistic situation may prevail, reducing the external validity or generalizability of the experiment. Some compromise is inevitable so that a reasonable balance may be established between control and generalizability—between internal and external validity.

Threats to internal validity

In educational experiments, or in any behavioral experiments conducted outside the laboratory, a number of extraneous variables are present in the situation or are generated by the experimental design and procedures. These variables influence the results of the experiment in ways that are difficult to evaluate. In a sense, they introduce rival hypotheses that could account for experimental change not attributable to the experimental variables under consideration. Although these extraneous variables cannot be completely eliminated, many of them can be identified. It is important that behavioral researchers anticipate them and take all possible precautions to minimize their influence through sound experiment design and execution.

A number of factors jeopardize the power of the experimenter to evaluate the effects of independent variables unambiguously. Donald T. Campbell and Julian C. Stanley[2] have discussed these factors in their excellent definitive treatment. They include the following:

Maturation.   Subjects change in many ways over a period of time, and these changes may be confused with the effect of the independent variables under consideration. Between initial and subsequent observations subjects may become tired, bored, wiser, or influenced by the incidental learnings or experiences that they encounter through normal maturation.

Contemporary history.   Specific external events beyond the control of the researcher may have a stimulating or disturbing effect upon the performance of subjects. The effect of a fire drill, the emotional tirade of a teacher, a pep session, the anxiety produced by a pending examination, or a catastrophic event in the community may significantly affect the test performance of a group of students.

In some classroom experiments these external events might have a similar effect upon both experimental and control subjects, but since they are specific events, they may affect one group but not the other. The effect of these uncontrolled external events is one of the hazards inherent in experiments carried on outside the laboratory. In laboratory experiments these extraneous variables can be controlled more effectively.

Testing.   The process of pretesting at the beginning of an experiment may produce a change in subjects. Tests may sensitize individuals by making them more aware of concealed purposes of the researcher and may serve as a stimulus to change. Pretesting may produce a practice effect that may make subjects more proficient in subsequent test performance. Testing presents a threat to internal validity that is common to pretest-posttest experiments.

Unstable instrumentation.   Unreliable instruments or techniques used to describe and measure aspects of behavior are threats to the validity of an experiment. If tests used as instruments of observation are not accurate or consistent, a serious element of error is introduced. If human observers are used to describe behavior changes in subjects, changes in their standards due to fatigue, increased insight or skill, or changes in criteria of judgment over a period of time are likely to introduce error.

[2]Donald T. Campbell and Julian C. Stanley, *Experimental and Quasi-Experimental Designs for Research* (Chicago: Rand McNally & Co., 1963). Chapter 5 in *Handbook of Research on Teaching*, N. L. Gage, ed. (Chicago: Rand McNally & Co., 1966), pp. 171–246.

Statistical regression. Statistical regression is a phenomenon that sometimes operates in pretest-posttest situations. Subjects who score highest on a pretest are likely to score relatively lower on a retest, whereas subjects who score lowest on the pretest are likely to score higher on a retest. In pretest-retest situations there is a normal regression toward the mean. The initially highest and lowest scoring subjects are not necessarily the highest and lowest achievers. They were the highest and the lowest only on that particular pretest occasion. Failure to recognize this regression effect may lead the researcher erroneously to attribute unwarranted gain to the lowest group and loss or small gain to the highest group.

Differential selection. Selection bias is represented by the nonequivalence of experimental and control groups, and its most effective deterrent is the random assignment of treatments to subjects. Selection bias is likely when, upon invitation, volunteers are used as members of an experimental group. Although they may appear to be equated to the nonvolunteers, their characteristics of higher motivation may introduce a bias that would invalidate reasonable comparison. Selection bias may be introduced when intact classes are used as experimental and control groups, because of scheduling arrangements an English class meeting during the fourth period may consist of particularly able students who are scheduled at that period because they are also enrolled in an advanced mathematics class.

Experimental mortality. Mortality, or loss of subjects, particularly likely in a long-term experiment, introduces a confounding element. Even though experimental and control groups are randomly selected, the survivors might represent a sample that is quite different from the unbiased sample that began the experiment. Those who survive a period of experimentation are likely to be healthier, more able, or more highly motivated than those who are absent frequently or who drop out of school and do not remain for the duration of the experiment.

Threats to external validity

External validity concerns the power of the experiment to generalize variable relationships to a wider population of interest. Let us presume that a valid relationship has been established between variables I and D in a high school classroom experiment. Does this relationship obtain in nonexperimental settings for other students in other schools, in other socioeconomic levels, in other types of communities, and in other geographic areas? There are a number of threats to external validity that the researcher must be aware of and attempt to mininize.

The artificiality of the experimental setting. In an effort to control extraneous variables the researcher imposes careful controls which may introduce a sterile or artificial atmosphere that is not at all like the real-life situation about which generalizations are desired. The reactive effect of the experimental process is a constant threat.

Placebo-Hawthorne effect. Knowledge of participation in an experiment may introduce the extraneous variable of bias in favor of the experimental group. The medical profession has long recognized that patients who receive any medication, regardless of its real efficacy, tend to feel better or perform more effectively. In medical experiments it is important to administer harmless or inert substitutes to the control group to offset the psychological effect of medication. These substitutes, or *placebos*, are indistinguishable from the real medication under investigation and neither experimental nor control subjects know whether they are receiving medication or the placebo. The effectiveness of the true medication is the difference between the effect of the medication and that of the placebo.

What seems to be a similar psychological effect was recognized in a series of experiments at the Hawthorne Plant of the Western Electric Company in Chicago a number of years ago. The studies concerned the relationships between certain working conditions and worker output efficiency. Illumination was one of these manipulated experimental variables. It was discovered that as light intensity was increased, worker output increased. After a certain peak was apparently reached it was decided to see what effect the reduction of intensity of illumination would have. To the surprise of the researchers, as intensity was decreased by stages, output continued to increase. The researchers concluded that the attention given the workers and their awareness of participation in an experiment apparently were important motivating factors. From these studies the term *Hawthorne Effect* was introduced into psychological literature.

It has been commonly believed that this reactive effect of knowledge of participation in an experiment, the Hawthorne Effect, is similar to the placebo effect. Researchers have devised nonmedical placebos to counteract it. One such device was used in connection with an experiment involving the comparison of traditional teaching materials with a new experimental program. The control, or traditional, materials were reprinted and labeled "Experimental Method" to minimize the reactive effect.

Recent studies by Desmond Cook[3] at Ohio State University have attempted to evaluate reactive effects of this type with what the author has reported as inconclusive results. Although it is believed that the

[3] Desmond L. Cook, *The Impact of the Hawthorne Effect in Experimental Designs in Educational Research.* Final Report, Project No. 1757. Contract No. OE-3-10-041. (Washington, D.C.: U.S. Office of Education, 1967).

Hawthorne Effect is a threat to experimental validity, it would seem that further study of the nature of this phenomenon is needed.

Contamination. Contamination is a type of bias introduced when the researcher has some previous knowledge about the subjects involved in an experiment. This knowledge of subject status may cause the researcher to convey some clue that affects the subject's reaction or may affect the objectivity of his judgment.

In medical research it is common practice to conceal from the subject the knowledge of who is receiving the placebo and who the experimental medication. This is known as a *blind*. Having someone other than the experimenter administer the treatments and record which subjects are receiving the medication and which the placebo provides an additional safeguard. This practice, known as a *double blind*, helps to minimize contamination.

Beginners in educational research have been known to contaminate a study by classifying student performance when they know the nature of the variable to be correlated with that performance. In a simple *ex post facto* study a member of the author's class proposed to determine the relationship between academic achievement and citizenship grades in her class. Since she proposed to assign the citizenship grades herself, it would seem apparent that an element of contamination would result. Her knowledge of the student's previous academic achievement would tend to precondition her judgment in assigning citizenship grades.

In educational studies of this type, researchers would minimize contamination if outside observers rated the subjects without any knowledge of their academic status.

Interference of prior treatment. In some types of experiments the effect of one treatment may carry over to subsequent treatments. In an educational experiment, learning produced by the first treatment is not completely erased and its influence may accrue to the advantage of the second treatment. This is one of the major limitations of the single-group, equated-materials experimental design in which the same subjects serve as members of both control and experimental groups.

Testing. We have noted that pretesting introduces a practice effect that may be a threat to the internal validity of an experiment. It may also pose a threat to the external validity, for generalization to populations that have not been pretested may lack validity.

Selection bias. It has been noted that selection bias is a threat to internal validity when it results in the comparison of nonequivalent experimental and control groups. It is also a threat to external validity when samples are selected from nonrepresentative populations. Educational researchers are rarely, if ever, able to randomly select samples from the wide population of interest; consequently, generalization from samples to populations is hazardous. Samples used in most classroom experiments are usually composed of intact groups, not randomly selected individuals. They are based upon an accepted invitation to participate. Some school officials agree to participate; others refuse. One cannot assume that samples taken from cooperating schools are necessarily representative of the target population. Such schools are usually characterized by faculties that have high morale, less insecurity, greater willingness to try a new approach, and a greater desire to improve their performance. Even if all schools were willing to participate in an experiment, few administrators will permit marked departures from the normal scheduling of classes and the random selection and assignment of students to experimental and control groups. In summary, in order to avoid selection bias, as it relates to external validity, random selection of subjects is essential.

Experimental design

Experimental design is the blueprint of the procedures that enable the researcher to test his hypotheses by reaching valid conclusions about relationships between independent and dependent variables. Selection of a particular design is based on the purposes of the experiment, the type of variables to be manipulated, and the conditions or limiting factors under which it may be conducted. The design deals with such practical problems as how subjects are to be selected for the experimental and control groups, the way variables are to be manipulated, the way extraneous variables are controlled, how observations are to be made, and the type of statistical analysis to be employed in interpreting variable relationships.

A complete discussion of experimental design would be too complex for this introductory treatment, therefore only a few designs will be described. Readers may wish to refer to Campbell and Stanley's[4] excellent treatment, in which 16 designs are described.

In discussing experimental designs a few symbols are used.

R random selection of subjects or assignment of treatments to experimental groups

X experimental variable manipulated

C control variable

[4]Donald T. Campbell and Julian C. Stanley, *Experimental and Quasi-Experimental Designs for Research* (Chicago: Rand McNally, 1966).

O observation or test

——   a line between levels indicates equated groups

PRE-EXPERIMENTAL DESIGN

The least adequate of designs is characterized by:

a. the lack of a control group, or
b. a failure to provide for the equivalence of a control group

1. The one-shot case study

$$X \quad O$$

Carefully studied results of a treatment are compared with a general expectation of what would have happened if the treatment had not been applied. This design provides the weakest basis for generalization.

Mr. Jones used a 25-minute film on racial integration in his junior high school history class. In a test administered after the showing of the film, the mean score was 86 (a high score indicated a favorable attitude toward acceptance of all racial groups). Mr. Jones believes that the mean score was higher than it would have been had the film not been viewed, and, as he recalled, higher than the mean score of a test that he had administered to a similar class several years before. He concluded that the film had been effective in reducing racial prejudice.

How could he attribute what he believed to be a better attitude to the viewing of the film? What would it have been for a similar group in the same community that had not seen the film? Without a control group, this design is the poorest available.

2. The one-group, pretest-posttest design

$$O_1 \quad X \quad O_2$$

This design provides some improvement over the first, for the effects of the treatment are judged by the difference between the pretest and the posttest scores. No comparison with a control group is provided.

In the same setting, Mr. Jones administered a pretest before showing the film and a posttest after the viewing. He computed the mean difference between the pretest and the posttest scores and found that the mean had increased from 52 to 80, a mean gain of 28 score points. He also apparently detected some temporary improvement in attitude toward racial integration. He concluded that there had been a significant improvement in attitude as a result of viewing the film. But what about the sensitizing effect of the pretest items that may have made the students aware of issues that they had not even thought of before? What would the gain have been if the pretest and the posttest had been administered to another class that had not viewed the film?

3. The static-group comparison design

$$X \quad O_1$$
$$X \quad O_2$$

This design compares the status of a group that has received an experimental treatment with one that has not. There is no provision for establishing the equivalence of the experimental and control groups, a very serious limitation.

A beginning researcher administered the 25-minute racial integration film to a group of elementary teachers in one school. He then administered the attitude scale and computed the mean score. At another elementary school he administered the attitude scale to teachers who had not viewed the film. A comparison of mean scores shows that the teachers who had viewed the film had a higher mean score than those who had not. He concluded that the film was an effective device in reducing racial prejudice.

What evidence did he have that the initial attitudes of groups were equivalent? Without some evidence of equivalence of the control and experimental groups, attributing difference to the experimental variable is unwarranted.

QUASI-EXPERIMENTAL DESIGNS

These designs provide control of when and to whom the measurement is applied but, because random assignment to experimental and control treatments has not been applied, the equivalence of the groups is unlikely. Of the many quasiexperimental designs, only two are described.

1. The nonequivalent, pretest-posttest design

$$O_1 \quad X \quad O_2$$
$$O_3 \quad X \quad O_4$$

This design is often used in classroom experiments when experimental and control groups are such naturally assembled groups as intact classes which may be similar. The difference between the mean of the O_1 and O_2 scores and the difference between the mean of the O_3 and O_4 scores (mean gain scores) are tested for statistical significance. Since this design may be the only feasible one, the comparison is justifiable, but the results should be interpreted cautiously.

Two first grade classes in a school were selected for an experiment. One group was exposed to the initial teaching alphabet approach to reading while the other was taught by the traditional alphabet approach. At the end of the school year both groups were administered a standardized reading test and the mean scores of the two groups were compared. The i/t/a group showed a significant superiority in test scores over the conventional alphabet group. However, without some evidence of the equivalence of the groups in intelligence, maturity, readiness, and other factors at the beginning of the experimental period, conclusions should be cautiously accepted.

2. The equivalent-materials, single-group, pretest-posttest design

$$M_A \quad O_1 \quad X \quad O_2; \quad M_B \quad O_3 \quad C \quad O_4$$

Because of the administrative difficulty of equating classroom experimental and control groups some researchers have suggested the advisability of using the same group of subjects (or the same class) as experimental and as control groups. The class may be used as an experimental group during the first cycle and as a control group during the second cycle. The order of exposure to experimental and control variables or treatments could be reversed—control first and experiment second.

This design has two apparently attractive features. It can be carried on with one intact group without a noticeable reorganization of the classroom schedule. In addition, artificiality can be minimized, for this procedure could be carried on without subjects' being aware that they are participating in an experiment. The testing and change in classroom procedures can be concealed within the ordinary classroom routines.

Ms. Smith hypothesized that the students in her class who were not used to an atmosphere of background music while doing their homework would learn to spell more efficiently in the classroom if music were provided. Since she was unable to arrange a parallel group experiment, she decided to use her class both as an experimental and a control group.

To equate the words to be learned she randomly selected two sets of 100 words from an appropriate graded word list. For cycle I, the control cycle, she pretested the class on word list A. Then for twenty minutes each day the students studied the words, using drill and the usual spelling rules. At the end of two weeks she retested the class and computed the mean gain score in correct spelling.

For cycle II, the experimental cycle, she pretested the class on word list B. Then for twenty minutes each day, with soft, continuous, music in the background, the independent variable, the students studied their word list, using the same drill and spelling rules. At the end of the second two-week period she retested the class and computed the mean gain score in correct spelling.

The mean gain score for the experimental cycle was significantly greater than the mean gain score for the control cycle. She concluded that the introduction of the experimental variable had indeed improved the effectiveness of the learning experience.

The apparent simplicity and logic of this design is somewhat misleading and when examined in light of the threats to experimental validity, the design's weaknesses become apparent.

1. It is often difficult to select equated materials to be learned. For types of learning other than spelling, finding learning materials equally interesting, difficult, and unfamiliar would be a serious problem.
2. As the student enters the second cycle he is older and more mature.
3. Outside events (history) would be more likely to affect the experience in one cycle than in the other.
4. There would be an influence of prior treatment carrying over from the first cycle to the second.
5. The effects of testing would be more likely to have a greater impact on the measurement of gain in the second cycle.
6. Mortality, or loss of subjects from the experiment, would be more likely in an experimental design spread over a longer period of time.
7. When the experimenter's judgment was a factor in evaluation, contamination, the experimenter's knowledge of subject performance in the first cycle, could possibly influence evaluation of performance in the second.

Some of the limitations of the equivalent-materials, single-group, pretest-posttest design can be partially minimized by a series of replications in which the order of exposure to experimental and control treatments is reversed. This process, known as *rotation*, is illustrated by this pattern in a four-cycle experiment.

$$\begin{array}{cccc} \text{I} & \text{II} & \text{III} & \text{IV} \\ O_1 \; X \; O_2 & O_3 \; C \; O_4 & O_5 \; C \; O_6 & O_7 \; X \; O_8 \end{array}$$

If the experimental treatment yielded significantly greater gains regardless of the order of exposure, its effectiveness could be accepted with greater confidence. However, it is apparent that this design is not likely to equate materials, subjects, or experimental conditions, and is acceptable only when an equated-group design cannot be arranged.

TRUE EXPERIMENTAL DESIGNS

In a true experiment the equivalence of the experimental and control groups is provided by random assignment of subjects to experimental and control treatments. While it is difficult to arrange a true experimental design, particularly in school classroom research, it is the strongest type of design and should be used whenever possible. Three experimental designs have been selected for discussion:

1. The posttest-only, equivalent-group design

$$
\begin{array}{ccc}
R & X & O_1 \\
\hline
R & C & O_2
\end{array}
$$

This design is one of the most effective in minimizing the threats to experimental validity. Experimental and control groups are equated by random assignment. At the conclusion of the experimental period the difference between the mean test scores of the experimental and control groups are subjected to a test of statistical significance, a t test, or an analysis of variance. The assumption is that the means of randomly assigned experimental and control groups from the same population will differ only to the extent that random sample means from the same population will differ as a result of sampling error. If the difference between the means is too great to attribute to sampling error, the difference may be attributed to the treatment variable effect.

Using a table of random numbers, the researcher selects 80 students from a school population of 450 sophomores. The 80 students are randomly assigned to experimental and control treatments, using the first 40 as the experimental group and the other 40 as the control group. The experimental group is taught the concepts of congruence of triangles by method X, while the control group is taught the same set of concepts by method C. All factors of time of day, treatment length in time, and other factors are equated. At the end of a three-week period the experimental and control groups are administered a test and the difference between mean scores is subjected to a test of statistical significance. The difference between mean scores is found to favor the experimental group, but not by an amount that is statistically significant. The researcher rightly concludes that the superiority of the X group could well have been the result of sampling error, and that there was no evidence of the superiority of the X method.

2. Pretest-posttest equivalent-groups design

$$
\begin{array}{cccc}
R & O_1 & X & O_2 & \quad X \text{ gain} = O_2 - O_1 \\
\hline
R & O_3 & C & O_4 & \quad C \text{ gain} = O_4 - O_3
\end{array}
$$

This design is similar to the previously described design, except that pretests are administered before the application of the experimental and control treatments and posttests at the end of the treatment period. Gain scores are compared and may be subjected to a t test or to an analysis of variance. An analysis of covariance, using pretest scores as covariates, is considered mere effective than a simple difference between gains t test. This is a strong design, but there is a possibility of the influence of the effects of testing and the interaction of testing and the experimental variable.

3. *The Solomon four-group design*

$$R \quad O_1 \quad X \quad O_2$$

$$R \quad O_3 \quad C \quad O_4$$
$$R \qquad\; X \quad O_5$$

$$R \qquad\; C \quad O_6$$

This design is really a combination of the two equivalent-groups designs previously described, the posttest-only design and the pretest-posttest design. It is thus possible to evaluate the main effects as well as the reactive effects of testing, history, and maturation. Since this design provides for two simultaneous experiments, the advantages of a replication are incorporated; however, the design is complex and would be difficult to set up with enough subjects to comprise four equivalent groups.

Ethics in human experimentation

Most medical and some psychological experiments involve an element of risk, however minor. A number of questions on the ethics of human experimentation have been raised. Some of these questions have been dealt with by enactments of legislatures, some by codes of professional ethics, and others remain unresolved issues. When is it justifiable to carry on experiments involving human beings when:

1. Subjects who are inmates of penal institutions may feel coerced to volunteer to participate by a need for money or in anticipation of more favorable treatment or recommendation for earlier parole.
2. Subjects are recruited by offers of financial reward, their disadvantaged economic condition thereby being exploited.
3. Parents volunteering the participation of minor children have no role in the decision process and no one to protect them from possibly dangerous effects.
4. Volunteers are recruited who do not have the competence to make rational judgments; senile, illiterate, or persons with low intelligence may not understand the possible dangers that may exist.
5. Individuals are encouraged to participate without a frank discussion of the possible dangers involved and a complete understanding of all risks.

Researchers have been known to justify risks to individuals in the name of science, but one might suspect that the prestige, ambition, or ego involvement of the experimenter is sometimes the prevailing motivation.

Experimentation using human subjects involves ethical implications. The issues go beyond courtesy or etiquette and concern the appropriate treatment of persons in a free society that values the dignity and worth of the individual.

Experimental invasion of privacy may involve the use of concealed observers, cameras, or microphones or the seeking of intimate information about a subject or his family. There may be deception through prevarication or through deliberately conveying a false impression in order to modify responses. Deception may also involve concealing from a subject the fact or the nature of his experimental manipulation. Such manipulation may involve tension- or frustration-producing stimuli to evaluate their effect upon human response. Certain types of experimentation may involve clinical treatment or the use of drugs.

Although it is not practicable to make specific rules about these procedures, certain general ethical principles may provide guidelines for the researcher.

Invasion of privacy may be justified if the advancement of knowledge is served and if the security and dignity of the subject are not jeopardized. The ethical researcher holds any information that he may gather about the subject in strict confidence and disguises the subject's identity in published reports. He informs the subject of the purpose of the investigation, either before the study or after its completion, as experimental circumstances dictate. In using treatments that may have a possibly injurious effect, the researcher takes all precautions to protect the physical and psychological well-being of the subject. Treatments are administered under the supervision of competent professional practitioners in clinical or research facilities where thorough precautions and safeguards may be assured. The subject should be informed of risks involved and his, or his agent's or guardian's, permission should be secured.

The American Psychological Association has formulated a code of ethics whose preamble states:

> The psychologist believes in the dignity and worth of the individual human being. He is committed to increasing man's knowledge of himself and others. While pursuing this endeavor he protects the welfare of any persons who may seek his service or of any subject, human or animal, that may be the object of his study. He does not use his professional position or relationship, nor does he knowingly permit his own service to be used by others, for purposes inconsistent with these values. While demanding for himself freedom of inquiry and communication, he accepts the responsibility this freedom

confers: for competence where he claims it, for objectivity in the report of his findings, and for consideration of the best interests of his colleagues and of society.[5]

One of the 19 listed principles of the code deals with the ethics of research.

Principle 16. Research Precautions.
The psychologist assumes obligations for the welfare of his research subjects, both animal and human.
a. Only when a problem is of scientific significance and it is not practicable to investigate it in any other way is the psychologist justified in exposing research subjects, whether children or adults, to physical or emotional stress as part of an investigation.
b. When a reasonable possibility of injurious aftereffects exists, research is conducted only when the subjects or their responsible agents are fully informed of this possibility and agree to participate nevertheless.
c. The psychologist seriously considers the possibility of harmful aftereffects and avoids them, or removes them as soon as permitted by the design of the experiment.
d. A psychologist using animals in research adheres to the provisions of the *Rules Regarding Animals*, drawn up by the Committee on Precautions and Standards in Animal Experimentation and adopted by the American Psychological Association.
e. Investigations of human subjects using experimental drugs (for example: hallucinogenic, psychotomimetic, psychedelic, or similar substances) should be conducted only in such settings as clinics, hospitals, or research facilities maintaining appropriate safeguards for the subjects.[6]

The ethical experimenter has obligations to his subjects, his professional colleagues, and the public. He does not discard unfavorable data that would modify the interpretation of his investigation. He makes his data available to his professional peers so that they may verify the accuracy of his results. He honors promises made to subjects as a consideration for their participation in a study. He gives appropriate credit to those who have aided him in his investigation, who have participated in the data analysis, or who have contributed to the preparation of the research report. He places scientific objectivity above personal advantage, and recognizes his obligation to society for the advancement of knowledge.

This discussion, which has examined the many limitations of the experimental method in behavioral research, may convey a sense of futility. As is true in many other areas of significant human endeavor, the researcher does not work under ideal conditions. He must do the best that he can

[5] *Ethical Standards of Psychologists* (Washington, D.C.: American Psychological Association, 1963), p. 2.
[6] *Ethical Standards*, p. 7.

under existing circumstances. He will find, however, that in spite of its
limitations, the well-designed and well-executed experiment provides a
legitimate method for testing hypotheses and making probability decisions
about the relationships between variables.

Some variables cannot be manipulated. The ethical problems that
would be raised if some others were manipulated indicates a place for such
nonexperimental methods as *ex post facto* research. The researcher starts
with the observation of dependent variables and goes back to the observation of independent variables that have previously occurred under uncontrolled conditions. Such studies are *not* experiments, for the researcher
has had no control over the events; they occurred before he began his
investigation. The description of cigarette smoking cancer research in
Chapter 5 is an example of *ex post facto* research.

Throughout this chapter the author has avoided a description of
factorial designs. The reader should not feel, however, that the experimental method is confined to the analysis of single-variable relationships.
Most significant experimentation involves the analysis of the interaction
of a number of variable relationships. However, the complexity of factorial
designs preclude their discussion in an elementary treatment. Advanced
students may wish to refer to such sources as Edwards, Kerlinger, and
Winer, listed in the chapter bibliography.

Summary

The experimental method provides a logical, systematic way to answer the
question, "If this is done under carefully controlled conditions, what will
happen?" To provide a precise answer the experimenter manipulates
certain influences, or variables, and observes how the condition or behavior of the subject is affected or changed. The experimenter controls or
isolates the variables in such a way that he can be reasonably sure that the
effects he observes can be attributed to the variables he has manipulated,
rather than to some other uncontrolled influences. In testing hypotheses,
or evaluating tentative answers to questions, the experimenter makes
decisions based upon probability rather than certainty. Experimentation,
the classic method of the laboratory, is the most powerful method for
discovering and developing a body of knowledge about the prediction and
control of events. The experimental method has been used with some
success in the school classroom, where, to some degree, variables can be
controlled.

The early applications of experimental method, based upon John
Stuart Mill's law of the single variable, have been replaced by the more
effective applications of factorial designs made possible by the contri-

butions of R. A. Fisher. His concept of equating groups by random selection of subjects and random assignment of treatments, and his development of the analysis of variance and the analysis of covariance have made possible the study of complex multivariate relationships that are basic to the understanding of human behavior.

The experimenter must understand and deal with threats to the internal validity of the experiment so that the variable relationships he observes can be interpreted without ambiguity. He must also understand and deal with threats to the external validity of the experiment so that his findings can be extended beyond his experimental subjects and generalized to a wider population of interest.

Experimental design provides a plan or blueprint for experimentation. Three pre-experimental, two quasi-experimental, and three true experimental designs have been presented and their appropriate use, their advantages and their disadvantages have been briefly discussed.

A brief discussion of the ethics of experimentation suggests some principles that should characterize the activities of the behavioral researcher.

Experimentation is a sophisticated technique for problem solving and may not be an appropriate activity for the beginning researcher. It has been suggested that teachers may make their most effective contribution to educational research by identifying important problems that they encounter in their classrooms and working cooperatively with research specialists in the conduct and interpretation of classroom experiments.

Exercises

1. In a classroom experiment, why is it more difficult to control extraneous variables than it would be in a pharmaceutical laboratory experiment?

2. What significant element distinguishes a quasi-experiment from a true experiment?

3. Why is an *ex post facto* study not an experiment?

4. A researcher, in proposing a research project, defines the dependent variable as achievement in mathematics. What is the difficulty that this definition presents? How would you improve it?

5. How could a double blind be applied in an educational experiment?

6. Under what circumstances could an independent variable in a study be a dependent variable in another study?

7. Why is randomization the best method for dealing with extraneous variables?

8. What effect could the Freedom of Information Act passed by Congress have upon experimental studies in education?
9. How could a high degree of experimental mortality seriously affect the validity of an experiment?
10. Read the report of an experiment in an educational research journal.
    a. Was the problem clearly stated?
    b. Were the variables defined in operational terms?
    c. Was the hypothesis clearly stated?
    d. Were the delimitations stated?
    e. Was the design clearly described?
    f. Were extraneous variables recognized? What provisions were made to control them?
    g. Was the population and the sampling method described?
    h. Were appropriate methods used to analyze the data?
    i. Were the conclusions clearly presented?
    j. Were the conclusions substantiated by the evidence presented?

Bibliography

AMERICAN PSYCHOLOGICAL ASSOCIATION. *Ethical Principles and the Conduct of Research with Human Participants.* Washington, D.C.: Ad Hoc Committee on Ethical Standards, 1973.

BAUERNFEIND, ROBERT H. "The Need for Replication in Educational Research." *Phi Delta Kappan* 50 (October 1968): 126–128.

BIJOU, SIDNEY W., and DONALD M. BAER. "The Laboratory-Experimental Study of Child Behavior." Chapter 4 in *Handbook of Research Methods in Child Development*, Paul H. Mussen, ed. New York: John Wiley & Sons, 1960.

BLALOCK, H. M. *Causal Inferences in Nonexperimental Research.* Chapel Hill, N.C.: University of North Carolina Press, 1964.

BRACHT, GLENN H., and GENE V. GLASS. "The External Validity of Experiments." *American Educational Research Journal* 5 (November 1968): 437–474.

CAMPBELL, DONALD T., and JULIAN C. STANLEY. *Experimental and Quasi-Experimental Designs for Research.* Chicago: Rand McNally & Co., 1966. Chapter 5 in *Handbook of Research on Teaching*, N. L. Gage, ed. Chicago: Rand McNally & Co., 1963.

COLLIER, RAYMOND, and STANTEY ELAM, eds. *Research Design and Analysis.* Second Annual Phi Delta Kappa Symposium on Educational Research. Bloomington, Ind.: Phi Delta Kappa, 1961.

CONROY, WILLIAM G. "Individual Privacy Rights and Research for Education." *Phi Delta Kappan* 56 (February 1974): 415–418.

COOK, DESMOND L. "The Hawthorne Effect in Educational Research." *Phi Delta Kappan* 44 (December 1962): 116–122.

COOK, DESMOND L. *The Impact of the Hawthorne Effect in Experimental Designs in Educational Research.* Final Report, Project No. 1757. Contract No. OE-3-10-041. Washington, D.C.: U.S. Office of Education, 1967.

DAYTON, C. M. *Design of Educational Experiments.* New York: McGraw-Hill Book Co., 1970.

EDWARDS, ALLEN L. "Experiments, Their Planning and Execution." Chapter 7 in *The Handbook of Social Psychology*, Vol. 1, Gardner Lindzey, ed., pp. 254–288. Cambridge, Mass.: Addison-Wesley Publishing Co., 1954.

EDWARDS, ALLEN L. *Experimental Design in Psychological Research.* New York: Holt, Rinehart & Winston, 1972.

"Ethical Aspects of Experimentation with Human Subjects." *Daedalus* (Spring 1969).

Ethical Standards of Psychologists. Washington, D.C.: American Psychological Association, 1963.

GARRETT, HENRY E. *Great Experiments in Psychology.* 3rd ed. New York: Appleton-Century-Crofts, 1951.

GEPHART, WILLIAM J. and DANIEL P. ANTONOPLOS. "The Effect of Expectancy and Other Research-Biasing Factors." *Phi Delta Kappan* 50 (June 1969): 579–583.

GLASS, GENE V. "Evaluating Testing, Maturation, and Treatment Effects in a Pretest-Posttest Quasi-Experimental Design." *American Educational Research Journal* 2 (March 1965): 83–87.

KATZ, JAY. *Experimentation with Human Beings.* New York: Russell Sage Foundation, 1972.

KERLINGER, FRED N. *Foundations of Behavioral Research.* 2d ed. New York: Holt, Rinehart & Winston, 1973.

LINDQUIST, E. F. *Design and Analysis of Experiments in Psychology and Education.* Boston: Houghton-Mifflin Co., 1965.

ROSENTHAL, ROBERT, and LENORE JACOBSON. *Pygmalion in the Classroom: Teacher Expectations and Pupils' Intellectual Development.* New York: Holt, Rinehart & Winston, 1968.

STANLEY, JULIAN C. "Controlled Experimentation in the Classroom." *Journal of Experimental Education* 25 (1957): 195–201.

STANLEY, JULIAN C. "A Common Class of Pseudo-Experiments." *American Educational Research Journal* 3 (March 1966): 78–87.

STANLEY, JULIAN C., ed. *Improving Experimental Design and Statistical Analysis.* Proceedings of the Seventh Annual Phi Delta Kappa Symposium on Educational Research. Chicago: Rand McNally & Co., 1967.

THORNDIKE, ROBERT L. "Pygmalion in the Classroom by Robert Rosenthal and Lenore Jacobson, Book Review." *American Educational Research Journal* 5 (November 1968): 708–711.

TOWNSEND, JOHN C. *Introduction to Experimental Method.* New York: McGraw-Hill Book Co., 1953.

UNDERWOOD, BENTON J. *Psychological Research.* New York: Appleton-Century-Crofts, 1957.

WEBB, EUGENE J. ET AL. *Unobtrusive Measures: Nonreactive Research in the Social Sciences.* Chicago: Rand McNally & Co., 1966.

WINER, B. J. *Statistical Principles in Experimental Design.* New York: McGraw-Hill Book Co., 1971.

WOLFENSBERGER, WOLF. "Ethical Issues in Research With Human Subjects." *Science* 155 (March 17, 1967): 47–51.

DESCRIPTIVE STUDIES: ASSESSMENT, EVALUATION, AND RESEARCH

Chapter 5

A descriptive study describes and interprets what is. It is concerned with conditions or relationships that exist, opinions that are held, processes that are going on, effects that are evident, or trends that are developing. It is primarily concerned with the present, although it often considers past events and influences as they relate to current conditions.

The term *descriptive study* conceals an important distinction, for not all descriptive studies fall into the category of research. In Chapter 1 the similarities and differences between assessment, evaluation, and research were briefly discussed. We will restate those similarities and differences in this discussion of descriptive studies.

Assessment describes the status of a phenomenon at a particular time. It merely describes a situation that prevails without value judgment, attempts no explanation of underlying reasons, and makes no recommendations for action. It may deal with prevailing opinion, knowledge, practices, or conditions. As it is ordinarily used in education, assessment describes the progress students have made toward educational goals at a particular time. The data are gathered by a testing program and a sampling procedure in such a way that no individual is tested over the entire test battery. It is not designed to determine the effectiveness of a particular process or program, but merely to estimate the degree of achievement of a large number of individuals who have been exposed to a great variety of educational and environmental influences. It does not propose or test hypotheses and does not deal with the many variables underlying the achievement or lack of achievement of those observed. It does not provide recommendations, but there may be some implied judgment as to the satisfactoriness of the situation or the fulfillment of society's expectations.

Evaluation adds the ingredient of value judgment of the social utility, desirability, or effectiveness of a process, product, or program, and it sometimes includes a recommendation for some course of action. School surveys are usually evaluation studies; educational products and programs are examined to determine their effectiveness in meeting accepted objectives, often with recommendations for constructive action.

Descriptive research, sometimes known as nonexperimental research, deals with the relationships between variables, the testing of hypotheses, and the development of generalizations, principles, or theories that have universal validity. It is concerned with functional relationships. The expectation is that if variable A is systematically associated with variable B, prediction of future phenomena may be possible and the results may suggest additional or competing hypotheses to test.

In carrying on a descriptive research project, in contrast to an experiment, the researcher does not manipulate the variables or arrange for events to happen. In fact, the events that are observed and described would have happened even though there had been no observation or analysis. Descriptive research involves events that have already taken place and are related to a present condition.

The method of descriptive research is particularly appropriate in the behavioral sciences, because many of the types of behavior that interest the researcher cannot be arranged in a realistic setting. Introducing significant variables may be harmful or threatening to human subjects. Ethical considerations often preclude exposing human subjects to potentially harmful manipulation. For example, it would be unthinkable to prescribe cigarette smoking to human subjects for the purpose of studying its possible relationship to throat or lung cancer, or to deliberately arrange auto accidents, except when manikins are used, in order to evaluate the effectiveness of seat belts or restraints in preventing serious injury.

Although some experimental studies of human behavior can be appropriately carried on, both in the laboratory and in the field, the prevailing research method of the behavioral sciences is descriptive. Under the conditions that naturally occur in the home, the classroom, the recreational center, the office, or the factory, human behavior can be systematically examined and analyzed.

The many similarities between these types of descriptive studies may have tended to cloud the distinctions between them. They are all characterized by disciplined inquiry, requiring expertise, objectivity, and careful execution. They all develop knowledge, adding to what is already known. They use similar techniques of observation, description, and analysis. The differences between them lie in the motivation of the investigator, the treatment of the data, the nature of the conclusions, and the use of the findings. Studies that illustrate these types of descriptive analysis are presented in this chapter.

Assessment and evaluation studies

THE SURVEY

The survey method gathers data from a relatively large number of cases at a particular time. It is not concerned with characteristics of individuals *as* individuals. It is concerned with the generalized statistics that result when data are abstracted from a number of individual cases. It is essentially cross-sectional.

Ninety-four percent of American homes have at least one television set. About three out of five students who enter the American secondary school remain to graduate. Fifty-six percent of adult Americans voted in the 1972 presidential election. The average American consumes about 103 pounds of refined sugar annually. The ratio of female births to male births in the United States in 1974 was 946 to 1000. The population of Indiana, according to the 1970 census, was 5,194,000. Data like these result from many types of surveys. Each statement pictures a prevailing condition at a particular time.

In analyzing political, social, or economic conditions, one of the first steps is to get the facts about the situation—or a picture of conditions that prevail or that are developing. These data may be gathered from surveys of the entire population. Others are inferred from a study of a sample group, carefully selected from the total population. And at times, the survey may describe a limited population which is the only group under consideration.

The survey is an important type of study. It must not be confused with the mere clerical routine of gathering and tabulating figures. It involves a clearly defined problem and definite objectives. It requires expert and imaginative planning, careful analysis and interpretation of the data gathered, and logical and skillful reporting of the findings.

THE CASE STUDY

When the focus of attention is directed toward a single case or a limited number of cases, the process is personalized. The case study is concerned with everything that is significant in the history or development of the case. The purpose is to understand the life cycle, or an important part of the life cycle, of an individual unit. This unit may be a person, a family, a group, a social institution, or an entire community. The case method probes deeply, and intensively analyzes interaction between the factors that produce change or growth. It emphasizes the longitudinal or genetic approach, showing development over a period of time.

Traditionally, in social work or in the field of guidance the term *case study* has assumed a more limited meaning. In this context emphasis is placed upon the study of an individual person, for the purpose of diagnosing his problems and recommending remedial measures for his rehabilitation. Here the emphasis is not upon the individual representing a type, but upon the individual as a unique personality, with his own constellation of problems and needs. Ordinarily, the social-work or guidance case study is not research-oriented, but is directed toward the solution of an individual's problems. A study of a number of these individual cases could be expanded into a research project, particularly where the typical aspects of each case are contrasted or compared for the purpose of arriving at a greater understanding of human behavior, or for the purpose of discovering new generalizations.

Case studies have been made of all types of communities, from the hamlet to the great metropolis. Case studies have been made of types of individuals—alcholics, drug addicts, juvenile delinquents, migratory agricultural workers, sharecroppers, industrial workers, members of a profession, executives, army wives, trailer court residents, members of a social class, Quakers, Amish, Jews, Negroes, American Indians, Chinese-Americans, Puerto Ricans, and many other ethnic or social groups. Such institutions as colleges, churches, factories, hospitals, corrective institutions, welfare agencies, fraternal organizations, and business groups have been studied as cases. In each case the element of typicalness is the focus of attention, with emphasis upon the many factors that characterize the type. These studies have been conducted for the purpose of arriving at greater understanding of the roles of their subjects in the American pattern of culture.

SOCIAL SURVEYS

A significant social survey was made in the late 1930s under the direction of the Swedish sociologist, Gunnar Myrdal, and sponsored by the Carnegie Foundation. Myrdal and his staff of researchers made a comprehensive analysis of the social, political, and economic life of the American Negro, yielding a great mass of data on race relations in America.[1]

---

[1]Gunnar Myrdal, *An American Dilemma* (New York: Harper & Row, Publishers, 1944).

The late Alfred Kinsey of Indiana University made a comprehensive survey of the sexual behavior of the human male,[2] based on data gathered from more than 12,000 cases. His second study of the behavior of the human female was published five years later. Although these studies have raised considerable controversy, they represent a scientific approach to the study of an important social problem, and have many implications for jurists, legislators, social workers, and educators.

Paul Witty[3] has studied the television viewing habits of school children, and has published annual reports on his investigations since 1950. These studies were conducted in the Chicago area, and indicate the amount of time devoted to viewing and the program preferences of elementary and secondary students, their parents, and their teachers. An effort was made to relate television viewing to intelligence, reading habits, academic achievement, and other factors.

Clifford R. Shaw and Henry D. McKay[4] have made a study of juvenile delinquency in Chicago yielding significant data on the nature and extent of delinquency in large urban communities.

The National Safety Council conducts surveys on the nature, extent, and causes of automobile accidents in all parts of the United States. State high school athletic associations conduct surveys on the nature and extent of athletic injuries in member schools.

PUBLIC-OPINION SURVEYS

In our culture, where so many opinions on controversial subjects are expressed by well-organized special-interest groups, it is important to find out what the people think. Without a means of polling public opinion, the views of only the highly organized minorities are effectively presented through the printed page, radio, and television.

How do people feel about diplomatic recognition of Red China, the foreign aid program, busing to achieve racial integration in the public schools, or the adequacy of the public schools? What candidate do they intend to vote for in the next election? Such questions can be partially answered by means of the public-opinion survey. Many research agencies carry on these surveys and report their findings in magazines and in syndicated articles in daily newspapers.

Since it would be impracticable or even impossible to get an expression of opinion from every person, sampling techniques are employed in such

[2]Alfred C. Kinsey et al., *The Sexual Behavior of the Human Male* (Philadelphia: W. B. Saunders Co., 1948); Alfred C. Kinsey et al., *The Sexual Behavior of the Human Female* (Philadelphia: W. B. Saunders Co., 1953).

[3]Paul Witty, "Children of the TV Era," Elementary English 64 (May 1967): 528–535.

[4]Clifford R. Shaw and Henry D. McKay, *Juvenille Delinquency in Urban Areas* (Chicago: University of Chicago Press, 1942).

a way that the resulting opinions of a limited number of people can be used to infer the reactions of the entire population.

The names Gallup, Roper, Harris, and Crossley are familiar to newspaper readers in connection with public-opinion surveys. These surveys of opinion are frequently analyzed and reported by such classifications as age groups, sex, educational level, occupation, income level, political affiliation, or area of residence. Researchers are aware of the existence of many publics, or segments of the public, who may hold conflicting points of view. This further analysis of opinion by subgroups adds meaning to the analysis of public opinion in general.

Those who conduct opinion polls have developed more sophisticated methods of determining public attitudes through more precise sampling procedures and by profiting from errors that plagued early efforts. In prediction of voter behavior several well-known polls have proved to be poor estimators of election results.

The failure of the 1936 *Literary Digest* poll to forecast accurately the results of the Landon-Roosevelt election has been attributed to a bias in sampling. The survey chose its respondents from automobile registration lists and from telephone directories. During the depression period, large numbers of voters, more often Democrats than Republicans, neither owned cars nor were telephone subscribers, and consequently were not represented in the sample.

In the 1948 election campaign a prominent poll predicted the election of Governor Thomas E. Dewey over President Harry S. Truman. Again the pollsters were wrong, possibly this time because they failed to recognize the shifting nature of public sentiment. Had the survey been made just prior to election day, a more accurate prediction might have resulted.

In addition to the limitations suggested, there is the hazard of careless responses, given in an off-hand way, that are sometimes at variance with the more serious opinions that are expressed as actual decisions.

Since 1969 the Gallup organization has conducted an annual nationwide opinion poll of public attitudes toward education. Using a stratified cluster sample of 1500 or more individuals over 18 years of age, the data have been gathered by personal interviews from seven geographic areas and four size-of-community categories. The responses were analyzed by age, sex, race, occupation, income level, political affiliation, and level of education. A wide range of problem areas has been considered; in the 1975 poll such problems areas confronting education were the use of drugs and alcohol; programs on drugs or alcohol; behavior standards in the schools; policies on suspension from school; work required of students, including amount of homework; requirements for graduation from high school; federal aid to public schools; the nongraded school program; open education; alternative schools; job training; right of teachers to strike; textbook censorship; and the role of the school principal as part of management.[5]

NATIONAL ASSESSMENT OF EDUCATIONAL PROGRESS[6]

This comprehensive educational survey was the first national assessment of educational achievement to be conducted in the United States. Originally financed by the Carnegie Foundation and the Fund for the Advancement of Education, with a supporting grant from the U. S. Office of Education, the Committee on Assessing the Progress of Education (CAPE) began its first survey in the spring of 1969. It gathered achievement test data by a sampling process such that no one individual was tested over the whole test battery or spent more than forty minutes in the process. Achievement was assessed every three years in four age groups (9, 13, 17, and young adults between 26 and 35) in four geographical areas (Northeast, Southeast, Central and West) for four types of communities (large city, urban fringe, rural, and small city) for several socioeconomic levels and ethnic groups.

Achievement has been assessed in art, reading, writing, social studies, science, mathematics, literature, citizenship, and music. Comparisons between individuals, schools or school systems have never been made.

The agency now conducting the assessment is the National Assessment of Educational Progress (NAEP) financed by the National Center for Educational Statistics, a division of the Department of Health, Education and Welfare. Periodic reports are provided for educators, interested lay adults, and through press releases to periodicals for the general public.

Science. Between 1969 and 1973, performance in science has declined on two-thirds of the test items with a total test score drop of two percentage points.[7] The gap between performance of whites and nonwhites, between males and females, and between inner-city and others has increased.

Politics and government.[8] Seventeen percent of 13-year-olds and 49 percent of 17-year-olds know that presidential candidates are nominated at national party conventions; 41 percent of 17-year-olds and 44 percent of young adults can correctly fill out a simple ballot, and 75 percent of

[5]"Seventh Annual Gallup Poll of Public Attitudes Toward Education," *Phi Delta Kappan* 57 (December 1975): 227–241.

[6]*How Much Are Students Learning?* (Detroit: Committee on Assessing the Progress of Education, 1968).

[7]Ahmann, J. Stanley et al., "Science Achievement: The Trend Is Down," *Science Teacher* 42 (September 1975): 23–25.

[8]Gaye Vandermyn, "Assessing Students' Political IQ," *American Education* 10 (June 1974): 21–25.

13-year-olds and 90 percent of 17-year-olds know that United States Senators are elected.

Consumer mathematics skills.[9]   Of 34,000 17-year-olds and 4200 young adults, fewer than 50 percent could determine the most economical size of a product, 1 percent of 17-year-olds and 16 percent of young adults could correctly balance a checkbook, 60 percent of 17-year-olds and 69 percent of young adults could calculate the mean of three salaries, and 10 percent of 17-year-olds and 20 percent of young adults could correctly calculate a taxi fare. Males consistently outperformed females on exercises involving buying and household situations.

Writing.[10]   In 1974 both 13-year-olds and 17-year-olds used a simpler vocabulary and wrote less coherently than their counterparts in the survey four years earlier. The 17-year-olds showed an increase in awkwardness in writing and had a greater tendency to write as they spoke.

Observations of this type tend to paint a discouraging picture of the educational achievement of American youth and young adults. While the data may tend to convey a biased judgment, there does seem to be evidence that a relatively large number of Americans do not have the skill and knowledge necessary to function successfully in modern society.

INTERNATIONAL ASSESSMENT[11]

The International Association for the Evaluation of Educational Achievement, with headquarters in Stockholm, Sweden, has been carrying on an assessment program in a number of countries since 1964. The first study, *The International Study of Achievement in Mathematics*, compared achievement in twelve countries: Austria, Belgium, England, Finland, France, West Germany, Israel, Japan, the Netherlands, Scotland, Sweden, and the United States. Short answer and multiple choice tests were administered to 13-year-olds and to students in their last year of the upper secondary schools, prior to university entrance. More than 132,000 pupils and 5000 schools were involved in the survey. Japanese students excelled all others, regardless of their socioeconomic status, while the U. S. students ranked near the bottom.

While the purpose of assessment is not to compare school systems, the data lead observers to make such comparisons. Critics of the first assess-

[9]Art Branscombe, "Checklist on Consumer Mathematics," *American Education* 11 (October 1975): 21–24.

[10]George Neill, "Writing Skills Drop: 20% Can't Cope, Studies Show," *Phi Delta Kappan* 57 (January 1976): 355.

[11]Torsten Husen, ed., *International Study of Achievement in Mathematics* (New York: John Wiley & Sons, 1967).

ment pointed out the inappropriateness of comparing 17-year-olds in the United States, where more than 75 percent are enrolled in secondary schools, with 17-year-olds in other countries in which those enrolled in upper secondary schools comprise a small, highly selected population.

More recent assessments reveal that, while 10 percent of the top United States students excelled similar groups in all other countries in reading, in science they occupied seventh place.[12]

Other assessments have been carried out and the number of participating countries has been increased to twenty-two.

DESCRIPTIVE STUDIES AND PROBLEM SOLVING

In solving a problem or charting a course of action several sorts of information may be needed. These data may be gathered through the processes of the descriptive method.

The first type of information is based upon *present conditions*. Where are we now? From what point do we start? These data may be gathered by a systematic description and analysis of all the important aspects of the present situation.

The second type of information involves *what we may want*. In what direction may we go? What conditions are desirable or are considered to represent best practice? This clarification of objectives or goals may come from a study of what we think we want, possibly resulting from a study of conditions existing elsewhere, or of what experts consider to be adequate or desirable.

The third type of information is concerned with *how to get there*. This analysis may involve finding out about the experience of others who have been involved in similar situations. It may involve the opinions of experts, who presumably know best how to reach the goal.

Some studies emphasize only one of these aspects of problem solving. Others may deal with two, or even three, of the elements. Although a study does not necessarily embrace all the steps necessary for the solution of a problem, it may make a valuable contribution by clarifying only one of the necessary steps—from description of present status to the charting of the path to the goal.

Descriptive studies may supply some, or all, of the needed information. An example will illustrate how descriptive studies can be used to help solve an educational problem.

Washington Township has a school building problem. Its present educational facilities seem inadequate, and if present developments continue, conditions may be much worse in the future. The patrons and

---

[12]Fred M. Hechinger and Grace Hechinger, "Are Schools Better in Other Countries?" *American Education* 10 (Feruary 1974): 6–8.

educational leaders in the community know that a problem exists, but they realize that this vague awareness does not provide a sound basis for action. Three steps are necessary to provide such a basis.

The first step involves a systematic analysis of present conditions. How many school-age children are there in the township? How many children are of preschool age? Where do they live? How many classrooms now exist? How adequate are they? What is the average class size? How are these present buildings located in relation to residential housing? How adequate are the facilities for food, library, health, and recreational services? What is the present annual budget? How is it related to the tax rate and the ability of the community to provide adequate educational facilites?

The second step projects goals for the future. What will the school population be in five, ten, or twenty years? Where will the children live? How many buildings and classrooms will be needed? What provisions should be made for special school services, for libraries, cafeterias, gymnasiums, and play areas to take care of expected educational demands?

Step three considers how to reach those goals, which have been established by the analysis of step two. What kind of buildings should be provided? Should schools be designed for grades one through eight, or should six-year elementary schools and separate three-year junior high schools be provided? How will the money be raised? When and how much should the tax rate be increased? When should the building program get under way?

Many of the answers to the questions raised in step three will be arrived at by analysis of practices of other townships, the expressed opinions of school patrons and local educational leaders, and the opinions of experts in the areas of school buildings, school organization, community planning, and public finance. Of course, this analysis of school building needs is but one phase of the larger educational problem of providing an adequate educational program for tomorrow's children. There remain problems of curriculum, pupil transportation, and school personnel. These problems can also be attacked by using similar methods of descriptive research.

SCHOOL SURVEYS

Many city, township, and county school systems have been studied by the survey method for the purpose of determining school needs. These surveys are sometimes carried on for a nominal fee as a service by the research bureau of a university in the area. Frequently, 'a large part of the data gathering is done by local educators, with the university staff providing direction and advisory services.

A study of the school system in Wayne Township, Marion County, Indiana, illustrates the type of cooperative survey described above.[13] Surveys of this type carefully study such items as the nature of the community, present plant and equipment, curriculum, staff personnel, pupil transportation, school budget, financial resources, and other phases of school administration. On the basis of present conditions and likely future demands, recommendations are made for community action.

A statewide survey of the public schools of Indiana[14] was conducted in 1947 by the Indiana School Study Commission, an agency created for the purposes of the survey. Directed by a 57-member committee of laymen and professional educators, a thorough study was made of all aspects of public education in Indiana. Hundreds of administrators, classroom teachers, and college people participated in the study, aided by seven out-of-state specialists who guided various phases of the survey. Recommendations for action were made on the basis of the findings, providing a sound basis for planning the future of public education in the state.

A survey known as the *Coleman Report on the Equality of Educational Opportunity*,[15] authorized by the U. S. Civil Rights Act of 1964, attempted, in the words of the act, "to assess lack of availability of equal educational opportunities for individuals by reason of race, color, religion or national origin in public educational institutions." Survey information was gathered for more than 3000 schools representing about 650,000 students in grades one, three, six, nine, and twelve. More than 60,000 teachers, several thousand principals, and several superintendents of school districts participated in the study.

The interpretation of the conclusions of this study has been extremely controversial.[16] Those demanding compulsory busing to achieve school racial integration have used the study to support the argument that integration is effective in improving the quality of education for minority children. Those who have opposed busing have observed the conclusion that about 4 percent of the factor of student academic achievement is attributable to the composition of the student body. Coleman, in subsequent papers and public statements, has pointed out that the report has been inter-

[13]School of Education, Indiana University, *A Cooperative Study of the Public School Enrollment and the School Building and Financial Needs of Wayne Township, Marion County, Indiana* (Bloomington, Ind.: Division of Research and Field Services, Indiana University, 1955.

[14]*An Evaluation of the Indiana Public Schools* (Indianapolis, Ind.: Indiana School Study Commission, 1949).

[15]James S. Coleman et al., *Equality of Educational Opportunity* (Washington, D.C.: Government Printing Office, 1965).

[16]Frederick Mosteller and Daniel P. Moynihan, eds., *On Equality of Educational Opportunity: Papers Deriving from the Harvard Faculty Seminar on the Coleman Report* (New York: Random House, Vintage Books, 1972).

preted or misinterpreted by social advocates on both sides of the controversy. There is little doubt that the report has had a significant effect upon social change in American education because of court interpretations of its findings.

COMMUNITY STUDIES

The community study is a thorough description and analysis of a group of people living together in a particular geographic location in a corporate way. The community study deals with such elements of the community as location, appearance, prevailing economic activity, climate and natural resources, historical development, mode of life, social structure, goals or life values and patterns, the individuals or power groups who exert the dominant influence, and impact of the outside world. It also evaluates the social institutions within the community that meet the basic human needs of health and protection, making a living, education, religious expression, and recreation. Such studies are case studies, with the community serving as the case under investigation. Communities that are chosen for study usually represent a typical pattern of social organization, size, type, or geographic location.

The community studies made by Robert and Helen Lynd and their associates at Muncie, Indiana, are well known. The first, reported in the *Middletown* in 1929,[17] and the second, *Middletown in Transition*[18] in 1937, describe the way of life of a typical midwestern, average-size city, tracing its development from the gas boom of the 1890s through World War I, the prosperity of the Twenties, and the depression of the Thirties. James West describes the nature of a very small community in the Ozark region in *Plainville, USA.*[19] Sherman and Henry[20] have studied the way of life of five "hollow" communities hidden away in the Blue Ridge mountains.

Some community studies have singled out particular aspects for special investigation. St. Clair Drake and H. R. Cayton[21] have described life in the Negro section of Chicago. August B. Hollingshead[22] has portrayed the status of adolescents in a small Illinois community. W. Lloyd Warner[23]

[17]Robert S. Lynd and Helen M. Lynd, *Middletown* (New York: Harcourt, Brace & Co., 1929).

[18]Robert S. Lynd and Helen M. Lynd, *Middletown in Transition* (New York: Harcourt, Brace and World, 1937).

[19]James West, *Plainville USA* (New York: Columbia University Press, 1945).

[20]Mandel Sherman and Thomas R. Henry, *Hollow Folk* (New York: Thomas Y. Crowell Publishing Co., 1933).

[21]August B. Hollingshead, *Elmtown's Youth* (New York: John Wiley & Sons, 1949).

[22]St. Claire Drake and H. R. Cayton, *Black Metropolis* (New York: Harcourt, Brace & World, 1945).

[23]W. Lloyd Warner and Paul S. Lunt, *Social Life in a Modern Community*, Vol. 1, "Yankee City Series." (New Haven: Yale University Press, 1941).

and his associates have delineated the social class structure of a New England community in their story of Newburyport, Massachusetts.

MARKET SURVEYS

Attempts to measure public reaction to consumer products or to evaluate the effectiveness of advertising are a specialized application of the public-opinion survey. This type of analysis has important implications for designers, manufacturers, distributors, and advertisers of products in their choice of color, composition, shape, and size of the product or the container in which it is packaged and displayed.

From a carefully selected sample the market researcher attempts to discover how the potential customer feels about the product. Using questionnaires or interviews, the opinions of the sample group are carefully gathered for analysis. Upon the basis of these data the producer and advertiser may present the most attractive or acceptable product, and predict with some degree of accuracy the likelihood of successful marketing.

Manufacturers in the modern competitive market are reluctant to risk the millions of dollars necessary to launch a new product or a new model without some evidence of probable public acceptance.

Motivation research

Another type of consumer analysis has been developed. Known as *motivation research*, it probes the hidden feelings and wishes of consumers. Using the technique of in-depth interviews, psychologists analyze unconscious motives of which the consumer himself is unaware.

For example, motivation researchers contend that an automobile is much more than a means of transportation: It is an expression of what an individual wants to be or what he thinks he is. The automobile is an instrument of self-expression. When interviewed as to what qualities they wanted in a car, individuals consistently ranked in order: economy, appearance, dependability, convenience, and safety. When asked what their friends considered most important, they ranked in order: appearance, size, and horsepower.

Motivation researchers conclude that the values that individuals attribute to their friends are really their own hidden motives. They are projecting their own desires for power and prestige, and when they themselves buy a new car, it is on the basis of appearance, size, and horsepower. Vance Packard has described the techniques of motivation research in *The Hidden Persuaders*.[24] This application of the descriptive method has

[24]Vance Packard, *The Hidden Persuaders* (New York: David McKay Co., 1957).

become an important element in market analysis, product design, and sales promotion.

Content or document analysis

Content analysis, sometimes known as document analysis, deals with the systematic examination of current records or documents as sources of data. Although documents usually consist of written or printed words or figures, they may be of the graphic type, and include paintings, drawings, cartoons, and photographs. Some studies may merely gather and classify factual data from the official reports of institutions or organizations. Other studies may classify and evaluate the contents of documents according to established criteria. The frequency of appearance or the proportion of space occupied may provide a basis for the analysis of other data.

It is well to remember that the emphasis in documentary materials is not always accurately evaluated by frequency of appearance or quantity of space occupied. The aspect of intensity through the use of prominence of position or emotionally loaded terms may well lend emphasis in ways quite unrelated to quantity alone.

In using documentary sources, one must bear in mind the fact that data appearing in print are not necessarily trustworthy. Documents used in descriptive research must be subjected to the same careful type of criticism employed by the historian. Not only is the authenticity of the document important, but the validity of its contents is crucial. The burden of proof lies with the researcher. It is his obligation to establish the trustworthiness of all data that he draws from documentary sources.

In documentary analysis the following may be used as sources of data: official records and reports, printed forms, textbooks, reference books, letters, autobiographies, diaries, compositions, themes or other prepared work, books, magazines, newspapers, college bulletins or catalogs, syllabi or courses of study, pictures, films, and cartoons.

The following purposes may be served through documentary analysis: (Examples of actual studies are given as illustrations.)

1. To describe prevailing practices or conditions.
   Entrance Requirements of Ohio Colleges as Revealed by an Analysis of College Bulletins
   Criteria for Primary Pupil Evaluation Used on Marion County Report Cards
2. To discover the relative importance of, or interest in, certain topics or problems.
   Public Information on Education as Measured by Newspaper Coverage in Three Indianapolis Daily Newspapers during the Month of December, 1958

    Statistical Concepts Presented in College Textbooks in Educational Research Published since 1940

3. To discover level of difficulty of presentation in textbooks or in other publications.

    The Vocabulary Level of Intermediate Science Textbooks
    Abstract Concepts Found in First Grade Readers

4. To evaluate bias, prejudice, or propaganda in textbook presentation.

    The Soviet Union As Presented in High School History Textbooks
    The Free Enterprise System As Pictured in High School Social Problems Textbooks
    Racial and Religious Stereotypes in Junior High School Literature Textbooks

5. To analyze types of errors in students' work.

    Typing Errors of First Semester Typing Students at Shortridge High School
    Errors in English Usage Found in Letters of Application for Admission to the University of Wisconsin

6. To analyze the use of symbols representing persons, political parties or institutions, countries, or points of view.

    Great Britain As a Symbol, As Represented in New York City Newspaper Cartoons in the Decade, 1930–1940
    The New Dealer As Depicted in the American Press from 1932 to 1942

7. To identify the literary style, concepts, or beliefs of a writer.

    Shakespeare's Use of the Metaphor
    Alexander Campbell's Concept of the Trinity, As Revealed in His Sermons
    John Dewey's Interpretation of Education as Growth

Content or document analysis should serve a useful purpose in adding important knowledge to a field of study, or yielding information that is helpful in evaluating and improving social or educational practices. Since there are so many significant areas of knowledge to be investigated, setting up studies for the pure joy of counting and tabulating has little justification. Such investigations as "The Uses of *Shall* and *Will* in the Spectator Papers," or "The Use of *Too*, Meaning *Also*, in the Works of Keats," would seem to add little useful knowledge to the field of English literature.

Activity analysis

The analysis of the activities or processes that an individual is called upon to perform is important, both in industry and in various types of social agencies. This process of analysis is appropriate in any field of work and at all levels of responsibility. It is useful in the industrial plant, where needed skills and competencies of thousands of jobs are carefully studied, jobs ranging in complexity from that of unskilled laborer to that of plant manager.

    In school systems the roles of the superintendent, the principal, the teacher, and the custodian have been carefully analyzed to discover what these individuals do and need to be able to do. The Commonwealth

Teacher Training Study[25] made under the direction of W. W. Charters and Douglas Waples described and analyzed the activities of several thousand teachers, and searched previous studies for opinions of writers on additional activities in which classroom teachers should engage.

This type of analysis may yield valuable information that would prove useful in:

1. Establishing the requirements for a particular job or position
2. Setting up a program for the preparation or training of individuals for various jobs or positions
3. Setting up an in-service program for improvement in job competence, or for upgrading of individuals already employed
4. Establishing equitable wage or salary schedules for various jobs or positions

Time-and-motion study

This more highly refined type of analysis in industrial plants consists of the observation and measurement of actual body movements involved in the performance of a production job. The stopwatch and the motion picture camera are frequently used to make the observation and measurement more exact.

Studies of this type may result in improved design of machinery and equipment, more effective placement and flow of materials, and reduction of waste motion and fatigue. All these factors may result in increased hourly output of both worker and machine.

Trend studies

The trend, or predictive, study is an interesting application of the descriptive method. In essence, it is based upon a longitudinal consideration of recorded data, indicating what has been happening in the past, what the present situation reveals, and on the basis of these data, what will be likely to happen in the future. For example, if the population in an area shows consistent growth over a period of time, one might predict that by a certain date in the future the population will reach a given level. These assumptions are based upon the likelihood that the factors producing the change or growth will continue to exert their influence in the future. The trend study points to conclusions reached by the combined methods of historical and descriptive analysis.

An excellent example of the trend study is presented in *An Economic*

[25] W. W. Charters and Douglas Waples, *The Commonwealth Teacher Training Study* (Chicago: University of Chicago Press, 1929).

Portrait of Indiana in 1970: Indiana's Economic Resources and Potential.[26] In this projection such elements as population, school enrollments at various levels, agricultural and industrial production, employment and the labor force, retail sales, electrical energy production, tax revenues, auto registrations, and the Indiana gross product are predicted.

This type of study furnishes valuable data for planning programs, in whatever area they may be. Of course, such predictions are estimates, representing tentative conclusions only. Wars, economic recessions, great technological discoveries, and many other unforeseen events could hasten or arrest the processes of growth or development.

The President's Committee on Higher Education[27] has used the process of trend analysis to forecast college enrollments by 1980. These trends have important implications for college officials, who must find ways of providing buildings and equipment, teaching staff, and financial support for a greatly expanded program of higher education. Basing these predictions on an ever-increasing number of secondary school graduates, and the constantly increasing proportion of graduates who continue their education, the Commission anticipated the flood of young people that would be knocking at college and university doors in coming years.

THE FOLLOW-UP STUDY

The follow-up study investigates individuals who have left an institution after having completed a program, a treatment, or a course of study. The study is concerned with what has happened to them, and what has been the impact upon them of the institution and its program. By examining their status or seeking their opinions, one may get some idea of the adequacy or inadequacy of the institution's program. Which courses, experiences, or treatments proved to be of value? Which proved to be ineffective or of limited value? Studies of this type enable an institution to evaluate various aspects of its program in light of actual results.

Dillon's[28] study of early school leavers has yielded information that may lead to the improvement of the curriculum, guidance services, administrative procedures, and thus the holding power of the American secondary school.

Project Talent[29] was an educational survey conducted by the University of Pittsburgh with support from the Cooperative Research Program of

[26] *An Economic Portrait of Indiana in 1970: Indiana's Economic Resources and Potential* (Bloomington, Ind.: School of Business, Indiana University, 1956).

[27] *Second Report to The President. President's Committee on Education beyond the High School* (Washington, D.C.: Government Printing Office, 1957).

[28] Harold J. Dillon, *Early School Leavers* Pub. #401. (New York: National Child Labor Committee, 1949).

[29] U.S. Office of Education. *Progress towards the Goals of Project Talent* (Washington, D.C.: Government Printing Office, 1965).

the U. S. Office of Education, the National Institutes of Health, the National Science Foundation, and the Department of Defense. The survey consisted of the administration of a two-day battery of aptitude, ability, and achievement tests, and inventories of the background characteristics of 440,000 students enrolled in 1353 secondary schools in all parts of the United States. Five basic purposes of the survey were stated:

1. To obtain an inventory of the capacities and potentialities of American youth
2. To establish a set of standards for educational and psychological measurement
3. To provide a comprehensive counseling guide indicating patterns of career success
4. To provide information on how youth choose their life work
5. To provide better understanding of the educational experiences which prepare students for their life work

In addition to the testing program, questionnaire follow-up studies have been conducted, and are planned at regular intervals, to relate the information gathered to patterns of aptitude and ability required by various types of occupations. The vast amount of data stored in the data bank, now available in the computer files, will make significant educational research possible and may provide a basis for possible changes in the educational patterns of American secondary schools.

Project Talent, described as an example of an educational survey, also provides an illustration of a follow-up study. One phase of the longitudinal study, conducted in 1964 and reported by Janet Combs and William W. Cooley[30] involved the follow-up of the ninth grade group who failed to complete the high school program. This group, which represented a random sample of the ninth grade secondary school population, provided an estimate of the characteristics of the dropout population, compared with those of a random sample of students who graduated but did not enter a junior college or four-year institution of higher learning. These two samples were compared on a number of characteristics, such as academic achievement, participation in extracurricular activities, work experiences, hobbies, contacts with school counselors, and self-reported personal qualities.

The students who graduated scored significantly higher on most of the characteristics, except self-reported qualities of leadership and impulsiveness. One unusual finding indicated that the dropouts earned as much as those who had finished high school and had been earning it longer. It was pointed out, however, that the study concerned students who were about 19 years of age, and that the economic advantages of finishing high school could not be adequately evaluated until later in life.

[30]Janet Combs and William W. Cooley, "Dropouts in High School and After School," *American Educational Research Journal* 5 (May 1968): 343–363.

Project Talent, now funded by the National Institute of Education,[31] has maintained contact with the original students and has completed the eleventh year follow-up survey. Many of the students expressed dissatisfaction with their schooling, and regretted that they had not gone on to college or vocational school and that they had married too early. More than half still live within 30 miles of their high schools, a surprising observation in a society that is believed to be extremely mobile. The more mobile half were the high academic achievers. Eighty percent of the men, but only 65 percent of the women expressed satisfaction with their jobs as meeting their long-range goals.

Genetic studies of genius

One of the most significant psychological research investigations of the present century is the series of studies concerning the nature and development of gifted children carried on at Stanford University under the direction of Lewis M. Terman. These investigations, spanning a period of almost sixty years, have been described in the series entitled *Genetic Studies of Genius,* published in five volumes, each describing a specific phase of the investigation.

Before 1921, no large group of gifted children had been studied intensively. Terman referred to this field as the darkest Africa of education, an area where positive knowledge of physical, mental, and personality traits of gifted children was so limited that sound educational procedures could not be planned.

In preparing these investigations five criteria or goals were agreed upon:

1. Subjects selected for study should represent an unbiased sample of their kind.
2. Procedures should be as objective as possible, and so clearly defined that the investigation could be repeated and conclusions checked.
3. The subjects should be followed as closely and as far into adult life as finances and other circumstances would permit.
4. A study should be made of the childhoods of a representative group of historical geniuses.
5. The investigation should not be a direct attack on the methods of teaching gifted children, but a search for facts that would help to provide a basis for special training in the education of the gifted.

In the Terman series of five published studies Vols. I, III, IV, and V are closely linked. Vol. I carefully analyzes the intellectual character and personality traits of 1000 gifted children. Vols. III, IV, and V followed the same group after periods of six, twenty-five, and thirty-five years, respectively.

[31]"Project Talent," *Phi Delta Kappan* 57 (January 1976): 360.

Study II is, in a sense, parenthetical, having no direct relation to the other three. It deals with gifted children, but approaches the analysis from another direction. Using historical data as evidence, the study goes back to the childhood and youth of 300 individuals who achieved eminence as adults. This study attempted to find the answer to the question, "What evidences of precocity or genius were revealed in the early lives of these 300 outstanding historic personalities?" We will describe each study briefly, pointing out the purposes, procedures, and significant conclusion reached.

I. THE MENTAL AND PHYSICAL TRAITS OF A THOUSAND GIFTED CHILDREN[32]

Financed by grants totaling more than $50,000 from the Commonwealth Fund and from Stanford University, Dr. Terman proposed an intensive study of the top one percent of the public school population of a number of cities and rural areas in Central California.

Because of the tremendous cost involved, it would have been impracticable to test all school-age children in order to find a group of subjects representative of all the gifted children in the area. A preliminary sifting method was adopted in order to select an experimental group. Teachers were asked to nominate children for possible selection in the following order:

1. Brightest child in the room
2. Second brightest
3. Third brightest
4. Youngest child
5. Brightest child in the previous year's class

Using these nominations in more than 20 California cities and adjacent rural areas, Stanford-Binet tests of intelligence were administered for the purposes of screening and selecting the gifted group to be studied. An intelligence quotient of 140 was first estimated to be the appropriate cutoff level for selection. The standard was later modified, however, to include some students with measured intelligence quotients above 132, whose ages exceeded eleven years. It was discovered that the brightest children over 11 years of age were rated too low by the Stanford-Binet Scale.

In addition to those nominated by their classroom teachers, a substantial number of gifted subjects were located through previous test records, special recommendations, and other sources.

Several experimental groups were established. The main experimental

[32]Lewis M. Terman et al., *The Mental and Physical Traits of a Thousand Gifted Children*, Vol. 1 (Stanford, Calif.: Stanford University Press, 1926).

group consisted of 643 gifted children in grades one through eight. The second group, for which less data were collected, included 356 gifted students residing in cities outside the principal area of the main survey. A third experimental group included 378 gifted high school students, and a fourth included a small number of pupils selected because of their special ability in such areas as art and music.

To serve as a basis for comparison, data gathered from a control group of about 800 nonselected students, attending the same schools, were used. A great deal of data were gathered for the individuals in the study, including the following:[33]

1. Intelligence as measured by the Stanford-Binet Test and the National Intelligence Test, Form B
2. A two-hour battery of educational achievement tests
3. A fifty-minute test of general information in science, history, literature, and the arts
4. A fifty-minute questionnaire test of interest in, and knowledge of, play, games, and amusements
5. A four-page interest blank filled out by the pupils
6. A two-month reading record kept by the pupils
7. A sixteen-page home information blank filled out by the parents. Such vital statistics as parents' age, race, nationality, occupation, education, income, family size, and eminent relatives were included. Parents also rated their child on 25 character traits
8. An eight-page school information blank filled out by the teacher, including ratings on the same 25 traits evaluated by the parents
9. Home and neighborhood ratings by field assistants as scored on the Whittier Scale for Grading Home Conditions, and a scale for rating neighborhoods
10. Medical data gathered from health records and health information supplied by parents on the home information blank. Each child was also examined periodically by a staff of qualified medical examiners. Thirty-seven anthropometric measurements were taken of each child. Such measurements as height; length, width, or circumference of limbs; head and chest measurements; strength of grip; breathing capacity; and weight were carefully recorded.

About 100 pages of data were collected for each child, including 65 pages of test and measurement data, and 35 pages of questionnaire data. The conclusions reached in this study resulted from the comparisons of data from the gifted or experimental groups with data from the control, or nongifted, groups. It should be noted that the differences described are differences between groups as revealed by measures of central tendency. The researchers pointed out that there was a great lack of homogeneity within both the experimental and the control groups. Often the differences among individuals within one of the groups were greater than the differ-

[33]*Ibid.*, p. 7.

ences between individuals in the experimental and the control groups.

Thus, the conclusions refer to the group as a whole and not to particular individuals. The experimental, or gifted, group, as a whole, evinced the following characteristics:

1. Physical superiority in all respects to the control or nongifted group
2. Acceleration in school. Eighty-five percent were accelerated one or more half-grades.
3. Fondness for school. They demonstrated marked superiority in subject matter mastery, as measured by achievement tests.
4. More interest in school subjects that are abstract (literature, science, mathematics), and less interest in the so-called practical subjects (penmanship, manual training, sewing)
5. Many-sided interest. One and three-quarters times as many gifted as control children had made hobby collections, and more than twice as many had made collections of a scientific nature.
6. Reading interests surpassing those of the nongifted group both in amount and in quality. The gifted group read more science, biography, travel, folk tales, informational fiction, and poetry; fewer books of adventure, mystery, and emotional fiction than the control group. The gifted child of 7 read more books than the nongifted child read at any age to 15 years.
7. Choice of older playmates than the nongifted. Gifted boys, although they showed less interest in competitive games, showed a higher masculinity index than that of control boys to age 13.
8. Decisive superiority over nongifted children in character and personality test scores in such traits as honesty, trustworthiness, modesty, moral judgment, and emotional stability
9. Earlier maturation. On the average, they walked one month earlier and talked three and one-half months earlier than the nongifted. Characteristics of gifted children first noticed by parents were quick understanding, insatiable curiosity, an extensive store of information, retentive memory, early speech, and unusual vocabulary. Nearly one-half of the gifted group had learned to read before starting school.
10. A home cultural level that was above average, but there was no evidence that their superiority was the product of deliberate parental stimulation

As a result of this investigation, the researchers concluded that there was no evidence that intellectual superiority was offset by inferiority in nonintellectual areas. Gifted children, as a group, revealed superiority in all of the qualities that were investigated and measured.

II. THE EARLY MENTAL TRAITS OF THREE HUNDRED GENIUSES[34]

The second phase of the *Genetic Studies of Genius* series deals with the study of 301 men and women of great historical eminence, to discover the degree of mental endowment that characterized these individuals in their childhood, youth, and young adulthood.

---

[34]Catherine M. Cox, *The Early Mental Traits of Three Hundred Geniuses*, Vol. 2 (Stanford, Calif.: Stanford University Press, 1926).

The researchers established three criteria for the selection of these individuals: (1) they should be individuals of unquestioned greatness; (2) their eminence should be based upon real achievement, not upon accident of birth or luck; (3) adequate records of their early lives should be available.

The period of 1450 to 1850 was selected—four centuries for which records were likely to be reasonably adequate, yet long enough past to enable the passage of time to sift the truly great from those who merely appeared to be great or who had won only temporary recognition.

The subjects selected for careful study were chosen from Cattell's list of *1,000 Most Eminent Men of History*. These men and women represented sixteen different nationalities and many fields of activity, and included in their number novelists, poets, historians, essayists, politicians, statesmen, scientists, soldiers, religious leaders, philosophers, artists, musicians, and revolutionary statesmen.

An individual case history was compiled for each eminent person using the method of research known as historiometry, the application of psychometric measures of personal traits based upon the historical evidence gathered from primary and some secondary sources of evidence. Such materials as letters, essays, poems, and diaries written by the subject; records of reading; school reports; and statements of parents, friends, and contemporaries were accepted as primary sources. Biographical materials written by competent historians and biographers were accepted as secondary sources of evidence.

Using these data, a panel of from three to five expert psychologists estimated two separate intelligence quotients for each eminent person, one based upon the data covering the period of early childhood and youth to the age of 17, and the other covering the period to age 26. In addition, each subject was rated independently by the panel on 67 character or personality traits.

The composite estimates of the raters comprised an estimated IQ score for each subject. It should be mentioned that each rater was a psychologist with a great deal of experience in the observation and testing of children and youth, knowing well the characteristics of young people of various levels of measured intelligence. Cox mentions the fact that the independent "estimates furnished by the raters showed a degree of agreement that should free them from the suspicion of being greatly influenced by personal bias."[35]

The mass of historiometric data, based upon evidence of the youthful behavior of these eminent individuals, points to three general conclusions:

[35] *Ibid.*, p. viii.

1. Not only was there evidence of above-average heredity, they also enjoyed superior environmental advantages.
2. Their childhood behavior indicates that they possessed unusually high IQ's. The mean IQ score for the group was probably between 155 and 165. Many scored above the 200 mark.
3. As a result of the analysis of other personality and character traits, there is evidence that these 300 geniuses, even in childhood, displayed not only high intellectual traits, but also such qualities as persistence of motive and effort, confidence in their abilities, and great strength or force of character.

III. THE PROMISE OF YOUTH[36]

The report in Vol. III is a follow-up study describing the status of the gifted group after a period of six years. The purpose of the follow-up study was to check on the correctness of some of the conclusions, and to obtain some evidence to supplement the data revealed in the original study of gifted children. Information was obtained regarding nearly 97 percent of the gifted group studied in 1921–22.

The method of data gathering was similar to that of the original study. Follow-up tests of intelligence, school achievement, and personality were administered, supplemented by data obtained from information blanks filled out by teachers, parents, and the children themselves. Field workers conducted personal interviews with the parents, children, and their teachers. Although the researchers recognized the desirability of getting more complete data than was possible because of limitations of time and funds, they reported that the data were complete enough to warrant reasonably conclusive findings.

Although the gifted group continued to display superiority, as indicated by intelligence tests scores, there was a slight drop in average IQ, the boys averaging a drop of three points, and the girls an average drop of thirteen points. The report concludes that changes in ability found over a period of time are possibly due to change-of-rate factors, and that such factors are correlated with sex. Boys are more likely than girls to have a high IQ as they advance in age, and are more likely than girls to retain a high IQ earlier evidenced. Both boys and girls of the gifted group were more accelerated in school than they were in the original survey.

The gifted group, as a whole, was relatively superior and relatively weak in the same school subjects as in 1921–22. The girls were relatively superior to boys in English and art, while the boys were better in science and mathematics.

In achievement, as measured by the Stanford Achievement Tests, the

---

[36]Barbara S. Burks, Dortha W. Jensen, and Lewis M. Terman, *The Promise of Youth: Follow-up Studies of a Thousand Gifted Children*, Vol. 3 (Stanford, Calif.: Stanford University Press, 1930).

girls tended to score relatively higher than the boys, in terms of what would be predicted from an analysis of their intelligence quotients. A similar superiority of girls over boys in average school marks received was also noted.

Gifted boys and girls tended to prefer reading to all other leisure-time activities, while collecting interests for both boys and girls declined after age 14. The gifted group, as a whole, continued to maintain its active participation in social as well as intellectual activities. The gifted subjects showed an even greater tendency to prefer companions older than themselves, and continued to display superior behavior and personality patterns.

Ninety-four percent of the boys and 91 percent of the girls had gone or had plans to go to college. About three times as many members of the gifted group were elected to Phi Beta Kappa as were other seniors at Stanford and the University of California. Those that married tended to choose a spouse who had about a year less schooling, and, in the majority of cases, who was less well-endowed intellectually.

As a general conclusion, it was reported that the composite picture of the gifted group had changed only in minor respects in six years.

IV. THE GIFTED CHILD GROWS UP[37]

Part IV of the *Genetic Studies of Genius* series presents a picture of Terman's original group of gifted children after a period of twenty-five years. The data presented in this report are the product of follow-up studies carried on in 1936, 1940, and 1945. By 1945 the average age of the group was 35, a period when adult careers clearly take form. This longitudinal type of study, covering a quarter of a century, enabled the researchers to follow a group of gifted individuals from childhood to adulthood, and to evaluate some of the influences of "giftedness" upon their development as creative contributors to society.

The additional data collected in the follow-up studies were gathered through personal interviews or by mail, through four-page information blanks filled out by each subject and by parents or relatives, the Strong Vocational Interest Test, a concept-mastery test, a marriage blank for both gifted subjects and their spouses, a personality and temperament test, and a Stanford-Binet Test of the subject's offspring above the age of two-and-a-half years, together with birth and developmental data on each child. In addition to the data mentioned, field workers made detailed reports based on their conversations with the subjects, their parents, their spouses, or other relatives. The researchers reported that the subjects

[37]Lewis M. Terman and Melita H. Oden, *The Gifted Child Grows Up. Twenty-five Years Follow-up of a Superior Group*, Vol. 4 (Stanford, Calif.: Stanford University Press, 1947).

were most cooperative, going to almost any lengths to aid in the conduct of the investigation.

Through the use of punched cards and machine tabulation, a thorough analysis of the great mass of data collected was accomplished. The completeness of the follow-up studies is attested by the fact that data were secured for 97.7 percent of the 1467 living subjects. Although it would be inappropriate to attempt to summarize all of the findings of the four studies, a few general conclusions are presented:

1. The health of the adult subjects was considerably superior to that of the general population. They excelled in stature and in freedom from serious defects, and showed a more favorable mortality rate than the general population of comparable age. In mental health and general adjustment the gifted group excelled the general population.
2. The incidence of delinquency was below that of the general population. Only four subjects served terms in penal institutions, three as juvenile offenders and one as an adult. The one adult, whose measured childhood intelligence quotient was 154, was sentenced to prison for forgery. It is noted that he was a model prisoner, and soon became editor of the prison newspaper.
3. As judged by the concept-mastery test given the adult group, there seems to have been evidence of a small mean decrease in mental function, which after correction for errors of measurement, may have been less than five IQ points.
4. Of the approximately 90 percent of the men who entered college, 70 percent graduated; of the 80 percent of the women entering, 67 percent graduated. The proportion of college graduates who completed advanced degrees was 51 percent of the men and 29 percent of the women. Forty percent of the men and about 32 percent of the women graduated from college with honors. Both men and women of the gifted group participated to a greater extent in extracurricular activities than did college students in general.
5. In occupational status, approximately 71 percent of the gifted men were individual or executive workers and, regardless of education, appeared to be assuming responsibility and leadership in far greater proportion than college graduates in general. Forty-five percent of the gifted men were in professions, eight times as high a proportion as that of California males in general.
6. In voting regularly the gifted group excelled the electorate in general, with 91 percent voting in national elections.
7. Gifted subjects tended to choose spouses who were less gifted, but who possessed intelligence equal to that of the average college graduate.
8. The mean intelligence quotient of the offspring who were given the Stanford-Binet Test was 128, a little below the average of their gifted parents. There were few cases of feeblemindedness and borderline mentality, however, and a high proportion of intelligence quotients of 150 or higher among the offspring of the gifted group.

It was discovered that gifted children grow up to be gifted and successful adults, maintaining their superiority in practically every trait and area of endeavor. The studies concluded with a series of important plans and proposals for continued investigation which should add much to this important area of human knowledge.

V. THE GIFTED GROUP AT MID-LIFE[38]

The fifth phase of the *Genetic Studies of Genius*, actually the fourth concerned with the longitudinal study of gifted children, was completed in 1958. Published after the death of Dr. Terman in his eightieth year, the study represents a follow-up of the gifted subjects in their mid-forties who had been under observation for 34 years. Approximately 97 percent of the original group provided the data for the 1950–52 study, and approximately 93 percent for the 1955 mail follow-up. Most of the information for the study was based on the General Information Blank. Some additional data were supplied through the concept-mastery test and through scores on the Stanford-Binet Test administered to the offspring of the subjects. A few of the major findings of the study are briefly presented: readers are urged to read the original studies for a more complete analysis.

The superiority of the gifted group was greatest in academic and intellectual accomplishment and in vocational achievement. Physically, the gifted group continued to reveal above-average status in health, and lower mortality rates. The gifted subjects did not differ from the control group in the extent of personality and adjustment problems, as indicated by incidence of alcoholism, divorce, sexual deviation, and delinquency.

Although it is understandable that a high proportion of the women were homemakers and did not seek gainful employment, their accomplishments were impressive. Seven were listed in *American Men of Science*, 2 in the *Directory of American Scholars*, and 2 in *Who's Who in America*. Publications of the women included 5 novels, 5 volumes of poetry, 70 poems, 32 professional or scholarly books, 50 short stories, 4 plays, 150 essays and articles, and more than 200 scientific papers. Five patents were obtained by the gifted women. Their intellectual stimulation and contribution to their husbands and children were impossible to measure.

The gifted men achieved prominence in nearly every field of activity—locally, nationally, and internationally. Eighty-six percent were engaged in professions or semiprofessions. Seventy were listed in *American Men of Science*, 10 in the *Directory of American Scholars*, and 21 in *Who's Who in America*.

Recognizing the fact that these gifted men and women were in their mid-forties, it can be assumed that their peak of recognition would come later, perhaps after 15 or 20 years. It might be predicted that listings in *American Men of Science* would probably be doubled, and in *Who's Who in America* trebled or quadrupled. In all areas of distinguished service the list could be expected to expand.

In summary, the study confirmed the earlier conclusions that the original group of gifted children grew up to be gifted adults who distin-

[38] Lewis M. Terman and Melita H. Oden, *The Gifted Group at Midlife*, Vol. 5 (Stanford, Calif.: Stanford University Press, 1959).

guished themselves in many areas of activity, and made extraordinary contributions to their homes, their communities, their nation, and the world.

Lee J. Cronbach and Robert T. Sears are completing a fifth follow-up study of the 1300 surviving members of the Terman group of gifted children, approximately 50 years after the original study.

A STUDY AND A REPLICATION

Replication, a fusion of the words *duplication* and *repetition,* is deliberately repeating a study, using identical procedures with different subjects, at a different time and in a different setting. Replication is always desirable to validate or to raise questions about the conclusions of a previous study. Rarely is an important finding made public unless the original study has been replicated. An interesting study and replication were concerned with teachers' knowledge of mental health principles.

E. K. Wichman[39] in his 1927 study compared the ranking of the seriousness of 50 behavioral problems, as viewed by a panel of 30 psychologists, psychiatrists, and psychiatric caseworkers, and a sample of 511 elementary classroom teachers. The members of each group ranked in order the 50 items from most serious to least serious. A comparison between the mean rankings of each group was made.

Aggressive behaviors that teachers considered most serious were judged to be much less serious by the clinicians. The withdrawing behaviors, considered most serious by the clinicians, were considered not serious by the teachers. The coefficient of correlation between the rankings of the two groups was low and negative ($r = -.11$). Of the 10 problems listed in Table 5–1 as most serious by both groups, only one common item, cruelty or bullying, was found.

TABLE 5–1   Behaviors Ranked by Teachers and Clinicians

511 teachers	Rank	30 clinicians
heterosexual activity	1	unsociableness
stealing	2	suspiciousness
masturbation	3	depressed/unhappy
obscene notes/talk	4	fearfulness
untruthfulness	5	resentfulness
truancy	6	bullying/cruelty
defiance	7	easily discouraged
bullying/cruelty	8	suggestibility
cheating	9	overcritical
destroying school property	10	sensitiveness

[39]E. K. Wickman, *Children's Behavior and Teacher's Attitudes* (New York: Commonwealth Fund, 1929).

Twenty-five years later George A. W. Stouffer[40] replicated the Wickman study to determine whether there was any change in the degree of agreement between clinicians and teachers. The same list of 50 behavioral items was used for comparison. A panel of 70 mental hygienists was selected from various parts of the country. A sample of 481 male and female elementary teachers was selected from all parts of the country, representing teachers of a variety of ethnic and socioeconomic groups, in both urban and rural areas. The sampling procedures closely approximated those used in the Wickman study.

Stouffer's study showed a much closer agreement between the judgments of the teachers and the clinicians. A positive coefficient of correlation of $+.52$ indicated that, although the two groups were not in complete agreement, the teachers were much more aware of mental health principles. Of course, this conclusion was based upon the assumption that the judgment of the clinicians represented a valid criterion.

One of the criticisms directed at the Wickman study was its failure to provide uniform directions and conditions for the ranking of the items by the clinicians and the teachers. Duplicating the Wickman procedure, Stouffer reported a coefficient of correlation of $+.52$. Substituting identical directions and conditions the coefficient of correlation between teachers and clinicians was $+.61$. It is interesting to note that the coefficient of correlation between the rankings of the clinicians in the Wickman study and in the Stouffer study was $+.87$.

Several interesting interpretations may be drawn from this replicated study:

1. As judged by agreement with clinicians, after 25 years, teachers seemed to be much more aware of the relative seriousness of many types of behavior. The change in coefficients of correlation was from $-.11$ to $+.52$.
2. The increased teacher awareness of mental health principles may have resulted from greater emphasis in teacher education programs upon the understanding of the social and emotional health of the child.
3. It is possible that an element of contamination may have accounted for some of the improvement, for some of the teachers in the Stouffer study may have been familiar with the findings of the Wickman study, reported in a number of educational psychology textbooks.
4. It would also seem realistic to expect some difference in the rankings of the seriousness of particular behavioral problems. Teachers are particularly sensitive to aggressive behavior, for they are charged with the responsibility of maintaining social control in a group situation in order that effective learning can go on. In addition, they are subject to certain community expectations and pressures in dealing with areas of sexual behavior.

   Clinicians usually deal with individual behavior problems and have little

[40]George A. W. Stouffer, "Behavior Problems of Children as Viewed by Teachers and Mental Hygienists," *Mental Hygiene* 34 (April 1952): 271–286.

responsibility for the control of groups. It would thus seem likely that they would take a more clinical, long-range view of the seriousness of certain types of problem behavior.

These studies by Wickman and by Stouffer have important implications for the understanding of the dynamics of behavior, and illustrate a useful method of evaluating programs for the preparation of classroom teachers.

Descriptive research

THE EX POST FACTO METHOD

Descriptive research seeks to find the answers to questions through the analysis of variable relationships. What factors seem to be systematically associated with certain occurrences, conditions, or types of behavior? Since it is often impracticable to arrange occurrences, an analysis of what actually does happen is the only feasible way to study causation.

For example, we would not arrange fatal automobile accidents in order to study their causes. But we can study the conditions associated with fatal accidents to attempt to find the factor or factors associated with them. Police departments, safety commissions, and insurance companies are constantly studying the problems of highway safety. If the causes of accidents could be determined, certain preventative measures could be adopted. Such factors as excessive speed, poor mechanical condition of the vehicles involved, driving under the influence of alcohol, and many others have been blamed.

By the methodology of descriptive research, the relative importance of these factors may be investigated. If, for example, excessive speed were associated with a high proportion of fatal accidents, state legislatures could attack the problem of highway safety by passing more stringent laws controlling speed, or by more rigid enforcement of existing speed laws. If a high proportion of vehicles involved in accidents revealed mechanical defects, compulsory periodic vehicle inspection might be effected. The need for engineering improvements in auto construction might also be suggested.

SEAT BELT RESEARCH

Seat belt research has had an important influence upon auto-safety equipment. Federal legislation requires that all new cars sold after January 1, 1968, be equipped with lap and shoulder belts. A Detroit news release cites research evidence that supports the effectiveness of safety belts.[41]

[41] *U.S. News and World Report* (January 29, 1968) Copyrighted article, p. 12.

Now that U.S. autos are being equipped with a maze of belts and harnesses for drivers and passengers, this question is being asked by many car buyers: Are they really useful, or are they more trouble than they are worth?

The answer, from the best available evidence, seems to be: The new harnesses can be an important factor in reducing injuries and death from accidents.

The widest research done to date on this subject was a Swedish survey of 28,780 accidents, showing how the use or non-use of shoulder harnesses affected the drivers and passengers. Main results of the survey were made public late in 1967. The survey by the manufacturers of Volvo autos also showed this: Use of a combined shoulder-lap belt reduced skull damage by 69 per cent for drivers and 88 per cent for passengers. Facial injuries dropped by 73 per cent for drivers and 83 per cent for passengers.

The U. S. auto industry has accepted the Federal Government edict that it provide the belts and harnesses—a total of 16 straps in each new auto. Now being worked on are plans to make them less unsightly and less awkward to use.

But dealers are finding a number of buyers unenthusiastic about all the belts. Some dealers asked if they could remove the belts at the request of the customers. The answer from manufacturers: No. The dealer, it was explained, might be breaking the law if he did so.

Some industry officials have also raised the question of whether the belts, themselves, can cause injury in case of accident. So far there has been no broad study in the United States to back this theory. The Swedish survey, however, did show this: In the 28,780 accidents studied, safety belts caused 34 injuries to drivers, 25 to front seat passengers. Most were minor injuries.

What a survey of accidents shows

Figures below show results of 28,780 traffic accidents in Sweden. In these accidents 98 per cent of the cars were equipped with lap and shoulder belts. But only 25 per cent of the drivers and 30 per cent of the front seat passengers were using the belts. This is what happened:

	Killed	Severely injured	Slightly injured
DRIVERS			
Among 6870 using belts	2	51	175
Among 21,910 not using belts	37	263	835
FRONT SEAT PASSENGERS			
Among 2699 using belts	1	22	109
Among 6032 not using belts	12	160	439

While these statistics may appear to present convincing evidence in favour of the use of lap and shoulder belts in reducing fatalities and serious injuries, one might speculate that motorists who are prudent enough to wear them are likely to be more careful drivers than those who do not.

Studies of juvenile delinquency may compare the social and educational backgrounds of delinquents and nondelinquents. What factors, if any, were common to the delinquent group? What factors, if any, were common to the nondelinquent group? Any factors common to one group, but not to the other, might serve as a possible explanation of the underlying causes of delinquency.

Some efforts have been made to associate good or poor teaching with the type of educational institution in which the teachers prepared. Those studies have proved inconclusive, possibly for a number of reasons. In addition to the difficulty of finding a valid and satisfactory criteria of good and poor teaching, many factors other than type of college attended seem to be significant. Such variables as quality of scholarship, socio-economic status, personality qualities, types of nonschool experiences, attitudes toward the teaching profession, and a host of others have possible relevancy.

The eight-year study[42]

In 1932 a number of leading colleges and universities agreed to a proposal of the Commission on the Relation of School and College of the Progressive Education Association to participate in an extensive study. The colleges agreed to accept students from a group of 30 selected secondary schools without entrance examinations and without regard to the pattern of course requirements ordinarily required for admission. The only requirements for admission were to be the recommendation of the principal, a complete record of the student's academic and extraclass activities, and his scores on scholastic aptitude and achievement tests given during the secondary school course.

The Progressive Education Association was concerned with better ways of setting up the secondary school curriculum. Freed from the traditional college entrance requirements, schools would then be able to build the type of curriculum they believed to be best. In the words of Max McConn in his preface to one of the published reports:[43]

> Is the traditional college entrance program the only safe and sound plan of preparation for college? Or can boys and girls be equally well, or even possibly better prepared for college through a considerable variety of widely different programs devised by competent secondary school teachers with their eyes fixed primarily on the conditions and demands of modern life, and the

[42]Dean Chamberlin et al., *Did They Succeed in College?* (New York: Harper & Row, Publishers, 1942). Used by permission of McGraw Hill Book Co., present copyright owner.

[43]*Ibid.*, p. xix.

individual capacities and interests of particular students, with only incidental reference to the impending college experience? Would students coming up through such a heterogeneous system be able to hold their own in a major college or would they be foredoomed to failure?

The hypothesis of the Commission on the Relation of School and College was that there are other ways of successfully preparing youth for college.

Selected to participate in the study were 30 secondary schools, public and private, large and small, and representing different geographic sections of the United States. The curriculum patterns were in no sense standardized. Each school was free to develop the type of courses and experiences it felt would best provide for the educational needs of its students. No two schools developed identical programs. Some introduced new courses, some combined existing courses, and others modified teaching-learning procedures within existing courses. Some set up a core curriculum, others emphasized the problems approach in more conventional courses. Broad field organization characterized some programs; others introduced correlated or fused courses.

Although the programs of the 30 schools were of widely differing patterns, they did have something basic in common. They emphasized teacher-pupil planning, laboratory-type learning experiences, democratic procedures, and the problem-solving approach to learning. They were also uninhibited by the usual restrictions of course unit requirements found in conventional secondary school programs.

In 1932 students in the 30 schools began to pursue innovative programs. By 1936 they were ready for college, and by 1940 the first class had completed the four-year college program. The results of the study are based upon those students who entered college in 1936 and who graduated in 1940, those who entered in 1937 for three college years, in 1938 for two college years, and in 1939 for one year in college.

PLAN OF THE STUDY

The study design consisted of matching a graduate of one of the 30 experimental schools with a graduate of a conventional high school, both of whom were enrolled at the same liberal arts college or university. These students were matched or equated on the basis of age, sex, intelligence, socioeconomic status, race, religious affiliation, expressed vocational objective, extraclass activity record, size of secondary school attended, and type of community. Most of the data were collected in 40 men's, women's, and coeducational colleges and universities.

In the comparison 1475 matched pairs were selected, making up an experimental group and a control group. During their college careers, the students in the experimental group were compared with students in the control group on the following criteria of success in college:

1. Intellectual competence as determined by academic grade point average, honors, prizes, and manifestation of interest in intellectual activities beyond course requirements
2. Cultural development and the use of leisure for worthy activities—concerts, theater, writing, art, athletics, hobbies, and participation in social, religious, and service-type activities
3. Practical competence, as revealed by evidence of manual skills, common-sense judgment, and ability to adapt to situations, to budget time and money wisely, and to obtain and hold a job
4. Philosophy of life, vocational objectives, ethical standards, and ideals
5. Emotional blance, as revealed by independence and attitudes toward parents and others
6. Social fitness—the ability to make and keep friends, evidence of poise, and social skills
7. Sensitivity to social problems—concern about social and economic problems on the campus and in the world at large, and willingness to assume citizenship responsibilities
8. Physical fitness—health habits developed and physical activities engaged in

To measure these qualities and competencies for comparative purposes, many types of evidence were employed:

1. Course grades
2. Reports from instructors, advisors, counselors, residence-hall heads, and activity supervisors
3. Special tests designed for the study
4. Questionnaires
5. Health reports
6. Interviews with the student
7. Reading and activity records
8. Samples of written work
9. Other college records

CONCLUSIONS

A comparison of the 1475 matched pairs of graduates of the 30 schools and the conventional high schools reveals the following characteristics of the graduates of the 30 schools:[44]

1. They earned a slightly higher grade point average in all subjects except the foreign languages. They received slightly more academic honors, and a higher percentage of nonacademic honors.
2. They were more often judged to possess intellectual curiosity and drive, and to be precise, systematic, and objective in their thinking. They were also more often judged to demonstrate a high degree of resourcefulness in meeting new situations.

[44] *Ibid.*, pp. 207–208.

3. They did not differ from the comparison group in number of times on probation, in ability to plan their time wisely, or in the quality of adjustment to
their contemporaries.
4. They participated more frequently and more often enjoyed appreciative
experiences in the arts, and participated more in all organized student
activities, except those of a religious or service nature.
5. They were more often judged to have developed clear ideas about the meaning
of education, a better orientation toward the choice of a vocation, and a more
active concern for what was going on in the world.

Although some of these differences were not great, they were consistent.
It is apparent that the graduates of the 30 schools were more successful
than graduates of the conventional schools, whether as judged by college
standards, by their contemporaries, or by the students themselves.

As an additional feature of the study, a special analysis was made of the
graduates of the six schools that departed most from tradition with the
graduates of the six that departed least. The graduates of the most innovative schools showed a marked superiority over those from the more
conventional schools, the difference being even greater than that existing
between the graduates of the total 30 schools and those of the conventional high schools.

In this study a slight advantage or even no difference between the
graduates of the 30 schools and the conventional schools would have
supported the hypothesis that there is no prescribed course pattern that
best prepares a student for college, and that students are not subjected to
the risk of college failure when secondary school teachers and administrators depart from traditional course requirements.

It is interesting to note that the conclusions reached by the Eight-Year
Study have apparently had a marked influence upon entrance requirements
in American colleges and universities.

THE IMPACT OF "SESAME STREET"

Minton[45] studied the effect of viewing the children's television program, "Sesame Street," on the reading readiness of kindergarten children.
Of three sample groups, a 1968, a 1969, and a 1970 group, only the 1970
group had viewed the program.

Reading Readiness and "Sesame Street"

Sample group	N	White	Black	Spanish-speaking
1968	482	431	51	18
1969	495	434	61	9
1970	524	436	88	25

[45]J. M. Minton, "Impact of Sesame Street on Reading Readiness," *Sociology of
Education* 48 (Spring 1975): 141–151.

Scores on the Metropolitan Reading Readiness Test battery, consisting of six subtests (word meaning, listening, matching, alphabet letter recognition, numbers, and copying text) were used to measure readiness. Using a pretest-posttest design, the mean gain scores of the 1970 group were compared with those of the 1968 and 1969 groups.

No significant differences at the .05 level were observed in total scores. On only one of the subtests, letter recognition, was a significant difference observed, favoring the 1970 group. When classified by socioeconomic status, advantaged children watched more and scored higher than disadvantaged children. The hypothesis that viewing "Sesame Street" would help to close the gap between advantaged and disadvantaged children was not supported; rather, the gap was widened.

Rogers[46] has summarized reports on the program's impact.

THE POST HOC FALLACY

One of the most serious dangers of *ex post facto* research is the *post hoc* fallacy, the conclusion that, because two factors go together, one is the cause and the other the effect. Because there seems to be a high relationship between the number of years of education completed and earned income, many educators have argued that staying in school will add an x number of dollars of income over a period of time for each additional year of education completed. Although there may be such a relationship, it is also likely that some of the factors that influence young people to seek additional education are more important than the educational level completed. Such factors as socioeconomic status, persistence, desire, willingness to postpone immediate gratification, and intelligence level are undoubtedly significant factors in vocational success. Staying in school may be a symptom rather than the prevailing cause.

Some critics of cigarette-cancer research have advanced a similar argument. The case that they propose follows this line of reason: Let us suppose that certain individuals with a type of glandular imbalance have a tendency toward cancer. The imbalance could induce a certain amount of nervous tension. Since excessive cigarette smoking is a type of nervous-tension release, these individuals would tend to be heavy smokers. The cancer could result from the glandular imbalance, rather than from the smoking which is a type of symptom. This error of confusing symptoms or merely associated factors with cause could lead researchers to deduce a false cause-effect relationship.

This illustration is not presented to discredit this type of cancer research. Substantial evidence does seem to suggest a significant relationship. Laboratory experiments have supported the relationship between the

[46]Janet M. Rogers, "Summary of Literature on Sesame Street," *Journal of Special Education* 6 (Spring 1972): 27–42.

coal-tar products that are distilled from cigarette combustion and malignant growth in animals. The association explanation, however, is one that should always be examined carefully.

Ex post facto research is widely and appropriately used, particularly in the behavioral sciences. In education, since it is impossible, impracticable, or unthinkable to manipulate such variables as aptitude, intelligence, personality traits, cultural deprivation, teacher competence, and some variables that might present an unacceptable threat to human beings, this method will continue to be used.

However, its limitations should be recognized:

1. The independent variables cannot be manipulated.
2. Subjects cannot be randomly assigned to treatment groups.
3. Causes are often multiple rather than single.

Since there is a danger of confusing symptoms with causes, *ex post facto* research should test not one, but all other logical alternate or competing hypotheses. Properly employed and cautiously interpreted, it will continue to provide a useful methodology for the development of knowledge.

Students who have completed a course in research methods should be sensitive to the operation of extraneous variables that threaten the validity of conclusions. In "Educational Piltdown Men," Gene V Glass[47] cautions educators of the need for critical analysis of reported research. He cites a number of interesting examples of carelessly conducted studies that resulted in completely false conclusions. Unfortunately, these conclusions were accepted by gullible readers and widely reported in popular periodicals and some educational psychology textbooks.

The author trusts that the experience of the introductory course in educational research will help students and educators to read research reports more carefully and to apply more rigorous standards of judgment.

Exercises

1. Why is it sometimes difficult to distinguish between an assessment study, an evaluation study, and a descriptive research project? Illustrate with an example.
2. Public opinion polls base their conclusions on a sample of approximately 1500 respondents. Is this an adaquate sample for a nationwide survey?

[47]Gene V Glass, "Educational Piltdown Men," *Phi Delta Kappan* 50 (November 1968): 148–151.

3. In a 1974 study, the West Virginia State Department of Education reported that counties with the highest per-pupil expenditure were the counties with the highest level of academic achievement, and that this "shows for the first time the clearest possible relationship between student achievement and the amount of money invested in the public schools." Can you suggest several competing hypotheses that might account for high academic achievement?

4. The Eight Year Study has been criticized for inadequate control of the independent variable. What may be the weakness of the research design?

5. What is the difference between a study and a research project?

6. In what ways do conducting longitudinal studies run the risk of the violation of confidentiality of personal information?

7. How can a study of money and investment trends help you provide for your future financial security?

8. Draw up a proposal for a follow-up study of your high school graduating class of five years ago. Indicate what information you believe would be helpful in improving the curriculum of the school.

9. Of what value are the findings of the annual Gallup poll of public attitudes toward education?

10. How could the survey type of study be helpful in arriving at solutions to the crime problem in large cities?

Bibliography

AHMANN, J. STANLEY ET AL. "Science Achievement: The Trend Is Down." *Science Teacher* 42 (September 1975): 23–25.

ANDERSON, C. ARNOLD. "The International Comparative Study of Achievement in Mathematics." *Comparative Education Review* 11 (June 1967): 182–196.

BACKSTROM, CHARLES H. and GERALD D. HURSH. *Survey Research.* Evanston, Ill.: Northwestern University Press, 1963.

BRANSCOMBE, ART. "Checkout on Consumer Mathematics." *American Education* 11 (October 1975): 21–24.

CHALL, JEANNE. *Learning to Read: The Great Debate.* New York: McGraw-Hill Book Co., 1967.

COLEMAN, JAMES S. ET AL. *Equality of Educational Opportunity.* Washington, D.C.: U.S. Office of Education, Government Printing Office, 1966.

COLEMAN, JAMES S. "International Assessment for Evaluation of Schools." *Review of Educational Research* 45 (Summer 1975): 355–386.

COLEMAN, JAMES S. "Racial Segregation in the Schools: New Research With New Policy Implications." *Phi Delta Kappan* 57 (October 1975): 75–77.

COLEMAN, JAMES S. "Social Research and Advocacy: A Response to Young and Bress." *Phi Delta Kappan* 57 (November 1975): 66–69.

COMBS, JANET and WILLIAM W. COOLEY. "Dropouts: In High School and after School." *American Educational Research Journal* 5 (May 1968): 343–363.

COOPER, DAN. "School Surveys." *Encyclopedia of Educational Research* (1960) 1211–1216.

DILLON, HAROLD J. *Early School Leavers.* New York: National Child Labor Committee, 1949.

ENNIS, ROBERT H. "On Causality." *Educational Researcher* 2 (June 1973): 4–16.

FLANNIGAN, JOHN C. *The American High School Student.* Pittsburgh: Project Talent Office, 1964.

GLASS, GENE V "Educational Piltdown Men." *Phi Delta Kappan* (November 1968): 148–151.

GLASS, GENE V and BLAINE R. WORTHEN. "Educational Evaluation and Research: Similarities and Differences." *Curriculum Theory Network* (Fall 1971).

GLASS, GENE V and BLAINE R. WORTHEN. "Educational Inquiry and the Practice of Education," in *Conceptual Frameworks for Viewing Educational Research: Development, Dissemination and Evaluation,* H. D. Schalock and G. R. Sell, eds. Monmouth, Ore.: Oregon College of Education, 1972.

GREELEY, ANDREW M. and PETER H. ROSSI. *The Education of Catholic Americans.* Chicago: Aldine Publishing Co., 1966.

HENDERSON, KENNETH B. and JOHN E. GOERWITZ. *How to Conduct a Follow-up Study.* Illinois Secondary School Curriculum Program Bulletin No. 11, Springfield, Ill.: Superintendent of Public Instruction, 1950.

HESS, ROBERT D. and JUDITH V. TORNEY. *The Development of Political Attitudes in Children.* Chicago: Aldine Publishing Co., 1967.

HIRSCHI, TRAVIS and HANAN C. SELVIN. *Delinquency Research: An Appraisal of Analytical Methods.* New York: Free Press, 1967.

HUSÉN, TORSTEN, ed. *International Study of Achievement in Mathematics.* 2 vols. New York: John Wiley & Sons, 1967.

HYMAN, HERBERT H. *Survey Design and Analysis.* Beverly Hills, Calif.: Glencoe Press, 1955.

International Association for the Evaluation of Educational Achievement. "Bibliography of Publications, 1962–1974." *Comparative Education Review* 18 (June 1974): 327–329.

LESSER, GERALD S. *Children Learn Lessons from Sesame Street.* New York: Random House, 1974.

MELLON, JOHN C. *National Assessment and the Teaching of English.* Urbana, Ill.: National Council of Teachers of English, 1974.

MINTON, J. H. "Impact of Sesame Street on Reading Readiness." *Sociology of Education* 48 (Spring 1975): 141–145.

MOSTELLER, FREDERICK and DANIEL P. MOYNIHAN, eds. *On Equality of Educational Opportunity: Papers Deriving from the Harvard Faculty Seminar on the Coleman Report.* New York: Random House, Vintage Books, 1972.

National Association of Science. *A Capsule Description of Changes in Science Achievement.* Science Report 04500. Washington, D.C.: Government Printing Office, 1975.

NEUWEIN, REGINALD A., ed. *Catholic Schools in Action: The Notre Dame Study of Catholic Elementary and Secondary Schools in the United States.* Notre Dame, Ind.: University of Notre Dame Press, 1966.

POLSKY, RICHARD M. *Getting to Sesame Street.* New York: Praeger, 1974.

POPHAM, W. JAMES. *Educational Evaluation.* Englewood Cliffs, N.J.: Prentice-Hall, 1975.

RAPH, JANE B., MERIAM L. GOLDBERG, and A. HARRY PASSOW. *Bright Underachievers: Studies of Scholastic Underachievement among Intellectually Superior High School Students.* New York: Teachers College Press, 1966.

ROGERS, JANET M. "A Summary of Literature on Sesame Street." *Journal of Special Education* 6 (Spring 1972): 270–272.

RYANS, DAVID G. *Characteristics of Teachers: Their Description, Comparison, and Appraisal.* Washington, D.C.: American Council on Education, 1966.

ST. JOHN, NANCY. *School Desegregation: Outcomes for Children.* New York: John Wiley & Sons, 1975.

VANDERMYN, GAYE. "Assessing Students' Political IQ.", *American Education* 10 (June 1974): 21–25.

WORTHEN, BLAINE R. and JAMES R. SANDERS. *Educational Evaluation: Theory and Practice.* Worthington, Ohio: Charles A. Jones Publishing Co., 1973.

YOUNG, BILOINE W. and GRACE B. BRESS. "Coleman's Retreat and the Politics of Good Intentions." *Phi Delta Kappan* 57 (November 1975): 159–166.

THE TOOLS
OF
RESEARCH

Chapter 6

To carry out any of the types of research investigation described in the three preceding chapters, data are gathered with which the hypothesis may be tested. A great variety of research tools has been developed to aid in the acquisition of data. These tools are of many kinds and employ distinctive ways of describing and quantifying the data. Each tool is particularly appropriate for certain sources of data, yielding information of the kind and in the form that would be most effectively used.

Many writers have argued the superiority of the interview over the questionnaire, or the use of the psychological test over the interview. The late Arvil S. Barr, University of Wisconsin teacher and researcher, resolved discussions of this sort by asking, "Which is better, a hammer or a handsaw?" Like the tools in the carpenter's chest, each is appropriate in a given situation.

Many behavioral researchers feel that there is too much dependence upon single methods of inquiry. Because each type of data-gathering device has its own particular bias, there is merit in supplementing one with another to counteract bias and generate more adequate data. Students of research should familiarize themselves with each of these tools of research and attempt to develop skill in their use and application.

The general category of inquiry forms includes data-gathering instruments through which respondents answer questions or respond to statements in writing. A questionnaire is used when factual information is desired. When opinions rather than facts are desired, an opinionnaire or attitude scale is used.

The questionnaire

Questionnaires administered personally to groups of individuals have a number of advantages. The person administering the instrument has an opportunity to establish rapport, to explain the purpose of the study, and to explain the meaning of items that may not be clear. The availability of a number of respondents in one place makes possible an economy of time and expense and provides a high proportion of usabie responses. It is likely that a principal would get completely usable responses from teachers in his building, or a teacher from students in the classroom. However, individuals who have the desired information cannot always be contacted personally without the expenditure of a great deal of time and money in travel. It is in such situations that the mailed questionnaire may make a useful contribution. The mailed questionnaire is probably both the most used and most criticized data-gathering device. It has been referred to as the lazy man's way of gaining information, although the careful preparation of a good questionnaire takes a great deal of time, ingenuity, and hard work. There is little doubt that the poorly constructed questionnaires that flood the mails have created a certain amount of contempt. This is particularly true when the accompanying letter pleads that the sender needs the information to complete the requirements for a graduate course, a thesis, or a dissertation. The recipient's reaction may be, "Why should I go to all this trouble to help this person get his degree?"

Filling out lengthy questionnaires takes a great deal of time and effort, a favor that few senders have any right to expect of strangers. The unfavorable reaction is intensified when the questionnaire is long, the subject trivial in importance, the items vaguely worded, and the form poorly organized. The unfavorable characteristics of so many questionnaires help to explain why so small a proportion of mailed questionnaires are returned. As a result of this sparse response, often as low as 40 percent to 50 percent, the data obtained are often of limited validity. The information in the unreturned questionnaires might have changed the results of the investigation materially. The very fact of no response might imply certain types of reactions, reactions that can never be included in the summary of data.

Unless one is dealing with a group of respondents who have a genuine interest in the problem under investigation, who know the sender, or who have some common bond of loyalty to a sponsoring institution or organization, the rate of returns is frequently disappointing, and provides a flimsy basis for generalization.

Although the foregoing discussion may seem to discredit the questionnaire as a respectable research technique, the attempt has been to consider the abuse or misuse of the device. Actually, the questionnaire has unique advantages and, properly constructed and admisistered, it may serve as a most appropriate and useful data-gathering device in a research project.

THE CLOSED FORM

Questionnaires that call for short, check responses are known as the *restricted*, or *closed-from*, type. They provide for marking a *yes* or *no*, a short response, or checking an item from a list of suggested responses. The following example illustrates the closed-form item:

Why did you choose to do your graduate work at this university? Kindly indicate three reasons in order of importance, using number 1 for the most important, 2 for the 2nd most important, and 3 for the 3rd most important.

	Rank
(a) Convenience of transportation	_____
(b) Advice of a friend	_____
(c) Reputation of institution	_____
(d) Expense factor	_____
(e) Scholarship aid	_____
(f) Other _____	_____
(kindly specify)	

Even when using the closed form, it is well to provide for unanticipated responses. Providing an "other" category permits the respondent to indicate what might be his most important reason, one that the questionnaire builder had not anticipated. Note the instruction "(kindly specify)," which enables the tabulator to properly classify all responses.

For certain types of information the closed-form qustionnaire is entirely satisfactory. It is easy to fill out, takes little time, keeps the respondent on the subject, is relatively objective, and is fairly easy to tabulate and analyze.

THE OPEN FORM

The *open-form*, or *unrestricted*, type of questionnaire calls for a free response in the respondent's own words. The following open-form item seeks the same type of information as previous closed-form item:

Why did you choose to take your graduate work at this university?

Note that no clues are given. The open form probably provides for greater depth of response. The respondent reveals his frame of reference and possibly the reasons for his responses. Since it requires greater effort on the part of the respondent, returns are often meager. This type of item is sometimes difficult to interpret, tabulate, and summarize in the research report.

Many questionnaires include both open- and closed-type items. Each type has its merits and limitations, and the questionnaire builder must decide which type is more likely to supply the information he wants.

Improving questionnaire items

Inexperienced questionnaire makers are likely to be naïve about the clarity of their questions. The author recalls a brilliant graduate student who submitted a questionnaire for the professor's approval. She seemed somewhat irritated and impatient at the subsequent questions and suggestions, and remarked that anyone with any degree of intelligence should know what she meant. At the advisor's suggestion she duplicated some copies and personally administered the questionnaire to a graduate class in research.

She was literally swamped with questions of interpretation, many that she could not answer clearly. There was considerable evidence of confusion about what she wanted to know. After she had collected the completed copies and had tried to tabulate the responses, she began to see the questionnaire's faults. Even her directions and explanation in class had failed to clarify the ambiguous intent of her questionnaire. Her second version was a much-improved instrument.

Many beginning researchers aren't really sure what they want to know. They use a shotgun approach, attempting to cover their field broadly in the hope that some of the responses will provide the answers for which they are groping. Unless the researcher knows exactly what he wants, however, he is not likely to ask the right questions, or to phrase them properly.

In addition to the problem of knowing what he wants, there is the difficulty of wording the questionnaire clearly. The limitations of words are particular hazards in the questionnaire. The same words mean different things to different people. The questionnaire maker has his own interpretation—the respondents may have many different interpretations. In the interview, or in conversation, we are able to clear up misunderstanding by restating our question, by inflection of the voice, by suggestions, and by a number of other devices. But the written question stands by itself, often ambiguous and misunderstood.

A simple example illustrates the influence of voice inflection alone. Consider the following question. Read it over, each time emphasizing the underlined word, noting how the change in inflection alters the meaning.

Were you there last night?
Were you there last night?
Were you there last night?
Were you there last night?
Were you there last night?

The questionnaire maker must depend on written language alone. It is apparent that he cannot be too careful in phrasing questions to insure their clarity of purpose. Although there are no certain ways of producing foolproof questions, certain principles can be employed to make items more precise. A few are suggested here, with the hope that students constructing questionnaires and opinionnaires will become critical of their first efforts and strive to make each item as clear as possible.

Define or qualify terms that could easily be misinterpreted.

What is the value of your house?

The meaning of the term *value* is not clear. It could mean the assessed value for tax purposes, what it would sell for on the present market, what you would be willing to sell it for, what it would cost to replace, or what you paid for it. These values may differ considerably. It is essential to frame specific questions such as, "What is the present market value of your house?"

As simple a term as *age* is often misunderstood. When is an individual 21? Most people would say that a person is 21 for the day of his twenty-first birthday until the day of his twenty-second. An insurance company would consider him 21 from the twenty-year, six-months date until the twenty-first-year, six-months date. Perhaps this question could be clarified by asking *age to nearest birthday*, or *date of birth*.

Hundreds of words are ambiguous because of their many interpretations. One has only to think of such words and phrases as *curriculum, democracy, progressive education, cooperation,* and *integration*—even such simple words as *how much* and *now.* To the question, "What work are you doing now?" the respondent might be tempted to answer, "Filling out your foolish questionnaire."

Be careful in using descriptive adjectives and adverbs that have no agreed-upon meaning. This fault is frequently found in rating scales as well as in questionnaires. *Frequently, occasionally,* and *rarely* do not have the same meanings to different persons.[1] One respondent's *occasionally* may be another's *rarely.* Perhaps a stated frequency—*times per week, times per month*—would make this classification more precise.

Beware of double negatives. Underline negatives for clarity.

Are you opposed to not requiring students to take showers after gym class? Federal aid should not be granted to those states in which education is not equal regardless of race, creed, or color.

Be careful of inadequate alternatives.

Married?   Yes_____ No_____

Does this question refer to present or former marital status? How would the person answer who is widowed, separated, or divorced?

How late at night do you permit your children to watch television?

There may be no established family policy. If there is a policy, it may differ for children of different ages. It may be different for school nights, or for Friday and Satuday nights when the late, late show may be permitted.

Avoid the double-barreled question.

Do you believe that gifted students should be placed in separate groups for instructional purposes and assigned to special schools?

One might agree on the advisability of separate groups for instructional purposes, but be very much opposed to the assignment of gifted students to special schools. Two questions are needed.

Underline a word if you wish to indicate special emphasis.

A parent should not be told his child's IQ score.
Should all schools offer a modern foreign language?

When asking for ratings or comparisons a point of reference is necessary.

[1]Milton D. Hakel, "How Often is Often?" *American Psychologist* 23 (July 1968): 533–534.

How would you rate this student teacher's classroom teaching?
Superior_____ Average_____ Below Average_____

With whom is the student teacher to be compared—an experienced teacher, other student teachers, former student teachers—or should the criterion be what a student teacher is expected to be able to do?

Avoid unwarranted assumptions.

Are you satisfied with the salary raise that you received last year?

A *no* answer might mean that I didn't get a raise, or that I did get a raise, but I'm not satisfied.

Do you feel that you benefited from the spankings that you received as a child?

A *no* response might mean that the spankings did not help me, or that my parents did not administer corporal punishment. These unwarranted assumptions are nearly as bad as the classic, "Have you stopped beating your wife?"

Phrase questions so that they are appropriate for all respondents.

What is your monthly teaching salary?

Some teachers are paid on a nine-month basis, some ten, some eleven, and some twelve. Three questions would be needed.

Your salary per month? _____
Number of months in school term? _____
Number of salary payments per year? _____

Design questions that will give a complete response.

Do you read the *Indianapolis Star?* Yes_____ No_____

A *yes* or *no* answer would not reveal much information about the reading habits of the respondent. The question might be followed with an additional item, as in Figure 6.1.

Provide for the systematic quantification of responses. One type of question that asks respondents to check a number of items from a list is difficult to summarize, especially if all respondents do not check the same

If your answer is *Yes*, kindly check *how often* and *what sections* of the *Star* you read.

SECTION	ALWAYS	USUALLY	SELDOM	NEVER
National and international news				
State and local news				
Editorial				
Sports				
Comic				
Society				
Financial				
Advertising				
Want Ad				
Syndicated features				
Special features				
Other (specify)				

FIGURE 6–1

number. One solution is to ask respondents to rank, in order of preference, a specific number of responses.

What are your favorite television programs? Rank in order of preference your first, second, third, fourth, and fifth choices.

The items can then be tabulated by inverse weightings.

1st choice	5 points
2nd choice	4 points
3rd choice	3 points
4th choice	2 points
5th choice	1 point

The relative populatity of the programs could be described for a group in terms of total weighted scores, the most popular having the largest total.

Consider the possibility of classifying the responses yourself, rather than having the respondent choose categories.   If a student were asked to classify his father's occupation in one of the following categories, the results might be quite unsatisfactory.

Unskilled labor	_____
Skilled labor	_____
Clerical work	_____
Managerial work	_____
Profession	_____
Proprietorship	_____

It is likely that by asking the child one or two short questions about his father's work, it could be classified more accurately.

1. At what place does your father work?
2. What kind of work does he do?

The student should bear in mind these few suggestions in constructing questionnaire items. There is no recipe or set of easy directions. It is a difficult job, one that requires a great deal of hard work, imagination, and ingenuity. (See reference by Stanley Payne listed in chapter bibliography.)

TEACHER MORALE QUESTIONNAIRE

1. Male _____ Female _____
2. Age _____
3. Marital status: single _____ married _____ divorced/separated _____ widowed _____
4. Number of dependent children _____; their ages _____
5. Number of other dependents _____
6. Highest degree held _____
7. Years of teaching experience _____
8. Years of teaching at present school _____
9. Teaching level; primary _____ intermediate _____ upper grades _____ Jr. H.S. _____ Sr. H.S. _____; If secondary, your major teaching area _____
10. Enrollment of your school _____
11. Your average class size _____
12. Population of your community or school district _____
13. Your principal is: male _____ female _____

In the following questions kindly check the appropriate column:

a. *excellent* b. *good* c. *fair* d. *poor*

	a	b	c	d

14. How does your salary schedule compare with those of similar school districts?

15. How would you rate your principal on these traits?

competence
friendliness
helpfulness
ability to inspire

16. How would you rate the consulting or advisory services that you receive?

encourage creativity
availability

17. Provision made for teacher free time

relaxation
preparation
lunch
conferences

18. How would you rate your faculty lounge?

19. How would you rate your faculty professional library?

books
periodicals
references

20. How would you evaluate the adequacy of teaching materials and supplies?

textbooks
references
AV aids
supplies

21. How would you evaluate the assignment of your nonteaching duties? (leave blank if item *does not apply*)

reports
meetings
halls
lunchroom
supervision of: { playground
study hall
extra-class
organizations

22. How would you rate the compatibility of your faculty?
23. How would you rate the parent support of your school?
24. How would you rate your morale as a teacher?
25. Kindly *rank in order of importance to you* at least *five* factors that you would consider most important in increasing your morale or satisfaction

with your working conditions: Rank 1, most important, 2 next in importance, etc.

_____ a. higher salary

_____ b. smaller class size

_____ c. more free time

_____ d. more adequate faculty lounge

_____ e. more compatible faculty

_____ f. more adequate teaching materials

_____ g. more effective principal

_____ h. better consulting services

_____ i. more effective faculty meetings

_____ j. assistance of a teacher aide

_____ k. more attractive classroom/building

_____ l. fewer reports to make out

_____ m. fewer nonteaching duties

_____ n. better provision for atypical students

_____ o. more participation in policy making

_____ p. fewer committee meetings

_____ q. teaching in a higher socioeconomic area

_____ r. teaching in a lower socioeconomic area

_____ s. other (kindly specify)

On the back of this sheet kindly add any comments that you believe would more adequately express your feelings of satisfaction or dissatisfaction with teaching.

FIGURE 6–2   Teacher Morale Questionnaire

CHARACTERISTICS OF A GOOD QUESTIONNAIRE

1. It deals with a significant topic, one the respondent will recognize as important enough to warrant spending his time on. The significance should be clearly and carefully stated on the questionnaire, or in the letter that accompanies it.
2. It seeks only that information which cannot be obtained from other sources such as school reports or census data.
3. It is as short as possible, only long enough to get the essential data. Long questionnaires frequently find their way into the wastebasket.
4. It is attractive in appearance, neatly arranged, and clearly duplicated or printed.
5. Directions are clear and complete, important terms are defined, each question deals with a single idea, all questions are worded as simply and as clearly as possible, and the categories provide an opportunity for easy, accurate, and unambiguous responses.
6. The questions are objective, with no leading suggestions as to the responses desired. Leading questions are just as inappropriate on a questionnaire as they are in a court of law.
7. Questions are presented in good psychological order, proceeding from general to more specific responses. This order helps the respondent to organize his own thinking, so that his answers are logical and objective. It may be well

to present questions that create a favorable attitude before proceeding to those that may be a bit delicate or intimate. If possible, annoying or embarrassing questions should be avoided.

8. It is easy to tabulate and interpret. It is advisable to preconstruct a tabulation sheet, anticipating how the data will be tabulated and interpreted, before the final form of the question is decided upon. This working backward from a visualization of the final analysis of data is an important step in avoiding ambiguity in questionnaire form.

If mechanical tabulating equipment is to be used, it is important to allow code numbers for all possible responses to permit easy transference to machine-tabulation cards.

PREPARING AND ADMINISTERING THE QUESTIONNAIRE

1. Get all the help you can in planning and constructing your questionnaire. Study other questionnaires, and submit your items for criticism to other members of your class or your faculty, especially to those who have had experience in questionnaire construction.

2. In the process of designing an inquiry form (questionnaire or opinionnaire) it is advisable to use a separate card or slip for each item. As the instrument is being developed items may be refined, revised, or replaced by better items without recopying the entire instrument. This procedure also provides desirable flexibility in arranging items in the most appropriate psychological order before the instrument is finally transferred to the stencil or ditto sheet for duplication.

3. Try out your questionnaire on a few friends and acquaintances. When you do this personally, you may find that a number of your items are ambiguous. What may seem perfectly clear to you may be confusing to a person who does not have the frame of reference that you have gained from living with and thinking about an idea over a long period.

    This "dry run" will be well worth the time and effort it takes. It may reveal defects that can be corrected before the final form is printed and committed to the mails. Once the instrument has been sent out, it is too late to remedy its defects.

4. Choose respondents carefully. It is important that questionnaires be sent only to those who possess the desired information—those who are likely to be sufficiently interested to respond conscientiously and objectively. A preliminary card, asking whether the individual would be willing to participate in the proposed study, is recommended by some research authorities. This is not only a courteous approach, but a practical way of discovering those who will cooperate in furnishing the desired information.

    In a study on questionnaire returns Harold W. See[2] discovered that a greater proportion of returns was obtained when the original request was sent to the administrative head of an organization, rather than directly to the person who had the desired information. It is possible that when a superior officer turns over a questionnaire to a staff member to fill out, there is an implied feeling of obligation.

[2]Harold W. See, "Send It to The President," *Phi Delta Kappan* 38 (January 1957): 130.

5. If questionnaires are planned for use in a public school, asking for the responses of teachers or pupils, it is essential that approval of the project be secured from the principal, who may then wish to secure approval from the superintendent of schools. Schools are understandably sensitive to public relations. One can understand the possibilities of unfavorable publicity that may result from certain types of studies made by individuals not officially designated to conduct research.

   School officials may also want to prevent the exploitation of teachers and pupils by amateur researchers, whose activities would require an excessive amount of time and effort in activities not related to the purposes of the school.

6. If the desired information is delicate or intimate in nature, consider the possibility of providing for anonymous responses. The anonymous instrument is most likely to produce objective responses. There are occasions, however, for purposes of classification, when the identity of the respondent is necessary. If a signature is needed, it is essential to convince the respondent that his responses will be held in strict confidence, and that his answers will in no way jeopardize the status and security of his position.

7. Try to get the aid of sponsorship. Recipients are more likely to answer if a person, organization, or institution of prestige has endorsed the project. Of course, it is unethical to claim sponsorship unless it has been expressly given.

8. Be sure to include a courteous, carefully constructed cover letter to explain the purpose of the study. The letter should promise some sort of inducement to the respondent for compliance with the request. Commercial agencies furnish rewards in goods or money. In educational circles a summary of questionnaire results is considered an appropriate reward, a promise that should be scrupulously honored after the study has been completed.

   The cover letter should assure the respondent that delicate information will be held in strict confidence. The explanation of sponsorship might well be mentioned. Of course, a stamped, addressed return envelope should be included. To omit this courtesy would be practically to guarantee that many of the questionnaires would go into the wastebasket. It has been suggested that two copies of the questionnaire be sent, one to be returned when completed, and the other for the respondent's own file.

9. Recipients are often slow to return completed questionnaires. To increase the number of returns, a vigorous follow-up procedure may be necessary. A courteous post card reminding the recipient that the completed questionnaire has not been received will bring in some additional responses. This reminder will be effective with those who have just put off or forgotten to fill out or mail the document. A further step in the follow-up process may involve a personal letter of reminder. In extreme cases a telegram, phone call, or personal visit may bring additional responses.

   It is difficult to estimate, in the abstract, what percentage of questionnaire responses is to be considered adequate or satisfactory. The importance of the project, the quality of the questionnaire, the care used in selecting recipients, the time of year, and many other factors may be significant in determining the proportion of responses. In general, the smaller the percentage of responses, the smaller the degree of confidence one may place in the adequacy of the data collected. Of course, objectivity of reporting requires that the proportion of responses received should always be included in the research report.

Questionnaires play an important part in educational research. The American Association of School Administrators and the Research Division of the National Education Association publish an annual bibliography, *Questionnaire Studies Completed.*[3] This report, published annually since 1937, provides educators with an alphabetized list of topics covered and a short abstract of each study. These studies deal with all phases of education, including such topics as school finance, teaching methods, personnel, transportation, curriculum, and legal aspects.

The opinionnaire, or attitude scale

The information form that attempts to measure the attitude or belief of an individual is known as an *opinionnaire*, or *attitude scale*. Since the terms *opinion* and *attitude* are not synonymous, a clarification is necessary.

How an individual feels, or what he believes, is his attitude. But it is difficult, if not impossible, to describe and measure attitude. The researcher must depend upon what the individual *says* are his beliefs and feelings. This is the area of opinion. Through the use of questions, or by getting an individual's expressed reaction to statements, a sample of his opinion is obtained. From this statement of opinion may be inferred or estimated his attitude—what he *really* believes.

The process of inferring attitude from expressed opinion has many limitations. An individual may conceal his real attitude, and express socially acceptable opinions. An individual may not really know how he feels about a social issue. He may never have given the idea serious consideration. An individual may be unable to know his attitude about a situation in the abstract. Until confronted with a real situation, he may be unable to predict his reaction or behavior.

Even behavior itself is not always a true indication of attitude. When politicians kiss babies, their behavior may not be a true expression of affection towards infants. Social custom or the desire for social approval make many overt expressions of behavior mere formalities, quite unrelated to the inward feelings of the individual. Even though there is no sure method of describing and measuring attitude, the description and measurement of opinion, in many instances, may be closely related to the real feeling or attitude of an individual.

With these limitations in mind, psychologists and sociologists have explored an interesting area of research, basing their data upon the expressed opinions of individuals. Several methods have been employed:

[3]National Education Association, Research Division, and American Association of School Administrators, *Questionnaire Studies Completed* (Washington, D.C.: The Association) 1937–date.

1. Asking the individual directly how he feels about a subject. This technique may employ a schedule or questionnaire of the open or closed form. It may employ the interview process, in which the respondent expresses his opinions orally.
2. Asking the individual to check in a list the statements with which he is in agreement.
3. Asking the individual to indicate his degree of agreement or disagreement with a series of statements about a controversial subject.
4. Inferring his attitude from his reaction to projective devices, through which he may reveal his attitude unconsciously. (A projective device is a data-gathering instrument which conceals its purpose in such a way that the subject cannot guess how he should respond to appear in his best light. Thus, his real characteristics are revealed.)

Two of these procedures have been used extensively in opinion research, and warrant a brief description.

THURSTONE TECHNIQUE

The first method of attitude assessment is known as the Thurstone Technique of Scaled Values.[4] A number of statements, usually twenty or more, that express various points of view toward a group, institution, idea, or practice are gathered. They are then submitted to a panel of a number of judges, who each arranges them in eleven groups, ranging from one extreme to another in position. This sorting by each judge yields a composite position for each of the items. When there has been marked disagreement between the judges in assigning a position to an item, that item is discarded. For items that are retained, each is given its median scale value, between one and eleven, as established by the panel.

The list of statements is then given to the subjects, who are asked to check the statements with which they are in agreement. The median value of the statements that they check establishes their score, or quantifies their opinion.

LIKERT METHOD

The second method, the Likert Method of Summated Ratings, which can be carried out without the panel of judges, has yielded scores very similar to those obtained by the Thurstone method. The coefficient of correlation between the scales was reported as high as +.92 in one study.[5] Since the Likert-type scale takes much less time to construct, it offers an interesting possibility for the student of opinion research.

The first step in constructing a Likert-type scale consists of collecting a number of statements about a subject. The correctness of the statements is not important. If they express opinions held by a substantial number of

[4]L. L. Thurstone and E. J. Chave, *The Measurement of Attitudes* (Chicago: University of Chicago Press, 1929).

[5]Allen L. Edwards and Katherine C. Kenney, "A Comparison of the Thurstone and Likert Techniques of Attitude Scale Construction," *Journal of Applied Psychology* 30 (February 1946): 72–83.

people, they may be used. It is important that they express definite favorableness or unfavorableness to a particular point of view. The number of favorable and unfavorable statements should be approximately equal.

After the statements have been gathered, a trial test should be administered to a number of subjects. Only those items that correlate with the total test should be retained. This testing for internal consistency will help to eliminate statements that are ambiguous or that are not of the same type as the rest of the scale.

The attitude or opinion scale may be analyzed in several ways. The simplest way to describe opinion is to indicate percentage responses for each individual statement. For this type of analysis by item, three responses are preferable to the usual five: agree, undecided, and disagree. If a Likert-type scale is used it may be possible to report percentage responses by combining the two outside categories: strongly agree and agree; disagree and strongly disagree.

strongly agree	undecided	disagree
agree		strongly disagree

For example, 70 percent of the male respondents agree with the statement, "Merit rating will tend to encourage conformity and discourage initiative."

LIKERT SCALE

The Likert scaling technique assigns a scale value to each of the five responses. Thus, the instrument yields a total score for each respondent, and a discussion of each individual item, while possible, is not necessary. Starting with a particular point of view, all statements favoring this position would be scored:

	Scale value
a. strongly agree	5
b. agree	4
c. undecided	3
d. disagree	2
e. strongly disagree	1

For statements opposing this point of view, the items are scored in the opposite order:

	Scale value
a. strongly agree	1
b. agree	2
c. undecided	3
d. disagree	4
e. strongly disagree	5

OPINIONNAIRE

The following statements represent opinions, and your agreement or disagreement will be determined on the basis of your particular beliefs. Kindly check your position on the scale as the statement first impresses you. Indicate what you believe, rather than what you think you should believe.

    a. I strongly agree
    b. I agree
    c. I am undecided.
    d. I disagree
    e. I strongly disagree

	a	b	c	d	e

1. Heaven does *not* exist as an actual place or location.
2. God sometimes sets aside natural law, performing miracles.
3. Jesus was born of a virgin, without a human father.
4. Hell does *not* exist as an actual place or location.
5. The inspiration that resulted in the writing of the Bible was no different from that of any other great religious literature.
6. There is a final day of judgment for all who have lived on earth.
7. The devil exists as an actual person.
8. Prayer directly affects the lives of persons, whether or not they know that such prayer has been offered.
9. There is another life after the end of organic life on earth.
10. When on earth, Jesus possessed and used the power to restore the dead to life.
11. God is a cosmic force, rather than an actual person.
12. Prayer does *not* have the power to change such conditions as a drought.
13. The creation of the world did *not* literally occur in the way described in the Old Testament.
14. After Jesus was dead and buried, he actually rose from the dead, leaving an empty tomb.
15. Everything in the Bible should be interpreted as literally true.

FIGURE 6–3   A Likert-type Opinionnaire

The opinionnaire illustrated in Figure 6.3 attempts to measure religious orthodoxy or conservatism. It is apparent that this type of instrument could be used to measure opinion in many controversial areas: racial integration, merit rating of teachers, universal military training, and many others.

The test scores obtained on all the items would then measure the respondent's favorableness toward the given point of view.

MERIT RATING OPINIONNAIRE

Male _____ Female _____ Age _____
Teaching level: elementary _____ secondary _____
Marital status: single _____ married _____ divorced/separated _____
widowed _____
Years of teaching experience _____ years.

The following statements represent opinions, and your agreement or dis-
agreement will be determined on the basis of your particular convictions.
Kindly check your position on the scale as the statement first impresses you.
Indicate what you believe, rather than what you think you should believe.

    a. I strongly agree
    b. I agree
    c. I am undecided
    d. I disagree
    e. I strongly disagree

	a	b	c	d	e
1. It is possible to determine what constitutes merit, or effective teaching. _____					
2. A valid and reliable instrument can be developed to measure varying degrees of teaching effectiveness. __					
3. Additional remuneration will *not* result in improved teaching. _____					
4. Merit rating destroys the morale of the teaching force by creating jealousy, suspicion, and distrust._____					
5. Mutual confidence between teachers and administrators is impossible if administrators rate teachers for salary purposes. _____					
6. Merit salary schedules will attract more high-quality young people to the teaching profession. _____					
7. Merit salary schedules will hold quality teachers in the profession. _____					
8. Parents will object to having their children taught by nonmerit teachers. _____					
9. Merit rating can be as successful in teaching as it is in industry. _____					
10. The hidden purpose of merit rating is to hold down salaries paid to most teachers by paying only a few teachers well. _____					
11. There is no justification for paying poor teachers as well as good teachers are paid. _____					
12. Apple-polishers will profit more than superior teachers from merit rating. _____					
13. Merit rating will encourage conformity and discourage initiative. _____					
14. The way to make teaching attractive is to reward excellence in the classroom. _____					
15. Most administrators do *not* know enough about teaching to rate their faculty members fairly. _____					
16. Salary schedules based on education and experience only encourage mediocre teaching. _____					

FIGURE 6–4   A Likert-type Opinionnaire on Merit Rating

If the opinionnaire consisted of 30 statements or items, the following score values would be revealing:

$$30 \times 5 = 150 \quad \text{Most favorable response possible}$$
$$30 \times 3 = 90 \quad \text{A neutral attitude}$$
$$30 \times 1 = 30 \quad \text{Most unfavorable attitude}$$

The scores for any individual would fall between 30 and 150; above 90, if opinions tended to be favorable, and below 90, if opinions tended to be unfavorable to the given point of view.

The author has used this device in a course which includes a unit dealing with intercultural relations. It is interesting to note whether information about minority groups tends to alter an individual's attitude or opinion toward those groups. Before the unit is begun, the students respond to a 30-statement opinionnaire devised by the author. The papers are filled out anonymously, and each student is instructed to mark his paper with some symbol known only to him, so that he can identify it at a later date.

Upon the completion of the unit several weeks later, the students respond to another copy of the same opinionnaire, again marking it with the symbol previously used. After the papers are scored, the instructor has a device which indicates possible changes in attitude or, at least, in expressed opinions. Invariably, there has been consistent growth in favorableness toward minority groups. Although the measure is crude, it does seem to support the hypothesis that knowledge about minority groups brings about a more favorable attitude toward them—in the classroom, at least. It is possible that the change in score is more significant than the magnitude of the score itself, for the validity of the instrument has not been, and cannot be, established.

This example of opinion analysis demonstrates how a teacher may use this technique to create class interest, even though it may fail to achieve the rigorous standards of fundamental research procedures.

It would be unwise to conclude this discussion without a recognition of the limitations of this type of opinion measurement. Obviously, it is somewhat inexact, and fails to measure opinion with the precision one would desire.

There is no basis for belief that the five positions indicated on the scale are equally spaced. The interval between "tend to agree" and "agree" may not be equal to the interval between "tend to agree" and "cannot say." It is also unlikely that the statements are of equal value in "for-ness" or "against-ness." That the respondent can validly react to a short statement on a printed form, in the absence of real-life qualifying situations, is unlikely. That equal scores obtained by several individuals indicate equal favorableness towards the given position is unlikely. Actually, different combinations of positions can yield equal score values, without necessarily indicating equivalent positions of attitude or opinion. Even though the opinionnaire provides for anonymous response, there is a possibility that an individual may answer according to what he thinks that he *should* feel, rather than how he *really* feels.

In spite of these limitations, the process of opinion measurement has merit, and until more precise measures of attitude are developed, this technique may serve a useful purpose in social research.

Q METHODOLOGY

Q methodology, devised by William Stephenson,[6] is a technique for scaling objects or statements. It is a method of ranking attitudes or judgments and is particularly effective when the number of items to be ranked is large. The procedure is known as a *Q*-sort, in which cards or slips bearing the statements or items are arranged in a series of numbered piles. Usually nine or eleven piles are established, representing relative positions on a standard scale. Some examples of simple polarized scales are illustrated.

most important	least important
most approve	least approve
most liberal	least liberal
most favorable	least favorable
most admired	least admired
most like me	least like me

The respondent is asked to place a specified number of items on each pile, usually on the basis of an approximately normal or symmetrical distribution. If nine piles were established, the assignment of slips or cards would be based upon an approximate stanine percentage distribution. From 50 to 100 items should be used.

Most like me							*Least like me*	
#	1	2	3	4	5	6	7	8	9
%	4	7	12	17	20	17	12	7	4

Self-concept *Q*-sort

Let us assume that a *Q*-sort has been designed to measure before-after therapy status of a subject. A few examples of appropriate traits are presented to be placed on the scale.

---

[6] William Stephenson, *The Study of Behavior* (Chicago: University of Chicago Press, 1953).

afraid	ignored	discouraged
suspicious	admired	energetic
successful	disliked	loved
enthusiastic	cheerful	hated
friendly	happy	stupid

A change in position of items from before-therapy to after-therapy would indicate possible change or improvement in self-esteem. Computing the coefficient of correlation between the pile positions of items before and after therapy would provide a measure of change. If no change in item placement had occurred the coefficient of correlation would be $+1.00$. If a completely opposite profile appeared the coefficient would be -1.00. While perfect $+1.00$ or -1.00 coefficients would be improbable, a high positive coefficient would indicate little change, whereas a high negative coefficient would indicate significant change.

Another type of Q-sort solicits the composite judgment of a selected panel of professors of educational research. The criterion of judgment involves the relative importance of research concepts that should be included in the introductory course in educational research. One hundred slips, each listing a concept, were to be sorted into nine piles, ranging from most important to least important. A few of the concepts that were considered are listed:

hypothesis	historical method
probability	survey
dependent variable	null hypothesis
coefficient of correlation	preparing a questionnaire
sources of reference materials	deductive method
preparing the research report	descriptive method
randomization	sampling
post-hoc fallacy	intervening variables
experimental method	independent variable
interviewing	Q-sorts
level of significance	standard deviation
the research proposal	nonparametric statistics
attitude studies	action research

The mean value of the positions assigned each item indicates the composite judgment of the panel as to its relative importance.

Two applications of the Q-sort technique have been illustrated in our simplified discussion. The first attempted to measure change in the attitude of an individual toward himself, the second the composite judgment of a group of individuals. Many types of analysis may be carried on in the area of attitudes by the use of Q methodology. Researchers contemplating the use of this techinque should carefully consider the theoretical assumptions underlying the criteria and the items selected.

Observation

As a data-gathering device, direct observation may make an important contribution to descriptive research. Certain types of information can best be obtained through direct examination by the researcher. When the information concerns aspects of material objects or specimens, the process is relatively simple, and may consist of classifying, measuring, or counting. But when the process involves the study of a human subject in action, it is much more complex.

One may study the characteristics of a school building by observing and recording such aspects as materials of construction, number of rooms for various purposes, size of rooms, amount of furniture and equipment, presence or absence of certain facilities, and other relevant aspects. Adequacy could then be determined by comparing these facilities with reasonable standards, previously determined by expert judgment and research.

In university athletic departments observation has been used effectively to scout the performance of the teams that will be encountered in inter-school football competition. Careful observation and recording of the skills and procedures of both team and individual players are made, and defenses and offenses are planned to cope with them. What formations or patterns of attack or defense are employed? Who carried the ball? Who does the passing, and where and with what hand does he pass? Who are the likely receivers, and how do they pivot and cut?

During a game a coaching assistant may sit high in the stands, relaying strategic observations by phone to the coach on the bench. At the same time, every minute of play is being recorded on film for careful study by the coaching staff and players. Who missed his tackle when that play went through for 20 yards? Who missed his block when play number two lost 6 yards? Careful study of these films provides valuable data on weaknesses to be corrected before the following Saturday's game. Through the use of binoculars, the phone, the motion picture camera, and the tape recorder, observations can be carefully made and recorded.

Although this example may seem inappropriate in a discussion of observation as a research technique, improving the performance of a football team is not altogether different from the problem of analyzing learning behavior in a classroom. The difference is one of degree of complexity. The objectives of the football team are more concretely identifiable than are the more complex purposes of the classroom. Yet some of the procedures of observation so effective in football coaching may also be systematically employed in studying classroom performance. In some schools teachers make short periodic classroom or playground observations of pupil behavior, which are filed in the cumulative folder. These recorded observations, known as anecdotal reports, may provide useful data for research studies.

The method of laboratory experimentation seeks to describe action or behavior that will take place under carefully arranged and controlled conditions. But many important aspects of human behavior cannot be profitably observed under the contrived conditions of the laboratory. The method of descriptive research seeks to describe behavior under less rigid controls, under more naturally occurring conditions. The behavior of children in a classroom situation cannot be effectively analyzed by observing their behavior in a laboratory. It is necessary to observe what they actually do in a real classroom.

This does not suggest that observation is haphazard or unplanned. On the contrary, observation as a research technique must always be expert, directed by a specific purpose, systematic, carefully focused, and thoroughly recorded. Like other research procedures, it must be subject to the usual checks for accuracy, validity, and reliability.

The observer must know just what to look for. He must be able to distinguish between the significant aspects of the situation and factors that have little or no importance to the investigation. Of course, objectivity is essential, and careful and accurate methods of measuring and recording are employed. The use of the check list, score card, or some other type of inquiry form may help to objectify and systematize the process.

The use of accurate instruments such as the scale, thermometer, stethoscope, audiometer, stopwatch, light meter, binoculars, camera, tape recorder, and other devices often makes possible observations that are more refined than mere sense observations. At times, the nature of an act may be more accurately analyzed when the action is slowed down, repeated, or re-examined. The use of the motion picture camera, time-lapse photography, or the audio and video tape recorder has facilitated the analysis of complex activities.

Both reliability and validity of observation are improved when observations are made at frequent intervals by the same observer, or when several observers record their observations independently. It is often important to establish conditions so that activities may take place in as natural a setting as possible, and are not unduly influenced by the presence of the observer or by his measuring or recording devices.

Newspaper reporters have confessed to minor crimes in order to get a true picture of existing prison conditions. Secret agents assume elaborate disguises and establish fictitious identities to find out what really happens inside a conspiracy. Hidden cameras and a one-way screen were used by Gesell to make significant observations of the behavior of infants. One-way windows have been used to observe the behavior of children in typical group activities, so that observers could see and hear without being either seen or heard.

RECORDING OBSERVATIONS

If it does not distract or create a barrier between observer and those observed, simultaneous recording of observations is recommended. This practice minimizes the errors that result from faulty memory. There are other occasions when recording would more appropriately follow some time after observation. The recording of observations should be done as soon as possible, while the details are still fresh in the mind of the observer. But many authorities agree that objectivity is more likely when the interpretation of the meaning of the behavior described is deferred until a later time, for simultaneous recording and interpretation often interfere with objectivity.

SYSTEMATIZING DATA COLLECTION

To aid in the recording of information gained through observation, a number of devices have been extensively used. Check lists, rating scales, score cards, and scaled specimens provide systematic means of summarizing or quantifying data collected by observation or examination.

CHECK LIST

The check list, the simplest of the devices, consists of a prepared list of items. The presence or absence of the item may be indicated by checking *yes* or *no*, or the type or number of items may be indicated by inserting the appropriate word or number. This simple "laundry-list" type of device systematizes and facilitates the recording of observations, and helps to assure the consideration of the important aspects of the object or act observed. Readers are familiar with check lists prepared to help buyers purchase a used car, choose a home site, or buy an insurance policy, indicating characteristics or features that one should bear in mind before making a decision.

RATING SCALE

The rating scale involves qualitative description of a limited number of aspects of a thing, or of traits of a person. The classifications may be set up in five to seven categories in such terms as:

superior	above average	average	fair	inferior
excellent	good	average	below average	poor
always	frequently	occasionally	rarely	never

Another procedure establishes positions in terms of behavioral or situational descriptions. These statements may be much more specific, and enable the judge to identify more clearly the characteristic to be rated. Instead of deciding whether the individual's leadership qualities are superior or above average, it may be easier to decide between "Always exerts a strong influence on his associates," and "Sometimes is able to move others to action."

One of the problems in constructing a rating scale lies in the difficulty of conveying to the rater just what quality one wishes evaluated. It is likely that a brief behavioral statement is more objective than an adjective that may have no universal meaning in the abstract.

Rating scales have several limitations. In addition to the difficulty of clearly defining the trait or characteristic to be evaluated, the halo effect causes raters to carry qualitative judgment from one aspect to another. Thus, there is a tendency to rate a person who has a pleasing personality high on other traits like intelligence or professional interest. This halo effect is likely to appear when the rater is asked to rate many factors, on a number of which he has no evidence for judgment. This suggests the advisability of keeping at a minimum the number of characteristics to be rated.

Another limitation of rating is the tendency of raters to be too generous. A number of studies have verified the tendency to rate 60 to 80 percent of an unselected group above average in all traits. Rating scales should carry the suggestion that raters omit the rating of characteristics that they have had no opportunity to observe.

SCORE CARD

The score card, similar in some respects to both the check list and the rating scale, usually provides for the appraisal of a relatively large number of aspects. In addition, the presence of each characteristic or aspect, or the rating assigned to each, has a predetermined point value. Thus, the score-card rating may yield a total weighted score that can be used in the evaluation of the object observed. Score cards are frequently used in evaluating communities, building sites, schools, or textbooks. Accrediting agencies sometimes use the score card in arriving at an overall evaluation of a school.

Score cards have been designed to help in estimating the socioeconomic status of a family. Such aspects as type of neighborhood, home (owned or rented), number of rooms, ownership of a piano, number of books in the library, number and type of periodicals subscribed to, telephone, occupation of father, and organizations parents belong to are all considered significant and have appropriate point values assigned.

The limitations of the score card are similar to those of the rating scale. In addition to the difficulty of choosing, identifying, and quantifying the significant aspects of the factor to be observed, there is the suspicion that the whole of a thing may be greater than the sum of its parts.

Colleges and universities are frequently evaluated in terms of such elements as size of endowment, proportion of faculty members holding the earned doctoral degree, pupil-teacher ratio, and number of volumes in the library. Although these aspects are important, the effectiveness of an institution may not be accurately appraised by their summation, for certain important intangibles do not lend themselves to score card ratings.

SCALED SPECIMEN

The scaled specimen, although not frequently encountered, provides an effective method for evaluating certain standards of performance. Thorndike's handwriting scales provide a number of graded samples to which one may compare the handwriting to be evaluated. Various intelligence-test scoring manuals provide scaled specimens for determining the mental age of children as revealed by their drawings.

CONTENT OR DOCUMENT ANALYSIS

The systematic examination of records or documents is a specialized application of data gathering by observation. Since this process has been discussed in some detail in the chapter on descriptive research (Chapter 5), it is not repeated here.

Observation, as a research data-gathering process, demands rigorous adherence to the spirit of scientific inquiry. The following standards should characterize the observer and his observations:

Observation is carefully planned, systematic, and perceptive. The observer knows what he is looking for, and what is irrelevant in a situation. He is not distracted by the dramatic or the spectacular.

The observer is aware of the wholeness of what is observed. Although he is alert to significant details, he knows that the whole is often greater than the sum of its parts.

The observer is objective. He recognizes his likely biases, and he strives to eliminate their influence upon what he sees and reports.

The observer separates the facts from the interpretation of the facts. He observes the facts, and makes his interpretation at a later time.

Observations are checked and verified, whenever possible, by repetition, or by comparison with those of other competent observers.

Observations are carefully and expertly recorded. The observer uses appropriate instruments to systematize, quantify, and preserve the results of his observations.

The interview[7]

The interview is, in a sense, an oral questionnaire. Instead of writing the response, the subject or interviewee gives the needed information verbally in a face-to-face relationship.

With a skillful interviewer, the interview is often superior to other data-gathering devices. One reason is that people are usually more willing to talk than to write. After the interviewer gains rapport, or establishes a friendly, secure relationship with the subject, certain types of confidential information may be obtained that an individual might be reluctant to put in writing. The interviewer can explain the purpose of his investigation, and can explain more clearly just what information he wants. If the subject misinterprets the question, the interviewer may follow it with a clarifying question. At the same time, he may evaluate the sincerity and insight of the interviewee. It is also possible to seek the same information, in several ways, at various stages of the interview, thus providing a check of the truthfulness of the responses.

Through the interview technique the researcher may stimulate the subject to greater insight into his own experiences, and thereby explore significant areas not anticipated in the original plan of investigation. The interview is also particularly appropriate when dealing with young children, illiterates, those with language difficulties, and those of limited intelligence.

If one were to study what junior high school students like and dislike in teachers, some sort of written schedule would probably be satisfactory. In order to conduct a similar study with first grade pupils, the interview would be the only feasible method of getting responses.

(When a graduate student in the author's class carried on such a study, she was surprised and amused to discover that first grade children frequently mentioned "she smells nice" as a favored characteristic of the teacher.)

The preparation for the interview is a critical step in the procedure. The interviewer must have a clear conception of just what information he needs. He must clearly outline the best sequence of questions and stimulating comments that will systematically bring out the desired responses. A written outline, schedule, or check list will provide a set plan for the interview, precluding the possibility that the interviewer will fail to get important and needed data.

The nature of the personal relationship between interviewer and subject requires an expertness and sensitivity that might well be called an art. The

[7]See Pauline V. Young, *Scientific Social Surveys and Research*, 4th ed. (Englewood Cliffs, N.J.: Prentice-Hall, 1966), Chapter 11.

initial task of securing the confidence and cooperation of the subject is crucial. Talking in a friendly way about a topic of interest to the subject will often dispel hostility or suspicion and, before he realizes it, the subject is freely giving the desired information. As is true in the use of the questionnaire, the interviewer must be able to assure the subject that his responses will be held in strict confidence. When interviews are not recorded by tape or other electronic device, it will be necessary for the interviewer to take written notes, either during the interview or immediately thereafter. It is suggested that the actual wording of the responses be retained. It is advisable to make the interpretation later, separating this phase of analysis from the actual recording of responses.

Recording interviews on tape is convenient and inexpensive, and obviates the necessity of writing during the interview, which may be a distracting influence, both to interviewer and to subject. Interviews recorded on tape may be replayed as often as necessary for complete and objective analysis at a later time. In addition to the words, the tone of voice and emotional impact of the response is preserved by the tapes.

As a data-gathering technique, the interview has unique advantages. In areas where human motivation as revealed in reasons for actions, feelings, and attitudes is concerned, the interview can be most effective. In the hands of a skillful interviewer, a depth of response is possible, a penetration quite unlikely to be achieved through any other means.

This technique is time consuming, however, and one of the most difficult to employ successfully. The danger of interviewer bias is constant. Since the objectivity, sensitivity, and insight of the interviewer are crucial this procedure is one that requires a level of expertness not ordinarily possessed by inexperienced researchers.

Psychological tests and inventories

As data-gathering devices, psychological tests are among the most useful tools of educational research, for they provide the data for most experimental and descriptive studies in education. Since we are able here to examine only limited aspects of the nature of psychological testing, students of educational research should consult other volumes for a more complete discussion.[8]

A psychological test is an instrument designed to describe and measure a sample of certain aspects of human behavior. Tests may be used to compare the behavior of two or more persons at a particular time, or one

[8] Lee J. Cronbach, *Essentials of Psychological Testing*, 3rd ed. (New York: Harper & Row, Publishers, 1970). Anne Anastasia, *Psychological Testing*, 3rd ed. (New York: Macmillan Co., 1968).

or more persons at different times. Psychological tests yield objective and standardized descriptions of behavior, quantified by numerical scores. Under ideal conditions, achievement or aptitude tests measure the best performance of which individuals are capable. Under ideal conditions, inventories attempt to measure typical behavior. Tests and inventories are used to describe status (or a prevailing condition at a particular time), to measure changes in status produced by modifying factors, or to predict future behavior on the basis of present performance.

In the simple classroom experiment described in the chapter on experimental research (Chapter 4), test scores were used to equate the experimental and control groups, to describe status in achievement before the application of teaching methods, to measure pupil mean gain resulting from the application of experimental and control teaching methods, and to evaluate the relative effectiveness of teaching methods. This example of classroom experimentation illustrates how experimental data may be gathered through the application of tests.

In descriptive research studies, tests are frequently used to describe prevailing conditions at a particular time. How does a student compare with those of his own age or grade in school achievement? How does a particular group compare with other groups in other schools, or in other cities?

In school surveys for the past forty years, achievement tests have been used extensively in the appraisal of instruction. Because tests yield quantitative descriptions or measure, they make possible more precise analysis than can be achieved through subjective judgment alone.

There are many ways of classifying psychological tests. One distinction is made between *performance tests* and *paper-and-pencil tests*. Performance tests, usually administered individually, require that the subject manipulate objects or mechanical apparatus while his actions are observed and recorded by the examiner. Paper-and-pencil tests, usually administered in groups, require the subject to mark his responses on a prepared sheet.

Two other classes of tests are *power* versus *timed* or *speed* tests. Power tests have no time limit, and the subject attempts progressively more difficult tasks until he is unable to continue successfully. Timed or speed tests usually involve the element of power, but in addition, limit the time that the subject has in which to complete certain tasks.

Another distinction is that made between *nonstandardized*, teacher-made tests and *standardized* tests. The test that the classroom teacher constructs is likely to be less expertly designed than that of the professional, although it is based upon the best logic and skill that the teacher can command, and is usually "tailor-made" for a particular group of pupils.

By contrast, the standardized test is designed for more general use. Each item and the total scores have been carefully analyzed, and validity and reliability established by careful statistical controls. Norms have been established, based upon the performance of many subjects of various ages living in many different types of communities and geographic areas. Not only has the content of the test been standardized, but the administration and scoring have also been set in one pattern so that those subsequently taking the tests will take them under like conditions. As far as possible, the interpretaion has also been standardized.

Although it would be inaccurate to claim that all standardized tests meet optimum standards of excellence, these instruments have been made as sound as possible in the light of the best that is known by experts in test construction, administration, and interpretation.

Psychological tests may also be classified in terms of their purposes—the types of psychological traits that they describe and measure.

ACHIEVEMENT TESTS

Achievement tests attempt to measure what an individual has learned—his present level of performance. Most tests used in schools are achievement tests. They are particularly helpful in determining individual or group status in academic learning. Achievement test scores are used in placing, advancing, or retaining students at particular grade levels. They are used in diagnosing strengths and weaknesses, and as a basis for awarding prizes, scholarships, or degrees.

Frequently, achievement test scores are used in evaluating the influences of courses of study, teachers, teaching methods, and other factors considered to be significant in educational practice. In using tests for evaluative purposes it is important not to generalize beyond the specific elements measured. For example, to identify effective teaching exclusively with the limited products measured by the ordinary achievement test would be to define effective teaching too narrowly. It is essential that researchers recognize that the elements of a situation under appraisal need to be evaluated on the basis of a number of criteria, not merely on a few limited aspects.

APTITUDE TESTS

Aptitude tests attempt to predict the degree of achievement that may be expected from individuals in a particular activity. To the extent that they measure past learning, they are similar to achievement tests. To the extent that they measure nondeliberate or unplanned learnings, they are different. Aptitude tests attempt to predict an individual's capacity to acquire improved performance with additional training.

Actually, capacity (or aptitude) cannot be measured directly. Aptitude can only be inferred on the basis of present performance, particularly in areas where there has been no deliberate attempt to teach the behaviors to be predicted.

Intelligence, which is generally thought of as inborn potentiality, is really measured by present ability. Whether an individual's achievement is relatively high, average, or low, we assume that it is a measure of how effectively he has profited from his informal opportunities for learning. To the extent that others have had similar opportunities, we predict his capacity or potentiality on the basis of how his ability compares with that of others his own age. This is a matter of inference rather than of direct measurement. Since it has proved useful in predicting future achievement, particularly in academic pursuits, we consider this concept of intelligence measurement a valid application.

Aptitude tests have been similarly designed to predict improved performance with further training in many areas. These inferred measurements have been applied to mechanical and manipulative skills, musical and artistic pursuits, and in many professional areas involving many types of predicted ability.

In music, for example, ability to remember and discriminate between differences in pitch, rhythm pattern, intensity, and timbre seems to be closely related to future levels of development in musicianship. Present proficiency in these tasks provides a fair predictive index of an individual's ability to profit from advanced instruction, particularly when the individual has had little formal training in music prior to the test.

Aptitude tests may be used to divide students into relatively homogeneous groups for instructional purposes, to identify students for scholarship grants, to screen individuals for particular educational programs, or to help guide individuals into areas where they are most likely to succeed.

INTEREST INVENTORIES

Interest inventories attempt to yield a measure of the types of activities that an individual has a tendency to like and to choose. One kind of instrument has compared the subject's pattern of interest to the interest patterns of successful practitioners in a number of vocational fields. A distinctive pattern has been discovered to be characteristic of each field. The assumption is that an individual is happiest and most successful working in a field most like his own measured profile of interests.

Another inventory is based on the correlation between a number of activities from the areas of school, recreation, and work. These related activities have been identified by careful analysis with mechanical, computational, scientific, persuasive, artistic, literary, musical, social-service, and clerical areas of interest. By sorting the subject's stated likes and dislikes into various interest areas, a percentile score for each area is obtained. It is then assumed that the subject will find his area of greatest interest where his percentile scores are relatively high.

Interest blanks or inventories are examples of self-report instruments in which the individual notes his own likes and dislikes. These self-report instruments are really standardized interviews in which the subject, through introspection, indicates feelings that may be interpreted in terms of what is known about interest patterns.

PERSONALITY MEASURES

Personality scales are usually self-report instruments. The individual checks responses to certain questions or statements. These instruments yield scores which are assumed or have been shown to measure certain personality traits or tendencies.

Because of the difficulty, inability, or unwillingness of individuals to report their own reactions accurately or objectively, these instruments may be of limited value. Part of this limitation may be due to the inadequate theories of personality upon which some of these inventories have been based. At best, they provide data useful in suggesting the need for further analysis. Some have reasonable empirical validity with particular groups of individuals, but prove to be invalid when applied to others. For example, one personality inventory has proven valuable in yielding scores that correlate highly with the diagnoses of psychiatrists in clinical situations. But when applied to college students, its diagnostic value has proved disappointing.

The development of instruments of personality description and measurement is relatively recent, and it is likely that continued research in this important area will yield better theories of personality and better instruments for describing and measuring its various aspects.

The Mooney Problems Check List[9] is an inventory to be used by a student in reporting his own problems of adjustment. The subject is asked to indicate on the check list the problems that trouble him. From a list of these items, classified into different categories, a picture of the student's problems, from his own viewpoint, is drawn. Although the most useful interpretation may result from an item analysis of personal problems, the device does yield a quantitative score which may indicate the degree of difficulty that a student feels he is experiencing in his adjustment. This instrument has been used as a research device to identify and describe the nature of the problems facing individuals and groups of individuals in a school.

The tendency to withhold embarrassing responses and to express those that are socially acceptable; the emotional involvement of an individual with his own problems; and lack of insight—all these limit the effectiveness of personal and social-adjustment scales. Some psychologists believe that

[9]Ross L. Mooney, *Problem Check List, High School Form* (Columbus, Ohio: Bureau of Educational Research, Ohio State University, 1941.)

the projective type of instrument offers greater promise, for these tests attempt to disguise their purpose so completely that the subject is unable to know how to appear in the best light.

The most commonly used projective tests involve the subject's interpretation of the meaning of various standardized ink-blot figures or pictured situations.

PROJECTIVE DEVICES

A projective instrument enables a subject to project his internal feelings, attitudes, needs, values, or wishes to an external object. Thus, the subject may unconsciously reveal himself as he reacts to the external object. The use of projective devices is particularly helpful in counteracting the tendency of a subject to try to appear in his best light, to respond as he believes he is expected to respond.

Projection may be accomplished through a number of techniques:

1. *Association.* The respondent is asked to indicate what he sees, feels, or thinks when presented with a picture, cartoon, ink blot, word, or phrase. The Thematic Apperception Test, the Rorschach Ink Blot Test, and various word-association tests are familiar examples.
2. *Completion.* The respondent is asked to complete an incomplete sentence or task. A sentence-completion instrument may include such items as:
   My greatest ambition is
   My greatest fear is
   I most enjoy
   I dream a great deal about
   I get very angry when
   If I could do anything I wanted it would be to
3. *Role-playing.* The subject is asked to improvise or act out a situation in which the subjects have been assigned various roles. The researcher may observe such traits as hostility, frustration, dominance, sympathy, insecurity, prejudice, or their absence.
4. *Creative or constructive.* Permitting subjects to model clay, finger paint, play with dolls, play with toys, or draw or write imaginative stories about assigned situations may be revealing. The choice of color, form, words, the sense of orderliness, evidence of tensions, and other reactions may provide opportunities to infer deep-seated feelings.

Qualities of a good test

In selecting tests for research purposes, several qualities are desirable.

VALIDITY

In general, a test possesses validity to the extent that it measures what it claims to measure. However, validity may be defined in a number of ways. *Logical* validity means that the test actually measures or is specifically related to the trait(s) for which it was designed. But the test title is no measure of logical validity. Some tests of skill in English usage consist of identifying errors of punctuation, spelling, agreement, and capitalization on a multiple-choice basis. Although items of this type are relatively easy to construct, they tend to overemphasize certain phases of good usage, and have a very limited relationship to real skill in usage or to the purposes of a good course in composition.

Empirical validity is concerned with the usefulness of a test in predicting successful performance, or how well it accomplishes a practical purpose. If a test is designed to pick out good candidates for appointment as shop foremen, and test scores show a high positive correlation with actual success on the job, the test has a high degree of empirical validity, whatever factors it actually measures. It predicts well. It serves a useful purpose.

But before a test can be evaluated on the basis of empirical validity, success on the job must be accurately described and measured. The criteria of the production of the department, the judgment of supervisors, or measures of employee morale might serve as evidence. Since these criteria might not be entirely satisfactory, however, empirical validity is not easy to assess. It is often difficult to discover whether the faults of prediction lie in the test, in the criteria of success, or in both. Many so-called intelligence tests have a high degree of empirical validity. Although there is great difference of opinion about the nature of intelligence, these tests have proved quite effective in predicting academic success. Perhaps they would be more appropriately labeled "academic aptitude tests." They do predict well. They serve a useful purpose.

Tests are often validated by comparing their results with a test of known validity. A well-known scale of personal adjustment, the Minnesota Multiphasic Personality Inventory, involved sorting nearly 500 cards into three categories, *yes*, *no*, and *cannot say*. The test equipment was expensive, and it could not be easily administered to large groups at the same time. A paper-and pencil form was devised, using the simple process of checking responses to printed items on a test form. This form could be administered to a large group at one time and then scored by machine, all with little expense. The results were so similar to the more time-consuming, expensive card-sorting process, that the latter has been largely replaced. This is the process of establishing concurrent validity; in this case, by comparing an expensive individual test with an easy-to-administer group test.

In like manner, performance tests have been validated against paper-and-pencil tests, and short tests against longer tests. Through this process, more convenient and more appropriate tests can be devised to accomplish the measurement of behavior more effectively.

Since there are other aspects of validity beyond the scope of this discussion, the reader is urged to consult the volumes on psychological testing cited in the chapter bibliography.

RELIABILITY

A test is reliable to the extent that it measures accurately and consistently, from one time to another. In tests that have a high coefficient of reliability, errors of measurement have been reduced to a minimum. Reliable tests, whatever they measure, yield comparable scores upon repeated administration. An unreliable test would be comparable to a stretchable rubber yardstick that yielded different measurements each time it was applied.

A test may be reliable, even though it is not valid. A valid test is always reliable.

OBJECTIVITY

A test should yield a clear score value for each performance, the score being independent of the personal judgment of the scorer.

ECONOMY

Tests that can be given in a short period of time are likely to gain the cooperation of the subject, and to conserve the time of all those involved in test administration. The matter of expense of administering a test is often a significant factor, if the testing program is being operated on a limited budget.

SIMPLICITY OF ADMINISTRATION, SCORING, AND INTERPRETATION

Ease of administration, scoring, and interpretation is an important factor in selecting a test, particularly when expert personnel or an adequate budget are not available. Many good tests are easily and effectively administered, scored, and interpreted by the classroom teacher, who may not be an expert.

INTEREST

Tests that are interesting and enjoyable help to gain the cooperation of the subject. Those that are dull or seem silly may discourage or antago-

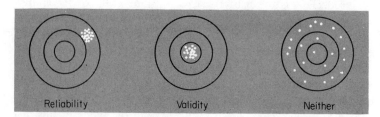

FIGURE 6-5 A Target Analogy of Reliability and Validity

nize the subject. Under these unfavorable conditions, the test is not likely to yield useful results.

It is important in selecting a test to recognize the fact that a good test does not necessarily possess all the desirable qualities for all subjects or for all levels of performance. Within a certain range of age, maturity, or ability, a test may be suitable. For other individuals outside that range, the test may be quite unsatisfactory and a more appropriate one needed.

The selection should be made after careful examination of the standardizing data contained in the test manual and extensive analysis of published evaluations of the instrument. Research workers should select the most appropriate standardized tests available. Detailed reports of their usefulness and limitations are usually supplied in the manual furnished by the publisher. The considered judgments of outside experts are also available. *The Mental Measurements Yearbook*,[10] the best single reference on psychological tests, contains many critical evaluations of published tests, each contributed by an expert in the field of psychological measurement. Usually, several different evaluations are included for each test. Since the reports are not duplicated from one volume to another, it is advisable to consult *Tests in Print* or previous *Yearbooks* for additional reports not included in the current volume. In addition to the reviews and evaluations, the names of test publishers, prices, forms, and appropriate uses are included. Readers are also urged to consult the listings and reviews of newly published psychological tests in the *Journal of Educational Measurement*.

In using psychological tests in educational research, it is important to recognize that standardized test scores are only approximate measures of the traits under consideration. This limitation is inevitable, and may be ascribed to a number of possible factors:

1. The choice of an inappropriate test for the specific purpose in mind
2. Errors inherent in any psychological test; no test is completely valid or reliable
3. Errors that result from poor test conditions, inexpert or careless administration or scoring of the test, or faulty tabulation of test scores
4. Inexpert interpretation of test results

Sociometry

Sociometry is a technique for describing social relationships that exist between individuals in a group. In an indirect way it attempts to describe attractions or repulsions between individuals by asking them to indicate whom they would choose or reject in various situations. Children in a school classroom may be asked to name the child, or several children in

---

[10]Oscar K. Buros, ed., *Seventh Mental Measurements Yearbook* (Highland Park, N.J.: Gryphon Press, 1972).

order of preference, that they would invite to a party, eat lunch with, sit next to, work with on a class project, or have as a friend.

The U. S. Air Force has used sociometry to study the acceptance of leadership in various situations. For example, the following question was used in a sociometric study of bomber crews: "What member of the crew, disregarding rank, would you select as the most effective leader, if your plane were forced down in a remote and primitive area?"

In some sociometric studies, negatively phrased items have been used: "If you were to work on a class project with another student, who would you *not* want to work with?" Sociometric studies have been made of many types of social groups, including classroom groups, fraternities and sororities, camp groups, factory and office groups, navy squadrons, air force crews, and entire communities.

THE SOCIOGRAM

Sociometric choices are represented graphically on a chart known as a sociogram. There are many variations of pattern, and the reader is urged to consult specialized references on sociometry.[11] A few observations will illustrate the nature of the sociogram.

In constructing a sociogram, boys may be represented by triangles and girls by circles. A choice may be represented by a single-pointed arrow, a mutual choice by an arrow pointing in opposite directions. Those chosen most often are referred to as stars, those not chosen by others as isolates. Small groups made up of individuals who choose one another are cliques.

The identifying initials of individuals are placed within the symbols. Symbols of those chosen most often are placed nearest the center of the diagram, with those chosen less often progressively outward. Those not chosen are, literally, on the outside. (See Figure 6-6.) It must be remembered that the relationship between individuals in a group is a changeable thing. Children's choices are most temporary, for stability tends to develop only with age.

Students of group relationships and classroom teachers may construct a number of sociograms over a period of time to measure changes that may have resulted from efforts to bring isolates into closer group relationships, or to transform cliques into more general group membership. The effectiveness of socializing or status-building procedures can thus be measured by the changes revealed in the sociogram. Since sociometry is a peer rating, rather than a rating by superiors, it adds another dimension to the understanding of members of a group.

[11] *How to Construct a Sociogram.* Horace Mann-Lincoln Institute of School Experimentation (New York: Bureau of Publications, Teachers College, Columbia University, 1947) and J. L. Moreno, *Who Shall Survive?* 2nd rev. ed. (New York: Beacon Press, 1953).

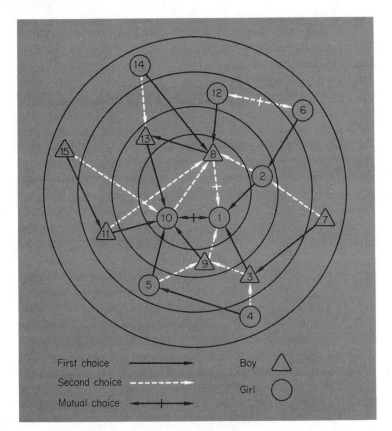

FIGURE 6-6   Sociogram Showing First and Second Choices in a Third Grade Class

"Guess-who" technique

A process of description closely related to sociometry is the "guess-who" technique. Developed by Hugh Hartshorne and Mark A. May,[12] the process consists of description of the various roles played by children in a group.

Children are asked to name the individuals who fit certain verbal descriptions.

This one is always happy.
This one is always picking on others.

[12]Hugh Hartshorne and Mark A. May, *Studies in Service and Self-Control* (New York: Macmillan Co., 1929).

This one is always worried.
This one never likes to do anything.
This one will always help you.

Items of this type yield interesting and significant peer judgments, and are useful in the study of individual roles. Of course, the names of children chosen should not be revealed.

Social-distance scale

Another approach to the description and measurement of social relationships is the social-distance scale, developed by E. S. Bogardus[13] at the University of Southern California. This device attempts to measure to what degree an individual, or a group of individuals, is accepted or rejected by another individual or group.

Various scaled situations, with score values ranging from acceptance to rejection, are established. The individual checks his position by choosing one of the points on the scale. For example, in judging acceptance of different minority groups, the choices might range between these extremes:

Complete acceptance	I wouldn't object to having a member of this group become a member of my family by marriage.
Partial acceptance	I wouldn't mind sitting next to a member of this group on a bus.
Rejection	I don't think that members of this group should be admitted into our country.

When applied to an individual in a classroom situation, the choices might range between these extremes:

Complete acceptance	I'd like to have him as my best friend.
Partial acceptance	I wouldn't mind sitting near him.
Rejection	I wish he weren't in my room.

Of course, in the real social-distance scale, illustrated by the sample items above, there would be a larger number of evenly spaced scaled positions (usually seven in number), giving a more precise measure of acceptance or rejection.

Devices of the type described here have many possibilities for the

[13] E. S. Bogardus, "A Social Distance Scale," *Sociology and Social Research* 17 (January–February 1933): 265–271.

description and measurement of social relationships and, in this important area of social research, may yield interesting and useful data.

Simple data organization

When the results of an observation, interview, questionnaire, opinion-naire, or test are to be analyzed, the problems of organization confront the researcher. The first problem is to designate appropriate logical and mutually exclusive categories for tabulation of the data. At times the hypothesis or question to be answered may suggest the type of organization. If the hypothesis involved the difference between the attitudes of men and women toward teacher merit rating, the categories *male* and *female* would be clearly indicated. In other instances the categories are not determined by the hypothesis and other subdivisions of the group under investigation may be desirable.

When analyzing the responses or characteristics of a group it is some-times satisfactory to describe the group as a whole. In simple types of analysis, when the group is sufficiently homogeneous, no breakdown into subgroups is necessary. But in many situations the picture of the whole group is not clear. The heterogeneity of the group may yield data that have little meaning. One tends to get an unreal picture of a group of subjects that are actually very different from one another, and the differ-ences are concealed by a description of a nonexistent or unreal average. In such cases it may be helpful to divide the group into more homogeneous subgroups or categories that have in common some distinctive charac-teristics that may be significant for the purpose of the analysis. Dis-tinguishing between the responses of men and women, between elementary and secondary teachers, between gifted and slow-learning children may reveal significant relationships.

For example, a new type of classroom organization may seem to have little impact on a group of students. But, after dividing the group into two subgroups, the gifted and the slow learners, some interesting relation-ships may become clear. The grouping may be effective for the bright students, but most ineffective for the slow learners.

Many studies employ the classification of data into dichotomous, or twofold, categories. When the categories are established on the basis of test scores, rankings, or some other quantitative measure, it may be advisable to compare those at the top with those at the bottom, omitting from the analysis those near the middle of the distribution. It is possible to compare the top third with the bottom third, or the top 25 percent with the bottom 25 percent. This eliminates those cases near the midpoint that tend to obscure the differences that may exist. By eliminating the middle portion, sharper contrast is achieved, but the risk of the regression effect is increased.

Comparisons are not always dichotomous. At times it is desirable to divide a large group into more than two categories, depending on the nature of the variables that are to be considered.

OUTSIDE CRITERIA FOR COMPARISON

In addition to the comparisons that may be made between subgroups, or *within* the larger group, the group may be analyzed in terms of some *outside criteria*. Of course, it must be assumed that reasonably valid and reliable measuring devices are available for making such comparisons. These "measuring sticks" may consist of standardized tests, score cards, rating scales, frequency counts, and physical as well as psychological measuring devices. Some of these outside criteria are:

1. *Prevailing conditions, practices, or performance* of a different but comparable unit, or comparable units. This comparison may be made with another community or other communities, school or schools, and class or classes. Comparisons may be made with groups representing best conditions or practices, typical or average status, or equated groups that have been matched in terms of certain variables, leaving one or a limited number of variables for comparison.
2. *What experts believe to constitute best conditions or practices.* These experts may comprise a specially selected panel, chosen for the purpose. A group of practitioners in the field who are assumed to be most familiar with the characteristics under consideration, or the survey staff itself, may constitute the body of experts. The judgments of recognized authorities who publish their opinions are frequently selected as criteria.
3. *What a professional group, a commission, an accrediting agency, or another scholarly deliberative body establishes as appropriate standards.* These standards may be expressed as lists of objectives, or may be quantitative measures of status for accreditation or approval. The *American Medical Association's* standards for accreditation of medical schools, the *North Central Association of Secondary Schools and Colleges* accreditation standards, or the standards of the *National Commission on Teacher Education and Professional Standards* for programs of teacher education are examples of evaluative criteria.
4. *Laws or rules that have been enacted or promulgated by a legislative or quasi-legislative body.* The areas of teacher certification regulations, school building standards, or health and safety regulations provide appropriate criteria for comparison.
5. *Research evidence.* The factors to be analyzed may be examined in the light of principles confirmed by scholarly research that has been published and generally accepted.
6. *Public opinion.* Although not always appropriate as a criterion of what should be, the opinions or views of "the man on the street" are sometimes appropriate as a basis for comparison.

Sorting and tabulating data

Tabulation is the process of transferring data from the data-gathering instruments to the tabular form in which they may be systematically examined. This process may be performed in a number of ways. In simple types of research, hand-tabulating procedures are usually employed. In more extensive investigations a card-tabulating process may be used, possibly including machine methods.

Most simple research studies employ the method of hand-sorting and recording, with tabulations written on tabulation sheets. To save time and to ensure greater accuracy, it is recommended that one person read the data while the other records them on the tabulation sheet. Marks are best recorded by fence tallies, ($\cancel{\text{////}}$) with a cross line every five tallies. In constructing tally form sheets it is important to provide enough space to record the tallies in each category.

The following discussion on hand tabulation emphasized the importance of careful planning before the sorting and tabulation begin.

Sorting and hand tabulation. Without careful planning, an inexperienced researcher may waste effort when tabulating responses on a set of questionnaires filled out by a group of teachers. After completing the tabulation, he may decide to compare the responses of elementary teachers with secondary teachers. This would involve retabulating the responses of the questionnaire. It might then occur to him that it would be interesting to compare the responses of the men with those of the women. Another handling of the questionnaires would be necessary

If he had decided upon his categories before tabulation, one handling of the questionnaires would have been sufficient. Sorting the questionnaires into two piles, one for elementary teachers and another for secondary teachers, then sorting each of these into separate piles for men and for women, would have yielded four stacks. Then by tabulating the responses of each of the piles separately, one planned operation would have yielded the same amount of information as three unplanned operations.

	ELEMENTARY	*SECONDARY*
men		
women		

Before tabulating questionnaires or opinionnaires, it is always important to decide upon the categories that are to be established for analysis. It has been shown that if this decision is delayed, it may be necessary to

	AGREE	*CANNOT SAY*	*DISAGREE*
Freshmen			
Sophomores			
Juniors			
Seniors			

FIGURE 6–7   Tabulation Form Providing for the Analysis of 12 Possible Response Categories Based upon Question 1 on an Opinionnaire

retabulate the items a number of times, needlessly consuming a great deal of time and effort.

If the data-gathering device called for a larger number of responses, the system of presorting would be similar. It would be advisable, however, to set up a separate tabulation sheet for each of the categories, because a single sheet would become unwieldy.

Figure 6–7 illustrates how a three-item opinionnaire response could be tabulated for a question such as the following:

"An honor system would eliminate cheating in examinations.
I agree _____.
I cannot say_____.
I disagree_____."

Students may apply these procedures to classify and tabulate similar types of data. These data sheets are not ordinarily presented in the report, but they may suggest ways in which some of the data may be presented as tables or graphic figures.

Tables and figures

The process of tabulation which has just been described is the first step in the construction of the tables that are included in a research report. It is likely that the beginning researcher thinks of tables purely as aids to understanding. Displaying data in rows and columns, according to some logical plan of classification, they may serve an even more important purpose in helping the researcher to see the similarities and relationships of his data in bold relief.

A discussion of the construction and use of tables and figures is presented in some detail in Chapter 9.

PERCENTAGE COMPARISONS

Presenting data by frequency counts has a number of limitations. If the groups to be compared are unequal in size, the frequency count may have little meaning. Converting to percentage responses enables the researcher to compare subgroups of unequal size meaningfully. Translating frequency counts into percentages indicates the number-per-hundred compared. By providing a common base the comparison is made clear.

There are several limitations that should be recognized in using percentage comparisons. Unless the number of frequencies is reasonably large, a percentage may be misleading and may seem to suggest a generalization that is unwarranted. It may be appropriate to indicate that, of four physicians interviewed, one believed that a particular medication would be harmful. To indicate that 25 percent of physicians interviewed believed that the medication would be harmful creates an image of a larger sample of physicians than was actually interviewed. It is essential that both frequency counts and percentage responses be included in the presentation and analysis of data.

In converting frequency counts to percentages, rounding to the nearest percentage point is preferable. Because the type of data presented in educational research is not too precise, there is little value in expressing percentages in decimal values. In other situations, however, such as the drug industry, where ratio scales of measurement are often used, it would be extremely important to carry a percentage reported to four or five decimal places, particularly when a trace of an element would be harmful if exceeded.

When using percentages in dichotomous comparisons it is only necessary to state the percentage in one of the categories. If 65 percent of the respondents are men, it is not necessary to indicate that 35 percent are women. Unnecessary duplication is evidence of poor reporting.

RANKING AND WEIGHTING ITEMS

There are times when response categories are not mutually exclusive. Preferences for certain things or reasons for an act are usually explained in terms of a number of factors, rarely single ones. It would be unrealistic to expect a respondent to indicate his favorite type of recreation or the single reason he decided to attend a particular university. In such instances it would be appropriate to ask the respondent to indicate two or three responses in order of importance or preference. This ranking of items makes possible a useful method of analysis. Items may be weighted in inverse order. For example, if three items are to be ranked, it would be appropriate to assign weightings as follows:

1st choice	3 points
2nd choice	2 points
3rd choice	1 point

A composite judgment of the importance of the items could be determined by the weighted totals or averages for all the respondents.

It should be remembered that when items are ranked in order, the differences between ranked items may not be equal. Ranking is not the most refined method of scaling.

EDGE-PUNCHED CARDS

Without the use of elaborate equipment, edge-punched cards may be used in data tabulation. Cards are provided with rows of numbered holes around their edges. Data are transferred to the cards by punching notches in the holes, according to a predetermined code. All possible responses can be coded to correspond to a particular hole or combination of holes.

Assume that the cards of male subjects are punched in hole 1 and secondary teachers, in hole 4, married individuals in hole 6, and those under 30 years of age in hole 9. To select the individuals who are male, married, secondary teachers under 30 years of age a *needle* would be successively inserted in holes 1, 4, 6, and 9. When the needle was lifted, those individuals' cards would fall loose, while the others would be held by the needle.

Subsequent insertion of the needle would make possible the rapid counting of frequencies of any coded response.

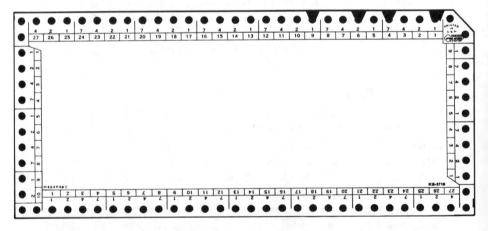

FIGURE 6–8   A $3\frac{1}{2}'' \times 7\frac{1}{2}''$ **Edge-punched Card with 78 Holes**[14]

[14]Used with permission of McBee Systems, Automated Business Systems, Division of Litton Industries, 600 Washington Ave., Carlstadt, N.J.

FIGURE 6–9   A 5″ × 8″ Double Edge-punched Card with 155 Holes

NUMERICAL CODE

To save space on a card, and time in notching and sorting, Keysort uses a special numerical code system. Only four holes are used for each set of numbers from 0 through 9, and these four holes are assigned the values of 7, 4, 2, and 1. By notching either a single number or a combination of two numbers, any number from 1 through 9 may be expressed. Ciphers are not notched.

The computer

The electronic digital computer is one of the most versatile and ingenious developments of the technological age. It is unlikely that complex modern institutions of business, finance, and government would have developed without the contributions of the computer. Making out payrolls, keeping stock inventories, maintaining credit balances, recording security transactions, reporting pupil data, providing individualized instruction, verifying tax teturns, maintaining subscription lists, navigating ships, piloting sophisticated aircraft, aiming intercontinental missiles, predicting earth-

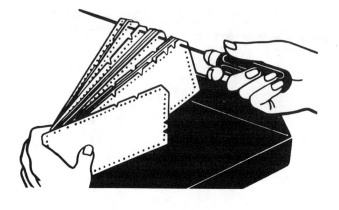

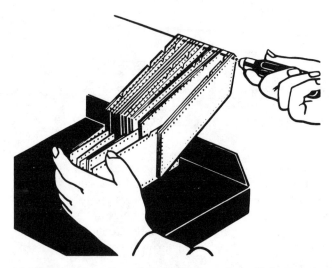

FIGURE 6–10   **Inserting Needle through the Holes Permits the Notched Cards to Fall, While the Others Remain on the Needle**

quakes and tornados, retrieving relevant legal decisions, and diagnosing diseases are some nonresearch applications.

To the researcher the use of the computer in the search for related literature and the analysis of complex data have made complicated research designs practicable. Performing calculations almost at the speed of light, the computer has become one of the most useful tools of research in the humanities and in the physical and behavioral sciences.

An early predecessor of the modern computer was a mechanical device developed by Charles Babbage, a nineteenth century English mathema-

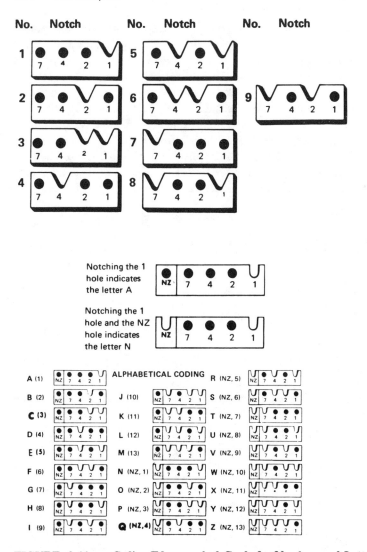

FIGURE 6–11   Coding Edge-punched Cards for Numbers and Letters

tician. Late in that century Herman Hollerith, a director of the United States Census Bureau, devised a hole-punched card to aid in the more efficient processing of census data. The punched card was a significant development for it is a very important part of modern computer date processing.

In the mid-1940s an electrical impulse computer was devised with circuits employing thousands of vacuum tubes. These computers were very large and cumbersome and required a great deal of space. The heat generated by the vacuum tubes required extensive air-conditioning equipment to prevent heat damage, and the uncertain life of the vacuum tubes caused frequent malfunction.

With the development of transistorized components, replacement of the vacuum tubes, smaller space requirements, increased component reliability, elimination of heat dissipation considerations, and other improvements the computer has become a much more effective device for the storage, processing, and retrieval of information.

The most advanced current models have incorporated micro-circuitry of even more compact size, improved storage capacity, and greater processing speed. Functions can be processed in nanoseconds or billionths of a second.

Computer technology involves a number of functions:

1. *Input.* Information or data are entered into the computer through the use of punched cards, mark sense cards, or optical scanning readers that translate printed page information to punched cards or magnetic tape.
2. *Storage.* Information is stored in magnetic cores, tapes, or disks, available for processing upon the demand of the program.
3. *Control.* The program written in computer language directs the computer to perform a series of operations in a designated sequence written by the programmer. FORTRAN IV (FORmula TRANslator) is a modified version of the original FORTRAN. Such directions as *do, go to, read, punch, call,* and *write* are FORTRAN language terms. FORTRAN IV is the prevailing language used for statistical calculations. ALGOL (ALGOrithmic Oriented Language) and COBOL (COmmon Business Oriented Language) are other widely used computer languages. Library and computer centers have many "canned" or prepared programs to perform a variety of statistical procedures so that the researcher need not always write his own.
4. *Output.* The output or retrieval process transfers the processed information or data from the computer to the researcher, using one of a number of devices to communicate the results. The output may be displayed on a screen, recorded on magnetic tape, or printed on paper by a rapid typing machine that can print as many as 1100 lines of up to 30 characters per minute.

The computer can perform many statistical calculations easily and quickly. Computation of means, standard deviations, coefficients of correlation, *t* tests, analysis of variance, and multivariate and factor analysis are some of the programs that are available at computer centers. However, simple calculations using small samples and few variables do not justify the use of the computer.

It has been said that the computer makes no mistakes; but program writers do make mistakes and any directions given the computer are faithfully executed. The computer doesn't think; it can only execute the directions of a thinking man. If poor data or faulty programs are introduced into the computer, the data analysis will lead to invalid conclusions.

The author recognizes that it would be impracticable to attempt to present a comprehensive explanation of the functions of the computer in a brief discussion. For complete understanding of computers and their application to data-processing, instruction in computer programming, some actual experience with computers and careful study of the literature in the field would be required.

Summary

From the instruments and procedures that provide for the collection and analysis of data upon which hypotheses may be tested, the researcher chooses the most appropriate.

The data-gathering devices that have proven useful in educational research include: questionnaires, opinionnaires, Q methodology, observation, check lists, rating scales, score cards, scaled specimens, document or content analyses, interviews, psychological tests and inventories, sociograms, "guess-who" techniques, and social-distance scales.

Some research investigations use but one of these devices. Others employ a number of them in combination. The student of educational research should make an effort to familiarize himself with the strengths and limitations of these tools, and should attempt to develop skill in constructing and using them effectively.

The analysis and interpretation of data represent the application deductive and inductive logic to the research process. The data are often classified by division into subgroups, and are then analyzed and synthesized in such a way that hypotheses may be verified or rejected. The final result may be a new principle or generalization. Data are examined in terms of comparisons between the more homogeneous segments within the whole group, and by comparison with some outside criteria.

The processes of classification, sorting, and tabulation of data are important parts of the research process. In extensive studies, mechanical methods of sorting and tabulating are used to save time and effort and to minimize error. In smaller projects, hand-sorting and hand-tabulating processes are usually employed.

The researcher must guard against the limitations and sources of error inherent in the processes of analysis and interpretation of data.

What are some of the limitations and sources of error in the analysis and interpretation of data that would jeopardize the success of an investigation?

Confusing statements with facts. A common fault is the acceptance of statements as facts. What individuals report may be a sincere expression of what they believe to be the facts in a case, but these statements are not necessarily true. Few people observe skillfully, and many forget quickly. It is the researcher's responsibility to verify all statements as completely as possible before they are accepted as facts.

Failure to recognize limitations. The very nature of research implies certain restrictions or limitations about the group or the situation described—its size, its representativeness, and its distinctive composition. Failure to recognize these limitations may lead to the formulation of generalizations that are not warranted by the data collected.

Careless or incompetent tabulation. When one is confronted with a mass of data, it is easy to make simple mechanical errors. Placing a tally in the wrong cell or incorrectly totaling a set of scores can easily invalidate carefully gathered data. Errors sometimes may be attributed to clerical helpers with limited ability and little interest in the research project.

Inappropriate statistical procedures. The application of the wrong statistical treatment may lead to invalid conclusions. This error may result from a lack of understanding of statistics or the limitations inherent in a particular statistical application.

Computational errors. Since the statistical manipulation of data often involves large numbers and many separate operations, there are many opportunities for error. Readers may be familiar with the story of the engineer who, after witnessing the collapse of his bridge, remarked, "I must have misplaced a decimal point." There is no way to eliminate completely human fallibility, but the use of either mechanical or electronic tabulating devices will help to reduce error.

Faulty logic. This rather inclusive category may embrace a number of the sources of error in the thought processes of the researcher. Invalid assumptions, inappropriate analogies, inversion of cause and effect, confusion of a simple relationship with causation, failure to recognize that group phenomena may not be used indiscriminately to predict individual occurrences or behavior, failure to realize that the whole may be greater than the sum of its parts, belief that frequency of appearance is always a measure of importance, and many other errors are limitations to accurate interpretation.

The researcher's unconscious bias. Although objectivity is the ideal of research, few individuals achieve it completely. There is great temptation to omit evidence unfavorable to the hypothesis, and to overemphasize favorable data. The effective researcher is aware of his feelings and the likely areas of his bias, and constantly endeavors to maintain the objectivity that is essential.

Lack of imagination. The quality of creative imagination distinguishes the true researcher from the compiler. Knowledge of the field of inquiry, skill in research procedures, experience, and skill in logical thinking are qualities that enable the adroit researcher to see relationships leading to possible generalizations that would escape the less skillful analyst. It is this ability to see all the implications in the data that produces significant discoveries.

Suggested activities

1. For what type of problem and under what circumstances would you find the following data-gathering techniques most appropriate:
   a. Schedule
   b. Questionnaire
   c. Interview
   d. Observation
   e. *Q*-sort
2. Construct a short schedule that could be administered in class. The following topics are suggested:
   a. Leisure Interests and Activities
   b. Reasons for Selecting Teaching as a Profession
   c. Methods of Dealing with School Discipline
   d. Political Interests and Activities
3. Construct a Likert-type opinionnaire dealing with a controversial problem. One of the following topics may be appropriate:
   a. Teacher Affiliation with Professional Organizations
   b. Teacher Strikes and Sanctions
   c. Religious Activities in the School Program
   d. The Nongraded School
4. Construct a short rating scale to be used for the evaluation of the teaching performance of a probationary teacher.
5. To what extent is the administration of personal and social adjustment inventories an invasion of a student's privacy?
6. Construct a specimen $4'' \times 6''$ edge-punched card with 32 holes. Number each hole and set up a code to correspond to responses from a questionnaire.

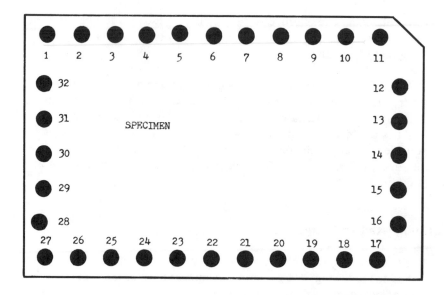

7. Using the edge-punched card as the questionnaire response form, devise a way for the respondents to indicate their responses directly on the card, so that it would not be necessary to transfer responses to the card from the questionnaire.

Bibliography

American Psychological Association Standards for Educational and Psychological Tests. Washington, D.C.: APA, 1974.

ANASTASI, ANN. *Psychological Testing*. New York: Macmillan Co., 1968.

BONNEY, MERLE F. "Sociometric Methods," in *Encyclopedia of Educational Research*. New York: Macmillan Co., 1960, pp. 1319–1323.

CARTWRIGHT, CAROL A. and G. PHILLIP CARTWRIGHT. *Developing Observation Skills*. New York: McGraw-Hill Book Co., 1974.

CONRAD, HERBERT S. "Clearance of Questionnaires with Respect to Invasion of Privacy, Public Sensitivities, Ethical Standards, Etc." *Journal of Educational Measurement* (Spring 1967): 22–28.

CRONBACH, LEE J. *Essentials of Psychological Testing*. New York: Harper & Row, Publishers, 1970.

DALE, EDGAR and JEANNE CHALL. "A Formula for Predicting Readability." *Educational Research Bulletin* 27 (January 1, 1948): 11–20.

EBEL, ROBERT L. *Essentials of Educational Measurement*. Englewood Cliffs, N.J.: Prentice-Hall, 1972.

EDWARDS, ALLEN L. and KATHERINE C. KENNEY. "A Comparison of the Thurston and Likert Techniques of Attitude Scale Construction." *Journal of Applied Psychology* 30 (February 1946): 72–78.

FENLASON, ANN. *Essentials of Interviewing.* New York: Harper & Row, Publishers, 1952.

FESTINGER, LEON and DANIEL KATZ. *Research Methods in the Behavioral Sciences.* New York: Holt, Rinehart & Winston, 1953. Chapters 2, 4, 6, 8, and 9.

FLESCH, RUDOLPH. *How to Test Readability.* New York: Harper & Row, Publishers, 1951.

GOODE, WILLIAM J. and PAUL K. HATT. *Methods in Social Research.* New York: McGraw-Hill Book Co., 1952. Chapters 10, 11, 13, 16 and 20.

GUTTMAN, LOUIS. "The Principal Components of Scalable Attitudes," in Paul F. Lazarsfeld, *Mathematical Thinking in the Social Sciences.* Beverly Hills, Calif.: Glencoe Press, 1954.

HERRIOTT, ROBERT E. "Survey Research Method," in *Encyclopedia of Educational Research.* New York: Macmillan Co., 1960, pp. 1400–1410.

HOPKINS, KENNETH D. and JULIAN C. STANLEY. *Educational and Psychological Measurement and Evaluation.* 5th ed., Englewood Cliffs, N.J.: Prentice-Hall, 1972.

HYMAN, HERBERT H. *Survey Design and Analysis.* Beverly Hills, Calif.: Glencoe Press, 1955.

HYMAN, HERBERT H. ET AL. *Interviewing in Social Research.* Chicago: University of Chicago Press, 1954.

Interview Manual. Ann Arbor, Mich.: Institute for Social Research, University of Michigan, 1969.

KAHN, ROBERT L. and CHARLES F. Cannell. *The Dynamics of Interviewing.* New York: John Wiley & Sons, 1957.

KERLINGER, FRED N. *Foundations of Behavioral Research.* New York: Holt, Rinehart & Winston, 1973. Chapters 22–24, 28–34.

KISH, L. *Survey Sampling.* New York: John Wiley & Sons, 1965.

LINDZEY, GARDNER, ed. *The Handbook of Social Psychology.* Cambridge, Mass.: Addison-Wesley, 1954. Chapters 9–13.

MEHRENS, WILLIAM A. and IRVIN J. LEHMANN. *Standardized Tests in Education.* New York: Holt, Rinehart & Winston, 1975.

MORENO, JACOB L. *Sociometry: Experimental Method and the Science of Society.* New York: Beacon Press, 1951.

MORENO, JACOB L. *The Sociometry Reader.* New York: Free Press, 1960.

MORENO, JACOB L. *Who Shall Survive?* New York: Beacon Press, 1953.

MURSTEIN, BERNARD I., ed. *Handbook of Projective Techniques.* New York: Basic Books, 1966.

MUSSEN, PAUL H., ed. *Handbook of Research Methods in Child Development.* New York: John Wiley & Sons, Inc., 1960. Chapters 3, 14–16, 18.

NOLL, VICTOR H. *Introduction to Educational Measurement.* Boston: Houghton Mifflin Co., 1965.

NUNNALY, JUM C. *Educational Measurement and Evaluation.* New York: McGraw-Hill Book Co., 1972.

OPPENHEIM, A. N. *Questionnaire Design and Attitude Measurement.* New York: Basic Books, 1966.

PARTEN, M. B. *Surveys, Polls and Samples: Practical Procedures.* New York: Harper & Row, Publishers, 1950.

PAYNE, STANLEY. *The Art of Asking Questions*. Princeton, N.J.: Princeton University Press, 1951.

REMMERS, H. H. *Introduction to Opinion and Attitude Measurement*. New York: Harper & Row, Publishers, 1954.

"School Surveys," in *Encyclopedia of Educational Research*. New York: Macmillan Co., 1960, pp. 1211–1216.

SELTIZ, CLAIRE, MARIE JAHODA, MORTON DEUTSCH and STUART W. COOK. *Research Methods in Social Relations*. New York: Holt, Rinehart & Winston, 1961. Chapters 5–8, 10, Appendix C.

SHAW, MARVIN E. and JACK M. WRIGHT. *Scales for the Measurement of Attitudes*. New York: McGraw-Hill Book Co., 1967.

STANLEY, JULIAN C. *Measurement in Today's Schools*. Englewood Cliffs, N.J.: Prentice-Hall, 1970.

STEPHENSON, WILLIAM. *The Study of Behavior: Q Technique and its Methodology*. Chicago: University of Chicago Press, 1953.

SUMMERS, GENE F., ed. *Attitude Measurement*. Chicago: Rand McNally & Co., 1970.

THURSTONE, LOUIS L. "The Measurement of Values." *Psychological Review* 41 (January 1954): 47–58.

TORGERSON, WARREN S. *Theory and Methods of Scaling*. New York: John Wiley & Sons, 1958.

WEBB, EUGENE J., DONALD T. CAMPBELL, RICHARD D. SCHWARTZ, and LEE SECHREST. *Unobtrusive Measures: Nonreactive Research in the Social Sciences*. Chicago: Rand McNally & Co., 1966.

YOUNG, PAULINE V. *Scientific Social Surveys and Research*. Englewood Cliffs, N.J.: Prentice-Hall, 1966.

Computers

BORKO, HAROLD, ed. *Computer Applications in the Behavioral Sciences*. Englewood Cliffs, N.J.: Prentice-Hall, 1962.

DAVIS, GORDON B. *An Introduction to Electronic Computers*. New York: McGraw-Hill Book Co., 1965.

LEE, R. M. *A Short Course in FORTRAN IV Programming*. New York: McGraw-Hill Book Co., 1967.

MARKER, R. W. P. McGRAW and F. D. STONE, eds. *Computer Concepts and Educational Information*. Iowa City, Iowa: Educational Information Center, 1966.

McCRACKEN, D. A. *Guide to FORTRAN Programming*. New York: John Wiley & Sons, 1961.

Personnel and Guidance Journal 49 (Nov. 1970) (entire issue devoted to technology in guidance).

SAXON, JAMES A. *COBOL, A Self-Instruction Manual*. Englewood Cliffs, N.J.: Prentice-Hall, 1970.

Scientific American 215 (September 1966) (entire issue devoted to computers).

VELDMAN, DONALD J. *FORTRAN Programming for the Behavioral Sciences*. New York: Holt, Rinehart & Winston, 1967.

YASAKI, Ed. "Educational Data Processing," *Datamation* 9 (June 1963): 24–27.

DESCRIPTIVE DATA ANALYSIS

Chapter 7

Since the following discussion is only a part of a general textbook on educational research, the treatment of statistical analysis is in no sense complete or exhaustive. Some of the most simple and basic concepts are presented. Students whose mathematical experience includes high school algebra should be able to understand the logic and the computational processes involved and should be able to follow the examples without difficulty.

The purpose of this discussion is twofold:

1. To help the student, as a consumer, develop an understanding of statistical terminology, and the concepts necessary to read with understanding some of the professional literature in educational research
2. To help the student develop enough competence and know-how to carry on research studies using simple types of analysis

The emphasis is upon intuitive understanding and practical application rather than on the derivation of mathematical formulas. Those who expect and need to develop real competence in educational research will need to take some of the following steps:

1. Taking one or more courses in behavioral statistics and experimental design
2. Studying more specialized textbooks in statistics, particulary those dealing with statistical inference (see Glass and Stanley, Guilford and Fruchter, Popham, Siegel, cited in the bibliography)
3. Reading research studies in professional journals extensively and critically
4. Carrying on research studies involving some serious "digging for oneself" in the use of statistical procedures

What is statistics?

Statistics is a body of mathematical techniques or processes for gathering, organizing, analyzing, and interpreting numerical data. Since research yields such quantitative data, statistics is a basic tool of measurement, evaluation, and research.

The word *statistics* is sometimes used to describe the numerical data that are gathered. Statistical data describe group behavior or group characteristics abstracted from a number of individual observations which are combined to make generalizations possible.

Everyone is familiar with such expressions as the average family income, the typical white-collar worker, or the representative city. These are statistical concepts and as group characteristics, may be expressed in measurement of age, size, or any other traits that can be described quantitatively. When we say that the average fifth grade boy is ten years old, we are generalizing about all fifth grade boys, not any particular boy. Thus the statistical measurement is an abstraction that may be used in place of a great mass of individual measures.

The research worker who uses statistics is concerned with more than the manipulation of data. Statistical method goes to the fundamental purposes of description and analysis, and its proper application involves answering the following questions:

1. What facts need to be gathered to provide the information necessary to answer the question or to test the hypothesis?
2. How are these observations to be selected, gathered, organized, and analyzed?
3. What assumptions underlie the statistical methodology to be employed?
4. What conclusions can be validly drawn from the analysis of the data?

Research consists of systematic observation and description of the characteristics or properties of objects or events for the purpose of discovering relationships between variables. The ultimate purpose is to develop generalizations that may be used to explain phenomena and to predict future occurrences. To conduct research, principles must be established so that the observation and description have a commonly understood meaning. Measurement is the most precise and universally accepted process of description assigning quantitative values to the properties of objects and events.

LEVELS OF MEASUREMENT

There are four levels of measures or scales, ranging from a rather crude description to a more precise and sophisticated level. The nature of the variable and the precision of the measuring instruments determine the appropriate level of measurement.

Nominal scale. A nominal scale is the lowest level method of quantification. A nominal scale indicates "telling apart" or describing differences between things by assigning them to such categories as professors, associate professors, assistant professors, instructors, or lecturers, and to such subsets as males or females.

TABLE 7–1   Academic Rank of Members of the Instructional Staff of Southland College

	Male	*Female*	*Total*
Professors	20	4	24
Associate professors	34	22	56
Assistant professors	44	30	74
Instructors	26	14	40
Lecturers	17	5	22
Totals	141	75	216

Nominal data are counted data. Each individual can be a member of only one set and all other members of the set have the same defined characteristic. Such categories as nationality, gender, educational level, occupation, or religious affiliation provide other examples. Nominal scales are nonorderable, but in some situations this simple enumeration or counting is the only feasible method of quantification and may provide an acceptable basis for statistical analysis.

Ordinal scale. Sometimes it is possible not only to indicate that things differ, but also to indicate that they differ in amount or degree. Ordinal scales permit ordering into *more than* or *less than* adjacent things. The criterion for highest to lowest ordering is expressed as relative position or rank in a group: 1st, 2nd, 3rd, 4th, 5th, . . . , nth. Ordinal measures have no absolute values and the differences between adjacent ranks may not be equal. Ranking spaces them equally though they may not be equally spaced. The following example illustrates this limitation:

Subject	Height in inches	Difference in inches	Rank
Jones	76		1st
Smith	68	8	2nd
Brown	66	2	3rd
Porter	59	7	4th
Taylor	58	1	5th

Interval scale.   A scale based on equal units of measurement indicates how much or how little of a given characteristic or property is present. The difference in amount of the characteristic possessed by persons with scores of 90 and 91 is assumed to be equivalent to that between persons with scores of 60 and 61.

The interval scale represents a decided advantage over nominal and ordinal scales because it indicates the actual amount of a trait or characteristic. Its primary limitation is its lack of a true zero. It does not have the capacity of measuring the complete absence of the trait. Psychological tests and inventories are interval scales and have this limitation.

Ratio scale.   A ratio scale has the equal interval properties of an interval scale but has two additional features:

1. The ratio scale has a true zero. It is possible to indicate the complete absence of a property. For example, the zero point on a centimeter scale indicates the complete absence of length or height.
2. The numerals of the ratio scale have the qualities of real numbers and can be added, subtracted, multiplied, and divided and expressed in ratio relationships. Five grams is one-half of ten grams, fifteen grams is three times five grams and on a laboratory weighing scale, two one-gram weights will balance a two-gram weight. One of the advantages enjoyed by practitioners in the physical sciences is the ability to describe variables in ratio scale form. The behavioral sciences are limited to describing variables in interval scale form, a less precise type of measurement.

Proceeding from the nominal scale (the least precise type) to ratio scale (the most precise) increasingly relevant information is provided. If the nature of the variables permits, the scale that provides the most precise description should be used.

PARAMETRIC AND NONPARAMETRIC DATA

In applying statistical treatments two types of data are recognized.

1. *Parametric data.* Data of this type are measured data, and parametric statistical tests assume that the data are normally or nearly normally distributed. Parametric tests are applied to both interval and ratio scaled data.

2. *Nonparametric data.* Data of this type are either counted or ranked. Nonparametric tests, sometimes known as distribution-free tests, do not rest upon the more stringent assumption of normally distributed populations.

Table 7–2 presents a graphic summary of the levels of quantitative description and the types of statistical analysis appropriate for each level; the concepts will be developed further later in the discussion.

TABLE 7–2   Levels of Quantitative Description

Level	Scale	Process	Data treatment	Some appropriate tests
4	Ratio	measured equal intervals true zero ratio relationship	parametric	*t* test analysis of variance analysis of covariance factor analysis Pearson's *r*
3	Interval	measured equal intervals no true zero		
2	Ordinal	ranked in order	nonparametric	Spearman's *rho* (ρ) Mann-Whitney Wilcoxon
1	Nominal	classified and counted		chi square median sign

DESCRIPTIVE AND INFERENTIAL ANALYSIS

To this point no reference has been made to the limits to which statistical analysis may be generalized. Two types of statistical application are relevant.

Descriptive analysis.   Descriptive statistical analysis limits generalization to the particular group of individuals observed. No conclusions are extended beyond this group and any similarity to those outside the group cannot be assumed. The data describes one group and that group only. Much simple action research involves descriptive analysis and provides valuable information about the nature of a particular group of individuals.

Inferential analysis.   Inferential statistical analysis always involves the process of sampling, and the selection of a small group that is assumed to be related to a larger group from which it is drawn. The small group is known as the sample; the large group the population. Drawing conclusions about populations based upon observations of samples is the purpose of inferential analysis.

A *statistic* is a measure based on observations of the characteristics of a *sample*. A *statistic* computed from a sample may be used to estimate a *parameter*, the corresponding value in the population from which the sample is selected.

Before any assumptions can be made it is essential that the individuals selected be chosen in such a way that the small group, or sample, approximates the larger group, or population. Within a margin of error, which is always present, and by the use of appropriate statistical techniques, this approximation can be assumed, making possible the estimation of population characteristics by an analysis of the characteristics of the sample.

It should be emphasized that when data are derived from a group without careful sampling procedures, the researcher should carefully state that his findings apply only to the group observed and may not apply to or describe other individuals or groups. The statistical theory of sampling is complex and involves the estimation of error of inferred measurements, error that is inherent in estimating the relationship between a random sample and the population from which it is drawn. The discussion of inferential data analysis is present later in the discussion.

The organization of data

The list of test scores in a teacher's grade book provides an example of unorganized data. Since the usual method of listing is alphabetical, the scores are difficult to interpret without some other type of organization.

Alberts, James	60
Brown, John	78
Davis, Mary	90
Smith, Helen	70
Williams, Paul	88

The array. Arranging the same scores in descending order of magnitude produces what is known as an array.

90
88
78
70
60

The array provides a more convenient arrangement. The highest score (90), the lowest score (60), and the middle score (78) are easily identified.

Thus the range (the difference between the highest and lowest scores, plus one) can easily be determined.

Illustrated in Table 7–3 is an ungrouped data arrangement in array form.

TABLE 7–3   **Scores of 37 Students on a Semester Algebra Test**

98	85	80	76	67
97	85	80	76	67
95	85	80	75	64
93	84	80	73	60
90	82	78	72	57
88	82	78	70	
87	82	78	70	
87	80	77	70	

Range $= 98 - 57 + 1 = 41 + 1 = 42$

GROUPED DATA DISTRIBUTIONS

Data are more clearly presented when scores are grouped with a frequency column included. Data can be presented in frequency tables with different class intervals, depending on the number and range of the scores.

Tables 7–4 and 7–5 illustrate the same distribution grouped in intervals of three and in intervals of five.

TABLE 7–4   **Scores on Algebra Test Grouped in Intervals of Three**

Score interval	Tallies	Frequency (f)	Includes
97–99	||	2	(97 98 99)
94–96	|	1	(94 95 96)
91–93	|	1	etc.
88–90	||	2	
85–87	⫽⫽	5	
82–84	||||	4	
79–81	⫽⫽	5	
76–78	⫽⫽ |	6	
73–75	||	2	
70–72	||||	4	
67–69	||	2	
64–66	|	1	
61–63		0	
58–60	|	1	
55–57	|	1	
		$N = 37$	

TABLE 7-5   Scores on Algebra Test Grouped in Intervals of Five

Score interval	Tallies	Frequency (f)	Includes
96–100	||	2	(96 97 98 99 100)
91–95	||	2	(91 92 93 94 95)
86–90	||||	4	etc.
81–85	JHT ||	7	
76–80	JHT JHT |	11	
71–75	|||	3	
66–70	JHT	5	
61–65	|	1	
56–60	||	2	
		$N = 37$	

It has been suggested that the number of intervals be set between ten and twenty. By dividing the range by 15, the approximate width and number of score intervals is established.

A score interval with an odd number of units may be preferable because its midpoint is a whole number rather than a fraction. Since all scores are assumed to fall at the midpoint (for purposes of computing the mean) the computation is less complicated.

Even interval of four: 8 9 10 11 (midpoint 9.5)
Odd interval of five: 8 9 10 11 12 (midpoint 10)

There is no rule that rigidly determines the proper score interval, and intervals of ten are frequently used.

Using the distribution presented in Table 7–3:

Highest score   98
Lowest score   57
Range   42
$\dfrac{42}{15} = 2.80$ Select an interval of three (rounded to a whole number).

Statistical measures

Several basic types of statistical measures are appropriate in describing and analyzing mass data in a meaningful way:

Measures of central tendency or averages
   Mean
   Median
   Mode
Measures of spread or dispersion
   Deviations
   Variance
   Standard deviation
Measures of relative position
   Percentile rank
   Percentile score
   Standard scores
Measures of relationship
   Coefficient of correlation

Describing characteristics of groups by using averages is understood by nonstatisticians. Climate of an area is often noted by average temperature or average amount of rainfall. We may describe students by grade point averages, or by average age. Socioeconomic status of groups is directed by average income and the return on an investment portfolio may be judged in terms of average income return on investment. But to the statistician, the term *average* is unsatisfactory for there are a number of types of averages, only one of which may be appropriate to use in describing given characteristics of a group. Of the many averages that may be used three have been selected as most useful in educational research: the mean, the median and the mode.

Measures of central tendency

THE MEAN (*M*)

The mean of a distribution is commonly understood as the arithmetic average. The term *grade point average*, familiar to students, is a mean value. It is computed by dividing the sum of all the scores by the number of scores. In formula form:

$$M_x = \frac{\Sigma X}{N}$$

where M = mean
   Σ = sum of
   X = scores in a distribution
   N = number of scores

Example

$$
\begin{array}{c}
X \\
6 \\
5 \\
4 \\
3 \\
2 \\
\underline{1} \\
\Sigma\,X = 21 \\
N = 6 \\
M_x = \tfrac{21}{6} = 3.50
\end{array}
$$

In using grouped data the formula is written:

$$M_x = \frac{\Sigma\,f\bar{X}}{N}$$

where $\bar{X}$ = the midpoint of each interval
f = the frequency (number of scores in each interval)

Each midpoint is multiplied by the frequency in each score interval, the products summed and divided by N. It is assumed that each score within an interval falls at the midpoint of the interval.

Ungrouped data method		*Grouped data method, intervals of three*			
X		X	f	$\bar{X}$	$f\bar{X}$
14		13–15	1	14	14
12		10–12	4	11	44
12		7–9	2	8	16
10		4–6	6	5	30
10		1–3	3	2	6
8				$\Sigma\,f\bar{X}$ =	110
7				N =	16
6				M =	6.88
6		where $\bar{X}$ = midpoint of interval			
5					
5					
4					
4					
3					
3					
2					
$\Sigma\,X$ = 111					
N = 16					
M = 6.94					

It is apparent that there is only a small difference between mean scores as computed by ungrouped or grouped data methods.

The mean is probably the most useful of all statistical measure, for, in addition to the information that it provides, it is the base from which many other important measures are computed.

THE MEDIAN (*Md*)

The median is a point (not necessarily a score) in an array, above and below which one-half of the scores fall. It is a measure of position rather than of magnitude and is frequently found by inspection rather than by calculation.

```
7
6                    3 scores fall above
5
4 —median
3
2                    3 scores fall below
1
```

When the number of scores is odd, the midscore is the median. When the number of scores is even, the median is the midpoint between the two middle scores.

```
6
5                    3 scores above
4
  —median = 3.50
3                    3 scores below
2
1
```

The median is not influenced by extreme scores at either end of a distribution. In the following examples the medians are identical.

```
    A              B
    7              50
    6              49
    5              30
    4 —Md          4 —Md
    3              3
    2              2
    1              0
```

In certain types of data distributions the median may be a more realistic measure of central tendency than the mean.

In a small school with five faculty members, the salaries are:

Teacher A	$20,000
B	8,800
C	8,400
D	8,200
E	8,000
	$53,400

$$M = \frac{53,400}{5} = \$10,680$$

The average salary of the group is represented with a different emphasis by the median salary ($8,400) than by the mean salary ($10,680), which is substantially higher than that of four of the five faculty members. Thus, the median is less sensitive than the mean to extreme values at either end of a distribution.

THE MODE (*Mo*)

6
5
4 ⎫
4 ⎭ —Mode
3
2
1

The mode is that score that occurs most frequently in a distribution. It is located by inspection rather than by computation. In grouped data distribution, the mode is assumed to be the midscore of the interval in which the greatest frequency occurs.

The modal age of fifth grade children is ten years. There are more ten year old fifth graders than any other age. A menswear salesman will verify the fact that there are more sales of size 40 suits than of any other size. Consequently, a larger number of size 40 suits are ordered and stocked, 40 being the mode.

In some distributions there may be more than one mode. A two mode distribution is bimodal, more than two, multimodal. If the number of auto accidents on the streets of a city were tabulated by hours of occurrence, it is likely that two modal periods would become apparent—between 7 and 8 a.m. and between 5 and 6 p.m., the hours when traffic to and from stores and offices was heaviest and when drivers were in the greatest hurry. In a normal distribution of data there is one mode and it falls at the midpoint. However, in some unusual distributions, the mode may fall at some other point. When the mode or modes reveal such unusual behavior, they do not serve as measures of central tendency but they do reveal useful information about the nature of the distribution.

Measures of spread or dispersion

Measures of central tendency describe location along an ordered scale. These are characteristics of data distributions that call for additional types of statistical analysis. The following scores were made by two groups of students.

	Group I			Group II	
Pupil	*Score*	*Academic grade*	*Pupil*	*Score*	*Academic grade*
Arthur	100	A	John	82	C
Betty	90	B	Katherine	81	C
Charles	80	C	Larry	80	C
Donna	70	D	Nancy	79	C
Edward	60	F	Mary	78	C

$$\Sigma X = 400 \qquad\qquad \Sigma X = 400$$
$$N = 5 \qquad\qquad N = 5$$
$$M = \tfrac{400}{5} = 80 \qquad\qquad M = \tfrac{400}{5} = 80$$
$$Md = 80 \qquad\qquad Md = 80$$

The mean and the median are identical for both groups. It is apparent that averages do not fully describe the differences in achievement between students in group I or those in group II. To contrast their performance it is necessary to use a measure of score spread or dispersion. Group II is homogeneous with little difference between adjacent scores. Group I is decidedly heterogeneous with performances ranging from superior to very poor.

RANGE
The range, the simplest measure of dispersion, is the difference between the highest and lowest score, plus one. For group I the range is 41 $(100 - 60 + 1)$. For group II the range is 5 $(82 - 78 + 1)$.

DEVIATION FROM THE MEAN (small x)
A score expressed as its distance from the mean is called a deviation score. Its formula is:

$$x = (X - M)$$

If the score falls above the mean the deviation score is positive $(+)$, if it falls below the mean the deviation score is negative $(-)$.

Using the same example, comparing groups I and II:

	Group I			Group II	
Pupil	X	(X − M)	Pupil	X	(X − M)
		x			x
Arthur	100	+20	John	82	+2
Betty	90	+10	Katherine	81	+1
Charles	80	0	Larry	80	0
Donna	70	−10	Nancy	79	−1
Edward	60	−20	Mary	78	−2
	$\Sigma X = 400$	$\Sigma x = 0$		$\Sigma X = 400$	$\Sigma x = 0$
	$N = 5$			$N = 5$	
	$M = 80$			$M = 80$	

It is interesting to note that the sum of the score deviations from the mean equals zero.

$$\Sigma (X - M) = 0$$
$$\Sigma x = 0$$

In fact, an alternative definition of the mean is:
The mean is that value in a distribution about which the sum of the deviation scores equals zero.

VARIANCE (σ^2)

The sum of the squared deviations from the mean, divided by N, is known as the variance. We have noted that the sum of the deviations from the mean equals zero ($\Sigma x = 0$). From a mathematical point of view it would be impossible to find a mean value to describe these deviations (unless the signs were ignored). Squaring each deviation score yields a positive score. They can then be summed, divided by N, and the mean of the squared deviations computed.

$$x^2 = + \text{ values}$$

| x | x^2 |

Example

| -2 | $+4$ |
| $+2$ | $+4$ |

The variance formula is:

$$\sigma^2 = \frac{\Sigma(X - M_x)^2}{N} \quad \text{or} \quad \frac{\Sigma x^2}{N} \qquad x = (X - M_x)$$

Thus the variance is a value that describes how all of the scores in a distribution are dispersed or spread about the mean. This value is very useful in describing the characteristics of a distribution and will be employed in a number of very important statistical tests.

STANDARD DEVIATION (σ)

The standard deviation is the positive square root of the variance and is also used as a measure of the spread or dispersion of scores in a distribution. The formula for standard deviation is:

$$\sigma = \sqrt{\frac{\Sigma(X - M)^2}{N}} \quad \text{or} \quad \sqrt{\frac{\Sigma x^2}{N}}$$

In the following example the variance and the standard deviation are computed

	x	x^2
82	+2	+4
81	+1	+1
80	0	0
79	−1	+1
78	−2	+4
	Σx^2 =	10

variance $\sigma^2 = \dfrac{10}{5} = 2$ standard deviation $\sigma = \sqrt{\dfrac{10}{5}} = \sqrt{2} = 1.414$

While the deviation approach provides a clear example of the meaning of variance and standard deviation, in actual practice the deviation method is too awkward to use in computing the variances or standard deviations for large score distributions. A much less complicated method uses the raw scores instead of the deviation scores. The number values tend to be large, but the use of a calculator facilitates the computation.

$$\text{variance } \sigma^2 = \frac{N\,\Sigma X^2 - (\Sigma X)^2}{N^2}$$

$$\text{standard deviation } \sigma = \sqrt{\frac{N\,\Sigma X^2 - (\Sigma X)^2}{N^2}}$$

The following example demonstrates the process of computation, using the raw score method:

X	X^2
90	8100
85	7225
83	6889
80	6400
70	4900
68	4624
68	4624
68	4624
65	4225
65	4225
61	3721

$$\Sigma X = 803 \qquad \Sigma X^2 = 59{,}557$$
$$N = 11$$

$$\sigma^2 = \frac{11(59{,}557) - (803)^2}{(11)(11)}$$

$$\sigma^2 = \frac{655{,}127 - 644{,}809}{121}$$

$$\sigma^2 = \frac{10{,}318}{121} = 85.27$$

$$\sigma = \sqrt{85.27} = 9.24$$

A number of time-saving calculations may be performed using grouped data rather than raw scores. However, the availability of inexpensive electronic calculators and the increasing use of computers have minimized the advantages of grouped data procedures. When calculators or computers are not available a number of grouped data calculations are helpful and are presented in Appendix F.

The standard deviation is a very useful device for comparing characteristics that may be quite different or that may be expressed in different units of measurement. The discussion that follows indicates that when the normality of distributions can be assumed, it is possible to compare the proverbial oranges and bananas. The standard deviation is independent of the magnitude of the mean and provides a common unit of measurement. To use a rather far-fetched example, imagine a man whose height is one standard deviation below the mean, and whose weight is one standard deviation above the mean. Since we assume that there is a normal relationship between height and weight (or that both characteristics are normally distributed) we have a picture of a short, overweight individual. His height, expressed in inches, is in the lowest 16 percent of the population, his weight, expressed in pounds, in the highest 16 percent.

This concept is developed later, but before the discussion of the use of the standard deviation as a means of describing status or position in a group, an examination of the normal distribution is appropriate.

The normal distribution

The earliest mathematical analysis of the theory of probability dates back to the eighteenth century. Abraham DeMoivre, a French mathematician, discovered that a mathematical relationship explained the probabilities associated with various games of chance. He developed the equation and the graphic pattern that describes it. During the nineteenth century a French astronomer, LaPlace, and a German mathematician, Gauss, independently arrived at the same principle and applied it more broadly to areas of measurement in the physical sciences. From the limited applications made by these early mathematicians and astronomers, the theory of probability or the curve of distribution of error has been applied to data gathered in the areas of biology, psychology, sociology, and other sciences. It has been found to describe the fluctuations of chance errors of observation and measurement.[1] Some understanding of the theory of probability and the nature of the curve of normal distribution is necessary for comprehension of many important statistical concepts, particularly in the area of standard scores, the theory of sampling, and inferential statistics.

The law of probability and the normal curve that illustrates it are based upon the law of chance or the probable occurrence of certain events. When any body of observations conforms to this mathematical form, it can be represented by a bell-shaped curve with definite characteristics (see Figure 7–1).

1. It is symmetrical around its vertical axis.
2. The terms cluster around the center (the mean).
3. The mean, median and the mode of the distribution have the same value.
4. The curve has no boundaries in either direction for the curve never touches the base line, no matter how far it is extended. The curve is a curve of probability, not of certainty.

[1]Sir Francis Galton (1822–1911) wrote, "I know of scarcely anything so apt to impress the imagination as the wonderful form of cosmic order expressed by the 'law of frequency or error'. This law would have been personified by the Greeks and deified, if they had known it. It reigns with serenity and in complete self-effacement amidst the wildest confusion. The huger the mob, the greater the apparent anarchy, the more perfect its sway .It is the supreme law of unreason. Whenever a large sample of chaotic elements are taken in hand and marshalled in the order of their magnitude, an unsuspected and most beautiful form of regularity proves to have been latent all along."

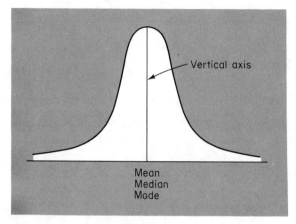

Vertical axis

Mean
Median
Mode

FIGURE 7–1   The Normal Curve

The operation of chance prevails in the tossing of coins or dice. It is believed that many human characteristics respond to the influence of chance. For example, if certain limits of age, race, and gender were kept constant, such measures as height, weight, intelligence, and even longevity would approximate the normal distribution pattern. But the normal distribution does not appear in data based upon observations of samples. There just aren't enough observations. The normal distribution is based upon an infinite number of observations beyond the capability of any observer; thus, there is usually some observed deviation from the symmetrical pattern. But for purposes of statistical analysis, it is assumed that many characteristics do conform to this mathematical form within certain limits, providing a convenient reference.

The concept of measured intelligence is based upon the assumption that this trait is normally distributed throughout limited segments of the population. Tests are so constructed (standardized) that scores are normally distributed in the large group that is used for the determination of norms or standards. Insurance companies determine their premium rates by the application of the curve of probability. A life insurer, basing its expectation on observations of past experience, can estimate the probabilities of the survival of a man from age 45 to 46. They do not purport to predict the survival of a particular individual, but from a large group they can predict the mortality rate of all insured risks.

A coin-tossing experiment may be used to illustrate the type of frequency distribution that conforms to the normal probability curve. If a fair coin is tossed either a head or a tail will turn up. The probability that a head will appear is one chance in two. ($P = .50$). The probability that two or more heads will turn up when several coins are tossed is a product of their probabilities. This principle is illustrated by the binomial equation discovered by DeMoivre. If 2 coins were tossed 4 times, the expected appearance of heads and tails would be:

$$(H + T)^2 = H^2 + 2HT + T^2$$
$$1 \quad\quad 2 \quad\quad 1$$

H^2 both heads: 1 out of 4

2 HT 1 head 1 tail: 2 out of 4

T^2 both tails: 1 out of 4

If fair coins were tossed, 4 at a time, sixteen times, the expected frequency, following the binomial equation, would be:

$$(H + T)^4 = H^4 + 4H^3T + 6H^2T^2 + 4HT^3 + T^4$$
$$1 \quad\quad 4 \quad\quad\; 6 \quad\quad\;\; 4 \quad\quad 1$$

$1H^4$	one chance in 16, all heads	$\frac{1}{16}$
$4H^3T$	four chances in 16, 3 heads, 1 tail	$\frac{4}{16}$
$6H^2T^2$	six chances in 16, 2 heads 2 tails	$\frac{6}{16}$
$4HT^3$	four chances in 16, 1 head 3 tails	$\frac{4}{16}$
$1T^4$	one chance in 16, all tails	$\frac{1}{16}$
Total 16 tosses		Total $\frac{16}{16}$

Since the number of tosses is relatively small, the discrepancy between observed appearance of heads and tails and the theoretical appearances would probably be significant. It has been noted that the curve of normal distribution is approximated as the number of observations approaches an infinite number.

In an interesting class assignment 20 students each tossed 4 coins 4 at a time 16 times. No student observed a theoretically normal distribution of heads and tails but the combined observations of the group came closer to the normal expected frequencies.

TABLE 7–6   **Expected and Observed Number of Heads Appearing When 20 Students Tossed 4 Coins 16 Times**

Number of heads	Theoretical/expected		Observed	
		$f \div 20$		$f \div 20$
0	20	1	25	1.25
1	80	4	70	3.50
2	120	6	125	6.25
3	80	4	84	4.20
4	20	1	16	.80
	$N = 320$	$N = 16$	$N = 320$	$N = 16$

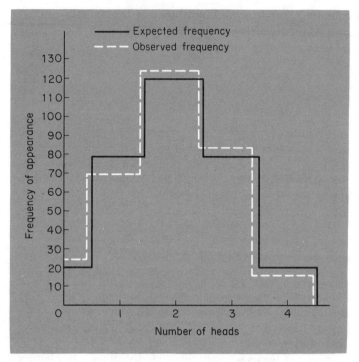

FIGURE 7–2   **Expected and Observed Number of Heads Appearing When 20 Students Tossed 4 Coins 16 Times**

Note the differences between the observed and expected frequencies. Yet there is a pattern of symmetry that would probably conform more closely to the normal curve pattern if the number of participants in the experiment was increased. When N in the expression $(H + T)^n$ becomes infinite in number, the resulting sides of the histogram grow shorter and shorter, finally approaching a curve, the normal curve. Since the tossing of coins may be used to illustrate the operation of chance, this experiment shows the operation of probability, the concept of sampling error (to be described in Chapter 8), and something of the nature of the normal curve (Figure 7–2).

The total area under the normal curve may be considered to approach 100 percent probability. Interpreted in terms of standard deviations, areas between the mean and various standard deviation distances from the mean under the curve show these percentage relationships (Figure 7–3).

Note the graphic conformation of the characteristics of the normal curve.

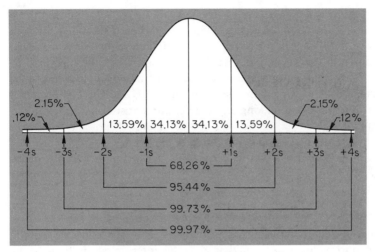

FIGURE 7-3   **Percentage of Frequencies in a Normal Distribution Falling Within a Range of a Given Number of Standard Deviations from the Mean**

1. The curve is symmetrical. The percentage of frequencies is the same for equal intervals below or above the mean.
2. The terms cluster or crowd around the mean. Note how the percentages in a given standard deviation distance are greatest around the mean and decrease as one moves away from the mean.

M to $\pm 1.00z$	34.13%
± 1.00 to $\pm 2.00z$	13.54%
± 2.00 to $\pm 3.00z$	2.15%

3. The curve is highest at the mean. The mean, median, and mode have the same value.
4. The curve has no boundaries. A small fraction of 1 percent of the space falls outside of ± 3.00 standard deviations from the mean.

The normal curve is a curve that also describes probabilities. For example, if height is normally distributed for a given segment of the population, the chances are 34.13/100 that a person selected at random will be between the mean and one standard deviation above the mean in height, or 34.13/100 that the person selected will be between the mean and one standard deviation below the mean in height, or 68.26/100 that the selected person will be within one standard deviation (above or below) the mean in height. Another interpretation would be that 68.26 percent of this population segment would be between the mean and one standard deviation above or below the mean in height.

For practical purposes the curve is usually extended to ± 3 standard deviations from the mean ($\pm 3z$). Most events, occurrences (or probabilities) will fall between these limits. The probability is 99.97/100 that these limits account for observed or predicted occurrences. This statement does not suggest that events or measures could not fall more than three standard deviations from the mean, but that the likelihood would be too small to consider when making predictions or estimates based upon probability. Statisticians deal with probabilities, not certainty, and there is always a degree of reservation in making any prediction. Statisticians deal with the probabilities that cover the normal course of events, not the extremely deviant events outside the normal range of experience.

The normal probability table provides a basis for estimating probabilities and an understanding of its interpretation is essential for students of statistics.

INTERPRETING THE NORMAL PROBABILITY TABLE

The values presented in the normal probability table (Appendix B) provide data for normal distributions that may be interpreted in these ways Figure 7–4):

1. The percentage of total space included between the mean and a given sigma distance (z) from the mean
2. The percentage of cases or the number when N is known, that fall between the mean and a given sigma distance from the mean
3. The probability that an event will occur between the mean and a given sigma distance (z) from the mean

$$z = \text{number of standard deviations from the mean}$$

$$z = \frac{X - M}{\sigma}$$

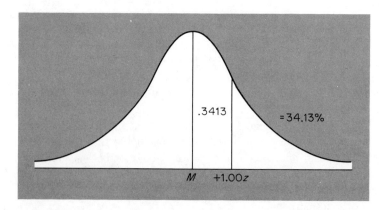

FIGURE 7–4   **The Space Included under the Normal Curve Between the Mean and $\pm 1.00z$.**

In a normal distribution:

1. The space included between the mean and $+1.00z$ is .3413 of the total area under the curve.
2. The percentage of cases that fall between the mean and $+1.00z$ is .3413.
3. The probability of an event occurring (observation) between the mean and $+1.00z$ is .3413.

Since the normal probability curve is symmetrical, the shape of the right side (above the mean) is identical to the shape of the left side (below the mean). Since the values for each side of the curve are identical, only one set of values is presented in the probability table, expressed to one hundredths of a sigma (standard deviation) unit (Figure 7–5).

What is the probability that a score falls

		Probability
above the mean	.5000	50/100
below the mean	.5000	50/100
above $+1.96z$	$.5000 - .4750 = .0250$	$2\frac{1}{2}/100$
below $+.32z$	$.5000 + .1255 = .6255$	$62\frac{1}{2}/100$
below $-.32z$	$.5000 - .1255 = .3745$	$37\frac{1}{2}/100$

STANDARD DEVIATION OF A DICHOTOMOUS VARIABLE

In certain types of nominal data only an *either/or* observation is possible. When a coin is flipped either a head or a tail appears. Such dichotomous variables as gain/loss, $+/-$, M/F, succeed/fail provide other examples. In certain types of analysis the variance and the standard deviation can be calculated and a normal distribution of observations can be assumed.

Another type of coin-tossing experiment illustrates the normal distribution of chance events.

If the coin is fair, the probability of a head appearing is .50. When the probability of an event is .50, the standard deviation of a dichotomous variable can be expressed in the formula:

$$\sigma_{DV} = \sqrt{\frac{N}{4}}$$

The mean would be computed as NP and a normal curve could be plotted as shown in Figure 7–6.

If 100 fair coins were tossed the following normal distribution might appear:

$$N = 100$$
$$P = .50 \qquad \sigma_{DV} = \sqrt{\frac{100}{4}} = \sqrt{25} = 5$$
$$NP = \text{mean} = 50$$

For differences between z values on opposite sides of the mean, add the values.

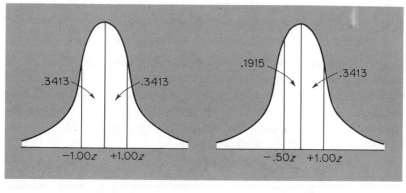

between $-1.00z$ and $+1.00z$	between $-.50z$ and $+1.00z$
$.3413 + .3413$	$.1915 + .3413$
$= .6826$	$= .5328$

For differences between z values on the same side of the mean, subtract the smaller value from the larger.

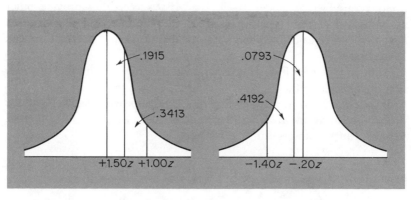

between $+.50z$ and $+1.00z$	between $-1.40z$ and $-.20z$
$.3413 - .1915$	$.4192 - .0793$
$= .1498$	$= .3399$

FIGURE 7–5   **Calculating the Area Between Sigma Points on Opposite and on the Same Sides of the Mean**

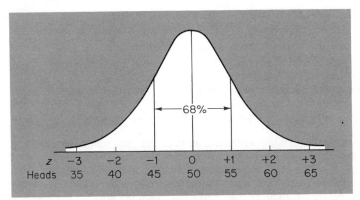

FIGURE 7-6   Distribution of the Mean Number of Heads Appearing When 100 Fair Coins Are Tossed

One would expect that 45–55 heads should appear in 100 tosses in about 68/100 repetitions. Another way of expressing it would be that there would be about a 68/100 probability that between 45 and 55 heads should appear.

If 400 coins were tossed:

$$
\begin{aligned}
N &= 400 \\
P &= .50 \qquad \sigma_{DV} = \sqrt{\frac{400}{4}} = \sqrt{100} = 10 \\
NP &= 200
\end{aligned}
$$

One would expect that between 190–210 heads would appear in 400 tosses, in about 68/100 repetitions of the experiment (Figure 7–7).

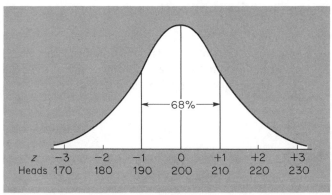

FIGURE 7-7   Distribution of the Mean Number of Heads Appearing When 400 Fair Coins Are Tossed

PRACTICAL APPLICATIONS OF THE NORMAL CURVE

In the field of educational research there are a number of practical applications of the normal curve, among which are:

1. To convert raw scores into standard scores
2. To calculate the percentile rank of scores in a normal distribution
3. To scale qualitative data by transforming them into numerical values. The data to be scaled may be responses to opinionaires, judgments, ratings, or rankings.
4. To normalize a frequency distribution, an important process in standardizing a psychological test or inventory
5. To test the significance of observed measures in experiments, relating them to the chance fluctuations or errors that are inherent in the process of sampling, and generalizing about populations from which the samples are drawn

Measures of relative position; standard scores

Standard scores provide a method of expressing any score in a distribution in terms of its distance from the mean in standard deviation units. The utility of this conversion of a raw score to a standard score will become clear as each type is introduced and illustrated. Five types of standard scores are considered.

1. Sigma Score (z)
2. Standard Score (Z or T)
3. College Board Score (Z_{cb})
4. Stanine Score
5. Academic Grading Scale

The reader is reminded that an assumption of the normality of the distribution is made when using any type of standard score.

THE SIGMA SCORE (z)

In describing a score in a distribution, its deviation from the mean, expressed in standard deviation units, is often more meaningful than the score itself. The unit of measurement is the standard deviation.

$$z = \frac{X - M}{\sigma} \quad \text{or} \quad \frac{x}{\sigma}$$

where X = raw score
M = mean
σ = standard deviation
$x = (X - M)$ score deviation from the mean

Example A	Example B
$X = 66$	$X = 57$
$M = 60$	$M = 62$
$\sigma = 4$	$\sigma = 5$

$$z = \frac{66 - 60}{4} = +\frac{6}{4} = +1.50 \qquad z = \frac{57 - 62}{5} = \frac{-5}{5} = -1.00$$

The raw score of 66 in example A may be expressed as a sigma score of $+1.50$, indicating that 66 is 1.5 standard deviations above the mean. The score of 57 in example B may be expressed as a sigma score of -1.00, indicating the 57 is one standard deviation below the mean.

In comparing or averaging scores on distributions where total points may differ, the use of raw scores may create a false impression or basis for comparison. A sigma score (z) makes possible a realistic comparison of scores and may provide a basis for equal weighting of the scores. On the sigma scale the mean of any distribution is converted to zero and the standard deviation equal to 1.

A teacher wished to get a student's equally weighted average (mean) achievement on an algebra test and an English test.

Subject	Test score	Mean	Highest possible score	Standard deviation
Algebra	40	47	60	5
English	84	110	180	20

It is apparent that the mean of the two raw test scores would not provide a valid summary if the student's performance for the mean would weight overwhelmingly in favor of the English test score. By converting each test score to a sigma scale they have been equally weighted and made comparable, for both test scores have been expressed on a scale with a mean of zero and a standard deviation of 1.

$$z = \frac{X - M}{\sigma}$$

$$\text{Algebra test score} = \frac{40 - 47}{5} = \frac{-7}{5} = -1.40$$

$$\text{English test score} = \frac{84 - 110}{20} = \frac{-26}{20} = -1.30$$

$$M = \frac{\Sigma X}{N} = \frac{-2.70}{2}$$

$$M = -1.35$$

The mean sigma score of -1.35 shows that, on an equally weighted basis, the performance of the student was fairly consistent: 1.40 standard deviations below the mean in algebra and 1.30 standard deviations below the mean in English.

Since the normal probability table describes the percentage of area lying between the mean and successive standard deviation units under the normal curve, (see Appendix B) the use of sigma scores has many other useful applications to hypothesis testing, determination of percentile ranks, and probability judgments.

STANDARD SCORE (Z)

$$Z = 50 + 10\frac{(X - M)}{\sigma} \quad \text{or} \quad 50 + 10z$$

Another version of a standard score, sometimes called a Z or T score, has been devised to avoid some confusion resulting from negative z scores (below the mean) and also to eliminate decimal values.

Adding 50 to the mean and multiplying the z score by 10 results in a scale of positive whole number values or convenient conversion. Using the scores in the previous example: $Z = 50 + 10z$

$$\text{Algebra } Z = 50 + 10(-1.40) = 50 + (-14) = 36$$
$$\text{English } Z = 50 + 10(-1.30) = 50 + (-13) = 37$$

Z scores are always rounded to the nearest whole number. A sigma score of $+1.27$ would be converted to a Z score of 63.

$$Z = 50 + 10(+1.27) = 50 + (+12.70) = 50 + 12.70 = 62.70 = 63$$

COLLEGE BOARD SCORE (Z_{cb})

The College Entrance Examination Board and several other testing agencies use another conversion that provides a more accurate measure by spreading out the scale (see Figure 7–8).

$$Z_{cb} = 500 + 100\frac{(X - M)}{\sigma} = 500 + 100z$$

The mean of this scale is 500.
The standard deviation is 100.
The range is 200–800.

STANINE, OR STANDARD NINE-POINT, SCALE

In their program of testing and classification, statisticians of the U. S. Air Force during World War II devised a single digit, nine-point scale, based on sigma scores. The word *stanine* is derived from the words stan-

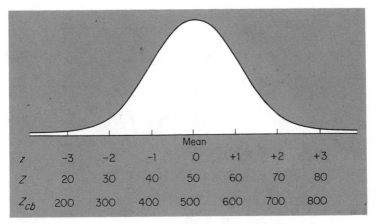

FIGURE 7–8   **A Comparison of Three Types of Standard Scores**

dard and nine. The total distribution is divided into 9 categories, each category except 1 and 9 (which are unbounded) one-half standard deviation in width (see Figure 7–9).

The percentages, based upon the normal probability table values, are rounded to the nearest whole number.

The stanine scale is used in some school districts and by some testing services to report norms.

ACADEMIC GRADING SCALE

While the concept of "grading on the curve" is in disrepute, it is based upon a sigma scale concept. It is a scale that divides achievement into five

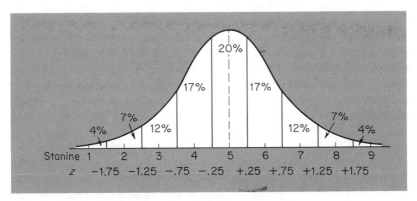

FIGURE 7–9   **The Stanine Scale Has a Width of One-half Sigma Unit for Each of the Nine Categories**

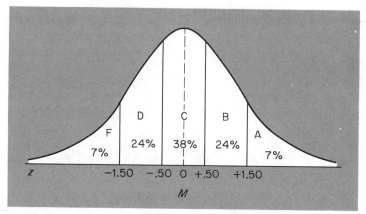

FIGURE 7-10 The Distribution of Academic Grades Based upon the Normal Curve

categories, A, B, C, D, F, using a standard deviation band for each grade designation except F and A (see Figure 7-10).

Rounded Percentages Based upon Normal Probability Table Values are:

			Percentage of cases
Above	$+1.50z$	A	7
$+50z$ to	$+1.50z$	B	24
$-.50$ to	$+.50z$	C	30
-1.50 to	$-.50z$	D	24
Below	$-1.50z$	F	7

In its early application there was an attempt to apply a useful concept for large unselected populations to small, often highly selected groups in which the normality of distribution had been destroyed. For example, in a college class of juniors or seniors where screening processes and selection have eliminated many who would have occupied the lower positions in an unselected distribution, the application was invalid.

All of the five scores described are examples of standard scores, for they are based upon sigma values, the standard deviation unit distance from the mean.

PERCENTILE RANK

Often useful to describe a score in relation to other scores, the percentile rank is the point in the distribution below which a given percentage of scores fall. If the 80th percentile rank is a score of 65, 80 percent of the scores fall below 65. The median is the 50th percentile rank, for 50 percent of the scores fall below it.

When N is small, the definition needs an added refinement. To be completely accurate, the percentile rank is the score in the distribution below which a given percentage of the scores fall, plus one-half the percentage of space occupied by the given score.

This point can be demonstrated by a rather extreme example.

Scores

50
47
43
___
39
30

Upon inspection it is apparent that 43 is the median or 43 occupies the 50th percentile rank. Fifty percent of the scores should fall below it, but only two out of five scores fall below 43. That would indicate 43 has a percentile rank of 40. But by adding the phrase, "plus one-half the percentage of space occupied by the score," we reconcile the calculation:

40% of scores fall below 43: each score occupies 20% of
the total space

40% + 10% = 50 (true percentile rank)

When N is large this qualification is unimportant because percentile ranks are rounded to the nearest whole number, ranging from the highest percentile rank of 99 to the lowest of zero.

High schools frequently rate their graduating seniors in terms of rank in class. Because schools vary so much in size, colleges find these rankings of limited value unless they are converted to some common basis for comparison. The percentile rank provides this basis by converting class rank into a percentile rank.

$$\text{Percentile rank} = 100 - \frac{(100RK - 50)}{N}$$

where RK = rank from the top

Jones ranks 27th in his senior class of 139 students. Twenty-six rank above him, 112 below him. His percentile rank is:

$$100 - \frac{(2700 - 50)}{139} = 100 - 19 = 81$$

When scores in a distribution are assumed to be normally distributed, percentile rank can be calculated from a sigma score. Assume that a score has been converted to a sigma score of $+1.00$ as in Figure 7–11.

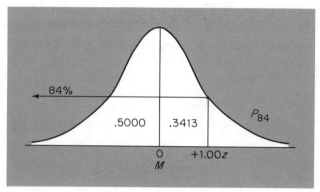

FIGURE 7–11   The Percentile Rank of $+1.00z$

Since the percentile rank is defined as the percentage of scores below a given score:

> 50% of scores fall below the mean
>
> 34.13% of scores fall between mean and $+1.00z$

Adding, 84 is the percentile rank for 84% if the scores fall below $+1.00z$ Assume that the score has been converted to a sigma score of $-1.00z$

> 50% of scores fall below the mean.
>
> 34.13% of scores fall between mean and $-1.00z$

Subtracting, 16 is the percentile rank for 50% − 34%; or 16% of the the scores fall below $-1.00z$. Thus the percentile rank may be determined by the percentage of space under the normal curve to the left of (below) the sigma point in question (Figure 7–12). To convert any raw score to a

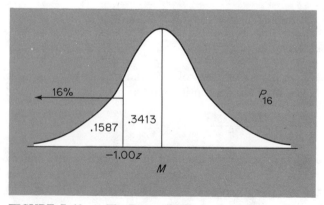

FIGURE 7–12   The Percentile Rank of $-1.00z$

percentile rank it is necessary to know the mean and standard deviation of the distribution. The score may then be converted to a sigma score.

$$z = \frac{X - M}{\sigma}$$

Examples

If the mean of a distribution is 80, and the standard deviation is 5:
(a)

$$X = 88$$

$$z = \frac{88 - 80}{5} = \frac{+8}{5} = +1.60$$

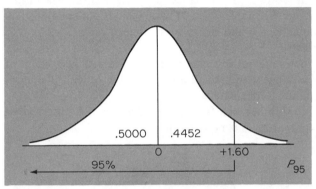

FIGURE 7–13   **Calculation of a Percentile Rank from a Given Score**

(b)

$$X = 70$$

$$z = \frac{70 - 80}{5} = \frac{-10}{5} = -2.00$$

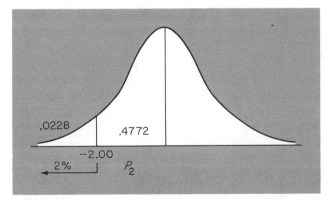

FIGURE 7–14   **Calculation of a Percentile Rank from a Given Score**

.5000 (below the mean) − .4772 = .0228

Measures of relationship

CORRELATION

Correlation is the relationship between two or more paired variables, between two or more sets of data. The degree of relationship may be measured and represented by the coefficient of correlation. This coefficient may be identified by either the Greek letter *rho* (ρ), the symbol *r*, or other symbols, depending upon certain assumptions about the data distributions and the way the coefficient has been calculated.

Teachers observe that students who have high intelligence quotients tend to receive high scores in mathematics tests, whereas those with low *IQ*'s tend to score low. When this type of relationship is obtained, the factors of measured intelligence and scores on mathematics tests are said to be positively correlated.

Sometimes variables are negatively correlated when a large amount of one variable is associated with a small amount of the other. As one increases the other tends to decrease.

When the relationship between two sets of variables is a pure chance relationship, we say that there is no correlation.

-1.00	0	$+1.00$
high in one trait	pure chance	high in one trait
low in the other	relationship	high in the other

These pairs of variables are usually positively correlated; as one increases the other tends to increase.

a. intelligence	academic achievement
b. productivity per acre	value of farm land
c. height	shoe size
d. family income	value of family home

These variables are usually negatively correlated. As one increases the other tends to decrease.

a. total corn production	price per bushel
b. time spent in practice	number of typing errors
c. prime interest rate	Dow Jones Industrial Average
d. age of an automobile	trade-in value

There are other traits that probably have no correlation.

a. body weight   intelligence
b. shoe size   monthly salary

The degree of linear correlation can be represented quantitatively by the coefficient of correlation. A perfect positive correlation is +1.00. A complete lack of relationship is zero (0). Rarely, if ever, are perfect coefficients of correlation of +1.00 or −1.00 encountered, particularly in relating human traits. Although some relationships tend to appear fairly consistently, there are variations or exceptions that reduce the measured coefficient from either a −1.00 or a +1.00 toward zero.

A definition of perfect positive correlation specifies that for every unit increase in one variable there is a proportional unit increase in the other. The perfect negative correlation specifies that for every unit increase in one variable there is a proportional unit decrease in the other. That there can be no exceptions explains why coefficients of correlation of +1.00 or −1.00 are not encountered in relating human traits. The sign of the coefficient indicates the direction of the relationship, and the numerical value its strength.

The scattergram and linear regression line.   When the relationship between two variables is plotted graphically, paired variable values are plotted against each other on the *X* and *Y* axis.

The line drawn through, or near, the coordinate points is known as the line of best fit or the regression line. It is the line from which the sum of the deviations of all the coordinate points has the smallest possible value. As the coefficient approaches zero (0) the coordinate points fall further from the regression line.

When the coefficient of correlation is either +1.00 or −1.00, all of the coordinate points fall on the regression line indicating that, when r = +1.00, for every increase in *X* there is a proportional increase in *Y*, and when r = −1.00, for every increase in *X* there is a proportional decrease in *Y*. There are no individual exceptions.

The slope of the regression line, or line of best fit, is not determined by guess or estimation but by a geometric process described later.

There are actually two regression lines. When r = +1.00 or −1.00 the lines are superimposed and appear as one line. As *r* approaches zero the lines separate further.

Only one of the regression lines is described in this discussion, the *Y* on *X* (or *Y* from *X*) line. It is used to predict unknown *Y* values from known *X* values. The *X* values are known as the predictor variable, the *Y* values, the predicted variables.

Plotting the slope of the regression line. The slope of the regression (Y from X) line is a geometric representation of the coefficient of correlation and is expressed as a ratio of the magnitude of the *rise* (if r is $+$) to

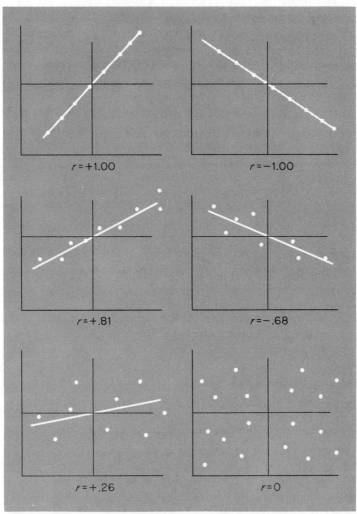

FIGURE 7–15   Scatter Diagrams Illustrating Different Coefficients of Correlation

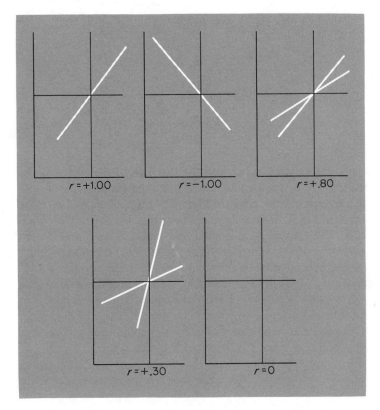

FIGURE 7–16   **Pairs of Regression Lines for Different Coefficients of Correlation**

the run, or as a ratio of the *fall* (if *r* is −) to the run, expressed in standard deviation units.

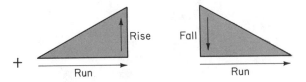

For example, if $r = +.60$, for every sigma unit increase (run) in X, there is a .60 sigma unit increase (rise) in Y.

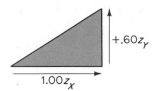

If $r = -.60$, for every sigma unit increase (run) in X, there is a .60 sigma unit decrease (fall) in Y.

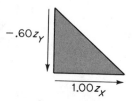

The geometric relationship between the two legs of the right triangle determines the slope of the hypotenuse or the regression line.

Since all regression lines pass through the intersection of the mean of X and the mean of Y lines, only one other point is necessary to determine the slope. By measuring one standard deviation of the X distribution on the X axis and a .60 standard deviation of the Y distribution on the Y axis, the second point is established.

The regression line (r) involves one awkward feature: all values must be expressed in sigma scores (z) or standard deviation units. It would be more practicable to use actual scores to determine the slope of the regression line. This can be done by converting to a slope known as b. The slope of the b regression line Y on X is determined by the formula:

$$b = r\frac{\sigma_Y}{\sigma_X}$$

For example, if $r = +.60$

$$\sigma_Y = 6$$

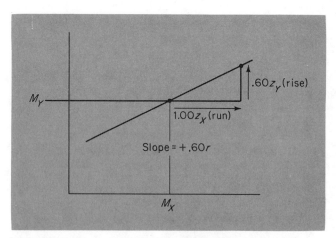

FIGURE 7–17   A Positive Regression Line, $r = +.60$

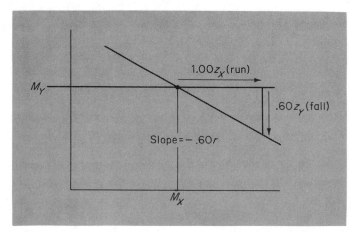

FIGURE 7–18   **A Negative Regression Line, $r = -.60$**

and

$$\sigma_X = 5$$

$$b = +.60\frac{6}{5} = \frac{3.60}{5} = +.72$$

Thus an r of $+.60$ becomes $b = +.72$. Now the ratio of the rise to the run has another value and indicates a different slope of the regression line (Figure 7–19).

RANK ORDER CORRELATION (ρ)

The simplest type of correlation analysis is known as the Spearman rank order coefficient of correlation. The paired variables are expressed as ordi-

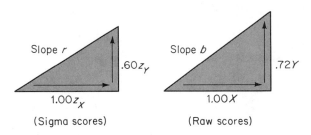

FIGURE 7–19   **Two Regression Lines, r and b. An r of $+.60$ is Converted to a b of $+.72$ by the Formula:**

$$b = r\frac{\sigma_Y}{\sigma_X}$$

nal values (ranked) rather than as interval or ratio values. It lends itself to an interesting graphic demonstration.

Pupil	IQ rank	Achievement in mathematics rank
A	1	1
B	2	2
C	3	3
D	4	4
E	5	5

Perfect positive coefficient of correlation

$$p = +1.00$$

Student ranking highest in IQ ranks highest in mathematics, lowest in IQ, lowest in mathematics achievement.

Pupil	Time spent in practice rank	Number of typing errors rank
A	1	5
B	2	4
C	3	3
D	4	2
E	5	1

Perfect negative coefficient of correlation

$$p = -1.00$$

Student ranking highest in amount of time spent in practice ranks lowest in number of errors.

Pupil	Height rank	IQ rank
A	1	3
B	2	4
C	3	2
D	4	1
E	5	5

Very low coefficient of correlation

$$p = +.10$$

There is probably little more than a pure chance relationship between height and intelligence.

COMPUTATION OF p (*rho*)

To compute the nonparametric Spearman rank order coefficient of correlation this rather simple formula is used:

$$\rho = 1 - \frac{6 \sum D^2}{N(N^2 - 1)}$$

where D = the difference between paired ranks
    $\sum D^2$ = the sum of the squared differences between ranks
    N = number of paired ranks

Judges Jones and Smith ranked ten pupils in a speech contest. The coefficient of correlation indicated the extent to which their judgments were in agreement.

Pupil	Jones' rank	Smith's rank	D	D²
A	1	1	0	0
B	3	2	1	1
C	4	5	1	1
D	7	9	2	4
E	6	6	0	0
F	9	8	1	1
G	8	10	2	4
H	10	7	3	9
I	2	4	2	4
J	5	3	2	4
$N = 10$				$\sum D^2 = 28$

$$\rho = 1 - \frac{6(28)}{10(100 - 1)} = 1 - \frac{168}{10(99)}$$

$$\rho = 1 - \frac{168}{990} = 1 - .17$$

$$\rho = +.83$$

A coefficient of correlation of +.83 shows a high degree of agreement between the judges.

The Spearman rank order coefficient of correlation computation is quick and easy. It is an acceptable method if data are available only in ordinal form, or if the number of paired variables is more than 9 or fewer than 30, with not more than a few ties in ranks. Teachers will find this method of computation useful when conducting studies using a single classroom group of students as subjects.

COMPUTATION OF PEARSON'S r

The most often used and most precise coefficient of correlation is known as the Pearson product-moment coefficient. It may be used when:

1. The data are expressed in interval or ratio score form.
2. The distributions of X and Y have a linear relationship.
3. The variances are approximately equal.
4. The distributions have no more than one mode.

The coefficient may be calculated by converting the raw scores to sigma scores and finding the mean value of their cross products.

$$r = \frac{\sum (z_X)(z_Y)}{N}$$

z_X	z_Y	$(z_X)(z_Y)$
+1.50	+1.20	+1.80
+2.00	+1.04	+2.08
−.75	−.90	+.68
+.20	+.70	+.14
−1.00	+.20	−.20
−.40	+.30	−.12
+1.40	+.70	+.98
+.55	+.64	+.35
−.04	+.10	−.00
−.10	+.30	−.03
		$\sum (z_X)(z_Y) = 5.68$

$$r = \frac{+5.68}{10} = +.568$$

If most of the negative z values of X are associated with negative z values of Y, and positive z values of X with positive z values of Y, the correlation coefficient will be positive. If most of the paired values are of opposite signs, the coefficient will be negative.

positive correlation $(+)(+) = +$ high on X, high on Y

$(-)(-) = +$ low on Y, low on Y

---

negative correlation $(+)(-) = -$ high on X, low on Y

$(-)(+) = -$ low on X, high on Y

The z score method is not often used in actual computation because it involves the conversion of each score into a sigma score. A raw score method computation is more convenient and is most often used when a calculator or computer is available.

$$r = \frac{N \sum XY - (\sum X)(\sum Y)}{\sqrt{N \sum X^2 - (\sum X)^2}\sqrt{N \sum Y^2 - (\sum Y)^2}}$$

The process involves setting up a table with five columns.

where $\sum X =$ sum of the X scores
$\sum Y =$ sum of the Y scores
$\sum X^2 =$ sum of the squared X scores
$\sum Y^2 =$ sum of the squared Y scores
$\sum XY =$ sum of the products of paired Y and Y scores
$N =$ number of paired scores

Variable X	Variable Y	X^2	Y^2	XY
24	13	576	169	312
20	9	400	81	180
18	12	324	144	216
17	20	289	400	340
15	11	225	121	165
12	16	144	256	192
10	5	100	25	50
8	2	64	4	16
6	7	36	49	42
4	1	16	1	4
$\sum X = 134$	$\sum Y = 96$	$\sum X^2 = 2174$	$\sum Y^2 = 1250$	$\sum XY = 1517$

$$r = \frac{10(1517) - (134)(96)}{\sqrt{10(2174) - (134)^2}\sqrt{10(1250) - (96)^2}}$$

$$r = \frac{15,170 - 12,864}{\sqrt{(21,740 - 17,956)}\sqrt{(12,500 - 9216)}}$$

$$r = +\frac{2306}{\sqrt{(3784)}\sqrt{(3284)}}$$

$$r = +\frac{2306}{\sqrt{12,426,656}} = +\frac{2306}{3525.15} = +.65$$

$$r = +.65$$

PREDICTION[2]

An important inferential use of the coefficient of correlation and the Y on X regression line is for prediction of unknown Y values from known X values.

Let us assume that a college admissions officer wishes to predict the likely academic performance of students considered for admission or for scholarship grants. He has built up a body of data based upon the past records of a substantial number of admitted college students over a period of several years. He has calculated the coefficient of correlation between their high school grade point averages and their college freshman grade point averages. He now can construct a regression line and predict the future college freshman GPA for any prospective student, based upon his high school GPA.

Let us assume that he found the coefficient of correlation to be $+.52$. The slope of the line could be used to determine any Y values for any X value. This process would be quite inconvenient, however, for all grade point averages would have to be entered as sigma (z) values.

---

[2]Because it is a method for estimating future performance of individuals on the basis of past performance of a sample, prediction is an inferential application of correlational analysis. It has been included in this chapter to illustrate one of the most useful applications of correlation.

A more practicable procedure would be to construct a regression line with a slope of b so that any college grade point average (Y) could be predicted directly from any high school grade point average. The b regression line and a carefully drawn graph would provide a quick method for prediction. For example:

$$r = +.52 \qquad b = r\frac{(\sigma_Y)}{(\sigma_X)}$$

$$\sigma_y = .50 \qquad b = +.52\frac{(.50)}{(.60)}$$

$$\sigma_x = .60 \qquad b = +.43$$

X_A student A's high school GPA, Y_A his predicted college GPA

X_B student B's high school GPA, Y_B his predicted college GPA

Another, and perhaps more accurate alternative, for predicting unknown Y's from known X's would be to use the regression equation, rather than the graph. The formula for predicting Y from X is:

$$\tilde{Y} = r\left(\frac{\sigma_y}{\sigma_x}\right)(X - M_x) + M_y$$

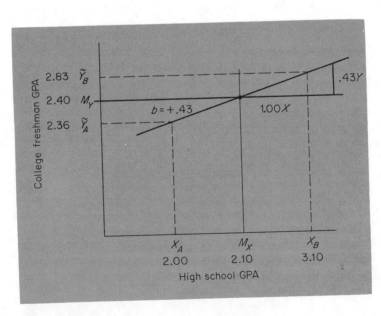

FIGURE 7-20   A Regression Line Used to Predict College Freshman GPA from High School GPA

Several examples using the following data will illustrate the computation.

$$r = +.52 \quad \text{coefficient of correlation between } X \text{ and } Y$$
$$\sigma_X = \quad .60 \quad \text{standard deviation of } X \text{ distribution}$$
$$\sigma_Y = \quad .50 \quad \text{standard deviation of } Y \text{ distribution}$$
$$M_x = \quad 2.10 \quad \text{mean of } X \text{ distribution}$$
$$M_y = \quad 2.40 \quad \text{mean of } Y \text{ distribution}$$
$$X = \quad \text{student's high school GPA}$$
$$\tilde{Y} = \quad \text{student's college freshman GPA}$$
$$b = \quad +.52\frac{(.50)}{(.60)}$$
$$b = +.43$$

Prediction for student A:

$$\tilde{Y} = r\left(\frac{\sigma_y}{\sigma_x}\right)(X - M_x) + M_y$$
$$\tilde{Y}_A = .52\left(\frac{.50}{.60}\right)(2.00 - 2.10) + 2.40$$
$$\tilde{Y}_A = .43(-.10) + 2.40$$
$$\tilde{Y}_A = -.04 + 2.40$$
$$\tilde{Y}_A = 2.36 \text{ student A's predicted college GPA}$$

Prediction for student B:

$$X_B = 3.10$$
$$\tilde{Y} = r\left(\frac{\sigma_y}{\sigma_x}\right)(X - M_x) + M_y$$
$$\tilde{Y}_B = +.52\frac{.50}{.60}(3.10 - 2.10) + 2.40$$
$$\tilde{Y}_B = .43(1.00) + 2.40$$
$$\tilde{Y}_B = .43 + 2.40$$
$$\tilde{Y}_B = 2.83 \text{ student B's predicated college GPA}$$

For student A, whose high school GPA was below the mean, the predicted college GPA was also below the mean. For student B, whose high school GPA was well above the mean, the predicted GPA was substantially above the mean. These results are consistent with a positive coefficient of correlation–high in X, high in Y; low in X, low in Y.

ERRORS IN PREDICTION

When the coefficient of correlation based upon a sufficient body of data has been determined as ±1.00 there would be no error of prediction. Prefect correlation indicates that for every increase in X, there was a proportional increase (when $+$) or proportional decrease (when $-$) in Y. There were no exceptions. But when r is less than $+1.00$ or -1.00, error of prediction is inherent since there have been exceptions to a consistent, orderly relationship. The regression line does not coincide or pass through all of the coordinate values used in determining the slope.

A measure for estimating this prediction error is known as the standard error of estimate (σ_{est}).

$$\sigma_{\text{est}_y} = \sigma_y\sqrt{1 - r^2}$$

As the coefficient of correlation increases, the prediction error decreases. When $r = \mp1.00$

$$\sigma_{\text{est}_y} = \sigma_y\sqrt{1 - r^2} = \sigma_y\sqrt{1 - (1)^2} = \sigma_y(0) = 0$$

When $r = 0$

$$\sigma_{\text{est}_y} = \sigma_y\sqrt{1 - (0)^2} = \sigma_y(1) = \sigma_y$$

When $r = 0$ (or when the coefficient of correlation is unknown) the best blind prediction of any Y from any X is the mean of Y. This is true because we know that most of the scores in a normal distribution cluster around the mean and that about 68 percent of them would probably fall within one standard deviation from the mean. In this situation the standard deviation of Y may be thought of as the standard error of estimate. When $r = 0$, $\sigma_{\text{est}_y} = \sigma_y$.

If the coefficient of correlation is more than zero, this blind prediction can be improved upon in two ways:

1. By plotting Y from a particular X from the regression line
2. By reducing the error of prediction of Y by calculating how much σ_y is reduced by the coefficient of correlation

For example; when $r = \pm.60$

$$\sigma_{\text{est}_y} = \sigma_y\sqrt{1 - (r)^2} = \sigma_y\sqrt{1 - (.60)^2} = \sigma_y\sqrt{1 - .36}$$
$$= \sigma_y\sqrt{.64} = .80\sigma_y$$

Thus the estimate error of Y has been reduced from σ_Y to $.80\sigma_Y$. Interpretation of the standard error of estimate is similar to the interpretation of the standard deviation. If $r = \pm.60$, the standard error of estimate of

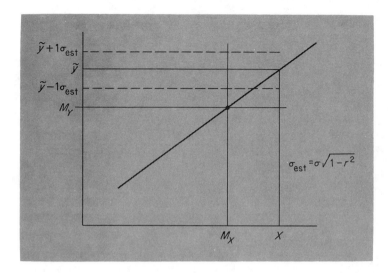

FIGURE 7–21   **A Predicted Y Score from a Given X Score, Showing the Standard Error of Estimate**

Y would be $.80\sigma_Y$. An actual performance score of Y would probably fall within a band of $\pm.80\sigma_Y$ from the predicted Y in about 68 of 100 predictions. In other words, the probability is that the the predicted score would not be more than one standard error of estimate from the actual score in about 68 percent of the predictions.

In addition to the applications described, the coefficient of correlation is indispensable to psychologists who construct and standardize psychological tests and inventories. A few of the basic procedures are briefly described.

STANDARDIZATION OF PSYCHOLOGICAL INSTRUMENTS

Computing the coefficient of correlation is the procedure used to evaluate the degree of validity and reliability of psychological tests and inventories.

The coefficient of validity.   A test is said to be valid to the degree that it measures what it claims to measure, or to the extent that it predicts accurately such types of behavior as academic success or failure, job success or failure, or stability or instability under stress. Tests are usually validated by correlating test scores against some outside criteria which may be scores on tests of accepted validity, successful performance or behavior, or the expert judgment of recognized authorities.

The coefficient of reliability. A test is said to be reliable to the degree that it measures accurately and consistently, yielding comparable results when administered a number of times. There are a number of ways of using the process of correlation to evaluate reliability:

1. Test-retest, correlating the scores on two or more successive administrations of the test (administration #1 vs. administration #2)
2. Equivalent forms, correlating the scores when groups of individuals take equivalent forms of the test (form L vs. form N)
3. Split halves, correlating the scores on the odd items of the test (numbers 1, 3, 5, 7, etc.) against the even items (numbers 2, 4, 6, 8, etc.). This method yields lower correlations because of the reduction in size to two tests of half the number of items. This may be correlated by the application of the Spearman-Brown prophecy formula.

$$r = \frac{2r}{1 + r}$$

If $r = +.60$,

$$r = \frac{1.20}{1 + .60} = +.75$$

Up to this point in the discussion we have considered only linear or straight line relationships which represent a consistent relationship between the variables.

CURVILINEAR CORRELATION

There are situations in which the relationship between sets of paired variables does not follow a straight-line pattern. The effect of rainfall on wheat production provides an interesting example. To a certain point, increased rainfall will bring increased crop yield, a positive correlation.

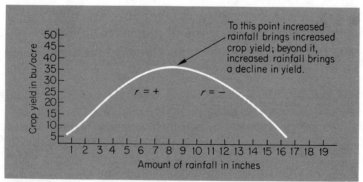

FIGURE 7–22 **Curvilinear Correlation between Amount of Rainfall per Acre and Crop Yield in Bushels**

But beyond a point, too much rain will operate negatively, bringing plant rot and a decline in yield (Figure 7–22).

A similar curvilinear relationship exists between the variables of human age and strength. To a certain point, strength increases with age (a positive correlation), but beyond that point, strength begins to decline (a negative correlation).

An interesting case of an opposite direction of change in correlation is illustrated by the value of an automobile that is kept long enough to become an antique. To a certain point the correlation is negative, for the value decreases as the age of the car increases. After a certain period, the car begins to gain in value, for as the age increases the value increases, a positive correlation. Thus the curve assumes the shape shown in Figure 7–23.

Curvilinear correlation is a complex type of measurement, and its computation goes beyond the treatment of this discussion.

PARTIAL AND MULTIPLE CORRELATION

It is possible to measure the relationship between more than two variables through the process of partial correlation. This is done by holding certain of the variables constant, or momentarily eliminating them from consideration, thus "partialling out" the influence of an independent factor. Partial correlation makes possible multiple correlations, useful in establishing the relative influence or weight of each of the factors in the relationship. For example, a university has computed a multiple regression equation (a prediction index) involving three weighted factors closely

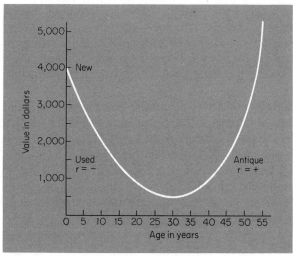

FIGURE 7–23   **Curvilinear Correlation Between the Age of an Automobile and Its Value in Dollars**

related to academic success in college:

1. Rank in high school graduating class
2. High school grade point average
3. Scores on college entrance examination board tests

These three, combined in proper proportion, have proved to be more accurate for predictive purposes than any one or two of the factors.

Frequently, textbook authors persent a crude criterion for the evaluation of a coefficient:

Coefficient (r)			Relationship
.00	to	.20	negligible
.20	to	.40	low
.40	to	.60	moderate
.60	to	.80	substantial
.80	to	1.00	high to very high

The foregoing table's crude analysis may be somewhat misleading. The significance of the coefficient of correlation depends upon the nature of the variables, the number of observations, the range of scores, and the purpose of the application. A test of the statistical significance of a coefficient is based upon the concept of sampling error, described in the next chapter.

MISINTERPRETATION OF THE COEFFICIENT OF CORRELATION

Several fallacies and limitations should be considered in interpreting the meaning of a coefficient of correlation. The coefficient does not imply a cause-effect relationship between variables. High positive correlations have been observed between the number of stork's nests and the number of births in northwestern Europe, and between the number of ordinations of ministers in the New England colonies and the consumption of gallons of rum.

These are inappropriate comparisons, for they may be merely symptoms of a common situation. As population increases both good things and bad things are likly to increase in frequency. Technological and social change may underlie the developments of many variables that have no logical relationship. Before a causal relationship between variables can be accepted, it must be established by logical analysis. The process of correlation merely quantifies a relationship. Confusing association with cause leads one to the *post-hoc* fallacy.

A NOTE OF CAUTION

Statistics is an important tool of the research worker, and an understanding of statistical terminology, methodology, and logic is important for the consumer of research. There are a number of limitations, however, that should be recognized in using statistical processes, and in drawing conclusions from statistical evidence.

1. Statistical process is the servant of logic and only has value if it verifies, clarifies, and measures relationships that have been established by clear, logical analysis. Statistics is a means, never an end, of research.
2. A statistical process should not be employed in the analysis of data unless the basic assumptions and limitations underlying its uses are clearly understood.
3. The conclusions derived from statistical analysis will be no more accurate or valid than the original data. To use an analogy, no matter how elaborate the mixer, a cake made of poor ingredients will be a poor cake. All the refinement of elaborate statistical manipulation will not yield significant truths if the data result from crude or inexact measurement.
4. All treatment of data must be checked and double-checked frequently to minimize the likelihood of errors in measurement, recording, tabulation, and analysis.
5. There is a constant margin of error wherever measurement by human beings is involved. This error is increased when qualities or characteristics of human personality are subjected to measurement, or when inferences about the population are made from measurements derived from statistical samples.

    When comparisons or contrasts are made, a mere number difference is, in itself, not a valid basis for any conclusion. A test of statistical significance should be employed to weigh the possibility that chance in sample selection could have yielded the apparent difference. To apply these measures of statistical significance is to remove some of the doubt from the conclusions.
6. Statisticians and liars are often equated in humorous quips. There is little doubt that statistical processes can be used to prove nearly anything that one sets out to prove. Starting with false assumptions, using inappropriate procedures, or omitting relevant data, the biased investigator can arrive at false conclusions. These conclusions are often particularly dangerous because of the authenticity that the statistical treatment seems to confer.

Distortion may be deliberate or unintentional. In research, omitting certain facts or choosing only those facts favorable to one's position is as culpable as actual distortion which has no place in research. The reader must always try to evaluate the manipulation of data, particularly when the report seems to be persuasive.

Research reports, particularly in the behavioral sciences, sometimes include elaborate statistical processes that serve no useful purpose, but are apparently included to lend an air of scholarship and dignity to a superficial, barren study. No statistical technique should be employed unless it adds clarity or meaning to the analysis of data. Never should it be used as window dressing to impress the reader.

Summary

This chapter deals with only the most elementary statistical concepts. For a more complete treatment the reader is urged to consult one of the references listed at the end of Chapter 8.

Statistical analysis is the mathematical process of gathering, organizing, analyzing, and interpreting numerical data, and is one of the basic phases of the research process. Descriptive statistical analysis involves the description of a particular group. Inferential statistical analysis leads to judgments about the whole population, to which the sample at hand is presumed to be related.

Data are organized in arrays in ascending or descending numerical order. Data are often grouped into class intervals, so that analysis is simplified and characteristics more readily noted.

Measures of central tendency (mean, median, and mode) describe data in terms of some sort of average. Measures of position, spread, or dispersion describe data in terms of relationship to a point of central tendency. The range, deviation, variances, standard deviation, percentile, sigma score, and standard score are useful measures of position, spread, or dispersion.

Measures of relationship describe the relationship of paired variables, quantified by a coefficient of correlation. The coefficient is useful in educational research in standardizing tests and in making predictions when only some of the data are available. It should be noted that a high coefficient does not imply a cause-effect relationship, but merely quantifies a relationship that has been logically established prior to its measurement.

Statistics is the servant, not the master, of logic, a means rather than an end of research. Unless basic assumptions are valid, unless the right data are carefully gathered, recorded, and tabulated, and unless the analysis and interpretations are logical, statistics can make no contribution to the search for truth.

Descriptive data analysis exercises

1. More than half the families in a community can have an annual income that is lower than the mean income for that community. Do you agree or disagree? Why?
2. The median is the midpoint between the highest and the lowest scores in a distribution. Do you agree or disagree? Why?
3. Compute the mean and the median of this distribution:
   74
   72
   70
   65
   63
   61

56
51
42
40
37
33

4. Determine the mean, the median, and the range of this distribution:

88
86
85
80
80
77
75
71
65
60
58

5. Compute the variance (σ^2) and the standard deviation (σ) of this distribution:

27
27
25
24
20
18
16
16
14
12
10
7

6. The distribution with the larger range is the distribution with the larger standard deviation. Do you agree or disagree? Why?

7. If five points were added to each score in a distribution how would it change:

   a. the range
   b. the mean
   c. the median
   d. the mode
   e. the variance
   f. the standard deviation

8. Using the assumed mean process described in Appendix F, calculate the mean, the variance, and the standard deviation.

Using a cumulative frequency column, compute the median, P_{40} and P_{80}.

f_c Scores	f	x'	fx'	fx'^2
125–129	4			
120–124	6			
115–119	12			
110–114	15			
105–109	20			
100–104	18			
95–99	7			
90–94	5			
85–89	2			
80–84	1			

9. John Brown ranked 27th in a graduating class of 367. What was his percentile rank?

10. A coin-tossing experiment where $N = 144$ and $P = .50$,

$$\sigma_{DV} = \sqrt{\frac{N}{4}}$$

Draw the curve depicting the distribution of probable outcomes of heads appearing for an infinite number of repetitions of this experiment. Indicate the number of heads for the mean, and at 1, 2, and 3 standard deviations from the mean, both positive and negative.

11. Assuming the distribution to be normal with a mean of 61 and a standard deviation of 5, calculate the following standard score equivalents:

X	x	z	Z
66			
58			
70			
61			
52			

12. Using the normal probability table in Appendix B, calculate the following values:

a. below $-1.25z$ _____ %

b. above $-1.25z$ _____ %

c. between $-1.40z$ and $+1.67z$ _____ %

   d. between $+1.50z$ and $+2.50z$ _____%
   e. 65th percentile rank _____z
   f. 43rd percentile rank _____z
   g. top 1% of scores _____z
   h. middle 50% of scores _____z to _____z
   i. not included between $-1.00z$ and $+1.00z$ _____%
   j. 50th percentile rank _____z
13. Assuming a normal distribution of scores, a test has a mean score of
   100 and a standard deviation of 15. Compute the following scores:
   a. score that cuts off the top 10% _____
   b. score that cuts off the lower 40% _____
   c. percentage of scores above 90 _____%
   d. score that occupies the 68th percentile rank _____
   e. score limits of the middle 68% _____ to _____

14.

	Mean	s	Tom	Dick	Harry
Algebra	90	30	60	100	85
History	20	4	25	22	19

Who had: _____
   a. the poorest score on either test _____
   b. the best score on either test _____
   c. the most consistent scores on both tests _____
   d. the least consistent scores on both tests _____
   e. the best mean score on both tests _____
   f. the poorest mean score on both tests _____
15. The coefficient of correlation measures the magnitude of the cause-
   effect relationship between paired variables. Do you agree or disagree?
   Why?
16. Using the Spearman rank order coefficient of correlation method,
   compute (p).

	X variable	Y variable
Mary	1	3
Peter	2	4
Paul	3	1
Helen	4	2
Ruth	5	7
Edward	6	5
John	7	6

17. Two sets of paired variables are expressed in sigma scores. Compute the coefficient of correlation between them.

z_X	z_Y
+.70	+.55
−.20	−.32
+1.50	+2.00
+1.33	+1.20
−.88	−1.06
+.32	−.40
−1.00	+.50
+.67	+.80
−.30	−.10
+1.25	+1.10
+.50	−.20

18. Using the Pearson product-moment raw score method, compute the coefficient of correlation between these paired variables:

X	Y	X^2	Y^2	XY
66	42			
50	55			
43	60			
8	24			
12	30			
35	18			
24	48			
20	35			
16	22			
54	38			

19. A class took a statistics test. The students completed all of the questions. The coefficient of correlation between the number of correct and the number of incorrect responses for the class was

_____.

20. There is a significant difference between the slope of the regression line r and that of the regression line b. Do you agree? Why?

21. Compute the standard error of estimate of Y from X when:

$$S_y = 6.20$$
$$r = +.60$$

22. Given the following information, predict the Y score from the given X, when $X = 90$, and:

   a. $r = +.60$

   $M_x = 80$ $S_x = 12$

   $M_y = 40$ $S_y = 8$

   b. $r = -.60$

INFERENTIAL
DATA
ANALYSIS

Chapter 8

The primary purpose of research is to discover principles that have universal application, but to study a whole population in order to arrive at generalizations would be impracticable, if not impossible. Some populations are so large that their characteristics could not be measured; before the measurement had been completed the population would have changed.

Imagine the difficulty of conducting a reading experiment with all American fifth grade children as subjects. The study of a population of this size would require the services of thousands of researchers, the expenditure of millions of dollars, and hundreds of thousands of class hours.

Fortunately, the process of sampling makes it possible to draw valid inferences or generalizations on the basis of careful observation or manipulation of variables within a relatively small proportion of the population. A measured value based upon sample data is a *statistic*. A population value inferred from a statistic is a *parameter*.

A population is any group of individuals that have one or more characteristics in common that are of interest to the researcher. The population may be all the individuals of a particular type or a more restricted part of that group. All public school teachers, all male secondary school teachers, all elementary school teachers, or all Chicago kindergarten teachers may be populations.

A sample is a small proportion of a population selected for analysis. By observing the sample, certain inferences may be made about the population. Contrary to popular opinion, samples are not selected haphazardly, but deliberately, so that the influence of chance or probability can be estimated.

Several types of sampling procedure are described here, each one particularly appropriate in a given set of circumstances. The most useful is the simple random sample. Most of the principles of statistical inference are based upon the assumption of random selection.

It is important to note that an unbiased sample is not necessarily an identical representation of the population. Successive samples drawn from the same population will differ, but it is possible to estimate their variations from the population and from each other. This topic is considered in greater detail later in this chapter in the discussion of the central limit theorem, sampling error, and the standard error of the mean.

Parametric tests

Parametric tests are considered to be the most powerful tests and should be used if their basic assumptions can be met. These assumptions are based upon the nature of the population distribution, and on the way the type of scale is used to quantify the data observations.

1. The observations are independent. The selection of one case is not dependent upon the selection of any other case.
2. The population values are normally distributed or, if not, the nature of their distribution is known.
3. The samples have equal or nearly equal variances. This condition is particularly important to determine when samples are small.
4. The variables described are expressed in interval or ratio scales. Nominal measures (frequency counts) and ordinal measures (ranking) do not qualify for parametric treatment.

Types of samples

THE SIMPLE RANDOM SAMPLE

The individuals or observations are chosen in a simple random sample in such a way that each individual or observation has an equal chance of being selected and that each choice is independent of any other choice.

If we wished to draw a sample of 50 individuals to observe from a population of 600 students enrolled in a school, we could place the 600 names in a container and, blindfolded, draw one name at a time until the sample of 50 was selected. The procedure is cumbersome and rarely used.

RANDOM NUMBERS

A more convenient way of choosing a random sample is by the use of a table of random numbers. Many such tables have been generated by computers producing a random sequence of digits. *The Million Random Digits with 100,000 Normal Deviates* of the RAND Corporation[1] and the *Table of 105,000 Random Digits* of the Interstate Commerce Commission[2] are frequently used.

When using a table, it is necessary to assign consecutive numbers to each member of the population from which the sample is to be selected. Then, entering the table at any page, row, or column, the sample can be selected from 100 to 999, three digits, and from 1000 to 9999, four digits selected. When a duplicated number or a number larger than the population size is encountered, it is skipped and the process continues until the desired sample size is selected.

As an illustration let us assume that a sample of 30 is to be selected from a serially numbered population of 835. Using a portion of a table of random numbers reproduced here, 30 three-digit numbers are selected by reading from left to right. When using the table of random numbers to select a sample, one must number the population members serially. Then, enter the table at any page, row or column at random, and the sample can be selected by reading to the left, right, up, down or diagonally. For populations to 99 in number, two digits are selected, from 100–999, three digits, and from 1000 to 9999, four digits.

These 30 numbered members of the population comprise the sample, if this group were to be divided into two equated groups of 15 each, the first 15 could compose one group and the second 15 the other. There are many varieties of random assignment, such as assigning the odd numbers to one group (1, 3, 5, 7, . . . , 29) and the even numbers (2, 4, 6, 8, 10–50) to the other. It is apparent that in order to select a random sample, conscious selection of any particular individual or observation must not enter the process. The size of the sample may or may not be significantly related to its adequacy. A large sample, carelessly selected, may be biased and inaccurate, whereas a smaller one, carefully selected, may be relatively unbiased and accurate enough to make satisfactory inference possible.

In addition to care in the sampling process, defining the population about which inferences are to be made is extremely important. When the now defunct *Literary Digest* drew its sample for the purpose of predicting the results of the 1936 presidential election, subjects were chosen

[1]RAND Corporation. *A Million Random Digits with 100,000 Normal Deviates* (New York: The Free Press, 1965).

[2]*Table of 105,000 Random Decimal Digits.* Washington, D.C.: Bureau of Transport Economics and Statistics, Interstate Commerce Commission, Statement No. 4914, File No. 261-A-1. Prepared for the Commission by H. Burke Horton and R. Tynes Smith III.

TABLE 8–1   An Abbreviated Table of Random Numbers

50393	13330	92982	17442	63378	02050
09038	31974	22381	24289	72341	61530
82066	06997	44590	23445	72731	61407
91340	84979	39117	89344	46694	95596

The sample

503	426	197	161	590	~~913~~	444
~~931~~	337	422	530	~~234~~	438	
333	802	381	820	457	497	
092	050	242	660	273	391	
~~982~~	090	~~897~~	699	~~161~~	178	
074	383	234	744	407	~~934~~	

In selecting this sample of thirty, seven numbers were deleted. Numbers 931, 982, 897, 913 and 934 were deleted because they were larger than the population of 835 described. Numbers 234 and 161 were deleted because they duplicated previous selections.

from the pages of telephone directories and from automobile registration lists. The prediction of Alfred Landon's victory over Franklin D. Roosevelt proved to be wrong and a postelection analysis revealed that the population for which the prediction was made was not the same population sampled. Large numbers of eligible voters did not own automobiles and were not telephone subscribers, and consequently were not included in the sample.

THE SYSTEMATIC SAMPLE

If a population can be accurately listed, or is finite, a type of systematic selection will provide what approximates a random sample. A systematic sample consists of the selection of each nth term from a list. For example, if a sample of 200 were to be selected from a telephone directory, with 200,000 listings, one would select the first name by selecting a randomly selected name from a randomly selected page. Then every thousandth name would be selected until the sample of 200 names was complete. If the last page were reached before the desired number had been selected, the count would continue from the first page of the directory. Systematic samples of automobile owners could be selected in similar fashion from a state licensing bureau list or file, or a sample of eighth grade students from a school attendance roll.

THE STRATIFIED RANDOM SAMPLE

At times it is advisable to subdivide the population into smaller homogeneous groups in order to get more accurate representation. For example, in making an income study of wage earners in a community, a true sample would approximate the same relative number from each socioeconomic level of the whole community. If the proportion were 15 percent professional workers, 10 percent managers, 20 percent skilled workers, and 55 percent unskilled workers, the sample should include approximately the same proportions in order to be considered representative. Within each subgroup a random selection should be used. This process gives the researcher a more representative sample than one selected from the entire community, which might be unduly weighted by a preponderance of unskilled workers.

In addition to, or instead of, socioeconomic status, such characteristics as age, sex, extent of formal education, racial origin, religious or political affiliation, or rural-urban residence might provide a basis for choosing a stratified sample. The characteristics of the entire population must be carefully considered together with the purposes of the study before a stratified sample is decided upon.

THE AREA OR CLUSTER SAMPLE

The area or cluster sample is a variation of the simple random sample, particularly appropriate when the population of interest is infinite, where a list of the members of the population does not exist, or when the geographic distribution of the individuals is widely scattered. Suppose for the purpose of a survey we wanted to select a sample of all public school elementary teachers in the United States. A simple random sample would be impracticable.

From the 50 states a random sample of 20 could be selected. From the 20 states all counties could be listed and a random sample of 80 counties selected. From the 80 counties all of the school districts could be listed and a random sample of 30 school districts selected. It would not be difficult to compile a list of all elementary teachers from the 30 school districts and a random sample of 500 teachers selected. This successive random sampling of states, counties, school districts, and finally of individuals would involve a relatively efficient and inexpensive method of selecting a sample of individuals.

This method of sampling is likely to introduce an element of sample bias because of the unequal size of some of the subsets selected. Only when a simple random sample would be impracticable is this method recommended.

THE CONVENIENT OR AVAILABLE SAMPLE

Educational researchers, because of the administrative difficulties in applying randomizing procedures, often use available classes as samples. This is a questionable procedure, for the ordinary methods of statistical inference are not validly applicable to such groups. Some of the weakness of educational research may be attributed to the drawing of random sampling inferences from nonrandom samples. Unless appropriate and more complex experimental designs are used to nullify uncontrolled factors, the research cannot be considered sound.

Statistical inference

PARAMETRIC STATISTICAL INFERENCE

The belief that an adequate sample is a small carbon copy of or has the identical characteristics of the population is a misconception shared by many laymen. If a large number of researchers selected random samples of 100 teachers from the population of all teachers in California, the mean weight of the samples would not be identical. A few would be relatively high, a few relatively low, but most of them would tend to cluster around the population mean. This variation of sample means is due to what is known as sampling error. The term does not suggest any fault or mistake in the *sampling process*, it merely describes the chance variations that are inevitable when a number of randomly selected sample means are computed.

Estimating or inferring a population characteristic (parameter) of a random sample (statistic) is not an exact process. It has been noted that successive means of randomly selected samples from the same population are not identical. Thus, if these means are not identical, it would be logical to assume that any one of them probably differs from the population mean. This would seem to present an insurmountable obstacle to the statistician, for he has only a sample to use as a basis for generalizations about a population. Fortunately, since the nature of the variations of sample means is known, it is possible to estimate the degree of error or variation of sample means on a probability basis.

THE CENTRAL LIMIT THEOREM

An important principle known as the central limit theorem describes the characteristics of sample means.

If a large number of equal-sized samples (greater than 30 in size) is selected at random from an infinite population:

1. The means of the samples will be normally distributed.
2. The mean value of the sample means will be the same as the mean of the population.
3. The distribution of sample means will have its own standard deviation. Known as the standard error of the mean, it is computed from this formula:

$$\sigma_M = \frac{\sigma}{\sqrt{N}}$$

where $\sigma =$ the standard deviation of individual scores
$N =$ the size of the samples
$\sigma_M =$ the standard error of the mean

To illustrate the operation of the central limit theorem, let us assume that the mean of a population is 180 and the standard deviation is 12. Figure 8–1 illustrates the relationship between the distribution of individual scores and the distribution of sample means when the sample size is 36. If $M = 180$, $N = 36$, and $\sigma = 12$:

$$\sigma_M = \frac{\sigma}{\sqrt{N}} = \frac{12}{\sqrt{36}} = \frac{12}{6} = 2$$

The standard error of the mean has a smaller value than the standard deviation of individual scores. This is understandable because in computing the means of samples, the extreme scores are not represented, for means are middle score values. Note the difference between the range and

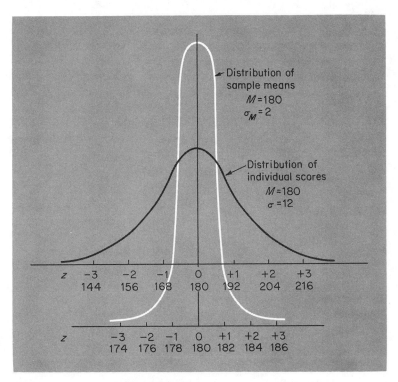

FIGURE 8–1 **Normal Distribution of Individual Scores and of Sample Means When $N = 36$**

standard deviation of individual scores and those of the sample means.
From the formula,

$$\sigma_M = \frac{\sigma}{\sqrt{N}}$$

it is apparent that as the size of the sample increases, the standard error
of the mean decreases. To cite extreme cases as illustrations; as the sample
N approaches infinity, the mean approaches the population mean and the
standard error of the mean approaches zero.

$$\sigma_M = \frac{\sigma}{\sqrt{\infty}} = \frac{\sigma}{\infty} \doteq 0$$

As the sample is reduced in size and approaches one, the standard error
of the mean approaches the standard deviation of the individual scores.

$$\sigma_M = \frac{\sigma}{\sqrt{1}} = \frac{\sigma}{1} = 1$$

As sample size increases the magnitude of the error decreases. Sample
size and sampling error are negatively correlated (see Figure 8–2).

It may be generalized that as the number of independent observations
increases, the error involved in generalizing from sample values to population values decreases, and accuracy of prediction increases.

To the statistician who must estimate the population mean from a
sample mean, his obtained sample mean would not be too far away from
the unknown population mean. One might say that the population mean

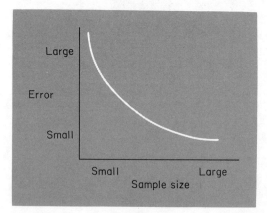

**FIGURE 8–2   The Relationship Between Sample Size and the Magnitude of
Sampling Error**

is "known only to God," but a particular mean calculated from a randomly selected sample can be related to the population mean in the following way.

The chances or probabilities are approximately:

> 68/100 that the sample mean will not be farther than 1 σ_M from the population mean
>
> 95/100 that the sample mean will not be farther than 1.96 σ_M from the population mean
>
> 99/100 that the sample mean will not be farther than 2.58 σ_M from the population mean.

Thus the value of a population mean, inferred from a randomly selected sample mean, can be estimated on a probability basis. In the example presented in Figure 8.1, since $\sigma_M = 2$ points, there is a 68/100 probability that the mean of any randomly selected sample of 36 would not be more than 2 points away from the population mean, and 95/100 probability that the sample mean would not be more than 4 points away.

THE SIGNIFICANCE OF THE DIFFERENCE BETWEEN THE MEANS OF TWO INDEPENDENT GROUPS

Since a mean is probably the most satisfactory measure for characterizing a group, researchers find it important to determine whether the difference between means of samples is significant. To illustrate the point an example might be helpful.

Let us assume that an experiment is set up to compare the effectiveness of two methods of teaching reading. Two groups are selected at random from the same population, one designated by random assignment as the experimental group and the other as the control group. The experimental group is taught by the initial alphabet method, and the control group by the traditional alphabet. At the end of a year a standardized reading test is administered and the mean score of each group is computed. The effectiveness of the experimental group method as compared to the effectiveness of the control group method is the issue, with the end-of-year mean scores of each group the basis for comparison.

A mere quantitative superiority of the experimental group mean score over the control group mean score is not conclusive proof of its superiority. Since we know that the means of two groups randomly drawn from the same population were not necessarily identical, any difference that appeared at the end of the experimental cycle could possibly be attributed to sampling error or chance. To be statistically significant, the difference must be greater than that reasonably attributed to sampling error. Determining whether a difference is significant always involves discrediting a sampling error explanation. The test of the significance of the difference between two means is known as a *t* test. It involves the computation of the ratio between experimental variance (observed difference between two sample means) and error variance (the sampling error factor).

$$t = \frac{M_1 - M_2}{\sqrt{\dfrac{\sigma_1^2}{N_1} + \dfrac{\sigma_2^2}{N_2}}} \quad \begin{array}{l} \text{experimental variance} \\[2em] \text{error variance (sampling error)} \end{array}$$

where M_1 = mean of experimental sample,
$\quad\ M_2$ = mean of control sample,
$\quad\ N_1$ = number of cases in first sample,
$\quad\ N_2$ = number of cases in second sample,
$\quad\ \sigma_1^2$ = variance of first sample,
$\quad\ \sigma_2^2$ = variance of second sample.

If the value of the numerator in this ratio is not significantly greater than the denominator, it is likely that sampling error, and not the effect of the treatment or experimental variable, is indicated. But before discussing the quantitative criteria determining statistical significance of the difference between means, two additional concepts should be considered:

1. the null hypothesis (H_0)
2. the level of significance

THE NULL HYPOTHESIS (H_0)

A null hypothesis states that there is no significant difference between two parameters. It concerns a judgment as to whether apparent differences are true differences or whether they merely result from sampling error. The experimenter formulates a null hypothesis, a no-difference hypothesis. What he hypothesizes is that any apparent difference between the mean achievement of the experimental and control sample groups at the end of the experimental cycle is simply the result of sampling error, as explained by the operation of the central limit theorem.

Students have complained that the statement of a null hypothesis sounds like double talk. They are understandably puzzled about the reasons for the negative statement that the researcher attempts to reject. The explanation is somewhat involved, but the logic is sound. Verification of one consequence of a positive hypothesis does not prove it to be true. Observed consequences that may be consistent with a positive hypothesis may also be compatible with equally plausible but competing hypotheses. Verifying a positive hypothesis provides a rather inconclusive test.

Rejecting a null or negative hypothesis provides a stronger test of logic. Evidence that is inconsistent with a particular negative hypothesis provides a strong basis for its rejection. Before a court of law a defendant is assumed to be not guilty, until the not-guilty assumption is discredited or rejected. In a sense, the not-guilty assumption is comparable to the null hypothesis.

If the difference between the mean achievement of the experimental and the control groups is too great to attribute to the normal fluctuations that result from sampling error, the experiment may refute or reject the null hypothesis, saying, in effect, that it is probably not true that the difference is merely the result of sampling error. The means no longer behave as random sample means from the same population. Something has happened to, or affected, the experimental group in such a way that it behaves like a random sample from a different or changed population. Thus the researcher may conclude that the experimental variable or treatment probably accounted for the difference in performance, as measured by the mean test scores. The experimenter is using a statistical test to discount chance or sampling error as an explanation for the difference.

If the difference between means was not great enough to reject the null hypothesis, the researcher accepts it. He concludes that there was no significant difference, and that chance or sampling error probably accounted for the apparent difference.

THE LEVEL OF SIGNIFICANCE

The rejection or acceptance of a null hypothesis is based upon some level of significance (alpha level) as a criterion. In psychological and educational circles the 5 percent (.05) alpha level of significance is often used as a standard for rejection. Rejecting a null hypothesis at the .05 level indicates that a difference in means as large as that found between experimental and control group means would not likely have resulted from sampling error in more than 5 out of 100 replications of the experiment. This suggests a 95 percent probability that the difference was due to the experimental treatment rather than to sampling error.

A more rigorous test of significance is the 1 percent (.01) *alpha* level. Rejecting a null hypothesis at the .01 level would suggest that as large a difference between experimental and control mean achievement would not likely have resulted from sampling error in more than 1 in 100 replications of the experiment.

When samples are large (more than 30 in size) the *t* critical value is expressed as a *z* (sigma score). If the *t* value equals or exceeds 1.96, we may conclude that the difference between means is significant at the .05 level. If the critical ratio value equals or exceeds 2.58 we may conclude that the difference between means is significant at the .01 level.

Using the example of the reading experiment previously described, let us supply the data and test the null hypothesis that there was no significant difference between the mean reading achievement of the initial teaching alphabet experimental group and the traditional alphabet control group.

Experimental _i t a_ group	Control _Traditional alphabet groups_
$N_1 = 32$	$N_2 = 34$
$M_1 = 87.43$	$M_2 = 82.58$
$S_1^2 = 39.40$	$S_2^2 = 40.80$

$$t = \frac{M_1 - M_2}{\sqrt{\frac{S_1^2}{N_1} + \frac{S_2^2}{N_2}}} = \frac{87.43 - 82.58}{\sqrt{\frac{39.40}{32} + \frac{40.80}{34}}}$$

$$= \frac{4.85}{\sqrt{1.23 + 1.20}} = \frac{4.85}{\sqrt{2.43}} = \frac{4.85}{1.56} \qquad t = 3.11$$

Since a _t_ value of 3.11 exceeds 2.58, the null hypothesis may be rejected at the .01 level of significance. If this experiment were replicated with ramdom samples from the same population, the probability is that a difference between mean performance as great as that observed would result from sampling error in fewer than 1 out of 100 replications. This test would indicate rather strong evidence that the treatment would probably make a difference in the teaching of reading when applied to similar populations of pupils.

TWO-TAILED AND ONE-TAILED TESTS OF SIGNIFICANCE

If a null hypothesis were established that there was no difference (other than a sampling error difference) between the mean IQ's of athletes and nonathletes, we would be concerned only with a difference, and not with the superiority or inferiority of either group.

There is no difference between the mean IQ's of athletes and nonathletes. In this situation we apply a two-tailed test.

If we changed the null hypothesis to indicate the superiority or inferiority of either group it might be stated:

Athletes do not have higher IQ's than nonathletes.
Athletes do not have lower IQ's than nonathletes.

Each of these hypotheses indicates a direction of difference. When a researcher is hypothesizing a direction of difference, rather than the mere existence of a difference, he uses a one-tailed test.

For a large sample two-tailed test, the 5 percent area of rejection is divided between the upper and lower tails of the curve ($2\frac{1}{2}$ percent at each end) and it is necessary to go out to ± 1.96 on the sigma scale to reach the area of rejection (Figure 8–3).

For a one-tailed test, since the 5 percent area of rejection is either at

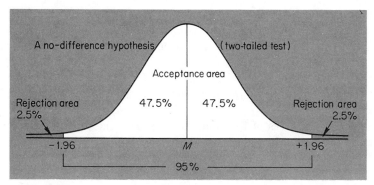

FIGURE 8–3   A Two-tailed Test at the .05 Level (2½ Percent at Each End)

the upper tail or at the lower tail of the curve, the *t* critical value is lower, for it is not necessary to go as far out on the sigma scale to reach the area of rejection (Figure 8–4). The *t* critical value in such a case is ±1.645.

A similar pair of curves would illustrate the difference between *t* critical areas of rejection at the 1 percent level of significance. The *t* values must equal or exceed these *t* critical values for the rejection of a null hypothesis.

Large Sample *t* Critical Values for Rejection of the Null Hypothesis

	.05 level	*.01 level*
Two-tailed test	1.96	2.58
One-tailed test	1.64	2.33

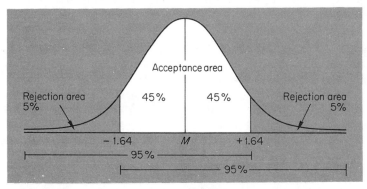

FIGURE 8–4   A One-tailed Test at the .05 Level (5 Percent at One End or 5 Percent at the Other End)

For small sample tests of the significance of the difference between two means the *t* critical values necessary for rejection of the null hypothesis are given in the *t* distribution table (see Appendix C), for the appropriate number of degrees of freedom.

For example, in comparing the significance of the mean IQ difference between samples of 8 athletes and 10 nonathletes, the number of degrees of freedom would be $N + N - 2 = 8 + 10 - 2 = 16$. From the *t* distribution table at 16 degrees of freedom, the *t* critical values necessary for the rejection of the null hypothesis would be:

	Level of significance	
16 degrees of freedom	*.05*	*.01*
Two-tailed test	2.120	2.921
One-tailed test	1.746	2.583

The test of the significance of the difference between two independent means to this point has concerned large samples, and the critical *t* values for rejection of the null hypothesis have been found in the normal probability table.

When small samples are used to infer population differences a different set of *t* critical values is used. But before discussing small sample tests, an important concept known as degrees of freedom should be considered.

DEGREES OF FREEDOM

The number of degrees of freedom in a distribution is the number of observations or values that are independent of each other, that cannot be deduced from each other. While this concept has been puzzling to students of statistics, several analogies and their application to estimation or prediction may help to clarify it.

1. Let us assume that a coin is tossed in the air. The statistician predicts that a head will turn up. If a head comes up he has made one correct, independent prediction. But if he predicted that a head would turn up and a tail would face down, he has made two predictions. Only one prediction however, is an independent prediction, for the other can be deduced from the first. The second added no new information. In this case there was one degree of freedom, not two.

The strength of a prediction is increased as the number of independent observations or degrees of freedom is increased.

2. When a mean is computed from a number of terms in a distribution the sum is calculated and divided by *N*.

$$M_x = \frac{\sum X}{N}$$

But in computing a mean, 1 degree of freedom is used up or lost, and subsequent calculations of the variance and the standard deviation will be based on $N - 1$ independent observations or $N - 1$ degrees of freedom. An example of the loss of a degree of freedom follows.

A *original distribution*	*B* *altered distribution*	
$+5$	15	
$+4$	8	These four terms can be altered
$+3$	5	in any way.
$+2$	7	
$+1$	-20	This term is dependent on, or
$X = +15$	$X = +15$	determined by, the other four
$N = 5$	$N = 5$	terms.
$M = +3$	$M = +3$	

In the altered distribution the fifth term must have a value of -20 for the sum to equal $+15$, the mean to be $+3$ and the sum of the deviations from the mean to equal zero. Thus four terms are independent and can be altered, but one is dependent or fixed and is deduced from the other four. There are $N - 1$ $(5 - 4)$ or 4 degrees of freedom.

When the variance or standard deviation of a sample is used to estimate a population variance or standard deviation, the denominator of the formula is $N - 1$, rather than N.

The variance or standard deviation calculated this way is known as *unbiased estimate* of the corresponding population value.

$$S^2 = \frac{\sum x^2}{N - 1}$$ an unbiased estimate of the variance of a population estimate from a sample

$$S = \sqrt{\frac{\sum x^2}{N - 1}}$$ an unbiased estimate of the standard deviation of a population estimate from a sample

Note that the symbols S^2 and S are used, rather than σ^2 and σ when sample calculations (statistics) are used to estimate population values (parameters). The denominator is always $N - 1$ in such calculations.

The computation using the number of degrees of freedom $(N - 1)$, rather than N in the denominator of the fraction, increases the magnitude of the quotient. This correction for the number of independent observations, or degrees of freedom, is particularly important when the sample is small. When N is large, the correction is negligible.

For example, when N is small, if $N = 5$ and $\sum x^2 = 80$:

$$\sigma^2 = \frac{\sum x^2}{N} \qquad\qquad x = (X - M)$$

$$\sigma = \sqrt{\frac{\sum x^2}{N}}$$

$$\sigma^2 = \frac{80}{5} = 16.00 \qquad \sigma = \sqrt{\frac{80}{5}} = \sqrt{16} = 4.00$$

$$S^2 = \frac{\sum x^2}{N - 1} \qquad\qquad S = \sqrt{\frac{\sum x^2}{N - 1}}$$

$$S^2 = \frac{80}{4} = 20.00 \qquad S = \sqrt{\frac{80}{4}} = \sqrt{20} = 4.48$$

Notice that the correction for the number of degrees of freedom makes a substantial difference in the calculated variance and standard deviation. When N is large, the correction for $N - 1$ degrees of freedom has little effect. If $N = 50$ and $\sum x^2 = 400$

$$\sigma^2 = \frac{400}{50} = 8.00 \qquad \sigma = \frac{400}{50} = 8.00 = 2.83$$

$$S^2 = \frac{\sum x^2}{N - 1} \qquad\qquad S = \sqrt{\frac{\sum x^2}{N - 1}}$$

$$S^2 = \frac{400}{49} = 8.16 \qquad S = \sqrt{\frac{400}{49}} = \sqrt{8.16} = 2.86$$

The correction for calculating the variance and standard deviation is important because unless the loss of a degree of freedom is considered, the calculated sample variance or standard deviation is likely to underestimate the population variance or standard deviation. This is true because the mean of the squared deviations from the mean of any distribution is the smallest possible value, and probably would be smaller than the mean of the squared deviation from any other point in the distribution. Since the mean of the sample is not likely to be identical to the population mean (because of sampling error), the use of the number of degrees of freedom, rather than N in the denominator, tends to correct for this underestimation of the population variance or standard deviation.

The strength of a prediction or the accuracy of an inferred value increases as the number of independent observations (sample size) is increased. Since large samples may be biased, sample size is not the only important determinant, but if unbiased samples are selected randomly from a population, large samples will provide a more accurate basis than will smaller samples for inferring population values.

STUDENT'S DISTRIBUTION (t)

When small samples (fewer than 30 observations in number) are involved, the t table, rather than the normal probability table, is used to determine statistical significance. This concept of small sample size was

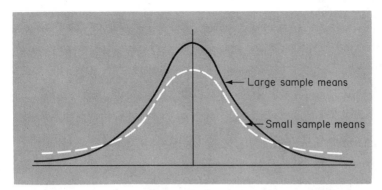

FIGURE 8–5   Distribution of Large and Small Sample Means

developed around 1915 by William Seely Gosset, a consulting statistician for Guinness Breweries of Dublin, Ireland. Since his employer's rules prohibited publication under the researcher's name, he signed the name "Student" when he published his findings.

Gosset determined that the distrubution curves of small sample means were somewhat different from the normal curve. Small sample distributions were observed to be lower at the means and higher at the tails or ends of the distributions.

Gosset's t critical values, carefully calculated for small samples, is reproduced in the t distribution table in Appendix C. The t critical values necessary for rejection of a null hypothesis are higher for small samples at a given level of significance (see Figure 8–5). Each t critical value for rejection is based upon the appropriate number of degrees of freedom.

As the sample sizes increase, the t critical values necessary for rejection of a null hypothesis diminish and approach the z values of the normal probability table.

Significance of the difference between two small sample independent means.   When the samples are small and their variances are equal or nearly equal, the method of pooled variances provides the appropriate test of the significance of the difference between two independent means.

The formula is a bit more involved than the one previously illustrated, but it provides a more powerful test of significance. The appropriate t critical value for rejection of the null hypothesis would be found for $N + N - 2$ degrees of freedom, using the t distribution table.

$$t = \frac{M_1 - M_2}{\sqrt{\dfrac{(N-1)S_1^2 + (N-1)S_2^2}{N_1 + N_2 - 2}\left(\dfrac{1}{N_1} + \dfrac{1}{N_2}\right)}}$$

HOMOGENEITY OF VARIANCES

In t tests for small samples there is one condition that must be met to justify the method of pooled variances. This condition is known as equality or *homogeneity of variances*. It does not literally mean that the variances of the samples to be compared must be identical, but only that they do not differ by an amount that is statistically significant. Differences that would be attributed to sampling error do not impair the validity of the process.

To determine whether the samples meet the criterion of equality of variances an F test is used.

$$F = \frac{S^2 \text{ (larger variance)}}{S^2 \text{ (smaller variance)}}$$

This F ratio is never less than one, for the larger variance is always divided by the smaller. To test for homogeneity of variances an F distribution table is used in much the same way as the t distribution table. F critical values are presented for determining the statistical significance of the calculated F critical ratio, based upon the appropriate rows and columns, each at $N - 1$ degrees of freedom.

A few .05 level of significance values from the F *distribution table* are presented. The complete table may be found in many statistics textbooks.

TABLE 8–2   **Distribution of F (.05 level) Degrees of Freedom for Larger $S^2(N - 1)$**

		9	10	11	12
Degrees of	9	3.18	3.13	3.10	3.07
freedom for	10	3.02	2.97	2.94	2.91
smaller S^2	11	2.90	2.86	2.82	2.79
$(N - 1)$	12	2.80	2.76	2.72	2.69

Unless the calculated F equals or exceeds the appropriate F critical value, it may be assumed that the variances are homogeneous and the difference is not significant.

For example, if two samples with 10 degrees of freedom (greater variance 38.40) and 12 *df* (smaller variance 18.06) were subjected to the test of homogeneity:

$$F = \frac{38.40}{18.06} = 2.13$$

An F critical value of 2.76 must be equaled or exceeded to determine that the difference between variances is significant at the .05 level. In this example since $2.13 < 2.76$ the researcher would conclude that the variances fulfilled the condition of homogeneity and that the method of pooled variances is appropriate. An example using small samples illustrates the process.

The mean score of 10 delinquent boys on a personal adjustment inventory was compared with the mean score of 12 nondelinquent boys, both groups selected at random. Test the null hypothesis that there is no statistically significant difference between the mean test scores at the .01 level of significance.

Delinquent boys	Nondelinquent boys
$M_2 = 9$	$M_1 = 14$
$S_2^2 = 20.44$	$S_1^2 + 19.60$
$N_2 = 10$	$N_1 = 12$

$df = 10 + 12 - 2 = 20$ (the variances are homogeneous)

$$F = \frac{20.44}{19.60} = 1.04$$

$$t = \frac{M_1 - M_2}{\sqrt{\frac{(N-1)S_1^2 + (N-1)S_2^2}{N_1 + N_2 - 2}\left(\frac{1}{N_1} + \frac{1}{N_2}\right)}}$$

$$t = \frac{14 - 9}{\sqrt{\frac{11(19.60) + 9(20.44)}{12 + 10 - 2}\left(\frac{1}{12} + \frac{1}{10}\right)}}$$

$$t = \frac{5}{\sqrt{\frac{215.60 + 183.96}{20}\left(\frac{11}{60}\right)}}$$

$$t = \frac{5}{\sqrt{19.98\left(\frac{11}{60}\right)}} = \frac{5}{\sqrt{3.66}}$$

$$t = \frac{5}{1.96} = 2.62$$

Since this is a two-tailed test, the t critical value for rejection of the null hypothesis at the .01 level of significance for 20 degrees of freedom is 2.831.

Since the calculated value is 2.62, it does not equal or exceed the t critical value necessary for rejection of the null hypothesis at the .01 level for 20 degrees of freedom; the hypothesis is accepted and we conclude that there is no significant difference.

Had we used the .05 level of significance for 20 degrees of freedom, the t critical value necessary for rejection would be 2.086, and we could have rejected the null hypothesis, for our calculated t critical ratio of 2.62 exceeds the 2.086 t table value.

Significance of the difference between the means of two matched or correlated groups. The two previous examples of testing the significance of the difference between two independent means assumed that the individuals were randomly assigned to the control and experimental groups. There are situations when it is appropriate to determine the significance of the difference between means of groups that are not randomly assigned. Two such situations are:

a. When the pairs of individuals who make up the groups have been matched by one or more characteristics—IQ, reading achievement, as identical twins, or on some other basis for equating the individuals
b. When the same group of individuals takes a pretest, is exposed to a treatment, and then is retested to determine whether the influence of the treatment has been statistically significant, as determined by mean gain scores

In such cases it is necessary to calculate the coefficient of correlation between:

a. The posttest scores of the matched pairs sample, or
b. The pretest and posttest scores of the participants in the experiment.

Using the coefficient of correlation the appropriate t test would be based upon this formula:

$$t = \frac{M_1 - M_2}{\sqrt{\frac{S_1^2}{N_1} + \frac{S^2}{N_2^2} - 2r\left(\frac{S_1}{\sqrt{N_1}}\right)\left(\frac{S_2}{\sqrt{N_2}}\right)}}$$

The number of degrees of freedom would be the number of pairs minus one. Two examples illustrate situations a and b:

Example a.

Two groups, each made up of 20 fifth grade students, were matched on the basis of IQ's. The use of film strips was the method used to teach the experimental group; the control group was exposed to a conventional "read and discuss" method.

The researcher wished to test the null hypothesis that there was no difference between the mean achievement of the two groups (a two-tailed test) at the .05 level.

$$F = 1.30 \text{ (variances are equal)}$$

X	C
$N_1 = 20$	$N_2 = 20$
$S_1^2 = 54.76$	$S_2^2 = 42.25$
$M_1 = 53.20$	$M_2 = 49.80$
$r = +.60$	$df = 19$

$$t = \frac{53.20 - 49.80}{\sqrt{\frac{54.76}{20} + \frac{42.85}{20} - 2(+.60)\left(\frac{7.40}{4.47}\right)\left(\frac{6.50}{4.47}\right)}}$$

$$t = \frac{3.40}{\sqrt{2.74 + 2.14 - 1.20(1.66)(1.45)}}$$

$$t = \frac{3.40}{\sqrt{4.84 - 2.89}}$$

$$t = \frac{3.40}{\sqrt{1.95}} = \frac{3.40}{1.40} = 2.43$$

Since the t value of 2.43 exceeds the t critical value of 2.093 for a two-tailed test at the .05 level at 19 degrees of freedom, the null hypothesis may be rejected.

Example b.

A typing teacher wished to determine the effectiveness of ten minutes of transcendental meditation upon the speed and accuracy of her class of 30 students. She administered a timed speed/accuracy test and recorded the score for each student. The next day, after ten minutes of class participation in a TM exercise she administered a similar timed speed/accuracy test.

She computed the mean scores for the pretest and the scores obtained after the TM experience and calculated the coefficient of correlation between the pairs of scores to be $+.84$.

She then tested the hypothesis that the TM experience would not improve the proficiency in speed and accuracy of typing of her class. She chose the .01 level of significance, using a one-tailed test.

$$F = \frac{37.21}{36.10} = 1.03 \text{ (variances are equal)}$$

Pretest	*Test after TM*
$N_2 = 30$	$N_1 = 30$
$S_2^2 = 37.21$	$S_1^2 = 36.10$
$M_2 = 44.80$	$M_1 = 49.10$
$r = +.84$	$df = 29$

$$t = \frac{49.10 - 44.80}{\sqrt{\frac{37.21}{30} + \frac{36.10}{30} - 2(+.84)\left(\frac{6.10}{5.48}\right)\left(\frac{6.01}{5.48}\right)}}$$

$$t = \frac{4.30}{\sqrt{1.24 + 1.20 - 1.68(1.11)(1.10)}}$$

$$t = \frac{4.30}{\sqrt{2.44 - 2.05}} = \frac{4.30}{\sqrt{.39}}$$

$$t = \frac{4.30}{.62} = 6.94$$

Since the t value of 6.94 exceeds the t critical value of 2.462 for a one-tailed test at the .01 level for 29 degrees of freedom, she rejects the null hypothesis, concluding that the meditation experience did improve performance proficiency.

ANALYSIS OF VARIANCE (ANOVA)

We have noted that the critical ratio z and t tests were employed to determine, after treatment, whether the means of two random samples were too different to attribute to chance or sampling error. The analysis of variance is an effective way to determine whether the means of *more than two samples* are too different to attribute to sampling error.

It would be possible to use a number of t tests to determine the significance of the difference between five means, two at a time, but it would involve ten separate tests. The number of necessary pair-wise comparisons of N things is determined by the formula:

$$\frac{N(N-1)}{2}$$

If $N = 5$

$$\frac{5(5-1)}{2} = \frac{20}{2} = 10$$

An analysis of variance would make this determination possible with a single test, rather than ten.

The question raised by the analysis of variance is whether the sample means differ from one another (among-groups variance) to a greater extent than the scores differ from their own sample means (within-groups variance). If the among-groups variance is not substantially greater than the within-groups variance, the samples are not significantly different and probably behave as samples from the same population.

$$F = \frac{\text{variance among groups}}{\text{variance within groups}}$$

The significance of the F ratio (so named for Sir Ronald Fisher) is found in an F table which indicates the F critical values necessary to reject the null hypothesis at selected levels of significance.

ANALYSIS OF COVARIANCE

The analysis of covariance represents an extension of analysis of variance, particularly appropriate when it has not been possible to compare randomly selected and randomly assigned samples, a common limitation in classroom experiments.

In such cases a pretest is administered to experimental and control groups before the application of the experimental variables. At the end of the experimental period a posttest is administered and the gain evaluated by a test of covariance, which in essence equates the pretreatment status of the samples.

Since analysis of variance and covariance are complex tests, only their basic purposes have been described. The volume by Popham listed in this chapter's bibliography is recommended as an excellent treatment.

Nonparametric tests

Nonparametric or distribution-free tests are used when:

1. The nature of the population distribution, from which samples are drawn, is not known to be normal;
2. The variables are expressed in nominal form (classified in categories and represented by frequency counts).
3. The variables are expressed in ordinal form (ranked in order, expressed as 1st, 2nd, 3rd, etc.).

Nonparametric tests, because they are based upon counted or ranked data rather than on measured values, are less precise, have less power than parametric tests, and are not as likely to reject a null hypothesis when it is false.

Many statisticians suggest that parametric tests be used, if possible, and that nonparametric be used only when parametric assumptions cannot be met. Others argue than nonparametric tests have greater merit than is often attributed to them because their validity is not based upon assumptions about the nature of the population distribution, assumptions that are so frequently ignored or violated by researchers employing parametric tests.

Of the many nonparametric tests, six of the most frequently used are described and illustrated here.

1. Chi square (χ^2) test
2. Median test
3. Mann-Whitney test
4. Sign test
5. Wilcoxon matched-pairs signed ranks test
6. Spearman rank order coefficient of correlation (ρ)

CHI SQUARE (χ^2)

The χ^2 test applies only to discrete data, counted rather than measured values. The test is a test of independence, the idea that one variable is not affected by, or related to, another variable. The χ^2 is not a measure of the degree of relationship. It is merely used to estimate the likelihood that some factor other than chance (sampling error) accounts for the apparent relationship. Since the null hypothesis states that there is no relationship (the variables are independent), the test merely evaluates the probability that the observed relationship results from chance. As in other tests of statistical significance, it is assumed that the sample observations have been randomly selected.

The computed χ^2 value must equal or exceed the appropriate χ^2 table critical value to justify rejection of the null hypothesis or the assumption of independence at the .05 or the .01 level of significance.

A finding of a statistical significant χ^2 value doesn't necessarily indicate a cause-effect relationship, a limitation that was observed when interpreting a coefficient of correlation. A significant χ^2 finding indicates that the variables probably do not exhibit the quality of independence, that they tend to be systematically related, and that the relationship transcends pure chance or sampling error.

There are situations when the theoretical or expected frequencies must be computed from the distribution. Let us assume that 200 residents of a college women's dormitory are blonde, brunette, or redhead. Is the variable, hair color, related to the number of dates the girls have in a three-week period? The null hypothesis would indicate that hair color is not related to frequency of dating—that the variables hair color and frequency of dating are independent.

Number of Dates

	Fewer than 10	11–15	More than 15	Total
Blondes	6 (12)	60 (56)	14 (12)	80*
Brunettes	14 (12)	48 (56)	8 (12)	80*
Redheads	10 (6)	32 (28)	8 (6)	40*
	30**	140**	30**	200 grand total

$fe(\ )$ $*\sum f$ row $**\sum f$ column

The expected frequency for each of the 9 cells is computed by the formula:

$$fe = \frac{(\sum f \text{ column})(\sum f \text{ row})}{\text{grand total}}$$

Computation of expected frequencies (fe):

$$\overset{**}{\underset{}{}}\overset{*}{\underset{}{}}$$

$$\frac{(30)(80)}{200} = (12) \quad \frac{(140)(80)}{200} = (56) \quad \frac{(30)(80)}{200} = (12)$$

$$\frac{(30)(80)}{200} = (12) \quad \frac{(140)(80)}{200} = (56) \quad \frac{(30)(40)}{200} = (6)$$

$$\frac{(30)(40)}{200} = (6) \quad \frac{(140)(40)}{200} = (28) \quad \frac{(30)(40)}{200} = (6)$$

COMPUTATION OF THE χ^2 VALUE

Formula:
$$\chi^2 = \frac{(f_0 - f_e)^2}{fe}$$

$$\frac{(6 - 12)^2}{12} = 3 \quad \frac{(60 - 56)^2}{56} = .28 \quad \frac{(14 - 12)^2}{12} = .33$$

$$\frac{(14 - 12)^2}{12} = .33 \quad \frac{(48 - 56)^2}{56} = 1.14 \quad \frac{(8 - 12)^2}{12} = 1.33$$

$$\frac{(10 - 6)^2}{6} = 2.67 \quad \frac{(32 - 28)^2}{28} = .57 \quad \frac{(8 - 6)^2}{6} = .67$$

$$\chi^2 = 3 + .28 + .33 + .33 + 1.14 + 1.33 + 2.67 + .57 + .67 = 10.32$$

$$\text{degrees of freedom} = (\text{rows} - 1)(\text{columns} - 1)$$
$$= (3 - 1)(3 - 1) = (2)(2) = 4$$

χ^2 critical values for 4 degrees of freedom

.01	.05	
13.28	9.49	$\chi^2 = 10.32$

The test indicates that there is a significant relationship between hair color and number of dates at the .05 but not at the .01 level of significance. If we wished to answer the question, "Is there a relationship between blonde hair and number of dates?" we would combine the brunette and redhead categories and use a χ^2 table with 6 rather than 9 cells.

Number of Dates

	Fewer than 10	11–15	More than 15	Total
Blondes	6 (12)	6 (56)	14 (12)	80
Nonblondes	24 (18)	80 (84)	16 (18)	120
	30	140	30	200

$$\frac{(30)(80)}{200} = (12)\frac{(140)(80)}{200} = (56)\frac{(30)(80)}{200} = (12)$$

$$\frac{(30)(120)}{200} = (18)\frac{(140)(120)}{200} = (84)\frac{(30)(120)}{200} = (18)$$

$$\frac{(6-12)^2}{12} = 3.00\frac{(60-56)^2}{56} = .29\frac{(14-12)^2}{12} = .33$$

$$\frac{(24-18)^2}{18} = 2.00\frac{(80-84)^2}{84} = .19\frac{(16-18)^2}{18} = .22$$

$\chi^2 = 3.00 + .29 + .33 + 2.00 + .19 + .22 = 6.03$ at 2*df*:

.01	9.21
.05	5.99

The null hypothesis may be rejected at the .05 but not at the .01 level of significance.

In a 2×2 table (4 cells) with 1 degree of freedom there is a simple formula that eliminates the need to calculate the theoretical frequencies for each cell.

Formula: $$\chi^2 = \frac{N[|AD-BC|]^2}{(A+B)(C+D)(A+C)(B+D)}$$

Let us use an example employing this formula. A random sample of auto drivers revealed the relationship between experiences of those who had taken a course in driver education and those who had not.

	Reported accident	No accident	
Had drivers' education	44*A*	10*B*	54
No drivers' education	81*C*	35*D*	116
	125	45	170

This is a 2×2 table with one degree of freedom

$$\chi^2 = 170\frac{[|(44 \times 35) - (10 \times 81)|]^2}{(54+10)(81+35)(44+81)(10+35)} = 170\frac{[|1540 - 810|]^2}{(54)(116)(125)(45)}$$

$$= \frac{170(730)^2}{35,235,000} = \frac{90,593,000}{35,235,000} = 2.57$$

The χ^2 value does not equal or exceed the critical χ^2 value (3.84) necessary to reject the null hypothesis at the .05 level of significance. There seems to be no significant relationship between completing the course in driver education and the number of individuals who had recorded auto accidents.

YATES CORRECTION FOR CONTINUITY

In computing a chi square value for a 2×2 table with one degree of freedom, the formula is modified when any cell has a frequency count of fewer than 10. This formula differs from the previous formula.

$$\chi^2 = \frac{N\left[|AD - BC| - \dfrac{N}{2}\right]^2}{(A + B)(C + D)(A + C)(B + D)}$$

EXAMPLE

A pharmaceutical company wished to evaluate the effectiveness of X-40, a recently developed headache relief pill.

Two randomly selected and assigned samples of patients who complained of headaches were given pills. The experimental group was given 6 X-40 pills daily, the control group 6 placebos (or sugar pills) daily, although they thought that they were receiving medication.) After a week they repeated their experience.

	X-40 X	Placebo C	
Headaches relieved	30_A	40_B	70
Headaches continued	4_C	10_D	14
	34	50	84

A χ^2 test using a 2×2 table at 1 degree of freedom was applied, with Yates correction. Was the effectiveness of the X-40 medication significant at the .05 level?

$$\chi^2 = \frac{84[|(30 \times 10) - (40 \times 4)| - 42]^2}{(30 + 40)(4 + 10)(30 + 4)(40 + 10)} = \frac{84[|300 - 160| - 42]^2}{(70)(14)(34)(50)}$$

$$= \frac{84(98)^2}{1,666,000} = \frac{84(9604)}{1,666,000} = \frac{806,736}{1,666,000}$$

$$\chi^2 = \frac{806,736}{1,666,000} = .48$$

The computed χ^2 is far below the χ^2 critical value (3.84) necessary for the rejection of the null hypothesis at the .05 level. The research concludes that the null hypothesis is accepted: There is no significant relationship between the use of X-40 pills at this dosage and headache relief. Any apparent effectiveness was probably the result of sampling error.

THE MEDIAN TEST

This nonparametric test determines the significance of the difference between the medians of two independent groups. It answers the question,

"Do medians of these randomly selected samples behave like medians from the same population?" Unlike the t test, which determines the significance of the difference between two means, the median test compares medians.

The median test is really an application of the χ^2 test, using a 2×2 table at 1 degree of freedom. The procedure consists of these steps:

1. Compute the median of the combined sample distributions.
2. Count the number of terms at or above the median and below the median for each group.
3. Compute the χ^2 value in a 2×2 table.

A researcher wished to compare the effect of medication upon the number of correct responses on a manipulation test. The experimental group received the medication while the control group received a placebo.

Since one of the cell frequencies < 10, Yates correction is the appropriate formula:

$$\chi^2 = \frac{N\left[|AD - BC| - \dfrac{N}{2}\right]^2}{(A + B)(C + D)(A + C)(B + D)}$$

$$\chi^2 = \frac{40[|(14 \times 14) - (6 \times 6)| - 20]^2}{(20)(20)(20)(20)}$$

$$\chi^2 = \frac{40[|196 - 36| - 20]^2}{(20)(20)(20)(20)}$$

$$\chi^2 = \frac{40[(160) - 20]^2}{160,000}$$

$$\chi^2 = \frac{40(19,600)}{160,000} = \frac{784,000}{160,000}$$

$$\chi^2 = 4.90$$

Since the χ^2 value of 4.90 exceeds the χ^2 critical value of 3.84 for 1 degree of freedom at the .05 level, the null hypothesis is rejected. There seems to be a significant difference between the scores of the experimental and control groups.

THE MANN-WHITNEY TEST

The Mann-Whitney U test is designed to test the significance of the difference between two populations, using random samples drawn from the same population. It is a nonparametric equivalent of the parametric t test. It is more powerful than the median test and lends itself to one- or two-tailed tests of the null hypothesis. It may be considered a useful alternative to the t test when the parametric assumptions cannot be met and when the observations are expressed in at least ordinal scale values.

The basic computation is U_1 and in experiments using small samples

TABLE 8–3   Manipulation Test Scores for Forty Subjects

X (Medication)		C (Placebo)		
56	24	58	16	
55	24	56	15	
43	23	52	15	Combined group
41	21	40	14	Md = 20
31	19	38	13	
31	17	28	12	
27	16	19	10	
26	13	18	10	
26	12	18	9	
25	9	17	8	

	At or above Md	Below Md
Experimental	14A	6B
Control	6C	14D

A, B, C, and D are all designations of cells.

the significance of an observed U may be determined by the U critical values of the Mann-Whitney tables.

When the size of either of the groups > 20, the sampling distribution of U rapidly approaches the normal distribution and the null hypothesis may be tested with reference to the z critical values of the normal probability table.

The values of the combined samples, N_1 and N_2 are ranked from the lowest to the highest rank, irrespective of groups, rank 1 to the lowest score, rank 2 to the next lowest, etc. Then the ranks of each sample group are summed individually and represented as $\sum R_1$ and $\sum R_2$.

There are two U's calculated by the formulas:

a. $U_1 = N_1 N_2 + \dfrac{N_1(N_1 + 1)}{2} - \sum R_1$

b. $U_2 = N_1 N_2 + \dfrac{N_2(N_2 + 1)}{2} - \sum R_2$

N_1 = number in one group $\sum R_1$ = sum of ranks in one group

N_2 = number in second group $\sum R_2$ = sum of ranks in second group

Only one U need be calculated, for the other can be easily computed by the formula.

$$U_1 = N_1 N_2 - U_2$$

It is the smaller value of U that is used when consulting the Mann-Whitney U table.

The z value of U can be determined by the formula:

$$z = \frac{U - \dfrac{N_1 N_2}{2}}{\sqrt{\dfrac{(N_1)(N_2)(N_1 + N_2 + 1)}{12}}}$$

It doesn't matter which U (the larger or the smaller) is used in the computation of z. The sign of the z will depend on which is used, but the numerical value will be identical.

A teacher wishes to evaluate the effect of two methods of teaching reading to two groups of 20 randomly assigned students, drawn from the same population.

The null hypothesis proposed is that there is no significant difference between the performance of the students taught by method A and the students taught by method B.

TABLE 8–4   **Performance Scores of Students Taught by Method A or by Method B**

A	Rank	B	Rank
50	3	49	2
60	8	90	36
89	35	88	33.5
94	38	76	21
82	28	92	37
75	20	81	27
63	10	55	7
52	5	64	11
97	40	84	30
95	39	51	4
83	29	47	1
80	25.5	70	15
77	22	66	12
80	25.5	69	14
88	33.5	87	32
78	23	74	19
85	31	71	16
79	24	61	9
72	17	53	6
68	13	73	18
$N_1 = 20$	$\sum R_1 = 469.5$	$N_2 = 20$	$\sum R_2 = 350.5$

$$U_1 = N_1 N_2 + \frac{N_1(N_1 + 1)}{2} - \sum R_1$$

After a period of four months' exposure to the two teaching methods, the scores of the students on a standardized achievement test were recorded. All scores were ranked from lowest to highest and the Mann-Whitney test was used to test the null hypothesis at the .05 level of significance.

$$U_1 = (20)(20) + \frac{20(21)}{2} - 469.50$$

$$= 400 + 210 - 469.50$$

$$= 140.50$$

$$U_2 = N_1 N_2 + \frac{N_2(N_2 + 1)}{2} - \Sigma R_2$$

$$= (20)(20) + \frac{20(21)}{2} - 350.50$$

$$= 400 + 210 - 350.50$$

$$= 259.50$$

Check:
$$U_1 = N_1 N_2 - U_2$$

$$140.50 = 400 - 259.50$$

$$140.50 = 140.50$$

$$z = \frac{U_1 - \frac{N_1 N_2}{2}}{\sqrt{\frac{N_1 N_2 (N_1 + N_2 + 1)}{12}}}$$

$$z = \frac{140.50 - \frac{400}{2}}{\sqrt{\frac{(20)(20)(41)}{12}}} = -\frac{59.5}{\sqrt{1366.67}} = -\frac{59.50}{36.97}$$

$$z = -1.61$$

Since the observed z value of -1.61 did not equal or exceed the z critical value of 1.96 for a two-tailed test at the .05 level, the null hypothesis was not rejected. The difference was not significant and the apparent superior performance of the A method group could well have resu'ted from sampling error.

THE SIGN TEST

The sign test may be used to evaluate the effect of an experimental treatment when certain limiting circumstances prevail:

1. The evaluation of the effect of the experimental variable or treatment cannot be measured, but can only be judged to result in superior or inferior performance.

2. The members of the experimental and control groups consist of more than 10 matched pairs, matched on the basis of IQ, aptitude, as members of sets if identical twins, or on some other basis for matching. The subjects may be matched with themselves in a preobservation, postobservation design, serving in one instance as a control group, and in another instance as an experimental group.

Let us assume that 26 pairs of matched individuals were randomly assigned to experimental and control groups. At the end of the experimental cycle each experimental subject was judged by an expert to be superior (+) or inferior (−) in performance to his matched subject in the control group.

The results were:

$N = 26$
18 experimental subjects judged superior   +18
7 experimental subjects judged inferior   −7
1 pair indicated no difference   0
Thus $N = 25$

In cases where no difference is discovered that pair is deleted from further consideration.

The null hypothesis to be tested: The performance of the experimental group did not exceed the performance of the control group at the .05 level of significance. Hypothesis: The number of pluses should equal the number of minuses. Under the null hypothesis using a one-tailed test to evaluate the superiority of performance of the experimental group, the following formula for a test of significance is applied, using the z critical values of the normal probability table:

$$z = \frac{(0 \pm .50) - \dfrac{N}{2}}{\sqrt{\dfrac{N}{4}}}$$

where O = number of signs of researcher's interest. When $O < N/2$, use $(0 + .50)$ in the formula; when $O > N/2$, use $(0 - .50)$ in the formula.

*$O = 18$ $N = 25$ (one no-difference observation)

*Superiority (+) signs were the researcher's interest. If in an experiment, loss of weight (−), for example, were of interest, the researcher would have counted the minus (−) signs.

Since $18 > N/2$, use $(O - .50)$ in the formula

$$z = \frac{(O - .50) - \dfrac{N}{2}}{\sqrt{\dfrac{N}{4}}} = \frac{17.50 - 12.50}{\sqrt{\dfrac{25}{4}}} = \frac{5}{2.50} = 2.00$$

Since the z critical ratio for a one-tailed test at the .05 level is 1.64, the null hypothesis is rejected and the superiority of performance of the experiment 1 group is probably established.

The reader is reminded that the sign test is appropriate for determining the difference between dependent, not independent samples. The non-parametric sign test is somewhat insensitive for it considers only the direction of superiority or inferiority, and does not reflect the magnitude or amount of the difference.

THE WILCOXON MATCHED-PAIRS SIGNED RANKS TEST FOR $N > 10$ PAIRS.

The Wilcoxon test is somewhat similar to the sign test, but is more powerful because it tests not only direction but also magnitude of difference between matched groups. If most of the differences favor one group, that group is probably superior. The null hypothesis would assume that the direction and magnitude of difference would be about the same.

The Wilcoxon test, like the sign test, deals with matched samples made up of matched pairs of individuals and is not applicable to independent samples.

The procedure involves a number of rather simple steps.

1. Let d indicate the difference between the pairs under the experimental and control treatment. There would be one d for each pair of scores.
2. Rank the d's without respect to sign, giving rank 1 to the smallest difference, 2 to the next smallest, etc. The number of ranks will equal the number of pairs.
3. Then to each rank affix the sign of the difference.
4. Total the ranks for the $+$ differences and total the ranks for the $-$ differences. If the sum of the $+$ ranks equaled the sum of the $-$ ranks, we would conclude that there was no difference between the effect of the experimental control treatment or variable.

When the scores of a pair are equal, that pair is deleted from the computation. When two or more differences between ranks are the same, the ranks are averaged. For example,

	Two equal differences	*Three equal differences*
Differences	20, 21, 21, 26, 27	18, 21, 21, 21, 28
Ranks	1, 2.5, 2.5, 4, 5	1, 3, 3, 3, 5
	$\dfrac{2 + 3}{2} = 2.5$	$\dfrac{2 + 3 + 4}{3} = 3$

The sum of the ranks of the smaller of the like-signed ranks is designated as T. A z formula is then applied and interpreted by the critical z values of the normal probability table.

$$z = \frac{T - \dfrac{N(N+1)}{4}}{\sqrt{\dfrac{N(N+1)(2N+1)}{24}}}$$

where N = number of pairs ranked
$\quad\ \ T$ = sum of the ranks of the smaller of the like-signed ranks

An example illustrates the computation and application of the Wilcoxon test.

Thirteen pairs of identical twins were separated, with one twin placed in a foster home and the other in an institution for homeless children. After a year they were tested for creativity, and their performance compared. The null hypothesis that there was no difference between the performance of the two samples was tested at the .05 level of significance.

$$z = \frac{9 - \dfrac{(12)(13)}{4}}{\sqrt{\dfrac{12(13)(25)}{24}}} = \frac{9 - 39}{\sqrt{162.50}} = \frac{30}{12.75}$$

$$z = -2.35$$

TABLE 8–5   Creativity Scores of Identical Twins Assigned to Foster Homes and to Institutions

Pair	Institution	Foster home	d	Rank of d
a	70	80	$+10$	11
b	62	69	$+7$	8
c	85	90	$+5$	6
d	70	68	-2	②
e	54	58	$+4$	4.5
f	49	58	$+9$	10
g/h	80	74	-6	⑦
i	79	80	$+1$	1
j	90	93	$+3$	3
k	64	75	$+11$	12
l	75	79	$+4$	4.5
m	81	89	$+8$	9
				$T = 9$

$N = 13 - 1 = 12$ (one no-difference pair)
T = sum of ranks of smaller like sign $(-)$

Since the obtained z value of -2.31 exceeds the z critical value of -1.96 for a two-tailed test at the .05 level, the null hypothesis is rejected. There is probably a difference too great to attribute to sampling error.

THE SPEARMAN RANK ORDER COEFFICIENT OF CORRELATION (p)

The concept of correlation was presented in Chapter 7 and both the parametric Pearson product-moment and the nonparametric Spearman *rho* were described.

STATISTICAL SIGNIFICANCE OF A COEFFICIENT OF CORRELATION

Throughout this chapter on inferential data analysis the idea of statistical significance and its relationship to the null hypothesis have been emphasized. An observed coefficient of correlation may result from chance or sampling error, and a test to determine its statistical significance is appropriate. In small sample correlations, chance could yield what might appear to be evidence of a genuine relationship.

The null hypothesis (H_0) states that the coefficient of correlation is zero. Only when chance or sampling error has been discredited on a probability basis can a coefficient of correlation be accepted as statistically significant. The test of the significance of r or p is determined by the use of the formula:

$$t_r = \frac{r\sqrt{N-2}}{\sqrt{1-r^2}} \quad \text{or} \quad t_p = \frac{p\sqrt{N-2}}{\sqrt{1-p^2}}$$

With $N-2$ degrees of freedom a coefficient of correlation is judged as statistically significant when the t value equals or exceeds the t critical value of the t distribution table.

If $r = .40$

$N = 25$

$$t = \frac{.40\sqrt{23}}{\sqrt{1-(.40)^2}} = \frac{1.92}{.92} = 2.09$$

On a two-tailed test at the .05 level with 23 degrees of freedom, the null hypothesis is rejected, exceeding the t critical value of 2.07. As sample size is decreased, sampling error increases. For a smaller sample, the coefficient must be larger to be statistically significant.

If $p = .40$

$N = 18$

$$t = \frac{.40\sqrt{16}}{\sqrt{1-(.40)^2}} = \frac{1.60}{.92} = 1.74$$

At 16 degrees of freedom the observed value of 1.74 fails to equal or exceed the t critical value of 2.12 at the .05 level of significance, and the null hypothesis must be accepted. With an N as small as 18, sampling error could account for a p of .40.

PRACTICAL SIGNIFICANCE

It is important to note that a finding that is significant may not be a measure of its usefulness in reaching a practical decision. A test of significance merely indicates that the relationship is genuine, that r (or p) is probably not 0.

A statistically significant finding indicates the probability that chance or sampling did not account for the observed relationship. When $N = 100$, a coefficient of $+.10$ is significant at the .01 level, but a coefficient of that magnitude would be too low for satisfactory prediction.

Summary

Statistics is an indispensable tool of the researcher that enables him to make inferences or generalizations about populations from his observations of the characteristics of samples. Although samples do not duplicate the characteristics of populations, and although samples from the same population will differ from one another, the nature of their variation is reasonably predictable. The central limit theorem describes the nature of sample means and enables the researcher to make estimates about population means (parameters) with known probabilities of error.

The pioneering contributions of Sir Ronald Fisher and Karl Pearson to statistics and scientific method, and William Sealy Gosset to small-sampling theory have made practicable the analysis of many of the types of problems encountered in psychology and education as well as in agricultural and biological research where they were first applied.

Parametric statistical treatment of data is based upon certain assumptions about the nature of distributions and the types of measures used. Nonparametric statistical treatment makes possible useful inferences without assumptions about the nature of data distributions. Each type makes a significant contribution to the analysis of data relationships.

Statistical decisions are not made with certainty, but are based upon probability estimates. The central limit theorem, sampling error, variance, the null hypothesis, levels of significance, and two-tailed and one-tailed tests have been explained and illustrated. Although this treatment has been brief and necessarily incomplete, the presentation of concepts may help the consumer of research to understand many simple research reports. Students who aspire to significant research activity, or who wish to interpret complex research studies with understanding, will need additional background in statistics and experimental design. They will find it helpful to participate in research seminars and to acquire competence through apprenticeship with scholars who are making contributions to knowledge through their own research activities.

Inferential data analysis exercises

1. Why is it stronger logic to be able to reject a negative hypothesis than to try to confirm a positive one?

2. A statistical test of significance would have no useful purpose in a purely descriptive study in which sampling was not involved. Do you agree? Why?

3. When a statistical test determines that a finding is significant at the .05 level, it indicates that there is a 5/100 probability that the relationship was merely the result of sampling error. Do you agree? Why?

4. Any hypothesis that can be rejected at the .05 level of significance can surely be rejected at the .01 level. Do you agree? Why?

5. The standard deviation of a sample is likely to be smaller in magnitude than the standard deviation of the population from which it is drawn. Do you agree? Why?

6. The t critical value necessary for the rejection of a null hypothesis (at a given level of significance and for a given number of degrees of freedom) is higher for a one-tailed test than it is for a two-tailed test. Do you agree? Why?

7. A manufacturer guaranteed that a particular type of steel cable had a mean tensile strength of 2000 pounds with a standard deviation of 200 pounds. In a shipment, 16 lengths of the cable were submitted to a test for breaking strength. The mean breaking strength was 1900 pounds. Using a one-tailed test at the .05 level of significance, determine whether the shipment met the manufacturer's specifications.

8. Two samples of mathematics students took a standardized engineering aptitude test. Using a two-tailed test at the .05 level of significance, determine whether the two groups were random samples from the same population.

Group A	Group B
$N = 25$	$N = 30$
$M = 80$	$M = 88$
$S = 8$	$S = 9$

9. An achievement test in spelling was administered to two randomly selected fifth grade groups of students from two schools. Test the null

hypothesis that there was no significant difference in achievement between the two fifth grade populations from which the samples were selected at the .05 level of significance. Use the method of separate variances.

School A	School B
$N = 40$	$N = 45$
$M = 82$	$M = 86$
$S = 12.60$	$S = 14.15$

10. One group of rats was given a vitamin supplement while the other group received a conventional diet. The rats were randomly assigned. Test the hypothesis that the vitamin supplement did not result in increased weight gain for the experimental group. Use a one-tailed test at the .05 level.

X	C
$N = 12$	$N = 16$
$S = 15.50$ g	$S = 12.20$ g
$M = 140$ g	$M = 120$ g

11. A consumer research agency tested two popular makes of automobiles with similar weight and horsepower. Eleven car A's provided a mean miles per gallon of 24.20 with an S of 1.40, while 11 car B's provided a mean miles per gallon of 26.30 with an S of 1.74. Using a two-tailed test at the .05 level, test the null hypothesis that there was no significant difference between the mean gasoline milage of the two makes of cars.

12. Calculate the number of degrees of freedom when:
   a. Estimating a population standard deviation from a sample standard deviation _____
   b. Computing the statistical significance of a coefficient of correlation _____
   c. Determining the significance of the difference between two means _____
   d. A 2×2 χ^2 table computation is involved _____
   e. A 3×5 χ^2 table computation is involved _____

13. In a survey to determine the preference of high school students for a soft drink, the results were:

	Brand A	Brand B	Brand C
Boys	25	30	52
Girls	46	22	28

Was there any relationship between the brand preference and the gender of the consumers? Use a two-tailed test at the .05 level of significance.

14. The number of correct responses on a coordination test was recorded for an experimental group that received a tranquilizer and a control group that received a placebo. Using a median test, test the null hypothesis that the medication had no effect at the .05 level of significance.

X	C
29	30
28	29
28	28
27	26
26	24
26	23
24	17
23	16
23	15
21	14
18	13
16	11
14	8
12	6
10	5

15. Twenty-six members of a local unit of the Weight Watchers Club were weighed two months after the conclusion of the enrollment period. Test the hypothesis that the program was not effective in enabling the former members to sustain their weight loss achieved in the program. Use a sign test at the .01 level of significance.

Initial weight	Two months after
159	148
175	170
170	160
200	189
160	163
140	144
125	120
204	200
228	214
270	250
165	164
149	153
122	120
130	144
150	148

Initial weight	Two months after
148	145
129	120
180	169
175	170
168	165
194	190
212	206
235	220
160	165
200	180
245	250

16. A group of 50 college freshmen was randomly assigned to experimental and control groups to determine the effectiveness of a counseling program upon academic averages. Use the Mann-Whitney test to test the null hypothesis that there was no difference between the academic performance of the experimental and control groups at the .05 level of significance.

Experimental	Control
2.10	2.01
3.00	2.69
1.96	3.07
2.04	2.14
3.27	2.82
3.60	2.57
3.80	3.44
2.75	4.00
1.98	3.01
2.00	2.55
2.98	2.77
3.10	3.09
3.69	2.72
2.66	3.34
2.56	2.81
2.50	3.05
3.77	2.67
2.40	1.90
3.20	1.70
1.71	1.57
3.04	1.39
2.06	2.09
2.86	3.68
3.02	2.11
1.88	2.83

17. Two groups of junior high school health class students were matched on the basis of intelligence quotients. One group was taught a unit on artificial resuscitation by a traditional lecture discussion method;

the other by a prediscussion and film strip presentation. At the conclusion of the unit the groups were tested. Test the null hypothesis that there was no difference in understanding between the groups at the .05 level of significance. Use the Wilcoxon matched-pairs signed ranks test.

	Lecture	Filmstrip
1.	60	70
2.	88	98
3.	78	79
4.	82	80
5.	60	75
6.	54	70
7.	80	87
8.	54	68
9.	50	78
10.	80	89
11.	60	84
12.	90	96
13.	70	88
14.	86	74
15.	60	78
16.	75	65
17.	88	92
18.	60	80
19.	92	70
20.	96	88

18. Compute the t value of the coefficient of correlation:

$$r = +.30$$
$$N = 18$$

Using Student's distribution, is this coefficient statistically significant at the .05 level for a one-tailed test?

Bibliography

BRADLEY, JAMES V. *Distribution-Free Statistical Tests*. Englewood Cliffs, N.J.: Prentice-Hall, 1968.

DOWNIE, N. M. and R. W. HEATH. *Basic Statistical Methods*. New York: Harper & Row, Publishers, 1965.

DuBOIS, PHILIP H. *An Introduction to Psychological Statistics*. New York: Harper & Row, Publishers, 1965.

EDWARDS, ALLEN. *Statistical Methods*. New York: Holt, Rinehart & Winston, 1967.

GARRETT, HENRY E. *Statistical Methods in Psychology and Education.* New York: David McKay Co., 1966.

GLASS, GENE V and JULIAN C. STANLEY. *Statistical Methods in Education and Psychology.* Englewood Cliffs, N.J.: Prentice-Hall, 1970.

GUILFORD, J. P. and B. FRUCHTER. *Fundamental Statistics in Psychology and Education.* New York: McGraw Hill Book Co., 1973.

HOROWITZ, LEONARD M. *Elements of Statistics for Psychology and Education.* New York: McGraw Hill Book Co., 1974.

MCCALL, ROBERT B. *Fundamental Statistics for Psychology.* New York: Harcourt Brace Jovanovich, 1975.

KISH, LESLIE. "Selection of the Sample." Chapter 5 in Leon Festinger and Daniel Kartz, eds., *Research Methods in the Behavioral Sciences.* New York: Holt, Rinehart & Winston, 1953.

NUNNALY, JUM C. *Introduction to Statistics for Psychology and Education.* New York: McGraw Hill Book Co., 1975.

POPHAM, W. JAMES. *Educational Statistics: Use and Interpretation.* New York: Harper & Row, Publishers, 1967.

ROBBINS, HERBERT and JOHN VAN RYZIN. *Introduction to Statistics.* Chicago: Science Research Associates, 1975.

SCHMIDT, MARTY J. *Understanding and Using Statistics: Basic Concepts.* Lexington, Mass.: D. C. Health & Co., 1975.

SIEGEL, SIDNEY. *Nonparametric Statistics for the Behavioral Sciences.* New York: McGraw Hill Book Co., 1956.

SILVERMAN, ELIOT N. and LINDA A. BRODY. *Statistics: A Common Sense Approach.* Boston: Prindle, Webber and Schmidt, 1973.

WEINBERG, GEORGE H. and JOHN A. SCHUMAKER. *Statistics: An Intuitive Approach.* Monterey, Calif.: Brooks/Cole Publishing Co., 1973.

WINER, B. J. *Statistical Principles in Experimental Design.* 2nd ed. New York: McGraw Hill Book Co., 1971.

YAMANE, TARO. *Elementary Sampling Theory.* Englewood Cliffs, N.J.: Prentice-Hall, 1967.

THE RESEARCH
REPORT

Chapter 9

Although research reports may differ considerably in scope of treatment, they are expected to follow a similar pattern of style and form that has become conventional in academic circles. These matters of style and form may seem unduly arbitrary to the student. However, they are based upon principles of clarity of organization and presentation, and it is essential that the graduate student in education be familiar with them if he is to communicate his ideas effectively.

STYLE MANUALS

Some graduate schools or departments have designated an official manual, or have established their own style manual, to which their theses or dissertations must conform. The student should find out which manual has been adopted officially by his institution or department. Beginning graduate students are disturbed when they discover that these manuals are not always in complete agreement on matters of typography or format. Careful examination, however, will reveal the fact that differences concern minor details. In general, they are in basic agreement on principles of correct presentation.

Regardless of which manual is used as a guide, it should be followed consistently in matters of form and style. The presentation of this chapter is consistent with one of the widely used form and style manuals.[1]

FORMAT OF THE RESEARCH REPORT

The research report, whether it be a thesis, dissertation, or a shorter term paper or report, usually follows a fairly standardized pattern. The following outline presents the usual sequence of topics:

A. Preliminary Section or Front Matter
1. Title Page
2. Acknowledgement (if any)
3. Table of Contents
4. List of Tables (if any)
5. List of Figures (if any)
B. Main Body of the Report
1. Introduction
   a. Statement of the problem—specific questions to be answered—hypotheses to be tested
   b. Significance of the problem
   c. Purposes of the study
   d. Assumptions and limitations
   e. Definition of important terms
2. Review of Related Literature or Analysis of Previous Research
3. Design of the Study
   a. Procedures used
   b. Sources of data
   c. Methods of gathering data
   d. Description of data-gathering instruments used
4. Presentation and Analysis of Data
   a. Text
   b. Tables
   c. Figures
5. Summary and Conclusions
   a. Restatement of the problem
   b. Description of procedures used
   c. Principal findings and conclusions
   d. Recommendations for further research
C. Reference Section
1. Bibliography
2. Appendix

Preliminary Section

The first page of the report is the title page. Although title page forms differ from one institution to another, they usually include: (1) the name

---

[1]William Giles Campbell and Stephen V. Ballou, *Form and Style: Theses, Reports, Term Papers* (Boston: Houghton Mifflin Co., 1974).

of the topic, (2) the name of the author, (3) the relationship of the report to a course or degree requirement, (4) the name of the institution where the report is to be submitted, and (5) the date of presentation.

The title should be concise and should indicate clearly the purposes of the study. It is well to keep in mind its possible usefulness to the reader who may scan a bibliography in which it may be listed. The title should not claim more for the study than it actually delivers. It should not be stated so broadly that it seems to provide an answer that cannot be generalized, either from the data gathered or from the methodology employed. For example, if a simple descriptive self-concept study were made of a group of children enrolled in a particular inner-city elementary school, the title should not read, "The Self-Concepts of Inner-City Children." A more appropriate title would be "The Self-Concepts of a Group of Philadelphia Inner-City Children."

The title should be typed in capital letters, single-spaced, and centered between the right and left margins of the page. Where more than one line is required, the words in the title are divided into lines so that each successive line is shorter than the one above it and is centered below it in an inverted pyramid style. This format is also used for table titles. Figure 9–1 illustrates a sample page used for a research report, submitted in partial fulfillment of the requirements of a course.

An acknowledgement page is included if the writer has received unusual assistance in the conduct of the study. If used, acknowledgements should be simple and restrained. Flattery and effusive recognition for routine participation by members of the writer's family, faculty advisors, librarians, and clerical helpers are considered unnecessary and in poor taste.

Table of contents. A good table of contents serves an important purpose in providing an outline of the contents of the report. The relationship between principal and minor divisions is indicated by capitalization of chapter numbers and titles, with subheadings in small letters and with capitalized principal letters. Page references for each topic are indicated.

List of tables and figures. If tables and figures are included in this report, a separate page is included for each list. The full titles of figures and tables, worded exactly as they appear in the text, are presented with corresponding numbers and page locations.

All pages in the preliminary section are numbered at the center of the bottom margin with lower-case Roman numerals (i, ii, iii, iv).

The Main Body of the Report

This section may be divided into five divisions. In a thesis or a dissertation these divisions may comprise chapters. In a shorter term

THE ATTITUDES OF A GROUP OF FIFTH GRADE TEACHERS
TOWARD THE WEEKDAY RELIGIOUS
EDUCATION PROGRAM

BY
MARY L. PORTER

A Term Report Submitted in Partial Fulfillment
of the Requirements in

Education 548: Introduction to Research

College of Education
BUTLER UNIVERSITY

June 6, 1969

FIGURE 9–1

paper or report they may consist of sections appropriately set off by centered headings.

1. The first section serves as an introduction to the area of consideration. A clear statement of the problem with specific questions to be answered or hypothesis to be tested is presented first. A consideration of the significance of the problem and its historical background is also appropriate. Specific purposes of the study are described, and all assumptions and limitations are recognized. All important terms are carefully defined, so that the reader may understand the concepts underlying the development of the investigation.

2. The second section reviews the important literature related to the study. Previous research studies are abstracted, and significant writings of authorities in the area under study are reviewed. This part of the research report provides a background for the development of the present study and brings the reader up to date. Since good research is based upon everything that is known about a problem, this part of the report gives evidence of the investigator's knowledge of the field. A brief summary, indicating areas of agreement or disagreement in findings, or gaps in existing knowledge, should be included.

3. The third section explains the design of the study in detail. The size of the samples and how they are selected, the variables and the controls employed, the sources and methods of gathering data, the reliability of instruments selected or constructed, and the statistical procedures used in the analysis are carefully described.

4. Section four includes the presentation and analysis of the data. This is the heart of the research report. Through textual discussion and tabular and graphic devices, the data are critically analyzed and reported. Tables and figures are used to clarify significant relationships. Good tables and figures are constructed and titled so that they are self-explanatory. Textual discussion may be used to point out generalizations and significant interpretations, but not to restate the information that they have presented. Good tables and figures are relatively simple, pointing up one or two significant relationships. If complex tables are developed, they should be placed in the appendix.

5. The fifth section consists of a summary. After a brief statement of the problem and a description of the procedures used in the investigation, the findings and conclusions are presented. Findings are statements of factual information based upon the data analysis. Conclusions are answers to the questions raised, or the statements of acceptance or rejection of the hypotheses proposed.

The summary is probably the most difficult section of the report to write. Beginning researchers are sometimes guilty of overgeneralizing on the basis of their limited data. There is a temptation to write persuasively,

TABLE OF CONTENTS

FIGURE 9–2

iv

v

FIGURE 9–3

to mount the soapbox. Previously held convictions, not tested by the analysis, creep into the discussion. The course instructor often has to comment, "Your study to this point has been good. Your summary is disappointing. What you have reported may possibly be true, but there is nothing in your study to justify or support your conclusions."

It is essential that the researcher cultivate the skepticism and the modesty of the scientist. These qualities of scholarly restraint are evidences of the objectivity of scientific analysis and good research reporting.

It may be appropriate in concluding this part of the report to indicate promising side-problems that have been uncovered and to suggest areas or problems for further investigation.

The summary section is the most used part of the research report. Readers who scan research literature to find significant studies examine this section before deciding whether or not further examination of the report is worthwhile.

Reference Materials

The bibliography is preceded by a sheet containing the word BIBLI-OGRAPHY, capitalized and centered on the page. The first page of the bibliography has the center title BIBLIOGRAPHY. References are arranged in alphabetical order, the last name of the author listed first. Each entry is placed flush with the left margin of the page, and subsequent lines are single-spaced and indented five spaces. A double space separates entries. If no author name is given, the name of the publication or the sponsoring organization is listed as the author.

In a short bibliography, books, pamphlets, monographs, and periodical references may be combined in the same list. If the number of references is large, the bibliography may be divided into sections, one for books, one for periodicals, and possibly one for special documents. Ordinarily, a selected bibliography is preferable to an exhaustive list. An annotation, or short statement giving the reader a clear idea of the nature of the reference and the topics that it covers, adds an important quality of usefulness to the bibliography. The annotating statement should be single-spaced, but separated from the bibliographic entry by a double space.

KING, EDMUND J. Other Schools and Ours. 4th ed. New York: Holt, Rinehart & Winston, 1973. 360 pp.

An interesting and perceptive analysis of school systems in Denmark, France, Great Britain, the United States, the Soviet Union, India, and Japan. The interaction of cultural influences and education is emphasized.

The appendix is preceded by a sheet containing the word APPENDIX, capitalized and centered on the page. The first page of the appendix is titled APPENDIX A, and pages are numbered serially, using Arabic numerals. Tables and data—important, but not essential to the understanding of the report—copies of cover letters used, and printed forms of questionnaires, tests, and other data-gathering devices may be placed in the appendix. Each separate entry heading is listed as APPENDIX A, APPENDIX B, etc.

In mounting pictures, standard forms, and other materials on the manuscript sheet stationers' rubber cement should be used. The naterials to be joined should each be coated and allowed to dry before being pressed together. The result will be a permanent bond that will not cause the paper to wrinkle.

STYLE OF WRITING

The research report should be presented in a style that is creative, clear, and concise. Although the phraseology should be dignified and straightforward, it need not be dull or pedantic. Even the most profound ideas can best be explained in simple language and short, coherent sentences.

Slang, hackneyed or flippant phrases, and folksy style should be avoided. Since objectivity is the primary goal, there should be no element of exhortation or persuasion. The research report should describe and explain, rather than try to convince or move to action. In this respect the research report differs from the essay or the feature article.

In the interests of objectivity the personal pronouns, I, we, you, my, our, and us should not be used. These personal pronouns can be avoided by the use of such expressions as "the investigator" or "the researcher." Instead of saying, "I selected ten students from each class," the passive voice construction would be preferable—"Ten students were selected from each class."

Only the last names of cited authorities are used. Titles such as professor, Dr., Mr., and Dean are omitted. The past tense should be used in describing research procedures that have been completed.

Abbreviations may be used in footnotes, tables, and figures, but they should not be used in the text of the report. A few such exceptions as IQ, PTA, NEA are appropriate, but if there is any doubt, words should be spelled out.

Discussion of quantitative terms. *Few* in number, *less* in quantity are the preferred forms of expression. Numbers beginning a sentence should always be spelled out. Fractions, round numbers, and numbers under 100 should be spelled out, except when they are combined. Use one-half, but $4\frac{1}{2}$ or 4.5. Percent (meaning per hundred) is spelled out except in tables and figures. Use Arabic numerals with percent (18 percent), unless they begin a sentence. Percentage means proportion. In numbers with more than three digits, commas should point off thousands or millions (1 ,324; 12,304,000).

Ordinarily, standard statistical formulas are not presented in the research report, nor are computations included. If a rather unusual formula is used in the analysis it is appropriate to include it.

Correct Usage

Of course, the ordinary rules of correct usage should prevail. A good dictionary, a spelling guide,[2] a handbook of style,[3] and Roget's Thesaurus are helpful references.

The author has noted frequent errors of spelling, agreement between subject and predicate, nonparallel construction, and inconsistent tense sequence. Students who have difficulty in written expression should have a competent friend or relative proofread their copy for correct usage before they type the final manuscript. Inability to write correctly is a serious limitation. Carelessness is an even greater fault.

Effective research report writing is not an easy task. Good reports are not written hurriedly. Even skillful and experienced writers revise many times before they submit a manuscript for publication.

TYPING THE REPORT

Many students type their own term papers or research reports. Anyone with reasonable proficiency and a willingness to learn proper procedures can do an acceptable job. In fact, typing a report is an excellent way to really learn proper form.

Typographical standards for the thesis or dissertation are more exacting. Strikeovers, crossovers, insertions, and erasures are not permitted. Therefore, only typists with great proficiency should attempt to prepare thesis or dissertation copy. Although the expense of professional typing may seem high, the saving of time and excessive effort usually make this arrangement the wiser choice.

It is the writer's responsibility to present manuscript material to the professional typist in proper form. Except for minor typographical matters, the correction of major errors is not the responsibility of the typist. After the material is received from the typist, the student should proofread it carefully before it is turned in.

[2]Twenty Thousand Words (New York: McGraw Hill Book Co., 1934.)
[3]John C. Hodges with Mary E. Whitten, eds., Harbrace College Handbook (New York: Harcourt, Brace & World, 1963).

Typography

1. Good quality of bond, $8\frac{1}{2}$ by 11 inches in size, of 13- to 16-pound weight, should be used for the original and first carbon copy of the thesis or dissertation. A lighter paper may be used for additional copies. For the term paper any bond paper is acceptable. Only one side of the sheet is used in typewritten manuscript.
2. Pica type, with ten spaces to the inch, is preferred to elite, which has twelve. The type must be clean, and a medium-inked black ribbon should be used. It is surprising what a new typewriter ribbon and clean type will do to produce effective copy. (Scotch Brand typewriter cleaner or an old toothbrush and some lighter fluid will remove lint and ink particles from the type.) Medium-weight, black carbon paper should be used for the copies. Carbon paper should be replaced often enough to insure clear and even copies. Special symbols not available on the typewriter keyboard should be carefully inserted, using black India ink.
3. To facilitate the proper placement of copy on the page a guide sheet may be constructed, showing the proper margins, the center of the copy portion, and the number of lines from the top and bottom margins. This sheet should be ruled in black ink and placed beneath the first sheet, so that the markings show through. The use of the guide sheet takes much of the guesswork out of copy placement. (See Figure 9–4.) Also helpful is Multicopy carbon paper, which has in the margin a numbered scale representing single-spaced lines.
4. The right margin should be one inch, the top margin $1\frac{1}{4}$ inches, the bottom margin $1\frac{1}{2}$ inches, and the left margin $1\frac{1}{2}$ inches.
5. Textual material should be double-spaced. Long lists of materials may be single-spaced.

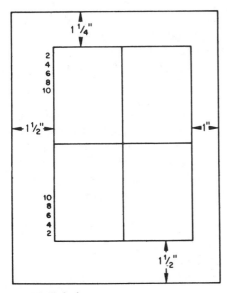

FIGURE 9–4

6. Paragraphs should be indented seven spaces for pica type, nine for elite.
7. Words should not be divided at the end of the line, unless completing them would definitely interfere with the margin. A few spaces runover is preferable. In dividing words, consult a dictionary for correct syllabication.
8. Direct quotations not over three typewritten lines in length are included in the text and are enclosed in quotation marks. Quotations of more than three lines are set off from the text in a single-spaced paragraph and indented four spaces from both left and right margins without quotation marks. Original paragraph indentations are retained.
9. The superscript is ordinarily placed at the end of the sentence of quoted material. Where several references are mentioned in one sentence, the superscript is placed after each name reference (Smith,[1] Jones,[2] and Brown[3] reported their findings).

FOOTNOTES

Footnotes serve a number of purposes. They enable the writer to substantiate his presentation by citations of other authorities, to give credit to sources of material that he has quoted or paraphrased, and to provide the reader with specific sources that he may use to verify the authenticity and accuracy of material used.

Occasionally, in research report writing, the footnote is used to present explanatory statements that, although important, would interfere with the logic and continuity of textual material. In serving these purposes footnotes are very useful devices. They should be used sparingly, however, and never included for the mere purpose of scholarly appearance.

Footnote citations may be inserted in parentheses at the end of the sentence. For example, (18:42) indicates that the citation refers to bibliography listing number 18, page 42. In another procedure all of the citations are placed on one page at the end of the chapter. Each institution or department usually specifies the type of footnote citation permitted or recommended.

Traditionally footnote citations are placed at the bottom of the page, and are separated from the text by a two-inch horizontal line drawn from the left margin, one double space below the last line of the text. The reference superscript is placed one-half space below the dividing line, the first footnote one line below the dividing line. Each footnote reference is indented the customary number of spaces. If there is a second line in the citation, it is flush with the left margin.

Footnotes are single-spaced, with double spacing between citations. Footnotes are numbered consecutively within a chapter, or consecutively within the entire report if chapter headings are not used.

In consecutive footnote reference the abbreviation Ibid. (Latin, *the same*) may be used. If the page reference is different, the new page citation follows:

[3]Fred N. Kerlinger, Foundations of Behavioral Research (New York: Holt, Rinehart & Winston, 1964), p. 217.

[4]*Ibid.* (indicates same page as previous reference)

[5]*Ibid.*, p. 232. (same work, but a different page)

When references to the same work occur within a page or two, op. cit. (Latin, *the work cited*) may be used, always with the surname of the author and the page reference. Op. cit. is used when another reference intervenes.

[1]Clinton I. Chase, Elementary Statistical Procedures (New York: McGraw Hill Book Company, 1967), p. 13.

[2]Philip H. DuBois, An Introduction to Psychological Statistics (New York: Harper & Row, Publishers, 1965), p. 24.

[3]Chase, *op. cit.*, p. 34.

When a second but nonconsecutive reference follows, referring to the same work and same page previously cited, loc. cit. may be used. Again the author's surname must be included.

[4]DuBois, *loc. cit.* (This reference is to page 24.)

Abbreviations

In bibliography or footnote references abbreviations may be used to conserve space. Students should be familiar with the following standard abbreviations:

art., arts.	article, articles
bk., bks.	book, books
c. (*circa*)	about (approximate date)
cf.	compare
chap., chaps.	chapter, chapters
col., cols.	column, columns
div., divs.	division, divisions
ed., eds.	editor, editors
ed., eds.	edition, editions
et al.	and others
e.g.	for example
et seq.	and the following
f., ff.	and the following
fig., figs.	figure, figures
ibid.	same reference
idem.	same person
i.e.	that is
illus.	illustrated
infra.	below
l., ll.	line, lines

loc. cit.	the place cited
mimeo.	mimeographed
ms.	manuscript
n.d.	no date given
n.n.	no name given
n.p.	no place given
no., nos.	number, numbers
op. cit.	previously cited
p., pp.	page, pages
par., pars.	paragraph, paragraphs
passim	here and there (scattered)
pt., pts.	part, parts
rev.	revised
sec., secs.	section, sections
sic.	thus
supra.	above
trans.	translated
vide.	see
vol., vols.	volume, volumes
(. . .)	omissions in quoted matter up to one paragraph in length—(for a full paragraph or more omitted, use a full line of alternating periods and spaces).

(All Latin abbreviations are underlined.)

BIBLIOGRAPHY AND FOOTNOTE FORM

The purpose of the bibliography is quite different from that of the footnote. The bibliography, located at the end of the main body of the report, lists in alphabetical order the references used by the writer in preparing the report. The footnotes, found at the bottom of the page, specifically cite the exact place where quoted or paraphrased materials may be found.

The typographical form of the bibliography listing and the footnote citation also differ. Note the following examples which illustrate the differences for a textbook reference:

Bibliography form:

VAIZEY, JOHN. Education in the Modern World. New York: McGraw Hill Book Company, 1967. 254 pp.

Footnote form:

[1]John Vaizey, Education in the Modern World (New York: McGraw Hill Book Company, 1967), p. 32.

Additional forms, both bibliography and footnote, most often used in educational writing are illustrated for each type of reference.

TABLE IX   A Comparison of Bibliography and Footnote Form

	Bibliography	*Footnote*
Indentation	overhanging—first line flush with margin, second line indented five spaces	[1]regular paragraph indentation
Name order	last name first (of first author when more than one author)	first name first
Placement	end of body of report— listed alphabetically by last name of first author	[1]bottom of page with superscript
Punctuation	Author name. Title. Place of publication: Publisher, date of publication.	[1]Author, Title (Place of publication: Publisher, date of publication).
Page reference	414 pp. (total number of pages in book or in article)	p. 23. (specific page location of reference)

Joint Authors

Bibliography form:

BARZUN, JACQUES and HENRY F. GRAFF. The Modern Researcher. New York: Harcourt, Brace & World, 1957. 386 pp.

Footnote form:

[1]Jacques Barzun and Henry F. Graff, The Modern Researcher 2nd. ed. (New York: Harcourt, Brace & World, 1970), p. 75.

More than Three Authors

Bibliography form:

SELLTIZ, CLAIRE ET AL. Research Methods in Social Relations. (Rev. in one vol.) New York: Holt, Rinehart & Winston, 1959.

Footnote form:

[1]Claire Selltiz et al. Research Methods in Social Relations (New York: Holt, Rinehart & Winston, 1959), p. 77.

Editor as Author

Bibliography form:

BUROS, OSCAR K., ed. The Sixth Mental Measurements Yearbook. Highland Park,
N.J.: Gryphon Press, 1965. 1163 pp.

Footnote form:

[1]Oscar K. Buros, ed., The Sixth Mental Measurements Yearbook (Highland Park,
N.J.: Gryphon Press, 1965), p. 179.

Author not Given

Bibliography form:

Author's Guide. Englewood Cliffs, N.J.: Prentice-Hall, 1955, 121 pp.

Footnote form:

[1]*Author's Guide* (Englewood Cliffs, N.J.: Prentice-Hall, 1955), p. 23.

Publication of an Association, Agency, or Society

If all of the publication is devoted to one topic, treat it as a book.
If the article is part of the publication, treat it as a periodical article.
Either the name of the article or the name of the sponsoring organization
may be listed first.

Bibliography form:

Modern Philosophies of Education. National Society for the Study of Education, Fifty-fourth Yearbook, Part I. Chicago: University of Chicago Press,
1955. 374 pp.

or

National Society for the Study of Education. Modern Philosophies of Education.
Fifty-fourth Yearbook, Part I. Chicago: The University of Chicago Press,
1955. 374 pp.

Footnote form:

[1]Modern Philosophies of Education, National Society for the Study of Education,
Fifty-fourth Yearbook, Part I (Chicago: The University of Chicago Press, 1955),
p. 220. Quoted by permission of the Society.

This particular organization asks for the inclusion of "Quoted by permission of the Society." Some organizations and publishers request certain
forms of acknowledgement when materials are quoted in the thesis, dissertation, or for a manuscript to be published in a book or periodical.
For term papers, permission to quote is not necessary.

Part of a Series

Bibliography form:

TERMAN, LEWIS M. and MELITA H. ODEN. The Gifted Child Grows Up. Vol. 4 of the Genetic Studies of Genius Series, Lewis M. Terman, ed. Stanford: Stanford University Press, 1947. 448 pp.

Footnote form:

[1]Lewis M. Terman and Melita H. Oden, The Gifted Child Grows Up, Vol. 4 of the Genetic Studies of Genius Series, Lewis M. Terman, ed., 5 vols. (Stanford: Stanford University Press, 1947), p. 7.

A Chapter Written by an Author Other than the Author or Editor of the Book

Bibliography form:

MACCOBY, ELEANOR E. and NATHAN MACCOBY, "The Interview: A Tool of Social Science," Chapter 12 in The Handbook of Social Psychology, Vol. 1, Gardner Lindzey, ed. Cambridge, Mass.: Addison-Wesley, 1954.

Footnote form:

[1]Eleanor E. Maccoby and Nathan Maccoby, "The Interview: A Tool of Social Science," Chapter 12 in The Handbook of Social Psychology, Vol. 1, Gardner Lindzey, ed. (Cambridge, Mass.: Addison-Wesley, 1954), p. 451.

A Translation

Bibliography form:

BEST, JOHN W. Como Investigar en Educacion. Gonzalvo Mainar, translator. Madrid: Morata, 1967. 397 pp.

Footnote form:

[1]John W. Best, Como Investigar en Educacion, Gonzalvo Mainar, translator (Madrid: Morata, 1967), p. 74.

Article in an Encyclopedia

Bibliography form:

BANTA, RICHARD E. "New Harmony." Encyclopædia Britannica (1968) 16: 305.

Footnote form:

Richard E. Banta, "New Harmony," Encyclopædia Britannica (1968) 16: 305.

Periodical Article

For periodical references, the differences between bibliography and footnote forms are similar to those for book references. Note that the name of the article is enclosed in quotation marks and the name of the publication is underlined. There are a few slight punctuation differences.

Bibliography form:

WALSH, J. HARTT. "Education in 2,000 A.D." Nation's Schools 57: 47–51 (April 1956).

Footnote form:

[1]J. Hartt Walsh, "Education in 2,000 A.D.," Nation's Schools 57: 50 (April 1956).

Quotation from a Primary Source that Cannot be Located

When using a quotation from a primary source quoted by an author, try to find the original source and quote it directly. If you cannot locate it, quote it, using both primary and secondary references.

Bibliography form:

KELLY, EARL P. "Education for What Is Real." New York: Harper & Row, Publishers, 1947. As cited by Edward A. Krug, Curriculum Planning. New York: Harper & Row, Publishers, 1950. p. 55.

Footnote form:

Earl P. Kelly, "Education for What is Real" (New York: Harper & Row, Publishers, 1947). As cited by Edward A. Krug, Curriculum Planning (New York: Harper & Row, Publishers, 1950), p. 55.

Newspaper Articles

Ordinarily newspaper items are not listed in the bibliography but they are cited in footnotes.

Footnote form:

[1]Editorial in The Indianapolis News, January 6, 1968.
[1]Associated Press Dispatch, The Milwaukee Journal, December 24, 1968, p. 1.
[1]The Chicago Daily News, February 3, 1968, p. 6.

Unpublished Materials

Bibliography form:

DEVOE, DONALD B. Bibliography on Uses of High Speed Computers in Psychology. Medford, Mass.: Tufts University, Institute for Applied Experimental Psychology, 1957. 5 pp. (Mimeographed).

Footnote form:

> [1]Donald B. Devoe, <u>Bibliography on Uses of High Speed Computers in Psychology</u> (Medford, Mass.: Tufts University, Institute for Applied Experimental Psychology, 1957), (Mimeographed) p. 2.

Thesis or Dissertation

Bibliography form:

BEST, JOHN W. <u>An Analysis of Certain Selected Factors Underlying the Choice of Teaching as a Profession</u>. Unpublished Doctoral Dissertation, University of Wisconsin, Madison, 1948.

Footnote form:

> [1]John W. Best, <u>An Analysis of Certain Selected Factors Underlying the Choice of Teaching as a Profession</u> (Unpublished Doctoral Dissertation, University of Wisconsin, Madison, 1948), p. 14.

Many dissertations are now reproduced in microfilm form.

PORTER, ROBERT M. <u>Relationship of Participation to Satisfaction in Small Group Discussions</u>. Doctoral Dissertation. Philadelphia: Temple University, 1955. 143 pp.
Abstract. Dissertation Abstracts 15: 2492–93; No. 12, 1955.

Speeches or statements made, but not published, are listed in the footnotes but not in the bibliography. When quoted in published reports, it is essential that the material be verified by the person who made the statement, and never used without his permission.

> [1]Statement by Paul Butler, personal interview, January 17, 1968.
> [1]Commencement address, Butler University, Indianapolis, Indiana, June 6, 1968.

Quotations from Letters

A letter is legally the property of the writer, not the recipient. When contents are quoted, the written permission of the writer or, if deceased, the permission of his heirs, is necessary.

> [1]*Letter*, Henry R. Smith to Paul T. Jones, December 7, 1968.

HEADINGS

When the manuscript is divided into chapters, each chapter begins a new page. The word *chapter* is capitalized, followed by a capitalized Roman numeral, centered and placed four spaces lower than the usual top line of the text. The chapter title is centered and capitalized, a double space below the heading. Textual material follows three spaces below the title.

A major division of a chapter or of a short term paper is introduced with a centered head written in full capitals. Textual materials that follow are placed three spaces below the centered head.

A subdivision of the section of the part of the discussion under the centered head is introduced by a freestanding side head, flush with the left margin. For further subdivision of the discussion, a paragraph side head is used, with the usual paragraph indentation.

CENTER HEAD (FULL CAPITALS)

Side Head (major words capitalized)

Paragraph side head. (only initial letter of first word capitalized)

PAGINATION

Page numbers are assigned to each page of the paper or report. The title page or the initial page of a section (chapter, major subdivision, bibliography, or appendix) does not have a page number typed on it, but a number is allowed for it in the series.

Page numbers are placed in the upper right-hand corner, one inch below the top of the page and aligned with the right margin. Page numbers of the preliminary section of the manuscript use small or lower-case Roman numerals (i, ii, iii), beginning with the title page and ending with the last page preceding the main body of the paper. The page containing Chapter I is page 1, but has no number typed on it. However, the next page is page 2. The bibliography and appendix are numbered serially and consecutively, following the last chapter.

Since correct pagination depends upon the final edited copy, assigning page numbers should be the final step before putting the manuscript into the binder or folder. Preliminary page numbers can be lightly penciled in and changed, if additions, deletions, or corrections are made.

TABLES

A table is a systematic method of presenting statistical data in vertical columns and horizontal rows, according to some classfication of subject matter. Tables enable the reader to comprehend and interpret masses of data rapidly, and to grasp significant details and relationships at a glance. Tables and figures should be used sparingly; too many will overwhelm the reader.

Good tables are relatively simple, concentrating on a limited number of ideas. Including too much data in a table minimizes the value of tabular presentation. It is often advisable to use several tables rather than to include too many details in a single one. It has been said that the mark of a good table is its effectiveness in conveying ideas and relationships independently of the text of the report.

If a table is large enough to occupy more than a half-page, it should be placed on a page by itself, carefully centered for a balanced effect. If it is short, occupying less than a half-page, it may be placed on the page with texual material, preferably following as closely as possible the textual discussion that relates to it.

Text references should identify tables by number, rather than by such expressions as, "the table above," or "the following table." Tables should rarely be carried over to the second or third page. If the table must be continued, the headings should be repeated at the top of each column of data on each page.

Tables should not exceed the page size of the manuscript. Large tables that must be folded into the copy are always cumbersome, and cannot be easily refolded and replaced. Large tables should be reduced to manuscript page size by photostating or some other process of reproduction. Tables that are too wide for the page may be turned sidewise, with the top facing the left margin, or binding, of the manuscript.

The word TABLE is centered between the page margins and typed in capital letters, followed by the table number in capital Roman numerals. Tables are numbered consecutively throughout the entire report or thesis, including those tables that may be placed in the appendix. The caption or title is placed two spaces below the word TABLE, and arranged in inverted pyramid form. No terminal punctuation is used. The main title should be brief, clearly indicating the nature of the data presented. Occasionally a subtitle is used to supplement a briefer main title, denoting such additional information as sources of data and measuring units employed.

Because they are completely unnecessary, such expressions as "table showing," "distribution of," or "frequency of" should be avoided.

The top of the table is placed three spaces below the last line of the title. Column headings, or box heads, should be clearly labeled, describing the nature and units of neasure of the data listed. Such terms as number, percent, and frequency may be abbreviated by the use of No., %, and f. The percentage symbol (%) should be placed at the top of the column, not with the numbers in the table.

If numbers are shortened by the omission of zeros, that fact should be mentioned in the subtitle (in millions of dollars—in thousands of tons). The stub, or label, for the rows should be clear and concise, parallel in grammatical structure, and if possible, no longer than two lines.

Numerical data are usually arranged in descending order of magnitude or frequency, so that cpmparisons by position can be noted readily. If there are several columns in the table, the first column to the left is arranged in descending order. When data are presented by states, the material is sometimes listed alphabetically by states to facilitate location. Lines of tabular data are single-spaced. Rulings or lines are used only if they facilitate the reading of the table. Few horizontal lines are needed. Vertical lines at left and right margins are omitted.

Decimal points should always be aligned in the column. When no data are available for a particular cell, indicate the lack by a dash, rather than by a zero. Double horizontal lines are placed at the top of the table separating it from the title. A horizontal line is also placed at the bottom to separate the table from the material which follows three spaces below.

When footnotes are needed to explain items in the table, small Arabic letters or typewriter key symbols are used. Numerical superscripts would be confused with the data contained in the table. Table footnotes are placed just below the table, rather that at the bottom of the page.

TABLE X
OCCUPATIONS OF FATHERS OF
UNIVERSITY OF WISCONSIN
SENIORS PREPARING TO
TEACH

Occupations	Men		Women	
	No.	%	No.	%#
Business proprietor	24	23	32	29
Skilled labor	19	18	10	9
Farming	17	17	19	17
Clerical-sales	16	16	18	16
Profession	15	15	20	18
Unskilled labor	6	6	6	5
No data	5	5	7	6
Total	102	100	112	100

\# Percentages rounded to equal 100%

* Adapted from John W. Best, An Analysis of Certain Selected Factors Underlying the Choice of Teaching as a Profession. (Unpublished Doctoral Dissertation, University of Wisconsin, Madison, Wisconsin, 1948), p. 47.

FIGURE 9–5

FIGURES

A figure is a device that presents statistical data in graphic form. The term figure is applied to a wide variety of graphs, charts, maps, sketches, diagrams, and drawings. When skillfully used, figures present aspects of data in a visualized form that may be clearly and easily understood. Figures should not be intended as substitutes for textual description, but included to emphasize certain significant relationships.

Many of the qualities that were listed as characteristics of good tables are equally appropriate when applied to figures.

1. The title should clearly describe the nature of the data presented.
2. Figures should be simple enough to convey a clear idea, and should be understandable without the aid of textual description.
3. Numerical data upon which the figure is based should be presented in an accompanying table, if they are not included in the figure itself.
4. Data should be presented carefully and accurately, so that oversimplification, misrepresentation, or distortion do not result.
5. Figures should be used sparingly. Too many figures detract from, rather than illuminate, the presentation.
6. Figures that occupy more than a half-page should be placed on a separate page. Those that are smaller and occupy less than a half-page may be placed on the same page as textual material.
7. Figures should follow, never precede, the related textual discussion.
8. Figures are referred to by number, never as "the figure above" or "the figure below."
9. Figures are numbered with Arabic rather than Roman numerals.
10. The title of the figure is placed below rather than above it.

There are several acceptable and frequently used title forms, any of which may be used if followed consistently throughout the report.

Paragraph form:

Figure 1. Absences of students at Washington School during November, 1968.

Underhung form:

Figure 1. Absences of students at Washington School during November, 1968.

Block form:

Figure 1. Absences of students at Washington School during November, 1968.

The Line Graph

The line graph or chart is especially useful in making predictions based upon trends, and in presenting relationships between several types of data

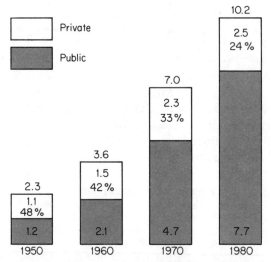

FIGURE 9–6   **Number in Millions of Past and Projected College and University Enrollments in Private and Public Institutions**

(see Figure 9–6). Changing status with the passing of time, or the relationships between variables, can be plotted on the vertical and horizontal axes.

The horizontal axis usually measures the independent variable, the vertical axis the measured characteristic. Graphic arrangement should proceed from left to right on the horizontal axis, and from bottom to top on the vertical. The zero point should always be represented, and scale intervals should be equal. If a part of the scale is omitted, a set of parallel jagged lines should be used to indicate that part of the scale omitted.

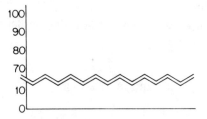

When coordinate graph paper is used, the lines connecting the intersecting points should be made heavy enough to distinguish them from the rulings on the paper. When several lines are drawn, they may be distinguished by using various types of lines—solid, dotted, or alternate dots and dashes. Black India ink is used.

A smoothed curve cannot be obtained by plotting any data directly.

Only when infinite data are obtained will the lines connecting the points approach a curved line. The figure formed by the lines connecting the points is known as a <u>frequency polygon.</u>

The Bar Graph or Chart

The bar graph may be arranged either horizontally or vertically, and represents data by bars of equal width, drawn to scale length. The numerical data may be lettered within the bar or outside it. A grid may be used to help quantify the graphic representation. A divided bar graph represents the components of a whole unit in one bar.

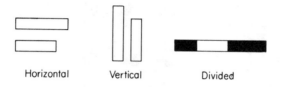

Horizontal   Vertical   Divided

When comparisons are made, bars or parts of the bars are contrasted by crosshatching. This crosshatching may be done with black India ink. This process is time-consuming, however, and many almost completed drawings have been spoiled by an ink smear in the process.

Pressure sensitive tape with various designs—of stripes, dots, circles, and checks—has largely replaced the inking process, and is available at art supply stores.[4]

In bar graphs the bars are usually separated by space. If the graph contains a large number of items, the bars may be joined to save space.

Horizontal bar graphs are usually used to compare components at a particular time. Vertical bars are used when making comparisons at different times.

In typed manuscript horizontal bars are easier to construct. Because of space limitations and typing problems, vertical bars are difficult to label.

The Circle, Pie, or Sector Chart

This type of chart shows the division of a unit into its component parts. It is frequently used to explain how a unit of government distributes its share of the tax dollar, how an individual spends his salary, or any other type of simple percentage distribution.

[4]Available from Chart-Pak, Inc., Leeds, Mass., or from Prestape, Inc., New York, New York, 10011.

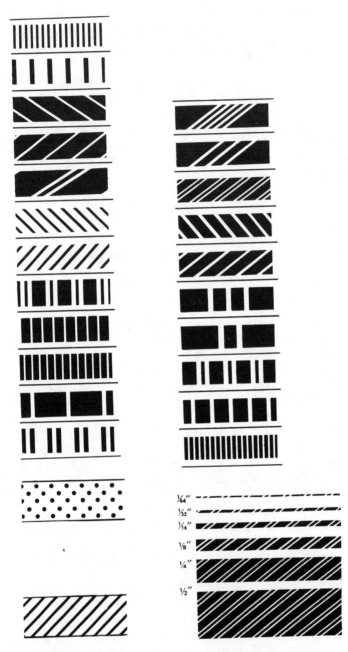

FIGURE 9–7 Commercially Prepared Pressure Sensitive Tapes for Use in Graphs

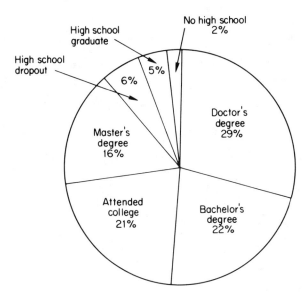

FIGURE 9-8   **Educational Backgrounds of 129 American Celebrities Listed in the *Current Biography 1966 Yearbook*.***

The radius is drawn vertically, and components are arranged in a clockwise direction in descending order of magnitude. The proportion of data is indicated by the number of degrees in each segment of the 360° circle (see Figure 9-8).

This kind of data should be typed or printed within the segment if possible. If there is not sufficient room for this identification, a small arrow should point from the identification term to the segment.

Maps

When geographic location or identification is important, maps may be used. Printed outline maps in $8\frac{1}{2} \times 11$ inch size are available at school-supply stores. Identification may be made by the use of dots, circles, or other symbols, and density or characteristics of areas represented by shading or crosshatching. A key or legend should always be supplied if shadings are used.

*Adapted from Adela Deming, "The Educational Attainments of Americans Listed in the Current Biography 1966 Yearbook" (Unpublished Report, Butler University, Indianapolis, Indiana, 1967), p. 7.

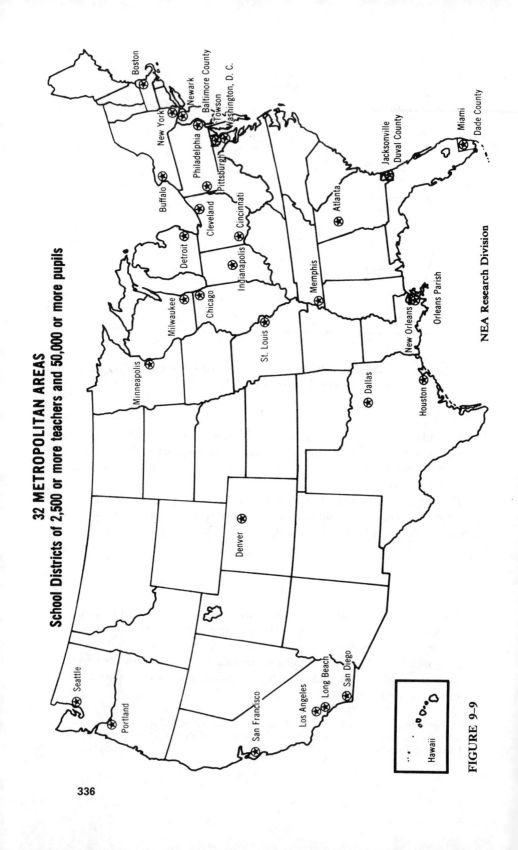

32 METROPOLITAN AREAS
School Districts of 2,500 or more teachers and 50,000 or more pupils

NEA Research Division

FIGURE 9–9

336

Organization Charts

To show staff functions, lines of authority, or flow of work within an organization, an organization chart is a helpful graphic device.

Units may be represented by circles, squares, or oblongs, with names lettered within the units. Distinctions between direct and indirect relationships may be indicated by the use of solid and dotted lines. Ordinarily, authority, supervision, or movement of materials flow from the top to the bottom of the chart, but variations can be indicated by the use of arrows.

EVALUATING A RESEARCH REPORT

Writing a critical analysis of a research report is a valuable experience for the student of educational research. Reports for this purpose may be taken from published collections[5] and such periodicals as the Journal of Experimental Education, the Journal of Educational Research, or one of the many other publications that publish reports of research in education or in the closely related fields of psychology or sociology.

Another source is the unpublished research reports written by students in previous classes in educational research, or the theses or dissertations found in the university library.

Through a critical analysis, the student may gain some insight into the nature of a research problem, the methods by which it may be attacked, the difficulties inherent in the research process, the ways in which data are analyzed and conclusions drawn, and the style with which the report is presented. (See Appendix G.)

The following questions are suggested as a possible structure for the analysis:

1. The Title
   a. Is it clear and concise?
   b. Does it promise no more than the study can provide?
2. The Problem
   a. Is it clearly stated?
   b. Is it properly delimited?
   c. Is its significance recognized?
   d. Are specific questions raised; hypotheses clearly stated?
   e. Are assumptions and limitations stated?
   f. Are important terms defined?
3. Review of Related Literature
   a. Is it adequately covered?
   b. Are important findings noted?

[5]Edwin Wandt, A Cross Section of Educational Research (New York: David McKay Co., 1965).

c. Is it well organized?
d. Is an effective summary provided?
4. Procedures Used
    a. Is the research design described in detail?
    b. Is it adequate?
    c. Are the samples described?
    d. Are relevant variables recognized?
    e. Are appropriate controls provided?
    f. Are data-gathering instruments appropriate?
    g. Are validity and reliability established?
    h. Is the statistical treatment appropriate?
5. Data Analysis
    a. Is appropriate use made of tables and figures?
    b. Is the textual discussion clear and concise?
    c. Is the analysis of data relationships logical and perceptive?
    d. Is the statistical analysis accurately interpreted?
6. Summary and Conclusions
    a. Is the problem restated?
    b. Are the procedures described in detail?
    c. Are findings concisely presented?
    d. Is the analysis objective?
    e. Are the findings and conclusions justified by the data presented and analyzed?

SUMMARY

The research report is expected to follow the conventional pattern of style and form used in academic circles. Although style manuals differ in some of the smaller details, the student is expected to be consistent in following the pattern of style contained in either the manual required by his institution, or the one that he is permitted to select.

The style of writing should be clear, concise, and completely objective. Of course, the highest standards of correct usage are expected, and careful proofreading is necessary before the final report is submitted.

Tables and figures may help to make the meaning of the data clear. They should be presented in proper mechanical form and should be carefully designed to present an accurate and undistorted picture.

The evaluation of a research project is a valuable exercise for the student of educational research. Using a pattern such as the one suggested, the critical analysis of the many aspects of another researcher's report helps the student to develop competency in his own research and reporting skills.

BIBLIOGRAPHY

BARZUN, JACQUES and HENRY F. GRAFF. The Modern Researcher. New York: Harcourt Brace Jovanovich, 1970.

CAMPBELL, WILLIAM G. and STEPHEN V. BALLOU. Form and Style: Theses, Reports, Term Papers. Boston: Houghton Mifflin Co., 1974.

GEPHART, WILLIAM J. Development of an Instrument for Evaluating Educational Research Reports. Cooperative Research Project #S-014. Washington, D.C.: U.S. Office of Education, 1964.

Harbrace College Handbook. New York: Harcourt, Brace & World, 1962.

KOEFOD, PAUL E., The Writing Requirements for Graduate Degrees. Englewood Cliffs, N.J.: Prentice-Hall, 1964.

PERRIN, PORTER G., Writer's Guide and Index to English. Chicago: Scott, Foresman & Co., 1968.

Publication Manual of the American Psychological Association. Washington, D.C.: The Association, 1974.

STRUNK, WILLIAM, and E. B. WHITE. The Elements of Style. New York: Macmillan Co., 1962.

TURABIAN, KATE L. A Manual for Writers of Term Papers, Theses, and Dissertations. Chicago: University of Chicago Press, 1973.

University of Chicago. A Manual of Style. Revised and enlarged. Chicago: University of Chicago Press, 1969.

HISTORICAL RESEARCH

Chapter 10

History is a meaningful record of man's achievement. It is not merely a list of chronological events, but a truthful integrated account of the relationships between persons, events, times, and places. Man uses history to understand the past, and to try to understand the present in light of past events and developments. Historical analysis may be directed toward an individual, an idea, a movent, or an institution. However, none of these objects of historical observation can be considered in isolation. No man can be subjected to historical investigation without some consideration of his interaction with the ideas, movements, or institutions of his times. The focus merely determines the points of emphasis toward which the historian directs his attention.

Table 10–1 illustrates several such historical interrelationships, taken from the history of education. For example, no matter whether the historian chooses for study the Jesuit Society, religious teaching orders, the Counter-Reformation, or Ignatius of Loyola, each of the other elements appears as a prominent influence or result and as an indispensable part of the account.

TABLE 10-1   Some Examples of the Historical Interrelationship between Men, Movements, and Institutions

		Institutions	
Men	*Movements*	*General type*	*Name*
Ignatius of Loyola	Counter-Reformation	Religious Teaching Order	Society of Jesus, 1534 (Jesuit Society)
Benjamin Franklin	Scientific Movement Education for Life	Academy	Philadelphia Academy, 1751
Daniel Coit Gilman G. Stanley Hall Wm. Rainey Harper	Graduate Study and Research	University Graduate School	Johns Hopkins University, 1876 Clark University, 1887 University of Chicago, 1892
John Dewey	Experimentalism Progressive Education	Experimental School	University of Chicago Elementary School, 1896
W. E. B. Dubois Walter White	Racial Integration in the Public Schools	Persuasion Organization	National Assn. for the Advancement of Colored People, 1909
B. R. Buckingham	Scientific Research in Education	Research Periodical, Research Organization	Journal of Ed. Research, 1920 American Educational Research Assn., 1931

The history of American education

Historical studies deal with almost every aspect of American education. Such investigations have pointed out the important contributions of both educators and statesmen. They have examined the growth and development of colleges and universities, elementary and secondary schools, educational organizations and associations, the rise and decline of educational movements, the introduction of new teaching methods, and the issues that have persistently confronted American education.

An understanding of the history of education is important to the professional worker in this field. It helps him to understand the *how* and the *why* of educational movements that have appeared and, in some cases, continue to prevail in the schools. It helps him to evaluate not only lasting contributions, but also the fads and "bandwagon" schemes that have appeared on the educational scene only to be discarded.

An examination of many developments of the past seems to confirm the observation that there is little in education that is really new. Practices hailed as innovative are often old ideas that have previously been tried and replaced by something new. Innovators should examine the reasons why such practices were discarded and consider whether their own proposals are likely to prove more successful. Several studies, briefly described, illustrate the historical background of some contemporary educational movements and issues.

Organized programs of individualized instruction introduced in a number of school systems in the 1960s seem to be similar in many respects to those introduced in a number of schools in the 1890s and in the first quarter of the twentieth century. First introduced at Pueblo, Colorado, and known as the Pueblo Plan, later modified and known as the Winnetka and Dalton Plans, these programs do seem to have common elements. Dispensing with group class activity in academic courses, students were given units of work to complete at their own rate before proceeding to more advanced units. Individual progress, based upon mastery of subject matter units, was the criterion for promotion or completion of a course. Preston W. Search[1] advocated this plan, and his influence upon Carleton Washburn in the elementary schools of Winnetka, Illinois, and Helen Parkhurst in the secondary schools at Dalton, Massachusetts, is generally recognized. Whether the Pueblo, Winnetka, or Dalton plans were fads or sound programs, the fact remains that they disappeared from the schools before reappearing in the 1960s.

The place of religion in public education is an issue that concerns many

[1] Preston W. Search, *An Ideal School: Looking Forward* (New York: Appleton-Century-Crofts, 1901).

people. In the period following World War II, in a series of Supreme Court decisions, religious instruction and religious exercises within the schools have been declared unconstitutional and in violation of the First Amendment of the United States Constitution. In 1963, in the case of *School District of Abington Township, Pennsylvania,* v. *Schempp,* the Court held that a Pennsylvania law requiring daily Bible reading was in violation of the First Amendment. Much resentment and criticism of the Supreme Court followed this decision and several efforts have been made to introduce amendments to the Constitution to permit religious exercises in the public schools.

The Bible reading issue was a bitter one more than 100 years ago. The "Philadelphia Bible Riots of 1840,"[2] resulted in the deaths of about 45 soldiers and civilians, serious injury to about 140, and property damage to homes and churches valued at nearly $500,000. Nativist–foreign-born, and Catholic-Protestant conflicts produced the tense atmosphere, but the Bible reading issue precipitated the riots. It is apparent that Bible reading is not an issue of recent origin, and that an understanding of previous conflicts places the issue in clearer perspective.

The contributions of Thomas Jefferson, Benjamin Franklin, Calvin Stowe, Horace Mann, Henry Barnard, William Holmes McGuffey, Daniel Coit Gilman, John Dewey, and many other eminent educators have been carefully examined in many studies and their impact on American education noted.

Richard E. Thursfield[3] studied Henry Barnard's *American Journal of Education,* published in 31 massive volumes between 1855 and 1881. He points out the *Journal's* vital contribution to the development of American education. Through its comprehensive treatment of all aspects of education it provided a readily available medium for the presentation and exchange of ideas of many of the great educators of the period. It has been stated that almost every educational reform adopted in the last half of the nineteenth century was largely due to the influence of the *Journal.* Among its contributors were Henry Barnard, Horace Mann, Bronson Alcott, Daniel Coit Gilman, William T. Harris, Calvin Stowe, and Herbert Spencer, in addition to many prominent foreign contributors.

Lawrence Cremin[4] examined the reasons for the rise and decline of the Progressive Education movement, including the major changes in philoso-

[2]Vincent L. Lannie and Bernard C. Diethorn, "For the Honor and Glory of God: The Philadelphia Bible Riots of 1840," *History of Education Quarterly,* 8 (Spring 1968): 44–106.

[3]Richard E. Thursfield, *Henry Barnard's American Journal of Education* (Baltimore: Johns Hopkins University Press, 1945.)

[4]Lawrence Cremin, *The Transformation of the School: Progressivism in American Education* (New York: Alfred A. Knopf, Inc., 1961).

phy and practices that transformed American education and the forces that brought the movement to a halt in the 1950s. Although some historians differ with some of his conclusions, Cremin's analysis is the definitive history of Progressive Education in America.

These historical studies are but a few of the thousands of books, monographs, and periodical articles that depict the story of American education. In addition to examining these works students are urged to consult the *History of Education Quarterly*, in which scholarly book reviews and critical analyses of contemporary historical research are presented.

History and science

There is some difference of opinion on the question of whether or not the activities of the historian can be considered scientific or whether there is such a thing as historical research.

Those who take the negative position may point out the following limitations:

1. Although the purpose of science is prediction, the historian cannot always generalize on the basis of past events. Because past events were often unplanned or didn't develop as planned, because there were so many uncontrolled factors, and because the influence of one or a few individuals was so crucial, the same pattern of factors is never repeated.
2. The historian must depend upon the reported observations of others, often witnesses of doubtful competence and sometimes of doubtful objectivity.
3. The historian is much like a person trying to complete a complicated jig-saw puzzle with many of the parts missing. On the basis of what is often incomplete evidence, he must fill in the gaps by inferring what has happened and why it happened.
4. History does not operate in a closed system such as may be created in the physical science laboratory. The historian cannot control the conditions of observation nor manipulate the significant variables.

Those who contend that historical investigation may have some of the characteristics of scientific research activity present these arguments:

1. The historian delimits a problem, formulates hypotheses or raises questions to be answered, gathers and analyzes primary data, tests the hypotheses as consistent or inconsistent with the evidence, and formulates generalizations or conclusions.
2. Although the historian may not have witnessed an event or gathered data directly, he may have the testimony of a number of witnesses who have observed the event from different vantage points. It is possible that subsequent events have provided additional information not available to contemporary observers. The historian rigorously subjects the evidence to critical analysis in order to establish its authenticity, truthfulness, and accuracy.

3. In reaching conclusions, the historian employs principles of probability similar to those used by physical scientists.
4. Although it is true that the historian cannot control the variables directly, this limitation also characterizes most behavioral research, particularly nonlaboratory investigations in sociology, social psychology, and economics.

HISTORICAL GENERALIZATION

There is some difference of opinion, even among historians, as to whether or not historical investigations can establish generalizations. Most historians would agree that some generalizations are possible, but they disagree on the validity of applying them to different times and places. Louis Gottschalk states the case of the comparative historian in this way:

> Sooner or later one or more investigators of a period or area begin to suspect some kind of nexus within the matter of their historical investigation. Though such "hunches," "insights," "guesses," "hypotheses"—whatever you may call them—may be rejected out of hand by some of them, the bolder or rasher among them venture to examine the possibility of objective reality of such a nexus, and then it is likely to become a subject of debate, and perhaps of eventual refinement to the point of wide recognition in the learned world. The process is not very different from the way analytical scholars in other fields proceed—Darwin, for example, or Freud. If this process serves no other purpose, it at least may furnish propositions upon which to focus future investigations and debates . . . .
>
> But do not these historical syntheses, no matter what their author's intention, invariably have a wider applicability than to any single set of data from which they rose? If Weber was right, isn't it implicit in his concept of the Protestant ethic that where a certain kind of religious attitude prevails, there the spirit of capitalism will, or at least may, flourish? . . . If Mahan was right, couldn't victory in war (at least before the invention of the airplane) be regarded as dependent on maritime control? If Turner was right, won't his frontier thesis apply to some extent to all societies that have frontiers to conquer in the future, as well as it has applied to American society in the past?[5]

M. I. Finley comments on generalization:

> Ultimately the question at issue is the nature of the historian's function. Is it only to recapture the individual, concrete events of a past age, as in a mirror, so that the progress of history is merely one of rediscovering lost data and of building bigger and better reflectors? If so, then the chronicle is the only correct form for his work. But if it is to understand—however one chooses to define the word—then it is to generalize, for every explanation is, or implies, one or more generalizations.[6]

[5]Louis Gottschalk, "Categories of Historical Generalization," in *Generalization in the Writing of History*, Louis Gottschalk, ed. (Chicago: University of Chicago Press, 1963), pp. 121–22.

[6]M. I. Finley, "Generalizations in Ancient History," in *Generalizations in the Writing of History*, Louis Gottschalk, ed. (Chicago: University of Chicago Press, 1963), p. 34.

William O. Aydelotte states the argument for generalization:

Certainly the impossibility of final proof of any historical generalization must be at once conceded. Our knowledge of the past is both too limited and too extensive. Only a minute fraction of what has happened has been recorded, and only too often the points on which we need most information are those on which our sources are most inadequate. On the other hand, the fragmentary and incomplete information we do have about the past is too abundant to prevent our coming to terms with it; its sheer bulk prevents its being easily manipulated, or even easily assimilated, for historical purposes. Further, historians deal with complex problems, and the pattern of the events they study, even supposing it to exist, seems too intricate to be easily grasped. Doubtless, finality of knowledge is impossible in all areas of study. We have learned through works of popularization how far this holds true even for the natural sciences, and, as Crane Brinton says, the historian no longer needs to feel that "the uncertainties and inaccuracies of his investigation leave him in a position of hopeless inferiority before the glorious certainties of physical science."[7]

The foregoing quotations are presented in support of the position that the activities of the historian are not different from those of the scientist. Historical research, as defined in this chapter, includes the delimitation of a problem, formulating hypotheses or generalizations to be tested or questions to be answered, gathering and analyzing data, and arriving at probablity-type conclusions or at generalizations based upon deductive-inductive reasoning.

THE HISTORICAL HYPOTHESIS

Allan Nevins[8] illustrates the use of hypotheses in the historical research of Edward Channing in answering the question: Why did the Confederacy collapse in April 1865? Channing formulated *four hypotheses* and tested each one in the light of the evidence gathered from letters, diaries, and official records of the army and the government of the Confederacy. He hypothesized that the Confederacy collapsed because of:

1. The military defeat of the Confederate army
2. The dearth of military supplies
3. The starving condition of the Confederate soldiers and the people
4. The disintegration of the will to continue the war

Channing produced evidence that seemed to refute the first three

[7]William O. Aydelotte, "Notes on the Problem of Historical Generalization," in *Generalizations in the Writing of History*, in Louis Gottschalk, ed. (Chicago: University of Chicago Press, 1963), pp. 156–157.

[8]Allan Nevins, *The Gateway to History*, Copyright c 1938, 1962, by D. C. Heath and Company. Lexington, Mass. (Boston: Raytheon Education Company, 1962), pp. 238–242.

hypotheses. More than 200,000 well-equipped soldiers were under arms at the time of the surrender, the effective production of powder and arms provided sufficient military supplies to continue the war, and enough food was available to sustain fighting men and civilians.

Channing concluded that hypothesis number 4, *the collapse of morale and the will to fight*, was substantiated by the excessive number of desertions of enlisted men and officers. Confederate military officials testified that they had intercepted many letters from home urging the soldiers to desert. Although the hypothesis sustained was not specific enough to be particularly helpful, the rejection of the first three did claim to dispose of some commonly held explanations. This example illustrates an historical study in which hypotheses were explicitly stated.

HYPOTHESES IN EDUCATIONAL RESEARCH

Hypotheses may be formulated in historical investigations of education. Several examples are listed.

1. The educational innovations of the 1950s and 1960s were based upon practices that previously had been tried and discarded.
2. Christian countries whose educational systems required religious instruction have had lower church attendance rates than those countries in which religious instruction was not provided in the schools.
3. The observation of European school systems by American educators during the nineteenth century had an important effect upon American educational practices.
4. The monitorial system had no significant effect upon American education.

Although hypotheses are not always *explicitly* stated in historical investigations, they are usually implied. The historian gathers evidence and carefully evaluates its trustworthiness. If the evidence is compatible with the consequences of the hypothesis, it is confirmed. If the evidence is not compatible, or negative, the hypothesis is not confirmed. It is through such synthesis that historical generalizations are established.

The activities of the historian, when education is his field of inquiry, are no different from those employed in any other field. The sources of evidence may be concerned with schools, educational practices and policies, movements, or individuals, but the historical processes are the same.

PROBLEMS IN HISTORICAL RESEARCH

The problems involved in the process of historical research make it a somewhat difficult task. A major difficulty is delimiting the problem so that a satisfactory analysis is possible. Too often, beginners state a problem much too broadly; the experienced historian realizes that historical research must be confined to a penetrating analysis of a limited problem, rather than involve only a superficial examination of a broad area. The weapon of research is the rifle, not the shotgun.

Since the historian may not have lived during the time he is studying and may be removed from the events that he investigates, he must often depend upon inference and logical analysis, using the recorded experience of others, rather than upon direct observation. To ensure that his information is as trustworthy as possible, he must rely on primary, or first-hand, accounts. Finding appropriate primary sources of data requires imagination, hard work, and resourcefulness.

Sources of data

Historical data are usually classified into two main categories:

1. *Primary sources* are eyewitness accounts. They are reported by an actual observer or participant in an event.
2. *Secondary sources* are accounts of an event that were not actually witnessed by the reporter. He may have talked with an actual observer or read an account by an observer, but his testimony is not that of an actual participant or observer. Secondary sources may sometimes be used, but because of the distortion in passing on information, the historian uses them only when primary data are not available.

PRIMARY SOURCES OF DATA

Documents, or the records kept and written by actual participants in, or witnesses of, an event. These sources are produced for the purpose of transmitting information to be used in the future. Documents classified as primary sources are constitutions, charters, laws, court decisions, official minutes or records, autobiographies, letters, diaries, genealogies, contracts, deeds, wills, permits, licenses, affidavits, depositions, declarations, proclamations, certificates, lists, handbills, bills, receipts, newspaper and magazine accounts, advertisements, maps, diagrams, books, pamphlets, catalogs, films, pictures, paintings, inscriptions, recordings, transcriptions, and research reports.

Remains or relics associated with a person, group, or period. Fossils, skeletons, tools, weapons, food, utensils, clothing, buildings, furniture, pictures, paintings, coins, and art objects are examples of those relics and remains that were not deliberately intended for use in transmitting information or as records. However, these sources may provide clear evidence about the past. The contents of an ancient burial place, for instance, may reveal a great deal of information about the way of life of a people—their food, clothing, tools, weapons, art, religious beliefs, means of livelihood, and customs.

Oral testimony, or the spoken account of a witness of, or participant in, an event. This evidence is obtained in a personal interview and may be recorded or transcribed as the witness relates his experiences.

PRIMARY SOURCES OF EDUCATIONAL DATA

Many old materials provide primary evidence that may be useful in studying the history of education. Although it would be impossible to list all the types of historical evidence, a number are listed.

Official records and other documentary materials. Included in this category are records and reports of legislative bodies and state departments of public instruction, city superintendents, principals, presidents, deans, department heads, educational committees, minutes of school boards and boards of trustees, surveys, charters, deeds, wills, professional and lay periodicals, school newspapers, annuals, bulletins, catalogs, courses of study, curriculum guides, athletic game records, programs (for graduation, dramatic, musical, and athletic events), licenses, certificates, textbooks, examinations, report cards, pictures, drawings, maps, letters, diaries, autobiographies, teacher and pupil personnel files, samples of student work, and recordings.

Oral testimony. Included here are interviews with administrators, teachers and other school employees, students and relatives, school patrons or lay citizens, and members of governing bodies.

Relics. Included in this category are buildings, furniture, teaching materials, equipment, murals, decorative pictures, textbooks, examinations, and samples of student work.

SECONDARY SOURCES OF DATA

Secondary sources are the reports of a person who relates the testimony of an actual witness of, or participant in, an event. The writer of the secondary source was not on the scene of the event, but merely reports what the person who *was* there said or wrote. Secondary sources of data are usually of limited worth for research purposes because of the errors that may result when information is passed on from one person to another. Most history textbooks and encyclopedias are examples of secondary sources, for they are often several times removed from the original, first-hand account of events.

Some types of material may be secondary sources for some purposes and primary sources for another. For example, a high school textbook in American history is ordinarily a secondary source. But if one were making a study of the changing emphasis on nationalism in high school American history textbooks, the book would be a primary document or source of data.

Historical criticism

It has been noted that the historian does not often use the method of direct observation. Past events cannot be repeated at will. Since he must get much of his data from the reports of those who witnessed or participated in these events, the data must be subjected to careful analysis to sift the true from the false, irrelevant, or misleading.

Trustworthy, usable data in historical research are known as *historical evidence*. It is that body of validated facts and information that can be accepted as trustworthy, as a proper basis for the testing and interpretation of an hypothesis. Historical evidence is derived from historical data by the process of criticism, which is of two types: *external* and *internal*.

EXTERNAL CRITICISM

External criticism establishes the authenticity or genuineness of data. Is the relic or document a true one rather than a forgery, a counterfeit, or a hoax? Various tests of genuineness may be employed.

The problem of establishing age or authorship of documents may involve intricate tests of signature, handwriting, script, type, spelling, language usage, documentation, knowledge available at the time, and consistency with what is known. It may involve physical and chemical tests of ink, paint, paper, parchment, cloth, stone, metals, or wood. Are these elements consistent with known facts about the person, the knowledge available, and the technology of the period in which the remain or the document originated?

INTERNAL CRITICISM

After the authenticity of a historical document or relic has been established, there is still the problem of evaluating its accuracy or worth. Although it may be genuine, does it reveal a true picture? What of the writer or creator? Was he competent, honest, unbiased, and actually acquainted with the facts, or was he too antagonistic or too sympathetic to give a true picture? Did he have any motives for distorting the account? Was he subject to pressure, fear, or vanity? How long after the event did he make a record of his testimony, and was he able to remember accurately what happened? Was he in agreement with other competent witnesses?

These questions are often difficult to answer, but the historian must be sure that his data are authentic and accurate. Only then may he introduce them as historical evidence, worthy of serious consideration. The following examples illustrate how the processes of historical criticism were used to expose a hoax and to establish the authenticity of an important historical discovery.

THE CARDIFF GIANT

An amazing series of events concerning the authenticity of a historical remain is related in "The Real Story of the Cardiff Giant," by Alan Hynd.[9] The Cardiff Giant was a 10' 4½" figure of a man, weighing about 3000 pounds, found in 1869, buried three feet beneath the surface of a farmer's field, near Cardiff, New York, about 13 miles south of Syracuse.

The huge figure was examined by two scientists from Yale University, who pronounced it a fossilized human figure. A delegation of archaeologists from the New York State Museum were of the opinion that the figure was an ancient statue. Ralph Waldo Emerson called it a *bona fide* petrified human being, while Dr. Oliver Wendell Holmes, the celebrated Harvard anatomist and father of the great jurist, declated that it was a statue of great antiquity. Scores of clergymen who came to see it enthusiastically claimed that the figure was a fossilized man of biblical times, proving the story of Genesis to be literally true.

The local owners turned down an offer by P. T. Barnum to buy the figure, whereupon Barnum commissioned a sculptor to make an exact replica of the Giant, which he later exhibited in his museum on Broadway in New York City, advertising it as the one, the only, the original Cardiff Giant. When the Cardiff owners sought an injunction against Barnum, the judge denied it, saying that the original was only a fake.

An unknown newspaper reporter, prompted by the growing feeling that the giant was a hoax, traced the shipment of a huge box labeled "machinery" to the farm near Cardiff, nearly a year before the Giant's discovery. Carefully tracing back detail upon detail, he discovered that a Mr. Hull had acquired a huge block of gypsum at Ft. Dodge, Iowa, and had shipped a box labeled "machinery," weighing exactly what the block of gypsum had weighed, to Chicago. From hotel, railroad, and drayage company records, he traced the shipment to a barn in the 900 block of North Clark Street in Chicago. The owner of the barn confessed his part in the scheme and implicated Hull, a stonecutter, and an artist who had fashioned the figure.

It was revealed that Hull, while visiting his sister in Ft. Dodge, Iowa, had gone to hear an evangelist who, while preaching about the sixth chapter of Genesis, had described in some detail and with much enthusiasm the "giants in the earth" mentioned there. Seeing a chance to make some easy money, Hull planned to have one of these giants fabricated, aged with sulphuric acid, secretly planted in the ground on his cousin's New York

[9]Alan Hynd, "The Real Story of the Cardiff Giant," originally published in "True, The Man's Magazine," later anthologized in *Grand Deception*, Alexander Klein, ed. (Philadelphia: J. B. Lippincott Co., 1955), pp. 126–135. Used here with permission of Fawcett Publications.

farm, and accidentally discovered by some well-diggers, ostensibly hired to dig a new well.

The rest was easy. Hull made no claims. The clergymen and the experts made the claims for him, and the controversy between them only added to the fame (and money-drawing power) of his stone figure.

Although this story does not actually illustrate scholarly research, the activities of the reporter represent a simple example of external criticism, for by following his hunch or hypothesis that the figure was recently man-made and not an ancient statue or a fossilized man, he tracked down and exposed the facts. This is quite remarkable in the light of the fact that prominent archaeologists, anatomists, and scholars had been completely fooled by the hoax.

The following example describes historical criticism of a more scholarly type, carried on by scientists and biblical scholars, in which historic documents were proven to be genuine.

THE DEAD SEA SCROLLS

One of the most interesting and significant historical discoveries of the past century was the finding of the Dead Sea Scrolls. This collection of ancient manuscripts was discovered in 1947 by a group of Bedouins of the Ta'amere tribe. Five leather scrolls were found, sealed in tall earthenware jars in the Qumran caves near Aim Feshkha, on the northwest shore of the Dead Sea.[10]

The Bedouins took the scrolls to Metropolitan Mar Athanesius Yeshue Samuel, of St. Mark's monastery in Jerusalem, who purchased them after discovering that they were written in ancient Hebrew. A consultation with biblical scholars confirmed the fact that they were very old and possibly valuable. They were later purchased by Professor Sukenik, an archaeologist of Hebrew University at Jerusalem, who began to translate them. He also had portions of the scrolls photographed to send to other biblical scholars for evaluation. Upon examining some of the photographs, Dr. William F. Albright of Johns Hopkins University pronounced them "the greatest manuscript discovery of modern times."

A systematic search of the Wadi Qumran area caves in 1952 yielded other leather scrolls, many manuscript fragments, and two additional scrolls of copper, so completely oxidized that they could not be unrolled without being destroyed. By 1956, scientists at the University of Manchester, England, had devised a method of passing a spindle through the scrolls, spraying them with aircraft glue, baking them, and then sawing

[10]A. Powell Davies, *The Meaning of the Dead Sea Scrolls* (New York: New American Library of World Literature, 1956), p. 9. Used with permission of the publisher.

them across their rolled-up length to yield strips which could be photo-graphed.[11]

There has been some question about the origin, the age, and the historic value of the scrolls. By careful and systematic external and internal criti-cism, however, certain facts have been established and are quite generally accepted by biblical scholars and scientists.

The scrolls are very old, probably dating back to the first century A.D. They are written in ancient Hebrew, and probably originated in a pre-Christian monastery of one of the Jewish sects. The writings contain two versions (one complete and one incomplete) of the Book of Isaiah, a commentary or *Midrash* on the Book of Habakkuk, a set of rules of the ancient Jewish monastery, a collection of about 20 psalms similar to those of the Old Testament, and several scrolls of apocalyptic writings, similar to the Book of Revelation.[12]

The contents of the copper scrolls and other fragments are in the pro-cess of translation. It is possible that more scrolls and writings may be discovered in the area, and it is likely that these ancient documents may throw new light on the Bible and the origins of Christianity.

It is interesting to note how these documents were authenticated, dated, and evaluated by:

1. Paleography, an analysis of the Hebrew alphabet forms used. These written characters were similar to those observed in other documents known to have been written in the first century.
2. A radiocarbon test of the age of the linen scroll coverings, conducted by the Institute of Nuclear Research at the University of Chicago. All organic matter contains radiocarbon 14, introduced by the interaction of cosmic rays from outer space with the nitrogen in the earth's atmosphere. The radioactivity constantly introduced throughout the life of the specimen ceases at death and disintegrates at a constant known rate. At the time of death, all organic matter yields 15.3 disintegrations per minute per gram of carbon content. The number of disintegrations is reduced by one-half after 5568, plus or minus 30 years. By measuring disintegrations by the use of a Geiger-type counter, it is possible to estimate the age of specimens within reasonable limits of accuracy. By the use of this technique the date of the scrolls was estimated at A.D. 33, plus or minus 200 years.
3. Careful examination of the pottery form in which the scrolls were sealed. These jars, precisely shaped to fit the manuscripts, were the type commonly used during the first century.
4. Examination of coins found in the caves with the scrolls. These dated Roman coins provided convincing evidence of the age of the scrolls.
5. Translation of the scrolls compared to other writings, both biblical and nonbiblical, of known antiquity.

[11]Davies, *op. cit.*, p. 18.
[12]Davies, *op. cit.*, p. 19.

Although external criticism has now produced convincing evidence of the genuineness and age of the Dead Sea Scrolls, internal criticism of their validity and relevance will be pursued by biblical scholars for many years to come, and may provide many new hypotheses concerning biblical writings and the early history of Christianity and the pre-Christian Jewish sects.

THE STONEHENGE (HANGING STONES)

For centuries a controversy has interested historians and archaeologists concerning the origin and purpose of the Stonehenge, a curious arrangement of stones and archways, each weighing more than forty tons, located on the Salisbury Plain, about 90 miles southwest of London. From the beginning of recorded history, writers have speculated about the stones. Their construction and arrangement have been attributed to many tribes and national groups who invaded or inhabited England. Modern radiocarbon dating of a deer antler found in the stone fill seems to place their time of erection at about 1900 to 1600 B.C. Their purpose has been explained in many legends that have developed—a city of the dead, a place of human sacrifice, a temple of the sun, a pagan cathedral, and a Druid ceremonial place.

More recently some scientists and historians have suggested that the Stonehenge was a type of astronomical computer calendar used by early Britons who were apparently sophisticated enough to compute the position of the sun and the moon at their various stages. Using an IBM 704 computer, Gerald S. Hawkins, an astronomer at the Smithsonian Astrophysical Observatory at Cambridge, Massachusetts, entered into the computer 240 stone alignments, translated into celestial declinations. Accomplishing in less than a minute a task that would have required more than four months of human calculator activity, the computer compared the alignments with the precise sun/moon extreme positions as of 1500 B.C. and indicated that they matched with amazing accuracy.

Hawkins suggests that the stone arrangements may have been created for several possible reasons: they made a calendar that would be useful for planting crops; they helped to create and maintain priestly power, by enabling the priest to call out the people to see the rise and setting of the midsummer sun and moon over the heel stone and midwinter sunset through the great trilithon; or possibly they served as an intellectual exercise. He concludes:

> In any case, for whatever reasons those Stonehenge builders built as they did, their final completed creation was a marvel. As intricately aligned as an interlocking series of astronomical instruments (which indeed it was) and yet architecturally perfectly simple, in function subtile and elaborate, in

appearance stark, imposing, awesome, Stonehenge was a thing of surpassing ingenuity of design, variety of usefulness and grandeur—in concept and construction an eighth wonder of the world.[13]

The account of this interesting historical-archaeological controversy illustrates the use of sophisticated computer technology to test an hypothesis related to the nature of the Stonehenge.

Writing the report

No less challenging than research itself is the writing of the report, which calls for creativity in addition to the qualities of imagination and resourcefulness already illustrated. Research reports should be written in a style that is dignified and objective. However, the historian is permitted a little more freedom in reporting. Homer Carey Hockett suggests that "the historian is not condemned to a bald, plain, unattractive style," and that "for the sake of relieving the monotony of statement after statement of bare facts, it is permissible, now and then, to indulge in a bit of color." He concludes, however, by warning that "above all, embellishments must never become a first aim, or be allowed to hide or distort the truth.[14]

An evaluation of graduate students' historical-research projects generally reveals one or more of the following faults:

1. Problem too broadly stated
2. Tendency to use easy-to-find secondary sources of data, rather than sufficient primary sources, which are harder to locate, but usually more trustworthy
3. Inadequate historical criticism of data, due to failure to establish authenticity of sources and trustworthiness of data. For example, there is often a tendency to accept a statement as necessarily true when several observers agree. It is possible that one may have influenced the other, or that all were influenced by the same inaccurate source of information.
4. Poor logical analysis resulting from:
   a. Oversimplification—failure to recognize the fact that causes of events are more often multiple and complex than single and simple
   b. Overgeneralization on the basis of insufficient evidence, and false reasoning by analogy, basing conclusions upon superficial similarities of situations
   c. Failure to interpret words and expressions in the light of their accepted meaning in an earlier period
   d. Failure to distinguish between significant facts in a situation and those that are irrelevant or unimportant

[13]Gerald S. Hawkins with John B. White, *Stonehenge Decoded* (Garden City, N.Y.: Doubleday & Company, 1965, London Souvenir Press, 1966), pp. 117–118. Used by permission of Doubleday & Company, Inc., and Souvenir Press.

[14]Homer C. Hockett, *Induction to Research in American History* (New York: Macmillan Co., 1948), p. 139. Used with permission.

5. Expression of personal bias, as revealed by statements lifted out of context for purposes of persuasion, assuming too generous or uncritical an attitude toward a person or idea (or being too unfriendly or critical), excessive admiration for the past (sometimes known as the "old oaken bucket" delusion), or an equally unrealistic admiration for the new or contemporary, assuming that all change represents progress
6. Poor reporting in a style that is dull and colorless, too flowery or flippant, too persuasive or of the "soap-box" type, or improper in usage

It is apparent that historical research is difficult and demanding. The gathering historical evidence requires long hours of careful examination of such documents as court records, records of legislative bodies, letters, diaries, official minutes of organizations, or other primary sources of data. Historical research may involve traveling to distant places to examine the necessary documents or relics. In fact, any significant historical study would make demands that few students have the time, the financial resources, the patience, or the expertise to meet. For these reasons, good historical studies are not often attempted for the purpose of meeting academic degree requirements.

School law research

Research in school law is an application fo the methodology of historical research. If one has access to a university law school library, almost all the necessary data involved in the research are available. However, the interpretation of legal problems involves an expertise that few graduate students in education possess. The ability to find the significant facts in a case and to distinguish the basic principles at issue is a skill that requires more than a superficial understanding of the law and of legal procedures.

For the student to carry on significant research in the area of school law, it would be desirable for him to have had several courses in school law, some law school training, and the aid of a school law specialist. Most graduate schools have such experts on their faculty.

The law is classified into two main categories:

Statutory law includes provisions written into state and federal constitutions, the legislative enactments of state legislatures and the Congress, and administrative laws and regulations having the force of law, promulgated by appointed bodies and commissions.

Case, or common, law includes the principles established by the courts in deciding issues not covered by statutory law, but based upon sound principles of public policy. It must be remembered that laws or regulations are of unknown validity until they have been tested in a court of law and their constitutionality verified by the authority of the highest courts of appeal, the supreme courts of the various states, or the Supreme Court of the United States.

M. M. Chambers has presented a list of suggestions on how to study and use law decisions.[15]

1. Observe what court is being reported and, if the case is on appeal, from what court or courts it has been appealed.
2. Observe the form in which the action is brought—whether it is a petition for a writ of mandamus, injunction, quo warranto, or prohibition; or a suit for pecuniary damages in tort or in contract; or an action in equity for the specific performance or reformation of a contract or for an accounting of partnership or corporation affairs; or a criminal action brought in the name of the state against a defendant accused of violation of a penal statute.
3. Segregate and digest the statement of the facts of the case before trying to understand the application of the law to the facts.
4. Determine what is the precise question of law which the court is called upon to decide. The courts' answer to this precise point is the decision of the case.
5. Note whether the decision seems to be in harmony with any broadly accepted rule of law. (Often the court will state the broad rule.)
6. Note whether the judge indulges in any discussion of points on which the court is not called upon to decide. Judicial pronouncements not directly related to the ratio dicidendi, or determination of the legal lissue in the case, are called dicta, and rank much lower than a decision in point of weight as precedents. Nevertheless, a mere dictum often is a figurative bomb packed full of brilliant philosophy which will illuminate its area of the law for years to come.
7. In view of the fact that all courts of last resort and most appellate courts are collegial—that is, consisting of several judges sitting *en banc*—note whether the decision and the opinion are concurred in by all the judges sitting, or whether one or more judges have filed specially concurring opinions or dissenting opinions. These may be important for the sake of the social philosophy they express. A large proportion of the essential wisdom to be extracted from the records of the United States Supreme Court for a generation past is to be found in the long line of brilliant dissenting opinions by the late Justice Oliver Wendell Holmes. These opinions were frequently concurred in by Justice Brandeis, later by Justices Stone, Roberts, and Chief Justice Hughes, finally coming to represent the social philosophy of a majority of the court in many particulars.
8. Try to orient the case in your own social and legal philosophy; evaluate the decision and the opinion critically, sympathetically, tolerantly; struggle to interpret it and express it vividly and meaningfully; make it live in the mind of your reader.
9. Get the complete caption and citation, including date.
10. Jot down the supporting authorities cited in the course of the opinion and follow them up, thus developing the history of the principles of law involved and disclosing trends.

[15]M. M. Chambers, "Legal Research in Education," *Review of Educational Research* 21 (December 1939): 462–463. Used by permission of the author.

Summary

History, the meaningful record of man's achievement, helps him to understand the present and, to some extent, to predict the future. Historical research is the application of scientific method to the description and analysis of past events.

The historian ordinarily draws his data from the observations and experiences of others. Since he is not likely to have been at the scene of the event, he must use logical inferences to supplement what is probably an incomplete account.

Primary sources may be "unconscious" testimony, not intended to be left as a record—relics or remains such as bones, fossils, clothing, food, utensils, weapons, coins, and art objects are useful. Conscious testimony, in the form of records or documents, is another primary source of information—examples are constitutions, laws court decisions, official minutes, autobiographies, letters, contracts, wills, certificates, newspaper and magazine accounts, films, recordings, and research reports.

Historical criticism is the evaluation of primary data. External criticism is concerned with the authenticity or genuineness of remains or documents. Internal criticism is concerned with the trustworthiness or relevance of materials. The story of the Cardiff Giant and the accounts of the Dead Sea Scrolls and the Stonehenge illustrate the processes of historical criticism.

The historical research studies of graduate students often reveal serious limitations. Frequently encountered are such faults as stating the problem too broadly, inadequate primary sources of data, unskillful historical criticism, poor logical analysis of data, personal bias, and ineffective reporting.

Research in school law is usually considered a phase of historical research, with statutes and court decisions providing the primary sources of data. This field of inquiry is not an appropriate one for the inexperienced student of law, for it requires an expertness that few graduate students possess. Some specialized law training, several courses in school law, and the counsel of a law expert are desirable, if not necessary, qualifications.

Suggested activities

1. Write a proposal for a historical study in a local setting. You may select a community, a school, a church, a religious or ethnic group, or an individual.

State an appropriate title, present you hypothesis, indicate the primary sources of data that you would search, and indicate how you would evaluate the authenticity and validity of your data.

2. Select a master's thesis of the historical type from the university library and analyze it in terms of:
   a. hypothesis proposed or questions raised
   b. primary and secondary sources of data used
   c. external and internal criticism employed
   d. logical analysis of data relationships
   e. soundness of conclusions
   f. documentation

Bibliography

BARZUN, JACQUES, and HENRY F. GRAFF. *The Modern Researcher.* 2nd ed. New York: Harcourt Brace Jovanovich, 1970.

BRICKMAN, WILLIAM W. *Guide to Research in Educational History.* New York: New York University Bookstore, 1949.

CARR, EDWARD H. *What Is History?* New York: Alfred A. Knopf, 1962.

CREMIN, LAWRENCE. *The Transformation of the School: Progressivism in American Education.* New York: Alfred A. Knopf, 1961.

EDGERTON, HAROLD E. "Stonehenge: New Light on an Old Riddle." *National Geographic,* 117 (June 1960): 846–866.

GARRAGHAN, GILBERT J. *A Guide to Historical Method.* New York: Fordham University Press, 1946.

GOTTSCHALK, LOUIS R. *Understanding History.* New York: Alfred A. Knopf, 1950.

GOTTSCHALK, LOUIS R., ed. *Generalization in the Writing of History. Report of the Committee on Historical Analysis of the Social Science Research Council.* Chicago: University of Chicago Press, 1963.

HAWKINS, GERALD S. with JOHN B. WHITE. *Stonehenge Decoded.* Garden City, N.Y.: Doubleday & Co., 1965.

HOCKETT, HOMER CAREY. *Introduction to Research in American History.* New York: Macmillan Co., 1948.

HOCKETT, HOMER CAREY. *The Critical Method in Historical Research and Writing.* New York: Macmillan Co., 1955.

KLEIN, ALEXANDER, ed. *Grand Deception.* Philadelphia: J. B. Lippincott Co., 1955.

LANNIE, VINCENT L. and BERNARD C. DIETHORN. "For the Honor and Glory of God: The Philadelphia Bible Riots of 1840." *History of Education Quarterly,* 8 (Spring 1968): 44–106.

NEVINS, ALLAN. *The Gateway to History.* Rev. ed. Boston: Raytheon Education Co., 1962.

PETERSON, CLARENCE S. *America's Rune Stone.* New York: Hobson Book Press, 1946.

SEARCH, PRESTON W. *An Ideal School: Looking Forward.* New York: Appleton-Century-Crofts, 1901.

STEBBINS, CATHERINE L. *Here I Shall Finish My Voyage: The Death Site of Father Jacques Marquette.* Onema, Mich.: Solle's Press, 1960.

THURSFIELD, RICHARD E. *Henry Barnard's American Journal of Education.* Baltimore: Johns Hopkins University Press, 1945.

RESEARCH
METHODS
BIBLIOGRAPHY

BABBIE, E. R. *Survey Research Methods.* Belmont, Calif.: Wadsworth Publishing Co., 1973.

BAKER, ROBERT L. and RICHARD E. SCHUTZ. *Instructional Product Research.* New York: American Book Co., 1972.

BARZON, JACQUES and HENRY F. GRAFF. *The Modern Researcher.* New York: Harcourt Brace Jovanovich, 1970.

BEST, JOHN W. *Research in Education.* Englewood Cliffs, N.J.: Prentice-Hall, 1970.

BORG, WALTER and MEREDITH D. GALL. *Educational Research: An Introduction.* New York: David McKay, 1971.

BUSWELL, GUY T. *Training for Educational Research.* Berkeley, Calif.: Center for the Study of Higher Education, University of California, 1966.

CAMPBELL, DONALD T. and JULIAN C. STANLEY. *Experimental and Quasi-Experimental Designs for Research.* Chicago: Rand McNally & Co., 1966.

CRENO, WILLIAM and MARILYN BREWER. *Principles of Research in Social Psychology.* New York: McGraw Hill Book Co., 1973.

EDWARDS, ALLEN L. *Experimental Design in Psychological Research.* New York: Holt, Rinehart & Winston, 1972.

CULBERTSON, JACK A. and STEPHEN P. HENCLEY, eds. *Educational Research: New Perspectives.* Danville, Ill.: Interstate Publishers and Printers, 1963.

ENGLEHART, MAX D. *Methods of Educational Research.* Chicago: Rand McNally & Co., 1972.

FESTINGER, LEON and DANIEL KATZ. eds. *Research Methods in the Behavioral Sciences.* New York: Holt, Rinehart & Winston, 1953.

FOX, DAVID J. *The Research Process in Education.* New York: Holt, Rinehart & Winston, 1969.

GAGE, N. L. *Handbook of Research on Teaching.* Chicago: Rand McNally & Co., 1966.

GALFO, ARMAND J. *Interpreting Educational Research.* Dubuque, Iowa: William C. Brown Co., 1975.

GEPHART, WILLIAM J. and ROBERT B. INGLE. *Educational Research: Selected Readings.* Columbus, Ohio: Charles E. Merrill Publishing Co., 1969.

GLASER, ROBERT ET AL. *Organization for Research and Development in Education.* Bloomington, Ind.: Phi Delta Kappa, 1966.

GOOD, CARTER V. *Essentials of Educational Research.* New York: Appleton-Century-Crofts, 1972.

GOODE, WILLIAM J. and PAUL K. HATT. *Methods in Social Research.* New York: McGraw Hill Book Co., 1952.

GORDON, IRA J. *Human Development: Readings in Research.* Glenview, Ill.: Scott Foresman & Co., 1965.

HARDWICK, CURTIS D. and LEWIS F. PETRINOVICH. *Understanding Research in the Social Sciences.* Philadelphia: W. B. Saunders Co., 1975.

HELMSTADTER, GERALD C. *Research Concepts in Human Behavior.* New York: Appleton-Century-Crofts, 1970.

ISAAC, STEPHEN and WILLIAM B. MICHAEL. *Handbook in Research and Evaluation.* San Diego, Calif.: Robert R. Knapp, Publisher, 1971.

KAPLAN, ABRAHAM. *The Conduct of Inquiry: Methodology for Behavioral Science.* San Francisco: Chandler Publishing Co., 1964.

KEPPEL, G. *Design and Analysis: A Researcher's Handbook.* Englewood Cliffs, N.J.: Prentice-Hall, 1973.

KERLINGER, FRED N. *Foundations of Behavioral Research.* New York: Holt, Rinehart & Winston, 1973.

KERLINGER, FRED N. ed. *Review of Research in Education I.* Itasca, Ill.: F. E. Peacock, Publishers, 1973.

KERLINGER, FRED N. and JOHN B. CARROLL eds. *Review of Research in Education II.* Itasca, Ill.: F. E. Peacock, Publishers, 1974.

KERLINGER, FRED N. ET AL. *Review of Research in Education III.* Itasca, Ill.: F. E. Peacock, Publishers, 1975.

LEHMANN, IRVIN J. and WILLIAM A. MEHRENS. *Educational Research: Readings in Focus.* New York: Holt, Rinehart & Winston, 1971.

LINDZEY, GARDNER, ed. *Handbook of Social Psychology. Vol. I,* Cambridge, Mass.: Addison-Wesley Publishing, Co., 1954.

MOULEY, GEORGE J. *The Science of Educational Research.* New York: Van Nostrand Reinhold Co., 1970.

NEALE, J. M. and R. M. LIEBERT. *Science and Behavior: An Introduction to Methods of Research.* Englewood Cliffs, N.J.: Prentice-Hall, 1973.

Runkle, Phillip and Joselh McGrath. *Research in Human Behavior.* New York: Holt, Rinehart & Winston, 1972.

Sax, Gilbert. *Empirical Foundations of Educational Research.* Englewood Cliffs, N.J.: Prentice-Hall, 1968.

Selltiz, Claire, Marie Jahoda, Morton Deutch, and Stuart W. Cook. *Research Methods in Social Relations.* New York: Holt, Rinehart & Winston, 1961.

Travers, Robert M. W. *An Introduction to Educational Research.* New York: Macmillan Co., 1969.

Travers, Robert M. W. *The Handbook of Research on Teaching.* 2d ed. Chicago: Rand McNally & Co., 1973.

Tuckman, Bruce W. *Conducting Educational Research.* New York: Harcourt Brace Jovanovich 1972.

Turney, B. and G. Robb. *Research in Education: An Introduction.* New York: McGraw Hill Book Co., 1973.

Van Dalen, Deobold B. *Understanding Educational Research.* New York: McGraw Hill Book Co., 1973.

Wandt, Edwin. *A Cross Section of Educational Research.* New York: David McKay Co., 1965.

Wiersma, William. *Research Methods in Education.* Itasca, Ill.: F. E. Peacock, Publishers, 1975.

APPENDIX A

Statistical Formulas

1. $>$ is greater than
   $<$ is less than

2. Mean M

$$M = \frac{\Sigma fx}{N}$$

$$M = AM + ci$$

$$c = \frac{\Sigma fx'}{N}$$

(assumed mean method)

3. Median Md

$$Md = L + i\frac{(.50N - f_c)}{f_w}$$

(grouped data computation)

Glossary of Statistical Symbols

$a > b$ a is greater than b
$b < a$ b is less than a

M arithmetic average
Σ sum of
     X, Y scores
     f frequency of appearance
     N number of scores
AM midpoint of assumed mean interval
c correction factor
i width of class interval
x' x prime: deviation from the assumed mean interval, expressed in number of intervals

Md the point in a distribution above and below which half the scores fall
L lower true limit of median interval

Statistical Formulas

Glossary of Statistical Symbols

f_e cumulative frequency of scores below interval in which median is located

f_w frequency of scores within median interval

4. Mode M_o

M_o mode: score that occurs most frequently in a distribution

5. Percentile rank P_r

$$P_r = 100 - \frac{(100R - 50)}{N}$$

P_r percentage of scores that fall below a given value, plus $\frac{1}{2}$ the percentage of space occupied by that score

R rank from the top of a distribution

6. Percentile score P_N

$$P_N = L + i\frac{(PN - f_c)}{f_w}$$

(grouped data computation)

P_N percentile score: the score in a distribution that corresponds to a particular percentile rank

L lower true limit of an interval

f_c frequency of scores that fall below interval that contains the particular score

f_w frequency of scores that fall within percentile rank interval

7. Variance σ^2
Standard deviation σ

$$\sigma^2 = \frac{\sum fx^2}{N} \quad x = (X - M)$$

$$\sigma = \sqrt{\frac{\sum fx^2}{N}}$$

(deviation computation)

$$\sigma^2 = \frac{N\sum X^2 - (\sum X)^2}{N^2}$$

$$\sigma = \sqrt{\frac{N\sum X^2 - (\sum X)^2}{N^2}}$$

(raw score computation)

σ^2 population variance: mean value of the squared deviations from the mean

σ population standard deviation: positive square root of the variance

$x = (X - M)$ deviation from the mean

8. Variance S^2
Standard deviation S

$$S^2 = \frac{\sum fx^2}{N - 1}$$

$$S = \sqrt{\frac{\sum fx^2}{N - 1}}$$

(deviation computation)

S^2 variance of a population estimated from a sample

S standard deviation of population estimated from a sample

Statistical Formulas

$$S^2 = \frac{N \sum X^2 - (\sum X)^2}{N(N-1)}$$

$$S = \sqrt{\frac{N \sum X^2 - (\sum X)^2}{N(N-1)}}$$

(raw score computation)

$$S^2 = i^2 \frac{(\sum fx'^2)}{N} - c^2$$

$$S = i\sqrt{\frac{(\sum fx'^2)}{N} - c^2}$$

(grouped data computation)

$$c = \frac{\sum fx'}{N}$$

Variance (S_{DV}^2) or standard deviation (S_{DV}) of a dichotomous variable

$$S_{DV}^2 = NP(1-P) \qquad S_{DV}^2 = \frac{N}{4}$$
$$S_{DV} = \sqrt{NP(1-P)}$$

(general formula) $S_{DV} = \sqrt{\dfrac{N}{4}}$

(when $P = .50$)

9. Standard error of the mean (S_M)

$$S_M = \frac{S}{\sqrt{N}} \qquad \sigma_M = \frac{\sigma}{\sqrt{N}}$$

10. Standard scores z, Z, Z_{cb}

$$z = \frac{X - M}{\sigma} \quad \text{or} \quad \frac{x}{\sigma}$$

$$Z(T) = 50 + 10\frac{(X - M)}{\sigma}$$

$$\text{or} \quad Z = 50 + 10z$$

$$Z_{cb} = 500 + 100z$$

11. Coefficient of correlation (r)

$$r = \frac{\sum (z_X)(z_Y)}{N}$$

$$r = \frac{N \sum XY - (\sum X)(\sum Y)}{\sqrt{N \sum X^2 - (\sum X)^2}\sqrt{N \sum Y^2 - (\sum Y)^2}}$$

$$p(rho) = 1 - \frac{6 \sum D^2}{N(N^2 - 1)}$$

Glossary of Statistical Symbols

i interval width
x' x prime: deviation from the assumed mean interval expressed in number of intervals

c correction factor

Dichotomous variable
an outcome is either-or: plus or minus, true or false, heads or tails
N number of events
P probability of an outcome

z sigma score
$Z(T)$ standard score
Z_{cb} College Board standard score

r Pearson product-moment coefficient of correlation

$p(rho)$ Spearman difference in ranks coefficient of correlation
D difference between each pair of ranks

Statistical Formulas	**Glossary of Statistical Symbols**

12. Statistical significance of r/p

$$t = \frac{r\sqrt{N-2}}{\sqrt{1-r^2}}$$

$$t = \frac{p\sqrt{N-2}}{\sqrt{1-p^2}}$$

Test of the statistical significance of a coefficient of correlation

13. Regression line slope

$$r = \frac{\text{rise}}{\text{run}} = \frac{z_Y}{z_X}$$

$$b = \frac{\text{rise}}{\text{run}} = \frac{Y}{X} \qquad b_Y = r\left(\frac{z_Y}{z_X}\right)$$

$$b_X = r\left(\frac{z_X}{z_Y}\right)$$

r the slope expressed in sigma (z) units

b the slope of the line expressed in raw scores

14. Regression equations

$$\tilde{Y} = b_Y(X - M_X) + M_Y$$

$$\tilde{X} = b_X(Y - M_Y) + M_X$$

Predicting a Y from a known X when the coefficient of correlation is known

$\tilde{Y}$ predicted Y

$\tilde{X}$ predicted X

15. Standard error of estimate S_{est}

$$S_{est} = S\sqrt{1 - r^2}$$

16. Standard error of the difference between two means
(independent variances; when variances are not equal)

$$S_{M_1 - M_2} = \sqrt{\frac{s_1^2}{N_1} + \frac{S_2^2}{N_2}}$$

(pooled variances; when variances are equal)

$$S_{M_1 - M_2} = \sqrt{\frac{(N_1 - 1)S_1^2 + (N_2 - 1)S_2^2}{N_1 + N_2 - 2}\left(\frac{1}{N_1} + \frac{1}{N_2}\right)}$$

17. Significance of the difference between two means

$$t = \frac{\text{difference between means}}{\text{standard error of the difference}}$$

$$t = \frac{M_1 - M_2}{\sqrt{\frac{(N_1 - 1)S_1^2 + (N_2 - 1)S_2^2}{N_1 + N_2 - 2}\left(\frac{1}{N_1} + \frac{1}{N_2}\right)}} \qquad \begin{array}{l}\text{(uncorrelated or}\\ \text{unmatched groups)}\end{array}$$

$$t = \frac{M_1 - M_2}{\sqrt{\frac{S_1^2}{N_1} + \frac{S_2^2}{N_2} - 2r\left(\frac{S_1}{\sqrt{N_1}}\right)\left(\frac{S_2}{\sqrt{N_2}}\right)}} \qquad \begin{array}{l}\text{(matched or correlated}\\ \text{groups)}\end{array}$$

18. Chi square χ^2

$$\chi^2 = \sum \frac{(f_o - f_e)^2}{f_e}$$

f_o observed frequencies

f_e expected frequencies

df degrees of freedom

Statistical Formulas   **Glossary of Statistical Symbols**

$$df = (f \text{ rows} - 1)(f \text{ columns} - 1)$$

$$\chi^2 = \frac{N\left[|AD - BC| - \frac{N}{2}\right]^2}{(A + B)(C + D)(A + C)(B + D)}$$

Computation for a 2×2 table

19. Median test

$$\chi^2 = +\frac{N\left[|AD - BC| - \frac{N}{2}\right]^2}{(A + B)(C + D)(A + C)(B + D)}$$

Statistical significance of the difference between the medians of two independent groups: at or above common median and below common median

20. Mann-Whitney test ($N > 20$)

$$U_1 = (N_1)(N_2) + \frac{N_1(N_1 + 1)}{2} - \sum R_1$$

$$U_2 = (N_1)(N_2) + \frac{N_2(N_2 + 1)}{2} - \sum R_2$$

$$z = \frac{U - \frac{(N_1)(N_2)}{2}}{\sqrt{\frac{(N_1)(N_2)(N_1 + N_2 + 1)}{12}}}$$

N_1 number in one group
N_2 number in second group
$\sum R_1$ sum of ranks of one group
$\sum R_2$ sum of ranks of second group
The significance of U is read from the U critical table. When $N > 20$, the z computation may be used with the normal probability table values.

21. Sign test (matched pairs)

$$z = \frac{(0 \pm .50) - \frac{N}{2}}{\sqrt{\frac{N}{4}}}$$

O number of signs of interest. When $O < N/2$, use $(O + .50)$; when $O > N/2$, use $(O - .50)$

22. Wilcoxon matched-pairs signed ranks test

$$z = \frac{T - \frac{N(N + 1)}{4}}{\sqrt{\frac{N(N + 1)(2N + 1)}{24}}}$$

N number of pairs ranked
T sum of the ranks of the smaller of the like-signed numbers

APPENDIX B

Percentage of Area Lying Between the Mean and Successive Standard Deviation Units Under the Normal Curve

$z\left(\dfrac{x}{\sigma}\right)$	.00	.01	.02	.03	.04	.05	.06	.07	.08	.09
.0	.0000	.0040	.0080	.0120	.0160	.0199	.0239	.0279	.0319	.0359
.1	.0398	.0438	.0478	.0517	.0557	.0596	.0636	.0675	.0714	.0753
.2	.0793	.0832	.0871	.0910	.0948	.0987	.1026	.1064	.1103	.1141
.3	.1179	.1217	.1255	.1293	.1331	.1368	.1406	.1443	.1480	.1517
.4	.1554	.1591	.1628	.1664	.1700	.1736	.1772	.1808	.1844	.1879
.5	.1915	.1950	.1985	.2019	.2054	.2088	.2123	.2157	.2190	.2224
.6	.2257	.2291	.2324	.2357	.2389	.2422	.2454	.2486	.2517	.2549
.7	.2580	.2611	.2642	.2673	.2704	.2734	.2764	.2794	.2823	.2852
.8	.2881	.2910	.2939	.2967	.2995	.3023	.3051	.3078	.3106	.3133
.9	.3159	.3186	.3212	.3238	.3264	.3290	.3315	.3340	.3365	.3389
1.0	.3413	.3438	.3461	.3485	.3508	.3531	.3554	.3577	.3599	.3621
1.1	.3643	.3665	.3686	.3708	.3729	.3749	.3770	.3790	.3810	.3830
1.2	.3849	.3869	.3888	.3907	.3925	.3944	.3962	.3980	.3997	.4015
1.3	.4032	.4049	.4066	.4082	.4099	.4115	.4131	.4147	.4162	.4177
1.4	.4192	.4207	.4222	.4236	.4251	.4265	.4279	.4292	.4306	.4319
1.5	.4332	.4345	.4357	.4370	.4383	.4394	.4406	.4418	.4429	.4441
1.6	.4452	.4463	.4474	.4484	.4495	.4505	.4515	.4525	.4535	.4545
1.7	.4554	.4564	.4573	.4582	.4591	.4599	.4608	.4616	.4625	.4633
1.8	.4641	.4649	.4656	.4664	.4671	.4678	.4686	.4693	.4699	.4706
1.9	.4713	.4719	.4726	.4732	.4738	.4744	.4750	.4756	.4761	.4767
2.0	.4772	.4778	.4783	.4788	.4793	.4798	.4803	.4808	.4812	.4817
2.1	.4821	.4826	.4830	.4834	.4838	.4842	.4846	.4850	.4854	.4857
2.2	.4861	.4864	.4868	.4871	.4875	.4878	.4881	.4884	.4887	.4890
2.3	.4893	.4896	.4898	.4901	.4904	.4906	.4909	.4911	.4913	.4916
2.4	.4918	.4920	.4922	.4925	.4927	.4929	.4931	.4932	.4934	.4936
2.5	.4938	.4940	.4941	.4943	.4945	.4946	.4948	.4949	.4951	.4952
2.6	.4953	.4955	.4956	.4957	.4959	.4960	.4961	.4962	.4963	.4964
2.7	.4965	.4966	.4967	.4968	.4969	.4970	.4971	.4972	.4973	.4974
2.8	.4974	.4975	.4976	.4977	.4977	.4978	.4979	.4979	.4980	.4981
2.9	.4981	.4982	.4982	.4983	.4984	.4984	.4985	.4985	.4986	.4986
3.0	.4987									

Example: Between the mean and $+1.00z$ is 34.13% of the area.
Between the mean and $-.50z$ is 19.15% of the area.

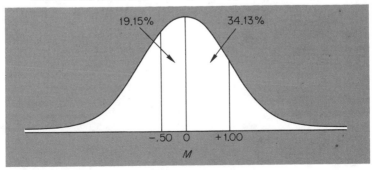

APPENDIX C

Critical Values of Student's Distribution (t)

df	Two-tailed test level of significance .05	.01	One-tailed test level of significance .05	.01
1	12.706	63.557	6.314	31.821
2	4.303	9.925	2.920	6.965
3	3.182	5.841	2.353	4.541
4	2.776	4.604	2.132	3.747
5	2.571	4.032	2.015	3.365
6	2.447	3.707	1.943	3.143
7	2.365	3.499	1.895	2.998
8	2.306	3.355	1.860	2.896
9	2.262	3.250	1.833	2.821
10	2.228	3.169	1.812	2.764
11	2.201	3.106	1.796	2.718
12	2.179	3.055	1.782	2.681
13	2.160	3.012	1.771	2.650
14	2.145	2.977	1.761	2.624
15	2.131	2.947	1.753	2.602
16	2.120	2.921	1.746	2.583
17	2.110	2.898	1.740	2.567
18	2.101	2.878	1.734	2.552
19	2.093	2.861	1.729	2.539
20	2.086	2.845	1.725	2.528
21	2.080	2.831	1.721	2.518
22	2.074	2.819	1.717	2.508
23	2.069	2.807	1.714	2.500
24	2.064	2.797	1.711	2.492
25	2.060	2.787	1.708	2.485
26	2.056	2.779	1.706	2.479
27	2.052	2.771	1.703	2.473
28	2.048	2.763	1.701	2.467
29	2.045	2.756	1.699	2.462
30	2.042	2.750	1.697	2.457
40	2.021	2.704	1.684	2.423
60	2.000	2.660	1.671	2.390
120	1.980	2.617	1.658	2.358
∞	1.960	2.576	1.645	2.326

APPENDIX D

Abridged Table of Critical Values for χ^2

	Level of significance	
df	*.05*	*.01*
1	3.84	6.64
2	5.99	9.21
3	7.82	11.34
4	9.49	13.28
5	11.07	15.09
6	12.59	16.81
7	14.07	18.48
8	15.51	20.09
9	16.92	21.67
10	18.31	23.21
11	19.68	24.72
12	21.03	26.22
13	22.36	27.69
14	23.68	29.14
15	25.00	30.58
16	26.30	32.00
17	27.59	33.41
18	28.87	34.80
19	30.14	36.19
20	31.41	37.57
21	32.67	38.93
22	33.92	40.29
23	35.17	41.64
24	36.42	42.98
25	37.65	44.31
26	38.88	45.64
27	40.11	46.96
28	41.34	48.28
29	42.56	49.59
30	43.77	50.89

APPENDIX E

Percentile Rank Equivalents of z Scores

Pr	z	Pr	z	Pr	z
1	−2.33	41	−.23	81	+.88
2	−2.05	42	−.20	82	+.92
3	−1.88	43	−.18	83	+.95
4	−1.75	44	−.15	84	+.99
5	−1.64	45	−.13	85	+1.04
6	−1.56	46	−.10	86	+1.08
7	−1.48	47	−.08	87	+1.13
8	−1.41	48	−.05	88	+1.18
9	−1.34	49	−.02	89	+1.23
10	−1.28	50	.00	90	+1.28
11	−1.23	51	+.02	91	+1.34
12	−1.18	52	+.05	92	+1.41
13	−1.13	53	+.08	93	+1.48
14	−1.08	54	+.10	94	+1.56
15	−1.04	55	+.13	95	+1.64
16	−.99	56	+.15	96	+1.75
17	−.95	57	+.18	97	+1.88
18	−.92	58	+.20	98	+2.05
19	−.88	59	+.23	99	+2.33
20	−.84	60	+.25		
21	−.81	61	+.28		
22	−.77	62	+.31		
23	−.74	63	+.33		
24	−.71	64	+.36		
25	−.67	65	+.39		
26	−.64	66	+.41		
27	−.61	67	+.44		
28	−.58	68	+.47		
29	−.55	69	+.50		
30	−.52	70	+.52		
31	−.50	71	+.55		
32	−.47	72	+.58		
33	−.44	73	+.61		
34	−.41	74	+.64		
35	−.39	75	+.67		
36	−.36	76	+.71		
37	−.33	77	+.74		
38	−.31	78	+.77		
39	−.28	79	+.81		
40	−.25	80	+.84		

APPENDIX F:
GROUPED DATA
COMPUTATIONS

Computing the mean

When the number of scores in a distribution is relatively large, and a calculator is not available, an alternative method is recommended. For computational purposes any interval in the distribution may be assumed to contain the mean. Using this interval as a reference point we may indicate interval deviations as X prime (X') or interval step deviations. Those above the mean interval are designated as $+1, +2, +3, \ldots$ Those below the mean interval are designated as $-1, -2, -3, -4 \ldots$ The interval deviations are then multiplied by the frequency (f) of scores in each interval (fx'); the sum of these products ($\sum fx'$) is divided by the number of scores (N). We have now computed the correction (c) in terms of intervals ($c = \sum fx'/N$).

The correction value is multiplied by the interval width (i) to convert the interval correction to score correction.

Adding the score correction (c)(i) to the midpoint of the assumed mean interval determines the mean.

$$M = AM + (c)(i)$$

The following problem illustrates the process:

Scores	f	x'	fx'	fx'^2
85–89	2	+6	12	+72
80–84	1	+5	5	+25
75–79	4	+4	16	+64
70–74	9	+3	27	+81
65–69	13	+2	26	+52
60–64	20	+1	20	+20
			Sum = 106	
55–59	16	0	+	
50–54	12	−1	−12	+12
45–49	7	−2	−14	+28
40–44	3	−3	−9	+27
35–39	2	−4	−8	+32
30–34	1	−5	−5	+25
	$N = 90$		Sum = −48	$\sum fx'^2 = 438$

$$c = \frac{\sum fx'}{N}$$

$$= +106$$

$i = 5$

$$\sum fx' = \frac{-\ 48}{+\ 58}$$

$$c = \frac{+58}{90} = +.64$$

$M = AM + ci$ $i = 5$

$M = 57 + 3.20$ $ci = (.64)(5) = +3.20$

$M = 60.20$

Computing the standard deviation

After having computed the means by the assumed mean method, computing the standard deviation involves one additional step. Using the same example, note the fx'^2 column. Each value is obtained by multiplying the x' value by the fx' value ($fx'^2 = (fx')(x')$).

These products are summed ($\sum fx'^2$) and divided by N. The square root of this quotient diminished by the correction score squared (c^2) produces the standard deviation in interval units. When multiplied by i, the interval width, the standard deviation is obtained.

$$\sigma = i\sqrt{\frac{\sum fx'^2}{N} - c^2} \qquad \begin{aligned} c &= +.64 \\ c^2 &= +.41 \end{aligned}$$

$$\sigma = 5\sqrt{\frac{438}{90} - .41}$$

$$\sigma = 5\sqrt{4.87 - .41}$$

$$\sigma = 5\sqrt{4.46}$$

$$\sigma = 5(2.11)$$
$$\sigma = 10.55$$

Computing the variance

If the variance score is desired the formula would be

$$\sigma^2 = i^2\left(\frac{\sum fx'^2}{N} - c^2\right)$$

$$\sigma^2 = 25\left(\frac{438}{90} - .41\right)$$

$$\sigma^2 = 25(4.46)$$

$$\sigma^2 = 111.50$$

The assumed mean methods of computing the mean, variance, or standard deviation will yield a correct score value, no matter what assumed mean interval is selected. The correction term (c) compensates for the selection of an interval that is too high or too low to actually contain the desired mean score.

A good way to check the accuracy of the computation is to recalculate the score, using a different assumed mean interval. If the resulting score is not the same, a computation error has been made.

Computing the median or any percentile score

To compute the median (or any percentile score) from a grouped data distribution it is necessary to introduce a cumulative frequency column, (f_c). Sometimes known as a "less than" column, the scores are summed by class intervals, counting from the bottom. Since the median or P_{50} is the point below which 50 percent of the scores fall, we must locate the 50 percent score from the bottom.

Another concept is essential. We must consider the true boundaries or limits of the interval. For example, the true limits of the interval 60–64 is 59.50 to 64.50. In this method of computation all of the scores in each interval are assumed to be equally spaced within the interval.

To the lower limit of the interval (L), identified as the median interval (.50N), we add the difference between .50N and the cumulative frequency of scores below this interval. This difference (.50$N - f_c$) is divided by the frequency of scores within the median interval (f_w). When multiplied by the i, which converts interval units to score units, and added to the lower limit of the median interval, the desired median score is obtained.

$$Md = L + \frac{i(.50N - f_c)}{f_w}$$

L = the lower true limit of the median interval

f_c = frequency of scores below the median interval

f_w = frequency of scores within the median interval

i = the interval width

Scores	f	f_c
85–89	2	90
80–84	1	88
75–79	4	87
70–74	9	83
65–69	13	74
60–64*	20	
55–59	16	41
50–54	12	25
45–49	7	13
40–44	3	6
35–39	2	3
30–34	1	1
	$N = 90$	

* interval containing the median (60–64)

f_c cumulative frequency of score below median interval (41)

f_w frequency within median interval (20)

$$Md = L + \frac{i(.50N - f_c)}{f_w}$$

$$Md = 59.50 + \frac{5(45 - 41)}{20}$$

$$= 59.50$$

$$= 59.50 + 1$$

$$Md = 60.50$$

This process and its formula may be generalized to compute any percentile score.

$$P_N = L + \frac{i(PN - f_c)}{f_w}$$

P_N = percentile score desired

Remember that the interval in which the desired percentile score falls must be located by counting from the bottom. P_N will indicate the interval. Using the same example let us compute P_{90}.

$PN = .90(90) = 81$, the 81st score from the bottom of the distribution.

The desired interval is 70–74; actually 69.50 to 74.50

$$f_c = 74$$

$$f_w = 9$$

$$P_N = L + \frac{i(PN - f_c)}{f_w}$$

$$P_{90} = 69.50 + \frac{5(81 - 74)}{9}$$

$$= 69.50 + \frac{35}{9}$$

$$P_{90} = 69.50 + 3.89$$

$$P_{90} = 73.39$$

$$P_{20} = 49.50 + \frac{5(5)}{12} \qquad PN = .20(90) = 18$$

$$= 49.50 + \frac{25}{12} \qquad \begin{aligned} L &= 49.50 \\ f_c &= 13 \end{aligned}$$

$$= 49.50 + 2.08 \qquad f_w = 12$$

$$P_{20} = 51.58$$

APPENDIX G: RESEARCH COURSE REPORT EVALUATION

RESEARCH REPORT EVALUATION

Name_____Date_____Grade_____

+ adequate   − inadequate

TITLE

clear and concise_____

PROBLEM

clearly stated_____
specific questions raised_____
clear statement of hypothesis_____
testable hypothesis_____
significance recognized_____
properly delimited_____
assumptions stated_____
important terms defined_____

DATA ANALYSIS

perceptive recognition of data relation-
    ships_____
effective use of tables_____
effective use of figures_____
concise report of findings_____
appropriate statistical treatment_____
logical analysis_____

SUMMARY

problem restated_____
questions/hypothesis restated_____
procedures described_____
concisely reported_____
supporting data included_____
conclusions based on data analysis___

FORM AND STYLE

typing_____

**REVIEW OF RELATED
LITERATURE**

adequately covered_____
well-organized_____
important findings noted_____
studies critically examined_____
effectively summarized_____

PROCEDURES

described in detail_____
adequate sample_____
appropriate design_____
variables controlled_____
effective data-gathering instruments or
    procedures_____

spacing_____
margins_____
balance_____
table of contents_____
list of tables_____
list of figures_____
headings_____
pagination_____
citations/quotations_____
footnotes_____
tables_____
figures_____
bibliography_____
appendix_____
spelling_____
punctuation_____
sentence structure_____
proof reading_____
clear and concise style_____

378

APPENDIX H:
FEDERAL INVOLVEMENT
IN EDUCATIONAL
RESEARCH

The federal government has encouraged, promoted, and supported educational activity since the beginning of the nineteenth century. Grants of public land, monetary appropriations, the establishment of special educational institutions, advisory services, dissemination of information, and loans and grants to institutions and individuals have all played an important part in the development of the American educational enterprise.

It has been relatively recently that the federal government has assumed responsibility for the support of educational research. The Eighty-third Congress enacted the Cooperative Research Act of 1954, but allocated no funds. It became operative in 1957 when congress appropriated a little more than one million dollars to improve education through research. The grants of supporting funds to individual colleges and universities, state departments of education, and local school systems provided tangible evidence of congressional awareness of the possible contribution of research to the improvement of education.

Rather than setting up agencies to carry on the needed research, the government entered cooperative agreements, providing funds to those educators who were committed to research and competent to conduct it. By 1960 the appropriations had been increased to 10 million dollars, and by 1966, to more than 100 million.

Although many sources of aid to educational research are scattered throughout various federal agencies, the primary responsibility for the administration of most of the funds lies within the National Institute of Education. Some of the other agencies administering research programs are the National Science Foundation; the Department of the Navy; the Social and Rehabilitation Service; the Office of Manpower, Automation and Training of the Department of Labor; the Office of Economic Opportunity; the Public Health Service, and the Department of Defense. A number of major legislative acts authorized and provided funds for educational research activity.

In 1965 a presidential task force took a critical look at the program of federally supported educational research. The committee approved of much that had been accomplished, but pointed out that there were a number of deficiencies:

1. The individual projects that had been submitted did not provide a coordinated approach to the solution of educational problems.
2. The dissemination of research findings was ineffective.
3. There was an apparent gap between research findings and their implementation. The committee recommended that human resources for research and development should be expanded by establishing training programs for developing research talent, and by utilizing the possible contributions of agencies and institutions previously not eligible for support.

These recommendations were implemented in 1966 by the creation of three new agencies:

1. Research and Development Centers
2. Regional Educational Laboratories
3. Educational Resources Information Centers

Research and development centers

Each center located at a host university which directed its operations focused professional and financial resources on research and development in a specialized problem area. These centers were established at institutions with the necessary interdisciplinary resources of established staff and experience. In one of the R and D centers, 25 professors, 50 other professionals, and a supporting secretarial staff, representing 13 academic departments of the university combined their efforts in experimentation, replication of experiments in additional settings, and large-scale field testing. Ten R and D centers were established.

1. *University of Pittsburgh*, learning research and instructional practices
2. *University of Oregon*, advanced study of educational administration

3. *University of Wisconsin*, cognitive learning
*4. *Harvard University*, individual and cultural differences in the learning process
*5. *University of Georgia*, programs of early and continuous stimulation
*6. *University of Texas*, teacher education
7. *Stanford University*, theory and practice of teaching
*8. *University of California, Berkeley*, higher education
9. *University of California, Los Angeles*, evaluation procedures
10. *Johns Hopkins University*, influence of social and administrative organization on the learning of students from diverse backgrounds

Regional educational laboratories

These laboratories were designed for the dissemination and implementation of research knowledge. Each laboratory, established as a nonprofit corporation, not affiliated with a university, served a particular geographical area, working with school systems, state educational agencies, and other organizations to promote and evaluate changes and innovations in teacher preparation, to disseminate promising educational programs and provide consultant services. Of the 20 regional laboratories that were established, financial support had been withdrawn from 10 by 1970 and from 4 more by 1975.

Educational resources information centers (ERIC)

The third type of agency, and one of the most successful, provided a network of specialized clearinghouses, designed to bring research findings and research-related information to teachers, administrators, researchers, and the public. Located at universities or other host organizations, each center was designated as a specialized information source, selecting, cataloging, indexing, and abstracting research information to be transmitted to the central ERIC agency in Washington. Sixteen ERIC centers currently provide these services:

Regional ERIC centers

Career education

Northern Illinois University
DeKalb, Illinois 60115

Counseling and personnel services

University of Michigan
Ann Arbor, Michigan 48104

*These centers have been discontinued.

Early childhood education

University of Illinois
Urbana, Illinois 61608

Educational management

University of Oregon
Eugene, Oregon 97403

Handicapped and gifted children

The Council for Exceptional Children
Reston, Virginia 22091

Higher education

George Washington University
Washington, D.C. 20036

Informational resources

Stanford Center for Research and
Development
Stanford, California 94305

Junior colleges

University of California at Los Angeles
Los Angeles, California 90024

Languages and linguistics

Center for Applied Linguistics
Arlington, Virginia 22204

Reading and communication skills

National Council of Teachers of
English
Urbana, Illinois 61801

Rural education and small schools

New Mexico University
Las Cruces, New Mexico 88003

Science, mathematics, and environmental education

Ohio State University
Columbus, Ohio 43210

Social studies/social science education

Social Science Education Consortium
Boulder, Colorado 90302

Teacher education

American Association of Colleges for
Teacher Education
DuPont Circle, Washington, D.C.
20036

Tests, measurement and evaluation

Educational Testing Service
Princeton, New Jersey 08540

Urban education

Teachers College, Columbia University
New York City, New York 10027

The central educational resources information agency

The central agency, located in Washington, provides the following coordinating services:

1. Publishes *Resources in Education*, a monthly abstract journal which includes résumés of research documents disseminated by the ERIC clearinghouses.
2. Contracts privately for the publication of *Current Index to Journals in Education* which provides a complete guide to periodic literature in more than

700 educational and education-related journals. More than 20,000 articles are indexed annually.

3. Publishes annually *ERIC Educational Documents Abstracts*, which includes all significant educational research reports
4. Publishes annually *ERIC Educational Documents Index*, a catalog of all research documents in the ERIC collection
5. Publishes the *Thesaurus of Eric Descriptors*, a definitive vocabulary of education, using the subject headings for indexing and retrieval of documents in the ERIC collection
6. Contracts for the reproduction and distribution of ERIC documents, available in paper copy form or in microfiche form. Each microfiche 4″ × 6″ film card with 24X reduction may contain up to 100 frames or pages of manuscript copy. These reproduced materials are available at a reasonable cost from:

> ERIC Document Reproduction Service
> Box 190
> Arlington, Virginia

7. Publishes annually a directory of more than 570 organizations that regularly receive monthly shipments of ERIC microfiche. Most of these organizations are university libraries, public libraries, state departments of education, ERIC clearing houses, foundations, or specialized institutes, not only in the United States but in many foreign countries.

The national institute of education

The National Institute of Education was established by an act of Congress in 1972 "to support the policy of providing an equal educational opportunity of high quality to every person, regardless of race, color, religion, sex, national origin, or social class".[1] Recognizing the primary role of the states and local governments, the federal government accepted the responsibility for providing leadership in the conduct and support of educational research. The legislation stated four objectives of the Institute:[2]

1. To help to solve or alleviate the problems and achieve the objectives of American education
2. To advance the practice of education as an art, science, and profession
3. To strengthen the scientific and technological foundations of education
4. To build an effective educational research and development system

Within the National Institute of Education, the Office of Research Grants was established to respond to all of these objectives, particularly on strengthening the scientific and technological foundations of education. Handicapped by organizational problems and inadequate congressional

---

[1] *National Institute of Education Grants for Research in Education.* (Washington, D.C.: Department of Health, Education and Welfare, 1973), p. 1.

[2] *Ibid.*, p. 2.

appropriations, it was apparent that the Institute had not realized the expectations of many of it proponents.

In March 1975, a committee of ten prominent educators completed a study of the operations of the institute and among their conclusions, several are listed here:[3]

1. The objectives of the agency are too broadly conceived and should be more sharply defined.
2. The relationship between the NIE and the Department of Health, Education and Welfare needs to be improved.
3. Too few individuals are involved in educational research and development activities. Efforts should be made to involve state and local agencies, and the participation of women and members of minority groups.
4. The present existing Regional Laboratories and Research and Development Centers should be reduced in number to not more than 6 to 8 strong agencies.
5. The National Institute of Education should provide a greater sense of direction and more effectively monitor the activities of the laboratories and centers.

The committee endorsed the potential role of the National Institute of Education as an effective agency and, paralleling the National Institutes of Health, trusted that it would eventually provide a much more effective vehicle for the promotion and dissemination of educational research and development than the uncoordinated efforts of the agencies that had previously attempted to attain this objective.

SEEKING RESEARCH FUND SUPPORT

Since policies change from year to year, it would not be practicable to suggest procedures for applying for a research grant from the National Institute of Education. Periodically, the agency selects a focus for research activity and has a general pattern of procedures to be followed:

1. A prospectus must be submitted for preliminary consideration for a grant.
2. To those submitting proposals, after evaluation of the preliminary prospectus, an invitation to submit a formal research proposal may be extended.

The process is highly competitive for funds are limited. In 1972, 203 research grants were made from more than 4,000 proposals.

For colleges and universities, public or private agencies, organizations, groups, or individuals that seek grant support, application forms should be obtained from The Office of Research Grants, Proposal Clearinghouse, National Institute of Education, 1832 M Street, Washington, D.C., 20208.

[3] *Research and Development Funding Policies of the National Institute of Education: Review and Recommendations* (Washington, D.C.: Department of Health, Education, and Welfare, August 1975).

ANSWERS TO STATISTICS EXERCISES

Chapter 7

1. Agree. The median could be lower than the mean if a large proportion of the families had low incomes.
2. Disagree. The median is that point in a distribution above and below which half of the scores fall. It may not be the midpoint between the highest and the lowest scores.
3. $M = 55.33$
   $Md = 58.50$
4. $M = 75$ Range $= 31$
   $Md = 77$
5.   Variance $= 41.33$
   Standard deviation $= 6.42$
6. Disagree. The range does not determine the magnitude of the variance or the standard deviation. These values indicate how all of the scores, not the most extreme, are clustered about the mean.
7. a. no change   d. $+5$
   b. $+5$ e. no change
   c. $+5$ f. no change
8. $M = 107.70$ variance $= 91$
   $Md = 107.50$ standard deviation $= 9.54$
   $P_{40} = 105.25$ $P_{80} = 116.17$
9. Percentile rank $= 93$.
10. $M = 72$ standard deviation $= 6$

z	-3	-2	-1	0	$+1$	$+2$	$+3$
heads	54	60	66	72	78	84	90

11.

X	x	z	Z
66	$+5$	$+1.00$	60
58	-3	$-.60$	44
70	$+9$	$+1.80$	68
61	0	0	50
52	-9	-1.80	32

12. a. 11% f. $-.18z$
    b. 89% g. $+2.33z$
    c. 87% h. $-.67_z$ to $+.67_z$
    d. 6% i. 32%
    e. $+.39z$ j. $0z$
13. a. 119   d. 107
    b. 96   e. 85 to 115
    c. 75%

14.

	Tom	Dick	Harry
algebra z	-1.00	$+.33$	$-.17$
history z	$+1.25$	$+.50$	$-.25$

a. Tom d. Tom
b. Tom e. Dick
c. Harry f. Harry

15. Disagree. The coefficient of correlation is an indication of the magnitude of the relationship, but does not necessarily indicate a cause-effect relationship.
16. rho $= +.61$
17. $r = +.65$
18. $r = +.53$
19. $r = -1.00$

most correct ↘ ↗ most incorrect
least correct ↗ ↘ least incorrect

20. Agree. $r = \dfrac{\text{rise}}{\text{run}}$ expressed in sigma units

$b = \dfrac{\text{rise}}{\text{run}}$ expressed in raw scores

The value of r cannot exceed ± 1.00
The value of b can exceed ± 1.00
21. $S_{est} = 4.96$
22. a. $\tilde{Y} = 44$
b. $\tilde{Y} = 36$

Chapter 8

1. Confirming a positive hypothesis provides a weak argument, for the conclusion may be true for other reasons. It does not preclude the validity of alternative or rival hypotheses. Rejecting a negative hypothesis employs stronger logic.
2. Agree. A test of statistical significance provides a basis for accepting or rejecting a sampling error explanation on a probability basis. Only when a sampling process is involved is a test of significance appropriate.
3. Agree. The level of significance determines the probability of a sampling error, rather than a treatment variable explanation. When a researcher finds an observation significant at the .05 level, he is admitting that there is a 5/100 chance of a sampling error explanation.
4. Disagree. The .01 alpha level is a much more rigorous criterion than the .05 level. However, any hypothesis that can be rejected at the .01 level can surely be rejected at the .05 level of significance.
5. Agree. The sum of the squared deviations from the mean of a sample is smaller than that calculated from any other point. According to the central limit theorem, the population mean would probably differ from the sample mean. Using the sample mean as a point of reference, the variance and the standard deviation of the population would probably be underestimated. This is partially corrected by considering the loss of one degree of freedom, reducing the size of the denominator in the formula by one, and increasing the size of the quotient.

6. Disagree. The t critical value for a one-tailed test is lower. The area of rejection is one side of the normal curve and it is not necessary to go out as far to reach it.

t critical values for rejection

	2t	1t
.05 level	1.96	1.64
.01 level	2.58	2.33

7. $t = -2.00$ Reject the null hypothesis. The cable did not meet the manufacturer's specifications.
8. $t = 3.49$.   Reject the null hypothesis. The means do not behave as sample means from the same population.
9. $t = 1.38$.   Accept the null hypothesis. There was no significant difference between the achievement of the two groups.
10. $t = 3.77$.   Reject the null hypothesis. The weight gain for the experimental group was significant.
11. $t = 3.13$.   Reject the null hypothesis. The difference in gasoline milage was significant.
12. a. $N - 1$
    b. $N - 2$
    c. $N + N - 2$
    d. 1
    e. 8
13. $\chi^2 = 14.06$.   Reject the null hypothesis. There seems to be a significant relationship between gender and brand preference.
14. $Md = 21$. $\chi^2 = .53$ Accept the null hypothesis. The effect of the medication does not seem to be significant.
15. $z = 2.54$.   Reject the null hypothesis. The program weight loss seems to have been sustained.
16. $z = .28$.   Accept the null hypothesis. The effect of the counseling program did not seem to be statistically significant.
17. $z = 2.13$.   Reject the null hypothesis. The difference in test scores of the two groups seems to be significant.
18. $t = 1.26$.   Accept the null hypothesis. The coefficient of correlation was not statistically significant.

AUTHOR
INDEX

SUBJECT
INDEX

A

Abbreviations in footnotes and bibliographies, 321–327

Abstracts, 57–61

Achievement tests, 185

Action research, 11–12

Activity analysis, 130

Adult Education in the United States, Handbook of, 66

Air University Library Index, 53

Almanacs, 64–66

American Almanac (Fact Book), 65

American Education, 76

American Jewish Yearbook, 68

American Jurisprudence, 64

American Library Directory, 77

American Men of Science, 74

American Reference Books Annual, 44

Analysis of variance (ANOVA), 288

Annual Review of Psychology, 59

Anonymity, questionnaires and opinionnaires, 168

Answers to statistical exercises, 385–387

Applied research, 11

Applied Science and Technology Index, 53

Aptitude tests, 185–186

Aristotle, 2

Array form, 216

Art, Encyclopedia of, 62

Art Index, 53

Assessment, 14, 116, 117

    International Assessment, 123–124

    National Assessment of Educational Progress, 122–123